ELIZABETH CADY STANTON AND THE
FEMINIST FOUNDATIONS
OF FAMILY LAW

Elizabeth Cady Stanton and the Feminist Foundations of Family Law

Tracy A. Thomas

NEW YORK UNIVERSITY PRESS
New York

NEW YORK UNIVERSITY PRESS
New York
www.nyupress.org

References to Internet websites (URLs) were accurate at the time of writing. Neither the author nor New York University Press is responsible for URLs that may have expired or changed since the manuscript was prepared.

Library of Congress Cataloging-in-Publication Data
Names: Thomas, Tracy A., author.
Title: Elizabeth Cady Stanton and the feminist foundations of family law / Tracy A. Thomas.
Description: New York : New York University Press, [2016] | Also available as an ebook. | Includes bibliographical references and index.
Identifiers: LCCN 2016023899| ISBN 9780814783047 (alk. paper) | ISBN 081478304X (alk. paper)
Subjects: LCSH: Domestic relations—United States—History—19th century. | Stanton, Elizabeth Cady, 1815-1902—Influence. | Feminist jurisprudence—United States—History—19th century. | Women's rights—United States—History—19th century.
Classification: LCC KF505 .T46 2016 | DDC 346.7301/5—dc23
LC record available at https://lccn.loc.gov/2016023899

New York University Press books are printed on acid-free paper, and their binding materials are chosen for strength and durability. We strive to use environmentally responsible suppliers and materials to the greatest extent possible in publishing our books.

Manufactured in the United States of America

10 9 8 7 6 5 4 3 2 1

Also available as an ebook

For Mom, who gave me the wings to fly.

CONTENTS

FIGURES

As a young girl, I was a voracious reader of women's biography. I moved to a new school in third grade, and the librarian there introduced me to a special section of the library filled with juvenile biographies of famous women. The shelves were divided into girls' biographies on the left, bound in burnt orange library covers, and the biographies of the boyhoods of famous men on the right, bound in an olive green color. When I quickly read through the smaller collection of girls' books, the librarian recommended I proceed to the boys' books; but I stubbornly refused. I was not interested in learning about the lives of men, and instead reread the stories of the first women scientists, doctors, authors, and artists. To this day, I have little interest in reading about the lives of men as presidents, generals, or politicians. My nightstand currently includes books on Margaret Fuller, Justice Sonia Sotomayor, Victoria Woodhull, and Georgia O'Keefe. My children learned never to ask me homework questions on wars or military leaders, but astutely selected Susan B. Anthony and women's rights for school projects requiring my assistance.

As those segregated shelves so starkly illustrate, women's history has been separated from mainstream history. From elementary school libraries to the legal academy, the history of women has been considered something other than the main story. The recovery of women's history has been the first step in integrating women's experience into the accepted narrative. Scholars from history and women's studies began in the early 1970s to discover and recount the stories of women, pioneers in their fields and leaders of social movements. At the popular level, this work influenced children's literature, which helped me line my daughter's shelves with books aimed at inspiring girl power through true stories of plucky heroines. At the intellectual level, much of this recovery work remains as researchers identify not only the famous firsts but also those women who followed and were an equally important part of history and the law. For the second step of integration, scholars of women's history work more subversively to infuse this recovered history into the commonly accepted understandings of legal developments and history. In this project of "engendering legal history," researchers tap into the power, as legal historian Felice Batlan describes, to "rewrite conventional narratives and challenge how we understand law."[1]

My intent in this book is both to recover and to integrate Stanton's history into the conventional narrative of the development of family law. Along the way, the book recovers more of the stories of feminism and women's suffrage, and the family values debates that dominated the nineteenth century. I first encountered Stanton's influence on family law sitting on my couch watching Ken Burns's PBS documentary on women's suffrage. I was intrigued by a few random references to Stanton's work on divorce and domestic violence—and frustrated by the scant detail I could find of these assertions in the legal and historical research. As a professor of family law, I was curious about the extent to which her feminism influenced the development of this field and supremely dissatisfied by the extant knowledge. Thus a feminist legal historian was born. The resulting book is more than the story of one woman. It is the story of the law—and women's persistent appeal to the law for equal rights in the family.

Miss Susan B. Anthony

Dear friend,

I do not know that the world is quite willing or ready to discuss the question of marriage. I feel in my innermost that the thoughts I sent your convention are true. It is in vain to look for the elevation of woman, so long as she is degraded in marriage. I say it is a sin, an outrage on our holiest feelings to pretend that anything but deep, fervent love & sympathy constitutes marriage. The right idea of marriage is at the foundation of all reforms. How strange it is, man will apply all the improvements in the arts & sciences to everything about him animate & inanimate, but himself. A child conceived in the midst of hate, sin, & discord, nurtured in abuse & injustice cannot do much to bless the world or himself. If we properly understand the science of life—it would be far easier to give to the world, harmonious beautiful, noble, virtuous children, than it is to bring grown up discord into harmony with the great divine soul of all. I ask for no laws on marriage . . . remove law and false public sentiment & woman will no more live as wife with a cruel, beastly, drunkard, than a servant, in this free country will stay with a pettish, unjust mistress. If law makers insist upon exercising their prerogative in some way on this question, let them forbid any woman to marry until she is twenty one. Let them fine a woman fifty dollars for every child she conceives by a Drunkard. Women have no right to saddle the state with idiots to be supported by the public. Only look at the statistics of the idiot asylums, nearly all the offspring of Drunkards. Woman must be made to feel that the transmitting of immortal life is a most solemn responsible act & never should be allowed, except when the parents are in the highest condition of mind & body. Man in his lust has regulated this whole question of sexual intercourse long enough; let the mother of mankind whose prerogative it is to set bounds to his indulgence, rouse up & give this whole question a thorough, fearless examination. . . . [I]f by martyrdom I can advance my race one step I am ready for it. I feel this whole question of woman's rights turns on the pivot of the marriage relation, & sooner or later it will be the question for discussion. I would not hurry it on neither would I avoid it. . . .

~ E.C. Stanton

Introduction

The "Radical Conscience" of Nineteenth-Century Feminism

Mother. Author. Orator.
Woman Suffrage Leader.
    —Elizabeth Cady Stanton gravestone, New York City

Elizabeth Cady Stanton was the principal feminist thinker, leader, and "radical conscience" of the nineteenth-century woman's rights movement. On her eightieth birthday in 1895, she was honored with a celebration of her fifty years as the figurehead of women's rights. Stanton was a popular national figure who directed the movement by organizing conventions, delivering speeches, lobbying legislatures, writing for newspapers, and headlining lecture tours. She popularized the ideas of women's rights to a general public enamored by her sharp wit, intellect, and maternal appearance. The pomp and pageantry of the birthday celebration, however, concealed Stanton's place at that time, pushed to the outskirts of the movement, ostracized by an organization growing more conservative and shocked by her radicalism. Her challenge to the biblically ordained inferiority of sex was the final straw, triggering sanction from her own organization. Stanton's persistent demands for easy divorce, free marriage, and biblical critique alienated fellow reformers gravitating more narrowly to the vote and the politics of domesticity. For Stanton, however, radical challenge to the family was critical to the women's rights agenda.[1]

Stanton initiated the women's rights movement on July 19, 1848, in Seneca Falls, New York. The site is now the location of the National Women's Rights Museum, where a waterfall cascades over a stone wall engraved with Stanton's words. There, Stanton issued her feminist manifesto, the Declaration of Sentiments, demanding women's right to vote.

This is generally all that history has remembered of Stanton. Her Declaration, however, asserted seventeen other demands for political, religious, social, and civil equality. These included the right to public office, marital property, divorce, education, employment, reproductive control, and religious autonomy. As Stanton explained, the institutions of government, church, family, and industry constituted "a fourfold bondage" of women, with "many cords tightly twisted together, strong for one purpose" of woman's subordination. They were all intertwined, so that "to attempt to undo one is to loosen all." As Stanton later explained, to break down this complexity required women to have "bravely untwisted all the strands of the fourfold cord that bound us and demanded equality in the whole round of the circle." Holistic reform was required to break down the complex system of women's oppression. Each right on the circle of life was at stake for woman's equality, "happiness and development," and comprehensive action "in all directions" was required. "We should sweep the whole board, demanding equality everywhere and the reconstruction of all institutions that do not in their present status admit of it."[2]

The family was one centerpiece of Stanton's feminist agenda. "The family, too, is based on the idea of woman's subordination, and man has no interest, as far as he sees, in emancipating her from that despotism, by which his narrow, selfish interests are maintained under the law and religion of the country." The family, governed by patriarchal laws and sentimental gender norms, created and perpetuated women's inferiority. "If the present family life is necessarily based on man's headship," Stanton argued, "then we must build a new domestic altar, in which the mother shall have equal dignity, honor and power." The private sphere of the family was not segregated from the public sphere, as both nineteenth-century suffrage reformers and twentieth-century feminists have argued, but instead was intertwined with the other institutional strands strangling equality. As a result, radical concrete change to the family institution was required in the forms of egalitarian partnerships, economic rights, free divorce, and maternal autonomy. Stanton's commitment to women's equality in marriage and the family was longstanding—from Seneca Falls to her last writings. As Stanton said, she "remained as radical on the marriage question at the age of eighty-six as [she] had been a half a century earlier."[3]

Stanton's family reforms seem less shocking today because most of them have become law. Her proposals to reconstruct marriage and the family, detailed in this book, are now mainstream. Women have separate and joint marital property rights. Spouses inherit equal shares of estates when one partner dies without a will. Common law marriage is prohibited in most states, and civil marriage requires procedural safeguards. Divorce is available for irreconcilable differences or for misconduct equally applicable to both spouses. The law supports domestic violence protections, reproductive choice, and maternal custody.

Recovering Stanton's feminist thinking on the family reveals the longevity and persistence of women's demands for family equality. Contrary to popular wisdom, these feminist ideas were not invented in the 1970s, but instead reach back more than a century as part of the original conceptualization of women's rights. This longer perspective bolsters the truth and credibility of such feminist demands, eschewing their characterization as a modern anomaly and demanding legitimization and consideration in the law. As these issues of family, marriage, work/life balance, pregnancy, and parenting continue to challenge the law and confound feminism, Stanton's work adds historical evidence of important principles that should be part of the legal equation. Her work shows that feminism and the family have not been historically in opposition, as we usually think. To the contrary, feminists have existed not apart from the family, but within it. Thus, understanding Stanton's views is critical to understanding both feminism and the family today.

The Personal Is Political

Knowing Stanton's story is the first step in understanding the depth and significance of her work, for that story shaped her thinking. As feminists in the twentieth century would say, "the personal is political." By this, they meant that women's private experiences are relevant and worthy of action in the legal and political sphere. Stanton's own experiences as a de facto lawyer and frustrated wife and mother informed her sharp critiques of gendered social norms and the laws that endorsed them.

Biographical accounts describe Elizabeth Cady Stanton as having a gregarious and charming personality armed with sarcasm and a brilliant mind. She had an opinion on every issue of the day. She was for dress reform of the Bloomer costume, bicycles for women, exercise in pregnancy, homeopathic medicine, and the Graham whole-wheat diet. She was against the death penalty, war, closing the Chicago World's Fair on Sunday, railroad monopolies, and Lincoln's reelection. Stanton was well read on law, literature, religion, political theory, and the emerging social sciences like anthropology. She was the first woman to run for Congress in 1866 and the first woman to testify before Congress.[4]

Stanton stands out from other nineteenth-century feminists not only for her intellect and philosophy but also for the extent to which law informed her advocacy. During a time when students trained for the law as apprentices to practitioners, Elizabeth obtained essentially the same training, though informally, under her father, Daniel Cady. Cady, "politically conservative and sternly Presbyterian," was a respected lawyer, federal and state legislator, and state judge who practiced law in his home. Cady was described as a man with a "giant intellect," who "wielded a ponderous logic that ground adversaries to powder."[5] Elizabeth, the favorite of his five surviving daughters, spent hours in her father's office reading law books, listening to clients, and watching her father work. She later described how she "studied three years in her father's office," and "read law" with him. It was this legal experience that Stanton credited as the source of her feminist awakening, as she watched her father give legal advice to widows and wives, revealing the "injustice and cruelty of the laws." Elizabeth observed her father's trials in the courthouse across the street, sparred with his apprentices at the nightly dinner table, and served as her father's law clerk and legal secretary. After time studying at Emma Willard's female seminary, Stanton returned home, where in her early twenties she continued to read law with her brother-in-law, Edward Bayard. She remained surrounded by the law throughout her life as her husband, four brothers-in-law, and four sons all trained in law.[6]

After her death, a journalist commented that "if the intellect of Elizabeth Cady Stanton had been possessed by a man, he would have had a seat on the Supreme Bench or in the Senate of the United States, but our country has no rewards for its great women."[7] Stanton was keenly aware of the glaring omission of women lawyers. "Where have they made any provision for her to learn the laws? Where is the Law School for our daughters?—where the law office, the bar, or the

Elizabeth Cady Stanton, age twenty.

bench, now urging them to take part in the jurisprudence of the nation?"[8] Her vicarious legal education, evident in her later advocacy, taught her to think like a lawyer, evaluating both sides of an issue, detailing rationales for positions, and bolstering arguments with legal authority and citation. Most significantly, Stanton gained an understanding of the instrumentality of the law: its ability to create social inequality as well as its power to remedy that inequality.

Stanton attributed her additional motivation for feminist reform to her frustrations as a wife and mother. She found joy and meaning in motherhood, but rebelled against the social and legal norms that confined her to that domestic sphere. Elizabeth married abolitionist Henry B. Stanton, who was then at the height of his fame and career as an antislavery speaker, having abandoned his study in seminary.[9] The short, plump Elizabeth and the tall, rangy, and older Henry made an "odd couple" "though both were drawn to the other's intellect, wit, self-assurance, and commitment to higher principles." She married against her father's wishes, as Cady opposed the marriage because of Stanton's radical politics and his lack of income or future prospects. The Stantons honeymooned at the 1840 World's Anti-Slavery Convention in London. Henry traveled there as representative of a group defecting from William Lloyd Garrison's antislavery society, preferring political action to moral suasion and seeking to avoid "the woman question" over the propriety of women speaking publicly as abolitionists. The London meeting became famous for its exclusion of female delegates and their banishment to the upper gallery, where Garrison joined them in boycott. Stanton spent her time taking it all in, and meeting new feminist mentor Lucretia Mott.[10]

Daniel Cady's predictions about his son-in-law proved true. Henry, an ambitious political operative and reluctant part-time lawyer, never achieved much financial or public success. After London, Henry studied law with Elizabeth's father. The Stantons moved to Boston, where Henry passed the bar exam and established a legal practice, hoping for a prominent role in politics there.[11] Elizabeth enjoyed Boston, immersing herself in politics, transcendentalism, and housekeeping in a well-appointed home provided by her father. But after just a few years in Boston, Henry moved the family in 1847 to the mill town of Seneca Falls in western New York, hoping for a good political district to launch his run for office. Again, Judge Cady provided the house, transferring to Elizabeth a run-down property he owned in Seneca Falls. Henry served as a New York state senator from 1849 to 1851. Always in search of political fame, Henry flitted from one party to the next—moving from the abolitionists to the Liberty Party, the Free Soil Party, the Democrats, and then to the Republicans, hoping for his own candidacy or position. He traveled most of the year, giving speeches, attending political conventions, or occasionally on legal business to Albany or Washington, D.C. Only when desperate for money would Henry return temporarily to the practice of law. While he developed an expertise in patent law and had several lucrative clients, the law never retained his interest for long.[12] "Politics was Stanton's first love." But abolitionists thought he had sold out his moral convictions for the pursuit of power, "ruined by ambition, desire of office and applause."[13]

Elizabeth grew increasingly resentful of Henry's assertion of privilege in the family and its restrictions on her own desires.[14] Henry had assumed they would have "a traditional middle-class marriage." "Mr. Stanton announced to me . . . that his business would occupy all his time, and that I must take entire charge of the housekeeping."[15] Elizabeth quickly tired of this arrangement. In a veiled reference to Henry, who was then in the state house, she ranted, "No man should give up a profitable business, leave his wife and children month after month, and year after year, and make his home desolate for any false ideas of patriotism, for any vain love of display or ambition, for fame and distinction."[16] While Henry played politics, Elizabeth was stuck at home, weighed down by the cares of single parenting and household management. She had seven children, with her last at age forty-three: Daniel (Neil) (1842), Henry (Kit) (1844), Gerrit (Gat) (1845), Theodore (1851), Margaret (1852), Harriot (1856), and Robert (Bob) (1859).[17]

In the midst of this chaotic family life, the thirty-two-year-old Stanton launched the women's rights movement from her hometown. The reason for her action, she said, was "the general discontent" she felt "with women's portion as wife, mother, housekeeper, physician, and spiritual guide, the chaotic conditions into which everything fell without her constant supervision, and the wearied, anxious look of the majority of women." To Stanton, women's haggard and limited reality was evidence of a need to take action "to remedy the wrongs of society in general, and of women in particular."[18] Stanton met with Lucretia Mott and Mott's sister and fellow Quakers around a dinner table, where they voiced their complaints of legal and religious subordination and vowed to plan an organized convention for woman's rights.

The women held their convention the following week on July 19 and 20, 1848, at the Wesleyan Chapel in Seneca Falls. It was attended by more than two hundred people, including notable reformers like Frederick Douglass.[19] Henry Stanton left town on the excuse of Free Soil business, but more likely to avoid any appearance of his political support for the woman question. Stanton resented Henry's absence and preoccupation, commenting in a speech shortly after the convention that if women had a vote, might not "office holders and seekers propose some change in her condition? Might not 'woman's rights' become as great a question as 'free soil'?"[20]

At the meeting, Stanton presented her Declaration of Sentiments attacking the political, civil, and religious wrongs of women. Seeking a dramatic impact emphasizing freedom and individual rights, Stanton modeled her founding document after the Declaration of Independence and borrowed its title from an American Anti-Slavery Society document. It enumerated the "long train of abuses and usurpations" and "history of repeated injuries" against women and demanded recognition of women's natural right to happiness and individual autonomy. Its outline of specific reforms mapped out what would become Stanton's feminist agenda, including family-specific reforms to marriage, divorce, domestic violence, and child custody. The Declaration also famously included a demand for women's right to vote that was considered the most radical.[21] As Stanton later recalled, "even good Lucretia Mott said it was an extravagant demand that would make our whole movement ridiculous." Mott thought it ridiculous not because it asked too much, as others feared, but because it contradicted her religious and abolitionist stance against political engagement and its corrupting moral influence.[22] Suffrage, though, emerged as the primary demand of the women's rights movement by century's end. Stanton, however, reminded people that the Declaration was about much more and that "the social wrongs of my sex occupied altogether the larger place" in the early movement.[23] As historians have shown, the early women's rights movement was a comprehensive movement, and its genius was "in linking rights to all the personal and political issues that affected women in the family, the church, and the state."[24]

Seneca Falls spawned woman's rights conventions in Massachusetts, New York, Ohio, and Pennsylvania, but Stanton's public role in this movement was limited by family responsibilities.[25] These years were increasingly frustrating for Stanton as she struggled to actualize her political self, constrained by family and Henry's lack of support.

> Men and angels give me patience! I am at the boiling point! If I do not find some day the use of my tongue on this question, I shall die of intellectual repression, a woman's rights convulsion! . . . How much I do long to be free from housekeeping and children, so as to have some time to read, and think, and write.[26]

Instead, her new partner, schoolteacher Susan B. Anthony, went in her place. Stanton was introduced to Anthony in 1851 on a street corner in Seneca Falls by their mutual friend, Amelia Bloomer, the editor of the temperance newspaper, the *Lily*. A bronzed statue today marks this historic spot. The two developed a political partnership, with Stanton doing the writing and theorizing and Anthony delivering the speeches and lobbying. As Stanton described their partnership, "it has been said that I forged the thunderbolts and she fired them."[27]

At age forty, Elizabeth considered traveling and lecturing for women's rights, but she was stymied by her family and constant pregnancies. She wrote to Anthony of her "struggle in deep waters." "I wish that I were as free as you. . . . But I am not." "The pressure on me just now is too great. Henry sides with my friends, who oppose me in all that is dearest to my heart. They are not willing that I should write even on the woman question. But I will both write and speak."[28] Stanton channeled her energy into writing, becoming a regular contributor to the *Lily* and the women's rights paper, the *Una*, and later sending articles to the *New York Tribune*.[29] It was not an easy compromise for her, and she was frequently angry and frustrated. "I pace up and down these two chambers of mine like a caged lioness, longing to bring to a close nursing and housekeeping cares. I have other work on hand, too." Sometimes the resentment overwhelmed her, as on one Fourth of July when Henry and the children went to the celebration and she was left alone at home to tend to baby Hattie. She sarcastically lamented that she, the mother, "as she who brought sin into the world and all our woe," was the one stuck "to perform all these duties, which no one else wishes to do."[30] As she wrote to Anthony,

> How rebellious it makes me feel when I see Henry going about where and how he pleases. He can walk at will through the whole wide world or shut himself up alone, if he pleases, within four walls. As I contrast his freedom with my bondage, and feel that, because of the false position of woman, I have been compelled to hold all my noblest aspirations in abeyance in order to be a wife, a mother, a nurse, a cook, a household drudge. I am fired anew and long to pour forth from my own experience the whole long story of woman's wrongs.[31]

Several years later, she was offered a paid three-month European lecture tour on woman's rights. She wrote to Anthony how she would easily leave her children with her as she had "more than once doubted the wisdom of sacrificing myself to them as I have done." The logistics, however, were unworkable, and Stanton concluded, "I fear the cup of bliss is not for me."[32]

Anthony was frustrated with her friend's domestic limitations, but she understood the situation. As she wrote to another colleague,

> Her husband, you know does not help or make it easy for her to engage in such work—and all her friends would throw mountains in her path—Mr. Stanton will be gone most of the Autumn—full of Political Air Castles— . . . he was gone 7 months last winter—the whole burden of home and children, therefore falls to her, if she leaves the post—all is afloat.

Anthony was aggravated. "I only scold now that for a moment's pleasure to herself or her husband, she should thus increase the load of cares under which she already groans." Anthony vowed, "I shall make a contract with the Father of my children to watch and care for them one half the time."[33]

Stanton returned to active duty in the women's movement in early 1860, after her youngest child turned one. Her father's death freed her from his controlling objection, endowed her with a fifty thousand dollar inheritance to support her family and her reform expenses, and renewed her relationship with her mother, who along with her sisters took over summer childcare.[34] Stanton gave three public speeches in a short period of time: testifying before the New York legislature on marital property, speaking to Garrison's American Anti-Slavery Society (from which her husband had defected), and delivering a speech on divorce reform to the Tenth National Woman's Rights Convention in New York City. Stanton's return, though, was short-lived, interrupted by the Civil War and the abeyance of women's rights activity.

Stanton detoured to the war effort and abolition, founding the Woman's National Loyal League. The league accomplished the unprecedented goal of obtaining four hundred thousand signatures, mostly from women, on petitions for a constitutional amendment banning slavery. In February 1864, the women's organization dramatically delivered six thousand petitions glued end to end and rolled into a trunk to the floor of the Senate and deposited on the desk of Charles Sumner. The petitions supplemented Senate proposals for constitutional amendments and helped convince President Lincoln to abandon his state-by-state approach and fully outlaw slavery nationally beyond the Emancipation Proclamation freeing slaves in the occupied South.[35]

The war also brought personal troubles, as the Stanton family encountered scandal arising out of Henry's new patronage job in New York City as deputy collector of the seaport custom house. His short tenure there ended when a congressional investigation revealed mismanagement and fraud in his department involving the waiver of shipping bonds for bribes given to his twenty-one-year-old son, Neil. Henry was indicted for failing to report five hundred dollars anonymously left in his office, earning three thousand dollars from drawing up legal papers and notarizing documents for shipping agents he then adjudicated, and hiring and failing to supervise his son. Forced to resign, Henry ended his political career, and he became a full-time journalist, working for the *Tribune* and then the *New York Sun* for the next twenty years as legal and political editor. Henry traded in a favor and secured Neil a patronage job in the Reconstruction government of Louisiana, where the ne'er-do-well son earned a small fortune. After the custom-house fiasco, Elizabeth and Henry separated even further, with Elizabeth purchasing her own country house in Tenafly, New Jersey, while Henry resided in the city.[36]

After the war, Stanton, now age fifty, finally launched her public career for women's rights. She restarted the women's rights conventions and became the first woman to run for Congress, garnering twenty-four votes. She and Anthony went to Kansas in 1867 to campaign for woman's suffrage on behalf of the American Equal Rights Association.[37] The Kansas legislature had two petitions on the ballot, one to add Negro suffrage and one to allow woman's suffrage. The two desperate women, faced with widespread political opposition by the dominant state Republicans, joined with the flamboyant, wealthy Democrat and racist George Francis Train. In Train, they found a vocal supporter of woman's suffrage, but Stanton and Anthony's fellow reformers were appalled that they would affiliate with him under any circumstances. Train, however, offered them significant financial support, including the promise of a woman's rights newspaper. That triggered even further outrage from their colleagues, though Stanton retorted that she "would take aid from the devil himself" if it would advance women's rights.

Back in New York, they launched their newspaper, the *Revolution,* which tackled all the radical issues of the day, including women's rights, divorce, marriage reform, infanticide, and other current debates.[38] It lasted, though, only three years until 1870 when financial problems forced it to fold, as Train's backing quickly disappeared after he was imprisoned in England and his assets confiscated for aiding Irish rebels. Many reformers refused to support the paper, criticizing even its name. Stanton dismissed her critics, saying that while others might prefer a name like "The Rosebud" (a slam on the *Lily*), there was "no name like the Revolution," as "the establishing of woman on her rightful throne is the greatest revolution the world has ever known or will know. To bring it about is no child's play."[39]

The Train affiliation exacerbated tensions between radical and conservative suffrage reformers, already heightened by Stanton's strident opposition to the Fifteenth Amendment granting black men the vote. With the proposed Fifteenth Amendment, the American Equal Rights Association abandoned its prior commitment to universal suffrage for both blacks and women, focusing instead only on Negro suffrage. Stanton was outraged at the betrayal of long-time allies and the rejection of women's suffrage. She refused to support the segregated pursuit of black suffrage and the directive that "this hour belongs to the Negro." "Do you believe," she retorted, "the African race is composed entirely of males?"[40]

Reformers, most of them former abolitionists, were appalled by Stanton's resort to vitriolic, racist language against the amendment. Stanton said, "Think of Patrick and Sambo and Hans and Yung Tung who do not know the difference between a monarchy and a republic, who can not read the Declaration of Independence or Webster's spelling-book, making laws" for revered women like Lucretia Mott[41]—though in an earlier exhortation, she added, "for our part, we prefer Bridget and Dinah at the ballot-box to Patrick and Sambo" as "we believe in equal rights to all, irrespective of sex or color."[42] She was offended that the "lower orders of men, natives and foreigners, Dutch, Irish, Chinese and African," would be entitled to citizenship before white women.[43]

Stanton defended her absolutist position against a hierarchy of "manhood suffrage," arguing that extending voting rights to black men, alone, inscribed an "aristocracy of sex" further entrenching male privilege. The Fifteenth Amendment enfranchised only men. And the Fourteenth

Amendment enforced its mandates by reducing congressional representation for states that denied the vote to "male inhabitants." An incensed
Stanton pointed out that this "inserted the word 'male' into the constitution for the first time" and that it would take "a century at least to get it
out again." Stanton's commitment to women's rights was unapologetically her primary allegiance. As she explained in her own defense, "they
say we are injudicious ofttimes in word and deed, saying many things
that should not be said, doing many things that should not be done; to
all of which we plead guilty and ask, what man or woman who has done
anything in this world must not honestly make the same confession."
Such was the price to pay for action, she suggested, as twenty years of
dedicated work for women's cause in which no one could show "one
duty left undone, one deadly breach not filled, one point of attack not
seen and met" inevitably resulted in some blunders, "for blunders are
human."[44]

The differences, however, proved too much and split the universal
suffrage movement. Conservative women pulled away in a New England group. In 1869, Stanton and Anthony abandoned the Equal Rights
Association and privately formed their own political organization dedicated to women's rights called the National Woman Suffrage Association (NWSA). Conservative women's rights reformers went their own
way, objecting to Stanton's stance on the Fifteenth Amendment, radical
position on free divorce, prohibition of male organizational leaders, and,
later, pursuit of a federal rather than state suffrage strategy. Male reformers like Theodore Tilton tried to reunite the groups, proposing in May
1870 a new "Union Woman's Suffrage Association" that would unite the
splintered groups with a distinct focus on women's rights. The Stanton
rivals refused, and instead, led by Lucy Stone and her husband Henry
Blackwell, issued a national call for a Cleveland Convention to establish
the new American Woman Suffrage Association (AWSA) as the leading
national voice of women's suffrage. The American organization, based
in Boston, started its own newspaper, the *Woman's Journal*, to compete
with Stanton's *Revolution*. Twenty years later, the two women's organizations would finally merge back, but not after the infighting and delay
wasted resources and diluted their political effectiveness.[45]

At this same time, in November 1869, Stanton joined the Lyceum Bureau and began a new phase of her career, traveling the country eight

months of the year for the next decade lecturing on women's rights.[46] As Stanton recalled, "the Lyceum Bureau was, at one time, a great feature in American life." The lyceum concept, founded by Josiah Holbrook in Massachusetts in 1826, was initially conceived as a populist forum for adult education, intellectual stimulation, and community improvement at the grassroots level. Since admission prices were low, one dollar for an entire season, "most people could afford to attend, and the popularity of the lyceum spread quickly." After the Civil War, the lyceum was commercialized with the advent of highly paid professional lecturers, and entertainment became the primary goal. Authors, spiritualists, phrenologists, and comedians joined social reformers in entertaining the audiences of "plain citizens," including farmers, shopkeepers, and women. Stanton praised her own lecturing skills, saying, "lyceum speaking, for which you are paid, involves a degree of popularity that calls for no end of miscellaneous eleemosynary eloquences, quite sufficient to exhaust the resources of an ordinary genius."[47] She proved successful in adapting her message to a popular audience, as her deliberately motherly persona blunted an otherwise controversial feminist message on divorce, marriage, and parenting. Women in particular came to the lyceum to be educated and entertained, and Stanton often spoke to them in a separate lecture on maternity. Stanton boasted how she was "converting many women to the cause of women's rights" and "stirring up the women generally to rebellion" on the lyceum circuit.[48]

The travel in the "gauntlet of the Lyceum" and "the long, weary pilgrimages, from Maine to Texas" took their toll on Stanton, then in her late fifties and early sixties. The lyceum allowed Stanton to earn desperately needed money for her children's college education, by some accounts more than one hundred thousand dollars per year in today's dollars. But she was lonely, missed her three children still at home, and hated the endless mishaps with weather, transportation, bad food, and "these detestable things called 'comforters,'" which she said were more like "tormentors" as they were so heavy and smothering.[49] In one letter from Iowa to a friend, Stanton bemoaned the weight gain from the constant travel. "I have one melancholy fact to state which I do so with sorrow and humiliation. I was weighed yesterday and brought the scales down at 240, just the speed of a trotting horse, and yet I cannot trot 100 feet without puffing." She tried to be optimistic. "As soon as I reach Omaha I intend to commence dieting. Yet I am well; danced the Virginia reel at Marlborough with Bob. But alas! I am 240!"[50] Stanton finally quit the lecture circuit in 1879 when her youngest child finished college.[51]

Stanton then turned to the tedious process of writing the massive *History of Woman Suffrage*. The first three volumes, edited by Stanton, Anthony, and Matilda Joslyn Gage, collected, sorted, and reviewed submissions from all the state and local women's organizations that had collectively comprised the grassroots efforts of the national women's movement. Their work mythologized the story of the origins of the women's movement and provided the next generation of activists with a usable past and reinforced Stanton and Anthony's leadership of the movement.[52] During the 1880s, Stanton traveled abroad several times, visiting her son Theodore in France, where he had married and was active in women's rights work, and living with her daughter Harriot Stanton Blatch in England, where she had married and started a family. Stanton worked with the radical Quaker branch of the British woman's rights movement to press for suffrage for married women against the moderate movement, which advanced only single women's suffrage, consistent with English law tying voting eligibility to property ownership. Building on her British connections, Stanton formed the International Council of Women, an innocuous European organization designed to exchange experiences among women's rights advocates globally and to celebrate the fortieth anniversary of Seneca Falls. She was in England when Henry died in 1887, though the two had been apart for a long while.[53]

Into her seventies and eighties, Stanton took on what she came to believe was the ultimate stumbling block for women's rights: the religious doctrine of women's inferiority. Seeking to tear down this foundational assumption undergirding all of law and society, Stanton devoted her last years to writing a feminist commentary of the Bible, the *Woman's Bible*. Stanton, with a supporting committee of women, took on "the chief block in the way of woman's advancement," the idea that women's inferiority was God ordained.[54] This heresy of questioning the Bible further ostracized her from the women's movement.

By now, the American woman's suffrage movement was strongly conservative, influenced by affiliations with the Woman's Christian Temperance Union (WCTU) and social purity reformers believing in the notion of women's moral superiority and the politics of domesticity. These groups embraced the ideology of wifely redemption by which women reform men, and thus save the family by restoring women's traditional and revered role in the family. In retrospect, this conservatism turned out to be detrimental to feminism at this time because it delayed and diverted the core feminist ideal promised by the early radical movement.[55] While the new conservative allegiances increased membership and support for the vote, it diluted the movement's broader feminist mission, as Stanton warned. As she passed the reins to the next generation in 1900, she said, "I would advise our coadjutors to beware of narrowing our platform." The success of a movement, she said, "does not depend on its numbers, but on the steadfast adherence to principle by its leaders." "We should not rest satisfied to sit on the doorpost of the great temple of human interests like Poe's raven simply singing 'suffrage evermore.'" "The ballot box," she said, "is but one of the outposts of progress, a victory that all orders of men can see and understand." But "only the few," Stanton said, "can grasp the metaphysics of this question, in all its social, religious, and political bearing."[56]

Stanton died in her sleep at the age of eighty-six while living with her children Maggie and Bob in New York City. Just two weeks before her birthday, she and Anthony had made plans to celebrate together. Anthony wrote, "it is fifty-one years since first we met, and we have been busy through every one of them, stirring up the world to recognize the rights of women." She continued, "we, dear old friend, shall move on to the next sphere of existence—higher and larger, we cannot fail to believe, and one where women will not be placed in an inferior position, but will be welcomed on a plane of perfect intellectual and spiritual equality."[57] Her gravestone monument, shaped like a queen chess piece, records her legacy as "Mother. Author. Orator. Woman Suffrage Leader." Stanton left her autobiography, *Eighty Years and More: Reminiscences, 1815–1897*, written more as feminist manifesto than memoir, in which she portrayed her personal life as political resistance to gender discrimination. Her feminist thought, however, remains scattered throughout her writings of speeches, addresses, and editorials responding to the specific issues of her day.

The controversy over Stanton did not end with her death. A new generation of younger, more conservative suffrage activists dis-

Elizabeth Cady Stanton, Robert Stanton, and Margaret
Stanton Lawrence, 1895.

avowed her anticlericalism and radical ideas, immediately rejecting her
legacy. Stanton's children, Harriot and Theodore, struggled to redeem
their mother's historical significance by publishing heavily edited and
whitewashed papers of her life and work.[58] Women's suffrage was not
achieved until the Nineteenth Amendment to the Constitution was ratified in 1920, seventy-two years after Seneca Falls. A statue commemorat-
ing the founding mothers of suffrage, Stanton, Anthony, and Mott, was
started and planned for the Capitol Rotunda, but was relegated to the
congressional basement. Efforts to restore the partially finished monument, dubbed "three women in a tub" after the nursery rhyme, met
with resistance from congressional Republicans, though it now stands
in its intended place. Seneca Falls became part of our national heritage,
though Stanton's home there is mostly empty of furnishings, memora-
bilia, or other insights into this original feminist.

Portrait Monument to Elizabeth Cady Stanton, Susan B. Anthony, and Lucretia Mott, U.S. Capitol, Washington, D.C. *Library of Congress.*

Multiple Feminisms

Stanton's political and legal reform was driven by feminist ideals, although "people in the nineteenth century did not say *feminism*."[59] They spoke of "woman's rights" or "the advancement or cause of woman," using the singular "woman" to symbolize the unity of the female sex. The word "feminism" did not come into popular use in America until 1910.[60] Historians traced its first usage to 1882 and French suffrage leader Hubertine Auclert's feminist newspaper, *La Citoyenne* (The Citizen). Stanton knew of Auclert and her work, and may have been familiar with the word "feminist" even if she did not adopt it as her own. Stanton's son, Theodore, then living in France, wrote to his mother of Susan Anthony's visit to Paris and their attendance at a woman's rights meeting "at which the brave, farseeing" Auclert "was the leading spirit." Theodore Stanton and Auclert were the French representatives to Stanton's International Council of Women in 1883. Stanton mentioned Auclert and her newspaper in the *History of Woman Suffrage*, and an 1888 letter from Auclert to Anthony regarding the council uses the term "feministe" throughout.[61] Whether such terminology was officially utilized, the core ideals of its meaning of feminism were clearly present and dominant in Stanton's theories. The feminist label accurately describes her thinking and provides a useful analytical tool for understanding her work.[62]

Stanton was an original feminist thinker, among the first to articulate feminist theories. She was familiar with the work of her few feminist predecessors and knew some of them in person. Stanton participated in transcendentalist writer Margaret Fuller's small-group conversations in Boston in 1843, when Fuller wrote the "The Great Lawsuit" and its expanded book form, *Woman in the Nineteenth Century*.[63] Fuller argued that each human soul should be allowed to achieve "fulness of being," which for women required the removal of male dominance, reform of marriage, and self-sufficiency in education and occupation. Stanton quoted Fuller's poem in concluding her first Address on Woman's Rights and launched similar small groups in Seneca Falls.[64] Stanton met and corresponded with abolitionist Sarah Grimké, sister-in-law to her husband Henry's close friend Theodore Weld, and her sister, Angelina, who together ignited "the woman question" as the first women to speak to public audiences on slavery. Stanton dissected and circulated Grimké's out-of-print feminist work, *Letters on the Equality of the Sexes* (1837), which challenged women's assumed biblical inferiority and legal disability.[65] Stanton read British writer Mary Wollstonecraft's *Vindication of the Rights of Woman* (1792) and its assertions of women's equal abilities and equal education, serializing the work in the *Revolution*.[66] And she paid homage to feminist utopian Frances Wright in speeches and on the front page of *History of Woman Suffrage*.[67] Stanton took these ideas and combined them with her vast knowledge of political, scientific, and social science theories to create a complex and holistic feminist theory designed to encompass all aspects of women's subordination. And then she put it into action.

"Feminism" generally is defined as a theory that opposes women's subordination to men and works to eliminate that hierarchy and injustice. It is characterized by methodologies that focus on gender as the primary category of analysis, validate and incorporate women's experiences, and evidence suspicion of seemingly objective rules. Modern feminist legal theory has divided into three main strands, emphasizing either women's sameness to men, their difference from men, or their dominance by men. Liberal feminist theory identifies subordination as a failure to view women as identical to men, and seeks formal rules of neutrality granting women individual rights. Difference feminism identifies unjust subordination in the failure to value women's different biological, relational, and/or cultural differences, such as mothering, moral reasoning, and caregiving. Radical or dominance feminism identifies subordination in the victimization and sexualization of women by men, resulting in harms like sexual harassment, pornography, and sexual assault and necessitating institutional restructuring.[68] Stanton's feminism embodies all of these multiple strands of feminist legal thought, though it is not often depicted that way.

Stanton is typically categorized as the "archetypical American equal-rights individualist" feminist focused simply on formal equality between women and men.[69] This categorization highlights Stanton's work to dismantle barriers to women's equality and give them the same rights as men. To modern feminists, this limits Stanton's relevance to ongoing feminist inquiry and advocacy. To nonfeminists, this narrow depiction supports their misappropriation of Stanton for conservative causes like domesticity and anti-abortion. For example, Christina Hoff Sommers in her 1994 book, *Who Stole Feminism? How Women Have Betrayed Women,* describes Stanton as an "Old Feminist" heroine who eliminated formal gender barriers to work and education, but then appropriately and deferentially stood by her man and her seven children at home. In another example, the anti-abortion group Feminists for Life features Stanton on posters and commemorative coffee mugs, misrepresenting her as someone who was "unapologetically and loudly pro-life" in her demand for equal rights for mothers.[70] These political cooptations, however, misunderstand the depth and complexity of Stanton's feminist theories.

Stanton's holistic feminism was unfettered by the modern demarcations that have circumscribed feminist theory. As historians have explained, early feminists understood feminism in a more fluid way, endorsing both sameness and difference in their appreciation of the nuances of women's subordination in different contexts.[71] For Stanton, all of the strands of feminist thought were instructive in understanding and challenging women's subjugation. Stanton viewed women as equal to, and not inferior to, men but also as differently situated with respect to their experiences bearing and raising children. She sought access to the rights men had but also extended rights to support women's experiences as mothers. To this, Stanton added an understanding that dominance of women by male systems of law, patriarchy, and religion were the causes of women's oppression, and that structural changes to the institutions of marriage, law, and the church were required.

Stanton's starting point was formal legal equality. She demanded women's rights "simply on the ground that the rights of every human being are the same and identical." She emphasized "that woman is man's equal—was intended to be so by the Creator, and the highest good of the race demands that she should be recognized as such." The foundational difficulty, Stanton said, was that lawmakers "cannot take in the idea that men and women are alike; and so long as the mass rest in this delusion, the public mind will not be so much startled by the revelations made of the injustice and degradation of woman's position."[72] The prevailing gender norms portrayed women as morally inferior, weak, and easily tempted away from moral righteousness, like Eve, who brought sin into the world. Stanton targeted this false belief in her earliest speech, debunking each claim that man was superior to woman intellectually, morally, and physically.[73] Establishing the "identity of the race in capabilities and responsibilities," Stanton assumed, logically and necessarily resulted in "the equality of human rights." And this is all one asks for woman, the same advantages, opportunities, and code of laws man claims for himself, no discriminations on the ground of sex, no "protection."[74]

Formal equality, though, was only the first step. As Stanton explained, "I have wrought heretofore mainly in behalf of the equality of the sexes because it has seemed to me that the recognition of that equality was as I still think it is, the first requisite, the first step on the road to social emancipation and social happiness." However, she explained, "I perceive more and more clearly every day that the recognition of the equality of woman with man in all the senses in which it is possible that they should be equal is not enough, that it is only a first step and nothing more."[75] Stanton appreciated the feminist insight that "formal, legal equality is necessary but not sufficient to attain substantive equality. Substantive equality requires dismantling major structural impediments to women's full participation in all spheres of civic life."[76]

Stanton's feminist attack demanded structural changes and what she called "social revolution." In terms now associated with radical feminism, Stanton framed the problem of women's inequality as women's systemic victimization. "We show by your statute books that your laws are unjust—that woman is the victim of avarice and power." Man was the oppressor, as his "subjection of woman . . . is rooted in selfishness and sensuality," which caused him to treat her as "the idol of his lust." Patriarchy was to blame and its continued assertion of male privilege in the law. Stanton demanded that all institutions built on this patriarchy— marriage, property, law, and the church—be radically restructured to recognize women's equal humanity and agency. Stanton applied this theory to deconstruct the marriage laws, emphasizing their victimizing role in sexualizing women, creating a haven for male licentiousness and perpetuating the husband's sexual prerogative.[77]

Stanton deconstructed the process by which law and social institutions enforced women's subjugation. Adopting what are now identified as feminist methodologies, Stanton critically analyzed the law,[78] suspicious of the existing law and questioning the underlying motivations that then revealed male bias and protection of power. "Our 'loyal defenders' are all looking out for themselves; they legislate our property and wages into their own pockets."[79] She saw clearly how male privilege was perpetuated by statutes and legal training, describing "beardless boys in your law offices, learning these ideas of one-sided justice— taking their first lessons in contempt for all womankind—being indoctrinated into the incapacities of their mothers, and the lordly, absolute rights of man over all women, children, and property," and expressing concern "that these are to be our future Presidents, Judges, Husbands, and Fathers."[80] She complained that law students and lawyers "cannot escape the legal view, which by constant reading, has become familiarized to their minds . . . written on the brow of every woman they meet," of the law's gendered language of "femme covert," "protection," and "female incapacities." Stanton criticized women's exclusion from the legal process of legislatures, juries, and courts, calling out men for their reluctance to share power with a new class of women.[81]

Stanton's feminism also integrated theories of women's difference.[82] "The advocates of woman's rights do not deny a difference in sex, but on the contrary, base their strongest arguments for equal rights on this very principle, because of its mutually protecting, elevating, invigorating power over the sexes."[83] In her first speech, she said that women's rights advocates "have no objection to discuss the question of equality, for we feel that the weight of argument lies wholly with us." However, "we wish the question of equality kept distinct from the question of rights, for the proof of the one does not determine the truth of the other."[84] The women's movement pragmatically started out on the equality ground, she later explained, "because we thought, from that standpoint, we could draw the strongest arguments for woman's enfranchisement. And there we stood firmly entrenched, until we saw that stronger arguments could be drawn from a difference in sex, in mind as well as body."[85]

The differences Stanton admitted were those of maternal and moral strength, as exemplified by the iconic loving mother or Mother Nature who calms male brute force obsessed with destruction, war, violence, and conquest.[86] These arguments were useful to Stanton in making alternative arguments for women's suffrage, affiliating conservative suffrage women focused on women's superior morality, and justifying opposition to the Fifteenth Amendment and its "manhood suffrage."[87] But beyond political pragmatism, Stanton fully and personally appreciated women's distinct burdens of maternity caused by pregnancy and childcare, and she disavowed the patriarchal attempts to control it. Maternity was not a curse, as religious dogma proclaimed, but rather a power deserving of recognition and support. The logical legal consequence of this difference, for Stanton, was to privilege women's maternal realities with positive, gender-specific rights like reproductive choice and maternal custody.[88] Her theory of maternal agency, however, contrasted sharply with the dominant ideology of maternalism in the nineteenth century.

The prevailing social ethic of "the cult of domesticity" reified women's morality, piety, and domestic work and then protected that sacredness in the home under the control of a man, either a husband or father. By the 1830s, domesticity was entrenched as ministers, educators, novels, and popular magazines prescribed specific behavior for women of housekeeping, educating young children, exhibiting heightened morality, and selflessly living for others. Woman's designated vocation and purpose of generating moral character through her presence in the home was thus identified as the essence of successful families. Home was the sanctuary where men sought refuge from the vexations and temptations of the business world. Thus, "the central convention of domesticity was the contrast between the home and the world." As a result, social behavior was segregated into two separate spheres based on sex: the public sphere for the man in work and politics, and the private domestic sphere for the woman in the home.[89]

Stanton soundly rejected this domesticity and its ideology of separate spheres as "nonsense."[90] Domesticity did not describe woman's true identity nor did the domestic sphere circumscribe woman's actualization. While Stanton recognized, and appreciated, women's unique burdens and capabilities as mothers, she did not view those domestic responsibilities as limitations on women's autonomy or public role. Rather, Stanton converted religious and moralistic talk of the different feminine element into an argument for power, and a basis for infusing that essential feminine element into the public sphere and into reconstruction of the state, church, and home.[91] Thus, "difference was both the agent of change . . . and the problem to be overcome."[92]

The distinguishing feature of Stanton's theory of difference was that it was not a basis for subordination, but rather for empowerment.[93] The problem was that society "confounds difference with inferiority."[94]

Stanton, in contrast, explained, "while admitting a difference, we claim that that difference gives man no superiority, no rights over woman that she has not over him." Going a step further, she asserted, "if a difference in sex involves superiority, then we claim it for woman; for as she is more complicated in her physical organization, fills more offices than man, she must be more exalted and varied in her mental capacities and endowments." Yet, ultimately, for Stanton, the point was not whether women's natures were the same or different from men's— for, she concluded, "the resemblances of sex are as great as their differences." The point was that "woman has the same right man has to choose her own place." Balance was required, and "the masculine and feminine elements in humanity must be in exact equilibrium." The existing social problem lay in the skewed balance and "undue depression of the feminine element."[95]

These views together comprehensively formed Stanton's feminism, designed to achieve women's full "freedom and individual happiness" by ending men's domination of women and actualizing women's own agency. At its core, Stanton's feminism, like that of "every mainstream legal feminist embraces antisubordination as its goal."[96] She explained, "the lesson of inferiority is taught everywhere, and in these terrible tragedies of life we have the result of this universal degradation of women."[97] Her ultimate objective was to dismantle all notions of women's inferiority and second-class status incorporated in laws, stereotypical ideologies, social institutions, and religion. Stanton's feminism first deconstructed law and social norms to expose and identify male dominance and its corollary, women's subjugation. As a result, she demanded the end of statutes establishing legal barriers for women, separate-spheres ideology of stereotypes of domesticity, marriages based on sexualization and victimization, and laws that devalued maternalism as inferior. Stanton then reconstructed these problematic institutions by substituting new frameworks for marriage, work, law, and the family.[98] Her solutions included egalitarian marital partnerships, women's economic self-dependency through education and employment, reproductive self-sovereignty, and women's participation in the legal and political process. Stanton was less concerned with moral questions of woman's true nature than with positive rights and tangible change to effectuate women's equality.

"I Have All the Rights I Want"

Stanton's feminism was pragmatic. She wanted not a theory, but reform. She activated her intellectual ideas in the context of many of the current events of the day, applying her ideas to identify the broader woman question in social, political, and religious issues. Stanton also used her feminism for political organizing power, using these ideas to bring women together to create the first social movement for women's rights.

Stanton's key insight was to treat women as a class—a group unified by common experiences and objectives. The cult of domesticity set up this social classification "by giving all women the same natural vocation" and by grouping them by gender all in the same domestic sphere.[99] Yet women, isolated in the home, uneducated, burdened with domestic cares, and scattered across class, race, ethnicity, and religion, failed to appreciate their commonalities and ways in which laws and social norms targeted their shared characteristic of gender. Stanton's goal was to bring women together, raising their consciousness and revealing shared realities that exposed institutional gender oppression while igniting a movement.[100]

From the start until the end of the women's movement, Stanton's continued frustration was the apathy of women. Stanton said "the chief obstacle" to women's rights was women themselves. She was exasperated by the constant refrain she heard from women: "I have all the rights I want."[101] Stanton criticized the "fashionable butterflies" too obsessed with frivolity and fashion to appreciate their own oppression. These "silly women," "lapped amidst luxuries," cared "more for their nodding plumes and velvet trains than for the statute laws by which their persons and properties are held—who blinded by custom and prejudice to the degraded position which they and their sisters occupy in the civil scale, haughtily claim they have all the rights they want."[102] She acknowledged the limitations of the "household drudges" too overburdened with daily cares to educate themselves on the law or to assert "the courage to compare their opinions with one another." She compared women to horses, trapped in a burning stable but too frightened to come out. Stanton warned that eventually these women would appreciate the need for such rights when confronted with the realities of marriage, maternity, and widowhood.[103]

Stanton emphasized this foundational truth of women's agency in her famous address, "The Solitude of Self." Speaking to a congressional judiciary committee and repeating her speech to a women's suffrage convention, Stanton poetically predicted how each woman must take responsibility for her own life, to be the "arbiter of her own destiny," like "an imaginary Robinson Crusoe with her woman Friday on a solitary Island." Women must be prepared to weather the "fierce storms of life" on their own. "No matter how much women, prefer to lean, to be protected and supported, nor how much men desire to have them do so, they must make the voyage of life alone, and for safety in an emergency must know something of the laws of navigation." She continued: "To guide our own craft, we must be captain, pilot, engineer; with chart and compass to stand at the wheel; to watch the wind and waves and know when to take in sail, and to read the signs in the firmament overall."[104]

Stanton's objective was to awaken women to their own subordination. Like the consciousness-raising efforts of the second-wave women's liberation movement of the 1960s, it was important for women to hear each other's stories, learn of injustices, and place their own individual circumstances within the context of the greater society. Stanton emphasized the common bond among women in order to sustain "united and vigorous action." Speaking to an international suffrage group, Stanton called for women to set aside differences in religion and culture in the name of unity. "We do not feel you are strangers and foreigners, for the women of all nationalities, in the artificial distinctions of sex, have a universal sense of injustice, that forms a common bond of union between them."[105]

To accomplish this unity, Stanton's strategy was to use the law as an organizing principle demonstrating women's shared subordination. She frequently supplemented her speeches and articles with citations to statutes, treatises, and cases. She resolved in the Declaration of Sentiments "that the women of this country ought to be enlightened in regard to the laws under which they live, that they may no longer publish their degradation, by declaring themselves satisfied with their present position, nor their ignorance, by asserting that they have all the rights they want."[106] Stanton noted that "the mass of the women of this nation know nothing about the laws, yet all their specially barbarous legislation is for woman." More specifically, Stanton used the law of domestic relations to underscore women's similar discriminatory treatment because of sex. She recited parable-like stories of women in family situations to help women connect with other women. She told stories of property, earnings, divorce, and domestic violence involving women who were wealthy, working-class, black, Mormon, Quaker, Irish, and Scottish to show that sex distinctions extended across class, race, and religion. Stanton's goal was to convert women's isolated experiences in the home into universal harms that would unify women behind group political action on behalf of "woman's rights." Sharing women's stories was intended to "transform an individual's experience of frustration, privation, or humiliation into consciousness of class-based disempowerment."[107]

Stanton's universalizing of women has been criticized by modern feminist scholars.[108] They condemn Stanton for essentializing women by assuming all women's interests to be the same and defining those interests in terms of her own interests as a privileged, white woman. The concern is that Stanton's feminism ignores relevant differences of identity and experience, and thus may "reinscribe privilege and social hierarchy," further perpetuating race or class discrimination.[109] This criticism stems from Stanton's racist remarks in opposition to the Fifteenth Amendment, her opposition to black suffrage, her support for educated suffrage, and her failure to work more for abolition, for black civil rights, and with black feminists.[110] It's possible to debate these assumptions—by acknowledging the prevalence of such racist notions at the time; looking to contrary evidence of Stanton's defense of black women, advocacy for the working class, friendship with leading black reformers like Robert Purvis and Sojourner Truth, and support for interracial marriage; or emphasizing her general pronouncements of equality regardless of race, religion, or class.[111] Whatever the conclusion reached, however, an important point often missed in this debate is the legal and political significance of universalizing women.

Collectivizing women as a group is important to formulating and pursuing a legal critique of the law. Stanton's classification of women as a singular group was instrumental because it provided the analytical mechanism by which to identify and challenge discrimination under the law. Identifying women as a class was an innovation necessary to legal reform. Modern sex discrimination and constitutional equality arguments depend upon the existence of an identifiable "suspect class" of sex to be legally actionable. The law compares classifications, grouping together those with an "immutable trait" of sex as an unchangeable, distinguishing characteristic used to stereotype and subordinate.[112]

Stanton worked to explain how the classifications based on sex were detrimental discrimination rather than beneficial protection. "This invidious classification of woman everywhere works a double wrong—it degrades her in her own estimation and in that of the man by her side." She emphasized the "stereotyped sneers" and "public sentiment of contempt" for women heard at every turn.[113] Drawing on the civil rights challenges based on race, Stanton analogized sex and race discrimination. "The prejudice against color, of which we hear so much, is no stronger than that against sex. It is produced by the same cause, and manifested very much in the same way. The negro's skin and the woman's sex are both prima facie evidence that they were intended to be in subjection to the white Saxon man." She concluded, "the discriminations against color and sex in the United States are both . . . forms of this same hateful spirit of caste."[114]

Stanton's universalizing of women was also critical to formulating legal challenge because it exposed broader systemic and structural harms. As legal scholar Martha Fineman has convincingly explained, without universality, institutional and structural inequalities of the workplace, the family, and the public sphere are obscured, leaving those wider systemic disadvantages unchallenged. When we deal with "law and the relationship between legal institutions and the structuring of power and authority, as well as their allocation among the individual, the state, and societal institutions, we employ a system dependent on the process of classification, generalization and universality." Universality allows for meaningful change on broad social-justice issues that "transcend those fragmented identities" of multiple and enumerable individual differences among women.[115] Stanton, operating at the beginning of the women's movement and legal challenges, particularly appreciated this importance of connecting women together to expose the systemic problems and support broad, revolutionary legal change.

Focus on the Family

Family has been the sticking point for feminism both legally and politically. Women's rights are often viewed as antifamily. Women and men have opposed women's rights over time, fearing a threat to and destruction of the family. The family and women's rights are often juxtaposed, seemingly in direct opposition to each other. In the nineteenth century, Stanton noted that "one common objection to this movement is that if the principles of freedom and equality which we advocate were put to practise, it would destroy all harmony in the domestic circle."[116] A century later in the women's liberation movement of the 1960s, critics similarly feared that change in women's social and legal status would devalue mothering and obliterate protections for women's important roles as mothers. Stanton was forthright in her view that such talk that women's political rights would destroy "domestic harmony is the sheerest humbug."[117] The "only happy households," she asserted, were those in which spouses "share equally in counsel and government" without subordination.[118] For Stanton, family was not a foil or opposition to women's rights: it was a central locality that demanded transformative change.

Stanton identified the family as an important institution for feminist reform for both practical and intellectual reasons. Practically, marriage was where most women then found themselves, and thus the common reality dictated how women experienced gender subordination. "As woman is the greatest sufferer, her chief happiness being in the home and with her children, and seldom having resources of her own, prevented by family cares from doing business in her own name and enjoying the dignity of independence by self-support, she is even more interested than man can possibly be as to the laws affecting family life."[119] Intellectually, Stanton understood how marriage created and entrenched gendered social norms. As historian Nancy Cott explains,

> The whole system of attribution and meaning that we call *gender* relies on and to a great extent derives from the structuring provided by marriage. Turning men and women into husbands and wives, marriage has designated the ways both sexes act in the world and the reciprocal relation between them. It has done so probably more emphatically than any other single institution or social force.[120]

Thus, attacking the source of the gendered norms in the family had the potential for significant reverberating effects on all public and civil inequalities.

Stanton's comprehensive challenge to the law of the family attacked the entrenched law of coverture. "Coverture," inherited from English common law, dictated that the legal identity and rights of a woman were lost when she married, "covered" by her husband. As English treatise writer William Blackstone described, "by marriage, the husband and wife are one person in law: that is, the very being or legal existence of the woman is suspended during the marriage, or at least incorporated and consolidated into that of the husband: under whose wing, protection, and *cover*, she performs every thing."[121] Left over from feudal times, coverture was based on a patriarchal system in which the lord, the husband, "protected" the wife, just as the lord had protected the peasant.[122] A married woman lost any right to own property, earn wages, draft a will, enter into a contract, testify in court, or sue or be sued. Her legal identity and her economic power were obliterated.[123] Even as a new specialized state law of "domestic relations" for husband/wife and master/servant developed in America in the 1830s, jurists and treatise writers held on to coverture, further embedding it in law.[124] That disabling of women's rights, Blackstone explained, was well intentioned, as the laws "are for the most part intended for her protection and benefit. So great a favourite is the female sex of the laws of England." "Protection!" Stanton said sarcastically; the law protects women like "the wolf the lamb or the eagle the dove he carries to his eyrie."[125]

Stanton challenged the law of coverture both symbolically and concretely. "Every line in the old common law of England on which the American system of jurisprudence is based, touching the interests of woman, is, in a measure, responsible for the wrongs she suffers today."[126] Normatively, she understood that coverture was a legal institution whose scope was "a tool of ideology at least as much as law." It taught women that they were inferior by mandating their complete subordination to men through legal disability, denying them dignity and independence.[127] Practically, she also demanded the tangible rights denied women under coverture's disabilities, seeking specific civil and social rights to property, contract, legal authority, and employment.[128] For coverture was intransient, fading only a little with the midcentury married women's property acts, and operating to deny women equal citizenship and profession in the U.S. Supreme Court.[129]

Coverture persisted despite the transformation of the legal concept of the family from patriarchy, to contract, to social institution. The patriarchal familial form inherited from English feudal times conceptualized marriage as a rigid hierarchy, with the husband as head of the household and part of the community governance extending power by divine right down from the king to the governor to the master of the house.[130] Post-Revolution, this derivative right of kings was replaced by the republican family constructed by the mutual consent of the parties free from governmental interference. Contract emerged as the dominant theory of law, politics, and commercialism, and it equally influenced the theory of the family. The contract theory still prioritized the husband's power, granting the woman power to consent to the initial marriage, but then assuming continued consent to all conditions and strictly segregating her role into the domestic sphere. Her importance in this sphere elevated over time from "republican motherhood," tasked with educating virtuous male citizens, to "true womanhood," responsible for all moral and family life, though always subordinated to the power of the husband.[131]

By the late nineteenth century, this private contract ideology, with its prioritization of individualism and private welfare, at least of the husband, triggered backlash and "near moral panic" as it was blamed for the social and moral disintegration of the family. Threats to the family were seen in industrialization, immigration, Mormon polygamy, women's rights, and prostitution. New social sciences of juvenile reform and social work emphasized the family as an important institutional protection for children. And this all led to a demand for stronger government regulation of the family and morality, and a reassertion of the sacred role of women in the home.[132]

Stanton fought against the dominant ideology at every stage, recognizing that women were victimized under all legal forms. "Men have tried all notions of marriage and family from monogamy to polygamy, and women the same under all, victims alike." Under all forms of the family, men retained control and agency, and women were relegated to the status of objects subject to that power. She objected to the continuing patriarchal ideas of the headship of the husband. "The same process of evolution that has given us a state without a king and a church without a Pope, will give us a family without 'a divinely ordained head,' in which the interests of father, mother, and child will be equally represented."[133]

She gravitated to the idea of the republican family with its precepts of individual rights, and used this legal language of contract to frame her concept of marital partnership with the free right to termination by divorce. Her contract theory, however, radically altered the prior marriage contract, reconstructing it as a partnership of fully equal and autonomous partners rather than two different, complementary gendered roles. Stanton rejected the sentimentalized, dominant ideology of "true womanhood" that depicted women as delicate and pious, appropriately relegated to submission, obedience, and domesticity under the control and protection of men.[134] Her ability to reframe the contractual notion of marriage, however, waned, as the public discourse rejected this private vision of marriage.

Stanton revolted against the family reformers' notion of marriage as a social institution that demanded the sacrifice of individual women. "We have so often heard the declaration that the individual must be sacrificed to society that we have come to think their interests be in different directions." Instead, she argued, "whatever promotes the best interests of the individual promotes the best interests of society, and vice versa." She saw protection of the family as a pretext for keeping women down. The goal for Stanton was to create full freedoms of power, opportunity, and choice for women in the family, not suppress them through more government regulation under the guise of "saving the family." Fundamentally, Stanton rejected defining women by their role in the family. These roles did not define women's true individuality, capacity for work, or intellect, but were mere incidents—secondary to their core personhood. Moreover, these roles of "woman, wife, widow, and mother" were not limitations as constructed by the ideology of domesticity, but instead were meaningful capacities that demanded substantive legal rights.[135] "Out of marriage, woman asks nothing at this hour but the elective franchise. It is only in marriage that she must demand her rights to person, children, property, wages, life, liberty, and the pursuit of happiness."[136]

Stanton envisioned radical structural change in the family based on women's full equality. "We are to-day in the midst of the greatest social revolution that the world has ever seen, because it goes down to the very foundation of society. This great idea of the equality of woman to man is knocking at the very doors of each of our homes."[137] And this scared people. Family became the foil for women's rights, juxtaposed as if in opposition. Proposals for suffrage or property rights met with opposition that such rights would cause the destruction of the family. "What will become of the family hearthstone," U.S. Senator Thomas Bayard from Delaware questioned in response to a proposed amendment to extend women's suffrage in the territories. "You will have a family with two heads—a 'house divided against itself.' You will no longer have that healthful and necessary subordination of wife to husband, and that unity of relationship which is required by a true and a real Christian marriage."[138]

At times, Stanton patiently appeased objectors, reassuring them that women's rights would not change the family, or at most, would improve it. "When this great work has been accomplished in every home and each one shall be the happy possessor of a higher marriage vow, we shall still be the possessors of not only home and family, but a better and purer order of things will be established."[139] And she dismissed the doomsayers who feared that "the advocates of Woman's Rights will ultimately abolish all distinctions of sex, make woman man, that the marriage relation will be annulled, cradles annihilated, and the stockings mended by the state; as if conjugal and maternal love depended on the puny legislation of man."[140] At other times, Stanton was less politic, boldly claiming that indeed, feminist reforms would upturn the existing oppressive family arrangements. "Fears are expressed that the ideas of Woman's Rights will disturb the whole family arrangements. I am proud to say that this will be the case."[141] She emphasized that the reform of marriage and the family for women's equality was both radical and progress.

> Conservatism cries out we are going to destroy the family. Timid reformers answer, the political equality of woman will not change it. They are both wrong. It will entirely revolutionize it. When woman is man's equal the marriage relation cannot stand on the basis it is on today. But this change will not destroy it. As human statutes and state constitutions did not create conjugal and maternal love, they cannot annul them. . . . Change is not death, neither is progress destruction.[142]

By claiming that women's rights would "upset the family relation," Stanton said, man "acknowledges that her present condition of subjection is not of her own choosing, and that if she had the power the whole relation would be essentially changed."[143] Quoting British philosopher John Stuart Mill's *Subjection of Women (1869)*, she said, "the male sex cannot yet tolerate the idea of living with an equal at the fireside, and here is the secret of the opposition to woman's equality in the State and the Church: men are not ready to recognize it at home."[144]

This book focuses on recovering and analyzing Stanton's feminist contributions to law of the family. It explores her work on marital property, marriage, divorce, domestic violence, reproductive choice, and mothering and the overarching feminist legal theory that drove her advocacy. It begins where Stanton did, with the issue of marital property rights, and then moves on to Stanton's broader structural critique of the patriarchal nature of marriage and her proposed reconstruction of marriage as a substantively equal partnership. It details her advocacy of divorce as a protection against domestic violence and as an entitlement for women's individual happiness, and the division this radical position on divorce caused among women's rights advocates. The book then examines Stanton's demands for gender-specific rights of prioritized control to women in reproductive choice and maternal custody. It concludes by exploring the striking parallels between Stanton's work and modern reforms that eventually adopted almost all of her tangible proposals for gender equality in the family.

Together, these chapters show that Stanton's theories on marriage and the family were not an evolution of thought over fifty years as much as they were a persistent application of her theories that repeated even as they developed. Stanton poured out her ideas early in the movement, with all of her ideas on marriage, divorce, and maternity foreshadowed by the Declaration of Sentiments and other early writings. She then revisited each piece of this complex and radical social challenge as current events, public interest, and her own consternation allowed. Stanton tailored her thoughts to the evolving social and political context, seeking public avenues for her radical views and taking pieces of new theories of politics, social science, and philosophy to bolster her arguments. Like an advocate, Stanton offered multiple arguments over the years in support of her ultimate position: the demand for women's full equality and agency within the family.

Writing Feminist Legal History

This is a work of feminist legal history. As history, it is focused on recovering the facts, filling in the knowledge gaps, and getting the story right. As legal, it situates Stanton's work in the context of the law, primarily concerned with understanding her advocacy in relation to domestic relations, sex equality, and access to justice. As feminist, this book "asks the woman question" as contemporary feminist theorists do by inquiring as to how the laws affected women, reading women and their experiences into the law, and utilizing critical methodologies to deconstruct and analyze the law and social norms.

This feminist legal history approach produces overall impressions that differ from the conventional understandings. First, it alters thinking about Stanton herself. It shows Stanton as a legal as well as a political actor focused on a comprehensive feminism. Her broad agenda included all issues of women's political, social, civil, and religious experience and encompassed complex and nuanced feminist thinking. She challenged the falsity of the public/private divide of separate spheres and identified the family as a key site of women's subjugation. Second, it revises oversimplified understandings of feminist legal history. A common description portrays the first-wave movement of the nineteenth century focused on the vote, a second-wave movement in the 1970s for employment and abortion, and a modern third-wave movement against reductionism to a few "women's" issues.[145] This work shows that early feminism as advanced by Stanton was a broad movement with a comprehensive agenda of political, economic, social, familial, civil, and religious justice. This comprehensive agenda, however, was not necessarily interchangeable, despite the historical tendency to lump all women's issues into one monolithic question, thereby shortchanging deep engagement. This work offers a counter approach of concentrating on one area of family rights. Third, the feminist legal history approach alters the view of the development of family law and of the issues relevant to that evolution. While family law was influenced by commercialization, codification, and industrialization, it was also challenged by feminist petition, even if legislators and judges resisted that challenge. Early feminists did challenge the private law of the family and the concrete and normative impact of designating women as inferior on the basis of her segregation into the separate domestic sphere.

The goal of this feminist legal history is to integrate its findings into the main narrative of law, salvaged from its second-class status on the sidelines. With visibility and acceptance, Stanton's work offers an applied legal history of evidence to contextualize continued debates over women's rights in the family.[146] As modern family law, for example, adopts objective economic formulas for alimony, Stanton's work calls us to question the underlying gendered assumptions of marital behavior. As subjective judicial standards of a child's "best interests" for custody operate on gendered assumptions of the "good mother" or overvalue unexpected paternal contributions, Stanton's work challenges these stereotypes and prioritizes rights based on the reality of which parent carries the burden of caregiving. And as reproductive choice faces religious preemption, Stanton's work calls us to question the religious interpretation and redirects us to understanding maternal power as a source of agency rather than incompetence. Ultimately, it's about recovering the rest of the story and letting it guide legal debates over women's rights as appropriate.

1

"What Do You Women Want?"

Many times and oft it has been asked us, with unaffected seriousness, "what do you women want? What are you aiming at?" Many have manifested a laudable curiosity to know what the wives and daughters could complain of. . . . We ask *no better laws than those you have made for yourselves. . . . [W]e ask for all that you have asked for yourselves in the progress of your development . . . ; and simply on the ground that the rights of every human being are the same and identical.*

—Elizabeth Cady Stanton, Address to the Legislature of
New-York, Feb. 14, 1854

The starting point for Stanton's women's rights advocacy was married women's property rights. A few months before the Seneca Falls convention, New York passed its first marital property statute, though it had debated the issue for almost a decade.[1] New York, like other states, was interested in marital property reform for reasons related to economic recession, debt protection, commercialization, and codification, resulting in the first generation of statutory change to coverture, beginning in the late 1830s. Stanton was familiar with this property debate, both the legal arguments and the key players, through her father's connections. Feminists found a relatively receptive audience for their property demands, in contrast to their more controversial requests for suffrage and divorce. Marital property thus emerged as one of the first opportunities for legislators as well as the public to confront the inequalities of sex.

Married women's property rights became the proxy for a broader societal discussion over gender. As Stanton explained, "[T]he property rights of married women . . . became the topic of general interest around many fashionable dinner-tables, and at many humble firesides. In this way all phases of the question were touched upon, involving the relations of the sexes, and gradually widening to all human interests—political, religious, civil, and social."[2] Capitalizing on the debate over marital property, Stanton and other feminists used this opportunity to bring their full range of women's rights issues to the lawmakers. "The drive for married women's property rights provided them with a perfect bridge, permitting the cautious to remain on the domestic side, the intrepid to invade the political side, and some to move gradually from one to the other."[3]

"What did women want?" Stanton was asked. Everything, she responded; all of the same rights as men. This formal simplicity, however, masked her more radical demands for systemic change to the law. What Stanton really wanted was a complete elimination of the legal and social system of coverture. This common law theory of marital rights inherited from England stripped married women of any legal autonomy and rights. The theory of coverture was that the legal identity of a married woman was "covered" by that of her husband upon marriage as the two became one under the law. Thus, married women's rights were subsumed into those of their husbands, and they lost all right to own, acquire, and control property during the marriage. As Stanton explained it, a husband "not only owns her, but her clothes, her wig, her false teeth, her cork leg if she has one, and if she met with an accident on the cars he recovers the price of her injuries!"[4] While the harsh effect of coverture could be technically mitigated by the equitable practice of creating premarital estates through equity, these trusts were available in few states, still vested control in male relatives, and were available only to those wealthy enough to petition the court and administer the estate.[5]

Stanton appreciated that coverture was a "legal institution whose scope was more expansive than the imposition of certain legal disabilities." Coverture not only denied married women specific legal rights, but it controlled women's larger societal position.

> It was a tool of ideology at least as much as law. The vocabulary of coverture was intended to express and enforce a total and complete subordination of married women to men at common law. It was a teaching device and its lessons were profound and unambiguous. It told women that they were inferior, it sanctified their inferiority through religious faith, and then made their subordination complete through legal disability.[6]

Stanton's goal was to go beyond the technicalities of obtaining women's ownership of assets and property and break down this system of social and legal norms altogether.

Stanton was uniquely positioned to advocate for property reform given her own experience as a married woman with property and as an apprentice in her father's law office. She recounted how she heard other women's stories of injustice from their loss of farms, homes, and income due to widowhood, creditors, and children, and how this shaped her sense of women's rights early on. Her home state of New York grappled with these issues, leading the national reform with its laws of 1848 and 1860.[7] The property issue thus spurred Stanton to political action, and she circulated petitions and lobbied legislators to gain their support for pending state legislation on married women's property acts. At the same time, Stanton critiqued the emerging legislation, recognizing its class limitations, its omission of earnings protections, and its failure to conceptualize marital property as jointly owned. She also appreciated the importance of the emerging property rights for women's citizenship status, arguing that the new rights supported their political enfranchisement. Marital property for Stanton was thus an avenue for achieving both egalitarian private rights of the family and systemic rights of public, democratic participation. Property thus became the entry point through which the rest of women's rights would follow.

Declaring Feminist Sentiments

Stanton attributed her feminist awakening to her personal experiences of the inequities of the property law for married women. These experiences included her observation of clients in her father's law office as well as her own property issues as the daughter of a wealthy father, but the wife of a poor husband. While these autobiographical accounts may have been exaggerated for political effect, Stanton cited these experiences with property law as instrumental to her own feminist development.[8]

Stanton's father, Daniel Cady, specialized in property law, handling both litigation and transactional matters of trusts, deeds, and dower.[9] Elizabeth spent many years observing her father at work, engaged in debate with her father's apprentices nightly at dinner, and later served as clerk for him, transcribing letters.[10] This de facto legal training exposed her to a wide variety of women's experiences under the property laws and raised her consciousness as to gender inequality. Stanton recalled how "the tears and complaints of the women who came to my father for legal advice touched my heart and early drew my attention to the injustice and cruelty of the laws." She identified this experience as "the primary school where I learned the a, b, c, of human rights and wrongs" and obtained the "first glimpse of an inferior and superior sex," which laid the foundation for her life's work.[11]

Stanton recounted several stories of inequities under the property law that fueled her advocacy of reform efforts. Looking back later in life, she recalled, "I see myself sitting in my father's office surrounded with students and law books, listening with indignation to the complaints of women robbed under the Common Law on which our statute laws were based." She told the story of one client, Flora Campbell, a widow, who sought legal help in retaining possession of her family farm, purchased with her money, that her husband had willed to her son. Daniel Cady counseled Flora that there was nothing the law could do, and Elizabeth was dismayed. Later, she threatened to cut every one of the "abominable laws" out of her father's law books, until he explained that it would make no difference, as the laws existed elsewhere. Stanton claims her father told her that when she grew up, she should go to Albany and talk to the legislators to tell them of the sufferings of women and widows and persuade them to pass new laws, though he was later opposed to her public career when she began to speak out for women's rights.[12]

Stanton also recalled tales of how her father's apprentices mocked her, pointing out "every aggravating law" and adding "the most exasperating comments." "The students, for their amusement, rehearsed to me each day, the laws they found in their reading that were unjust to women." She told a story of how they teased her when as a child of about ten, she showed them her new Christmas presents of a coral necklace and bracelets. One taunted, "If you were my wife, these jewels would be mine, and you could never wear them but when I gave you permission. I could sell them or give them away. Everything you have would belong to me." "These young fellows little dreamed that they were training me to overturn their pretentions to hold the reins of government."[13]

Stanton herself experienced some of these limitations of the marital property laws. She struggled with financial insecurity all of her married

Stanton house, Seneca Falls, New York, 2004. *Courtesy of Tracy Thomas.*

life. Henry had little financial success in life, being interested more in uncompensated political activities. Her father helped by providing her with a place to live both in Boston and then in Seneca Falls. When she moved to Seneca Falls, Daniel Cady transferred to his daughter property he owned there, a dilapidated house worth about two thousand dollars (fifty-five thousand dollars today).[14] When Stanton arrived in the village, "she saw only a neglected building surrounded by weeds," as the house had been "empty for some time and was badly in need of repairs." Elizabeth was left to fix up the house herself, as Henry, who had initiated the move, stayed behind in Boston to edit the antislavery newspaper, the *Emancipator*.[15]

Daniel Cady attempted to convey the house separately to his daughter by expressly excluding Henry from any ownership in the property. Cady, a property lawyer, tried to draft around the law by executing a quit-claim deed granting legal ownership of the house to his daughter "Elizabeth and to her heirs" "in consideration of the love and affection" he held for her and explicitly titling the property in the name of "Elizabeth Cady Stanton" rather than the conventional "Mrs. Henry Stanton." At his death in 1859, Daniel Cady bequeathed the sixty acres of farmland around the house to Elizabeth, dividing his remaining lands among his four daughters and providing for his wife fully in lieu of dower.[16]

Coverture continued to limit Stanton's ability to act unilaterally, though she tried to contract around it. When she sold the Seneca Falls property to move to New York City in 1862, the deed conveying the house to John Edwards for $1,650 included the language that "Henry consents in writing to Elizabeth's" sale of the property, despite Daniel Cady's intent that Henry have no right in the property. In a second deed of 1866 conveying the remaining farmlands for ten thousand dollars to James Lay, the grantors included both Elizabeth and Henry Stanton but conditioned any legal ownership of "the said Henry, believing that he has no interest in the land but executing this deed to obviate all doubts about that subject."[17] When Elizabeth later tried to purchase a house outside New York City in Tenafly, New Jersey, she expressed her frustrating that coverture again prevented her from owning property separately. "And now, with our own inheritance, we buy a home in New Jersey, and lo! we find that in this benighted state, a married woman can neither own, sell, or will what would be hers absolutely in the state of New York. Legislators of New Jersey, this will not do!"[18] These experiences taught her that marital property rights affected women in their daily lives, and, as a common reinforcement of married women's lack of rights, required change.

Stanton directed her own self-awareness of the constraints of the property laws toward raising the consciousness of other women, and men, about this problem. The Declaration of Sentiments featured demands for women's economic rights. Stanton's manifesto included a broad theoretical attack on the structure of coverture. One of the wrongs of man was that "he has made her, if married, in the eye of the law, civilly dead." The Declaration addressed the issue of marital property: "He has taken from her all right in property, even to the wages she earns." And it made the explicit connection between property and citizenship. "After depriving her of all rights as a married woman, if single and the owner of property, he has taxed her to support a government which recognizes her only when her property can be made profitable to it."[19]

Stanton house, Tenafly, New Jersey. *Courtesy Borough of Tenafly, New Jersey.*

This economic feminism and the demands for marital property rights were accepted by both conservative and radical women at the time, unlike the more subversive claim for suffrage.[20] As chronicled in Stanton's *History of Woman Suffrage*, the grassroots women's organizations that popped up after Seneca Falls in states like Ohio, Massachusetts, and Vermont focused their lobbying and recruitment on issues of property rights. Loss of the family home and personal property, the disabilities of dower in a widow's one-third share of her husband's property at his death, lack of ownership of wages earned, and creditor issues filled the pages of the women's grievances. When feminists pointed out how the law made wives financial dependents, "they made concrete the injury of disfranchisement in a way that abstract appeals to rights could not."[21] Property issues, thus, were able to recruit new members to the cause of women's rights and to the more debatable demand for suffrage.

But convincing women of the injustices of the property law was still difficult, as women fell back on ingrained biblical notions of men's superiority. Stanton recounted how "a very devout woman asked me, if that would not be an infringement on the divinely ordained headship of man and opposed to the principles of the Bible." So she "turned to the 27th of Numbers and read her about the five daughters of Zelophehad." The five unmarried women, having no brothers, petitioned Moses to inherit their deceased father's estate. Under Jewish law, property passed to the eldest son, or to the next male relative. Stanton emphasized that "these girls plead [sic] their own case," and that the governing men were greatly impressed with the justice of the demand, and the clear, concise way in which the plaintiffs presented their case. Though Moses was puzzled by the novel demand, so contrary to law, his appeal to the Lord was clear. And "the Lord *said* the daughters of Zelophehad *speak right*." That Old Testament authority convinced Stanton's objector, who responded, "Why! . . . I never read that before," and signed the petition forthwith.[22] The Zelophehad example, however, did not fully support Stanton's petition. While it exemplified women's boldness in asserting their rights, the precedent established only the rights of single women, which coverture allowed. Moreover, the story did not end well. When the daughters later tried to marry outside of the tribe, the Jewish leaders denied their rights, afraid that valuable land would transfer outside their control.[23] Biblical authority would not be the way to further married women's property rights, though it helped to convince at least a few signers.

Married Women's Property Acts

New York first passed legislation addressing married women's property rights in April 1848, just before Seneca Falls. The state enacted a statute protecting married women's separate property, acquired prior to marriage, by designating the wife as the sole owner of that property, thereby insulating it from her husband's creditors.[24] The New York law was one of many married women's property acts sweeping the nation beginning in the late 1830s to retain women's separate ownership of property. These laws were passed in three waves: first, debt protection statutes; then separate estates for married women; and finally, after the Civil War, earnings statutes. Almost every state adopted a form of the first-generation credit-protection statutes, exempting wives' property from their husbands' creditors. Others then created separate estates for women to hold, but usually not control, property acquired prior to marriage or inherited after marriage. The impetus for the marital property reforms was the recessed Jacksonian economy and the desire to protect family assets from creditors. The broader codification movement also drove the property changes as reformers sought to eliminate the vagaries and practices of equity by replacing it with more legislative control of statutory law.[25] More specifically, legal reformers sought to codify the equitable device of the antenuptial estate that retained a woman's premarital property separate for her own use but required that it be controlled and managed by a trustee of her father, brother, or other third party.[26]

In Stanton's home state of New York, she explained how "conservatives, radicals, and good society all joined hands and secured this act of justice" in the married women's property bill.[27] Reform of the New York marital property system emanated from efforts to deal with three problems: the instability of the economy, the inequities of the legal system, and women's rights.[28] Stanton recalled how the "selfishness of man was readily enlisted in securing woman's civil rights," from fathers seeking to bequeath property to daughters away from profligate husbands and husbands seeking to protect property from business debts. Stanton teased at the "wise selfishness" of "solid, thrifty Dutch fathers," who were "daily confronted with the fact that the inheritance of their daughters, carefully accumulated, would at marriage, pass into the hands of dissipated, impecunious husbands, reducing them and their children to poverty and dependence."[29] The codification movement attacked the elitism, high fees, and inefficiency of the state's equity courts, and instead sought uniform statutory laws made by elected legislators. In particular, the codification reforms sought to eliminate the equitable premarital trusts, on the belief that such trusts facilitated fraud on creditors by creating dual equitable and legal title, but also sought to retain the exception permitting a wife's separate legal ownership of property.[30]

The originator of the New York bill was motivated as Stanton was by concerns of gender equality. Thomas Herttell, a sixty-five-year-old assemblyman and judge, first proposed the idea in 1836 to the judiciary committee of the state assembly as a woman's rights initiative, arguing that the bill was needed to facilitate the natural rights of women's equality and to protect women from their husband's creditors.[31] His bill was wide-ranging, granting married women rights to separate property and their earnings, to write wills, and to have guardianship of their children.[32] Herttell argued on the basis of equality: "The doctrine, or just and moral principle of 'equal rights' cannot consistently, and does not righteously justify laws, giving to one sex powers and privileges relative to property which are denied to the other. The 'natural and inalienable right of life, liberty, and the pursuit of happiness,' is common to both sexes." Herttell presented his bill in legalistic form, arguing that the denial of women's equality violated the constitutional right to due process of law. He argued that taking a woman's property acquired either before or after marriage was tantamount to theft as the coercive law took the property of one and arbitrarily gave it to another. Such arbitrary deprivation of property without reason or compensation was a classic violation of due process. He backed up his assertions of right by comparing single women's right to property and the arbitrariness of the law that changed that inherent equality only by virtue of marriage. "Has marriage deprived them of their senses and their wits, as well as of their rights of property, which they possessed before marriage?" He argued, if anything, that a married woman was more able to manage property than a single one. "With the additional incitement of maternal solicitude for the well-being of her children, has not a married woman even more inducement to the discreet appropriation of her property to their maintenance, than an unmarried woman . . . ?"[33]

At first, support for these feminist ideals was limited. "Organized women's support for Herttell's bill appears to have been limited to one petition with six signatures collected by reformer Ernestine Rose, and one other petition with meager support from Utica."[34] An 1848 petition, submitted to the legislature months before Seneca Falls, included signatures of "forty-four ladies" from the towns of Darien and Covington, who cited the Declaration of Independence to challenge the laws "depriving us of property, of the means of acquiring it, and even of individuality."[35] Stanton helped Rose's petitioning effort, and along with Paulina Wright Davis and later Susan B. Anthony, organized petitioning campaigns to generate public support for New York marital property reform.[36] However, she called petitioning work "the most depressing work reformers ever did," as doors were slammed in their faces and "rudeness was the rule, courtesy the exception."[37] Instead, Stanton spent more time lobbying behind the scenes with prominent jurists and supporters of the New York property bills, taking advantage of the social networks established through her father during her lengthy stays in Albany from 1843 to 1846. Stanton recalled her meetings with "Judge Hurlbut and a large circle of lawyers and legislators" like Governor William Seward and Joshua Spencer and "exerting herself to strengthen their convictions in favor of the pending bill." Judge Hurlbut had written a tract, "Human Rights," on the equality of women, "with a lawyer's prejudice," first preparing a paper against the rights of women and then rebutting every argument.[38]

In 1844, the New York Assembly Judiciary Committee issued a report finally joining the issue of married women's separate property, though it rejected feminist reform. The committee dismissed feminist petitioners' requests for "an entire and radical change" to the marital law by adopting something similar to the community property regimes of Louisiana and France, whereby the wife could maintain separate property. The committee mocked feminists' claims of harm to domestic harmony, loss of self-respect, and individual happiness, finding no evidence of the claimed wrongs. They were "trying to discover what evils" there were from the property laws, but found that there simply were none. Instead, they reified the common law of coverture as "the perfection of reason," since it existed for centuries in England, controlled in America from the first settlement, and was relied upon by learned jurists, "as pure men as ever lived." Citing stare decisis, they said that a "small evil or slight inconvenience" is better tolerated than unsettling and remodeling settled law. As a matter of policy, the committee concluded that to maintain marital unity, necessary for moral and social order and the protection of children, in the merger of spouses, "one or the other must become the lesser star in the constellation and yield some rights." Given the "physical and moral delicacy of woman," it was obvious that the husband was better equipped to "command the rough battle" and "arduous duties" of marital rights. The committee, however, did propose a substitute bill seeking to reinstate the common law equitable practice of antenuptial trusts and marital settlements that had been "inadvertently" lost with the revisions to state law. They concluded that it was more appropriate for the wife to be protected by the intervention of a third-party trustee than for her to have individual control.[39]

Public debate on the married women's property bills finally aired at the 1846 New York Constitutional Convention. Before this, little debate had taken place on the married women's bills as discussion had been relegated to judiciary committees, where bills failed to emerge for vote. At the constitutional convention, the primary goal was simplification and administration of the courts. The convention provided for the election of judges and abolished courts of chancery, merging equity and law in the common law courts. The elimination of equity, and accordingly married women's separate equitable estate, eased the way to considering a similar statutory right. The delegates to the convention, some state legislators and others lawyers, farmers, and businessmen, initially voted to insert a married women's clause into the state constitution.[40] The main proposal was to permit married women to hold individual premarital and inherited property separately, similar to the preexisting equitable estate. Initially, debates in early October supported the separate estate on grounds of economic protection of women, as well as some feminist-like arguments as to women's independence.[41] The clause passed by fifty-eight to forty-four.

Three days later, the convention rescinded the vote, and on revote, the act lost fifty-nine to fifty. The debate was reopened by conservative New York City lawyer Charles O'Conor, who supported slavery as a "just, benign and beneficent institution."[42] He challenged the clause on alleged religious grounds, arguing that the "sacred institution of marriage" should remain untouched by law reform, as marriage was of "divine origin," and that control by the husband "is the price which female wants and weakness must pay for their protection." And he raised the fear of the female economic competitor, arguing that a wife with a separate estate "might rival her husband in trade or become the partner of his rival." Yet, despite this final defeat, the constitutional convention had "crystallized the issues" and created some "expectation that passage of a married women's act was merely a question of time."[43]

Less than two years later, the issue of married women's property "sailed through" the New York legislature, passing the Assembly by a vote of ninety-three to nine and the Senate by a vote of twenty-eight to one in April 1848. By this time the issue of marital property had been pending for twelve years, it had finally obtained public debate and support at the constitutional convention, most states had already adopted some form of married women's property acts, and women's petitioning increased from the paltry five signatures to six thousand. An 1846 judiciary committee report concluded that it was satisfied that chancery law was adequate to protect a wife's separate estate "if only it were more generally understood by the public" and accessible in statutory form.[44] The successful bill originated with Judge John Fine, who lost in a judicial race against Daniel Cady in 1847.[45] The new law allowed married women to hold separately property owned prior to marriage, free from the control, disposal, or debts of their husbands.[46] It also permitted married women to acquire separate property after marriage by inheritance or gift that would remain their separate property. A revision in 1849 granted women the right to "convey and devise" their separate inherited property.[47] These new laws did little more than restore the equitable separate estate, as intended, but it was a starting point for meaningful legal reform for women.

Limitations of the Early Statutes

The married women's property statutes were a symbolic first step for women's property rights and for redesigning the social vision of marriage under coverture. Stanton proclaimed New York as "the first State to emancipate wives from the slavery of the old common law of England, and to secure to them equal property rights."[48] The marital property laws had practical and symbolic significance for the women's movement, which Stanton trumpeted as concrete examples of women's legal agency. She said that for

> thirty years we tried to get the laws so amended as to secure to woman all her civil and political rights. Reading the barbarous code when but twelve years old, and with the same kind of interest that we did "Jack the Giant Killer," we vowed we would never rest until every woman in the state of New York was secure in the property she inherited from her father, in the wages she earned and the children of her love; and we have triumphed.[49]

But Stanton was also quick to point out the failure of these statutes to address women's economic reality, including their earnings and their uncompensated labor in the home.[50] Stanton vigorously objected to claims made that the New York statute afforded husbands and wives complete equality in all matters except suffrage. She argued that "the wife has never had an equal right to the joint earnings of the copartnership, as no valuation has ever been placed on her labor in the household. . . . This is *the vital point* of interest to the vast majority of married women, since it is only the *few* who ever possess anything through separate earnings or inheritance."[51]

As Stanton noted, the separate estate for wives was of limited practical value to most women. Only a few wealthy women inherited separate property from their fathers. Working-class married women who earned money outside the home as domestic workers, seamstresses, or factory workers did not have ownership of their earnings. The majority of women at that time performed household labor, working for the family cooking, cleaning, sewing, caring for children, nursing the sick, or working in family endeavors like farms, dairies, and taverns. This family labor did not create any ownership rights in the wife, but instead was considered a gift or moral service performed for the family.[52]

Moreover, the New York courts, like most other state courts, interpreted the married woman's property act narrowly, retaining restrictions of coverture.[53] "A hostile judiciary constrained the transformative possibilities of the reform legislation, by interpreting the statutes to preserve common-law understandings of marriage."[54] The close parallels between the language of the separate estate statutes and their predecessors of the equitable antenuptial trusts "made narrow construction almost inevitable."[55] The early property acts were designed for economic security and debt protection, and "were thus drafted and construed in accordance with equitable precedents, to give wives limited disposition powers over the property to which they now had legal title." Courts trying to resolve the commercial confusion created by this hybrid property regime vacillated between family protection and protection of creditor interests, but did not consider the empowerment of wives.[56]

Stanton was impatient as male legislatures slowly awakened to the full nature of the problem of women's disabilities as to property. In 1850, Stanton wrote a sarcastic article under her pseudonym "S.F." (Sun Flower) for Amelia Bloomer's temperance newspaper, the *Lily*, lauding the New York legislature's proposed bill allowing a married woman to withdraw the full amount of her earnings she deposited into a savings account. She poked fun at an earlier version of the bill that permitted a woman to withdraw only $250 of each $1,000 she deposited and mocked the generosity of the expanded revision.

> Let the women of the Empire State return countless thanks to their sires and sons. Only think of it! A woman!! be she married or single, can now deposit her *own* money in a bank, and draw it *all* out again *herself*. The length, the breadth, the height and the depth of this act of mercy and justice is only equalled by the fact that our Legislatures have been but fifty short years in arriving at its truth.[57]

During this time in the early 1850s, the women's movement concentrated its efforts on marital property reform. Feminists argued for a redistribution of property, "'joint property' laws that would recognize wives' claims to marital assets to which husbands otherwise had title." The antebellum feminists argued that "wives were entitled to joint rights in marital property by reason of the labor they contributed to the family economy." Stanton raised the issue of joint property at an 1848 meeting in Rochester held a few weeks after the Seneca Falls convention.[58] Replying to one man who asserted the doctrine of marital unity, Stanton said "she thought the Gospel, rightly understood, pointed to a oneness of equality, not subordination, and that property should be jointly held."[59] At the 1851 convention in Worcester, Massachusetts, Stanton coauthored resolutions on joint property providing "that since the economy of the household is generally as much the source of family wealth as the labor and enterprise of man, therefore the wife should, during life, have the same control over the joint earnings as her husband, and the right to dispose at her death of the same proportion of it as he."[60] A few years later she challenged the New York legislature to understand the joint contributions in acquiring marital property: "Think you that the woman who has worked hard all her days, in helping her husband to accumulate a large property, consents to the law that places this wholly at his disposal?"[61] Speaking to a U.S. Senate committee decades later, Stanton renewed her demand that a wife and mother must have an equal right "to the joint earnings of the co-partnership."[62] This petition for transformation of marital property norms, however, gained little traction beyond the few states that adopted community property regimes of French and

Spanish origin theoretically giving the wife a right to own, but not manage, one-half of the property acquired during marriage.[63]

Feminists instead directed their efforts to support the more viable political movement to reform property statutes to grant wives their own separate rights to property.[64] These statutes expanded the marital property reforms to working-class women, assisting those women who earned wages. Legislators were more open to considering the narrower idea of earnings laws and were willing to appease women with these laws in the face of increasing pressure to grant women the right to vote.[65] The vote threatened women's access to political power, while the earnings laws continued ideas about women's need for self-protection. Some feminists, like Antoinette Brown Blackwell, considered these earnings laws pragmatic first steps, pursued for economic realities rather than principles of marriage equality better reflected in joint property constructs.[66]

New York was at the forefront of this later generation of marital property laws. Male supporters of the New York married women's property bill sought out Stanton because they wanted a woman to argue the cause of the female sex. Stanton was then immersed in the chaos and drudgery of raising five children under the age of ten, while Henry, then a state senator, lived most of the year in Albany. Stanton agreed to write an address to enumerate the gendered effects of the laws, but sought research help from others, frustrated by her caregiving restraints. Writing to Susan Anthony, Stanton pleaded,

> Can you get any acute lawyer . . . sufficiently interested in our movement to look up just eight laws concerning us—the very worst in all the code? I can generalize and philosophize easily enough myself; but the details of the particular laws I need, I have not time to look up. You see, while I am about the house, surrounded by my children, washing dishes, baking, sewing, etc., I can think up many points, but I cannot search books, for my hands as well as my brains would be necessary for that work. . . . Men who can, when they wish to write a document, shut themselves up for days with their thoughts and their books, know little of what difficulties a woman must surmount.[67]

A few days later, she wrote Anthony again, pouring out her frustrations about rambunctious children and no childcare help, lamenting that her

Elizabeth Cady Stanton with Henry, 1854.

address was "not nearly finished" nor was she satisfied with it and that she would have to "sit up nights" to get it done in time.[68] Anthony responded to Stanton's plea by coming to help take care of the children while Stanton finished the address, though the children hated visits from the stern Anthony, who was so different from their easygoing mother.

Stanton then went to the state capital at Albany to present her ideas. Stanton read her address in front of a state Woman's Rights Convention on February 14, 1854, and then submitted it in written form with petitions of ten thousand to the legislative members, where it was referred to a select committee designated to consider "the just and equal rights of women." Family mythology, perpetuated by Stanton herself, claimed that this speech caused Stanton's father such distress that he threatened to disown her, but that he had a change of heart and ultimately helped her add the many legal citations seen in the speech.[69]

Stanton's 1854 address to the New York legislature took the opportunity of the proposed property reform to present a broader attack on the needed legal reforms for all aspects of women's lives. Stanton demanded systemic change: "The thinking minds of all nations call for change. There is a deep-lying struggle in the whole fabric of society; a boundless grinding collision of the New with the Old." She sought "redress of our grievances" through "a new code of laws" that provided "the full recognition of all our rights as citizens of the Empire State."[70] She addressed all of the issues that would become the platform of the women's movement, including suffrage, juries, marriage, marital property, earnings, domestic violence, dower, maternal custody, and guardianship of children. She detailed the legal disabilities of women, organized into four parts of women's lives, as woman, wife, widow, and mother.

On the property issue, Stanton acknowledged the legal significance of the earlier New York married women's property act that created legal identity for women with inherited property. "The wife who is so fortunate as to have inherited property, has, by the new law in this state, been redeemed from her lost condition. She is no longer a legal nonentity." She made the lawyer's argument about statutory construction: "This property law, if fairly construed, will overturn the whole code relating to woman and property." She argued that the right to property implied the right to buy and sell, will, and bequeath. "Herein is the dawning of a civil existence for woman, for now the 'femme covert' must have the right to make contracts." She jested, "so, get ready, gentlemen; the 'little justice' will be coming to you one day."[71]

However, she went on to acknowledge the irrelevance of that law for many women, who did not inherit family property. The more common question of property rights was that of earned income. "If by great economy she accumulates a small sum, which for future need she deposit, little by little, in a savings bank, the husband has a right to draw it out, at his option, to use it as he may see fit." Stanton continued: "Though the whole support of the family be thrown upon the wife, if the wages she earns be paid to her by her employer, the husband can receive them again. If, by unwearied industry and perseverance, she can earn for herself and children a patch of ground and a shed to cover them, the husband can strip her of all her hard earnings, turn her and her little ones out in the cold northern blast." She added that the law must reach "all the laboring women, who are loudly demanding remuneration for their unending toil—those women who teach in our seminaries, academies and common schools for a miserable pittance; the widows, who are taxed without mercy; the unfortunate ones in our work houses, poor houses and prisons." "Now do you *candidly* think," she asked rhetorically, "these wives do not wish to control the wages they earn—to own the land they buy—the houses they build?"[72]

Reports of the Assembly's discussion of Stanton's speech reveal that the legislators condemned Stanton and the other "unsexed women." An article in the Albany paper reported the opinion of one legislator: "[I]t is well known that the object of these unsexed women is to overthrow the most sacred of our institutions, to set at defiance the Divine law which declares man and wife to be one, and establish on its ruins what will be in fact and in principle but a species of legalized adultery."[73] A statement released by a select committee of the legislature offered a theological rationale. "A higher power than that from which emanates legislative enactments has given forth the mandate that man and woman shall not be equal . . . and civil power must, in its enactments, recognize this inequality. We cannot obliterate it if we would, and legal inequalities must follow."[74]

Yet, at the end of March, a select Assembly Committee proposed a bill entitling wives to claim their own earnings where their husbands were drunkards or deserters, and gave wives a veto in apprentice or guardianship decisions of their children.[75] The earnings provision would have simply codified the existing common law precedents of recognizing certain wives as "sole-traders" because of their husband's consent, absence, desertion, or nonsupport. The committee rejected the more subversive visions of marriage that Stanton and other feminist supporters advanced, reaffirming the headship of the husband in the family. While the bill did not pass, it signaled to women's rights activists that reform was now a possibility.[76]

The women's rights reformers accelerated their petitioning efforts. Anthony "took up the laboring oar," canvassing fifty-four of sixty counties during the first half of 1855 to collect enough signatures for "mammoth petitions with which to bombard the Legislature at every annual session."[77] One of these petitions for suffrage and marital property reforms with thirteen thousand signatures was submitted to the 1855 select committee.[78] That committee's report, however, ridiculed the women's petition, arguing facetiously that it was the gentlemen, in fact, who were the sufferers of oppression. "The ladies always have the best place and choicest tidbit at the table. They always have the best seat in the cars, carriages and sleighs, the warmest place in the winter, and the coolest place in the summer." Commenting on married couples who had both signed the same petition, they recommended that the parties "apply for a law authorizing them to change dresses, that the husband may wear petticoats and the wife the breeches."[79] Stanton continued her efforts by drafting and writing from the confines of her home.[80] She appealed to women using temperance argumentation:

> Do you know, women of New York, that under our present laws married women have no right to the wages they earn! Think of the 40,000 drunkards' wives in this state—of the wives of men who are licentious—of gamblers—of the long line of those who do nothing; and is it no light matter that all these women who support themselves, their husbands, and families, too, shall have no right to the disposition of their own earnings!

And she commanded them to action: "Roll up, then, your Petitions on this point, if no other, and secure to laboring women their wages at the coming session."[81]

In 1860, the New York legislature considered an act to grant married women the right to their own earnings. Anthony provided a copy of the new Massachusetts earnings law to the sponsor of the bill in the New York Senate.[82] But she and other women's rights reformers continued to rely on Stanton's oratory and lobbying efforts to push the bill through. "Mrs. Stanton must move heaven and earth now to secure this bill, and she can, if she will only try."[83] Stanton had promised, "Dear Susan, I am ready, willing, and happy to do next month the appointed work at Albany. However, I cannot, my dear friend, move heaven and earth; but I will do what I can with pen and brain."[84] The forty-three-year-old Stanton was still encumbered by parenting burdens, now with seven children ages newborn to seventeen. Stanton did not make it to Albany in time to affect the vote, but the legislature passed the earnings bill by a large majority.[85]

Stanton delivered her speech to a joint session of the legislative judiciary committees several days later, while the bill awaited the governor's signature. Her address mentioned virtually nothing about property or earnings, but instead used the occasion to make the broader demands for women's citizenship and challenged the systemic inequality of the law.[86] She begged the lawmakers to "let us alone." "Let us take care of ourselves, our property, our children, our homes. . . . There has been a great deal written and said about 'protection.' We as a class, are tired of one kind of protection, that which leaves us everything to do, to dare, and to suffer, and strips us of all means for its accomplishment." Her demand was to "strike down all special legislation for us."[87]

The earnings act passed in March 1860, granting a wife rights to earnings "acquired by trade, business, labor or services" carried on or performed "on her sole and separate account." It somewhat expanded wives' capacity to "bargain, sell and convey" their separate property, extending that right of control beyond inherited property as provided in the 1849 law to premarital and earned separate property. However, the law now required, for all conveyances by a wife, the written assent of the husband, with a judicial bypass exception in the case of a dissolute or irrational husband.[88] It created "capacity for women to act as a legal agent on her own behalf," allowing women to be sued on matters related to her separate property and earnings, and allowing women to sue for damages.[89] It created equal guardianship rights over children and equalized wives' and husbands' share of intestate inheritance by reducing the husband's share to one-third. The *New York Times* reported the significance of the bill: "It is the most sweeping innovation ever made upon any established usage—reversing entirely the old system, rooting it up in fact."[90] The earnings act proved the ability of feminists to exert political pressure. "Every provision of the 1860 statute . . . was a specific goal of the women's movement. . . . The New York Earnings Act, in other words, was the significant legislative realization of demands for women by women."[91] Two years later, however, the New York legislature repealed much of the law. It revoked the guardianship and inheritance provisions, but retained the earnings right and improved a wife's ability to convey property by eliminating the required husband's consent.[92] As Stanton and Anthony had feared, without pressure from the women's rights community, distracted by the Civil War and abolition efforts, women's legal gains were unsecured.

The New York courts as well limited the reach of the new law, acknowledging "the radical change of the common law" embodied in the earnings statute but nevertheless interpreting the earnings laws narrowly to preserve a husband's traditional right to his wife's labor.[93] The courts determined that the purpose of the statute was to protect wives from hardship or dissolute husbands, and thus concluded that under the statute a wife's earnings belonged to the husband unless "necessary for a wife's protection that she should control the proceeds of her labor."[94] Even where a wife labored for a third party, the courts held that her earnings presumptively belonged to the husband unless exceptional circumstances applied, such as the wife living separately from her husband, laboring for her own support, or requiring protection from her husband's drunkenness or idleness.[95] Toward the end of the century, wives began to be successful in recovering their own earnings, and the presumptions of a husband's ownership of his wife's earnings were legislatively overruled in New York in 1902, forty years after passage of the earnings act.[96]

Stanton continued to advocate for marital property rights through the pages of the *Revolution* and to use those rights to unify the women's movement.[97] When a prominent male legislator tried to credit the benevolence of men with passage of marital property reform, Stanton quickly retorted that all credit was due women. She highlighted women's own agency in bringing about the change. "Women have fought their own battle," she said. "We are not indebted to 'the law-making sex' for one step in progress. Every concession has been wrung from our opponents. The page of history is black with the oppressions of women, lightened only by their own protests and appeals."[98]

An Insult to Widows

Stanton also attacked the existing laws and customs affecting widows. Just after the Declaration of Sentiments, the Woman's Rights Convention held in Rochester in August 1848 resolved "[t]hat the assumption of law to settle the estates of men who die without wills, having widows, is an insult to woman, and ought to be regarded as such by every lover of right and equality."[99] Stanton took on the conventional wisdom that the common law provided "a generous gift to the wife" because of her special place under the law.[100] "Whenever we attempt to point out the wrongs of the wife, those who would have us believe that the laws cannot be improved, point us to the privileges, powers and claims of the widow." To the contrary, she argued. At the husband's death, the law "instantly spies out this widow, . . . and announces to her the startling intelligence that but one-third of the house and lot, and one-half the personal property, are hers. The law has other favorites with whom she must share the hard-earned savings of years."[101]

Dower was the common law right of intestacy, determining a widow's right to property in the absence of her husband's will.[102] Dower gave the wife a life interest in one-third of the real property of her husband.[103] She was entitled to her share before debts were paid, thus granting some protection against her husband's creditors. In many states by the nineteenth century, dower also included one-half of the husband's personal property, and had already included her "paraphernalia" of bare necessities, usually defined as bed, clothing, spinning wheel, tea kettle, and Bible. In contrast, husbands were "tenants by the curtesy" entitled to a life estate in all of his wife's real property (unless no children were born of the marriage) and all of her personal property that he acquired at marriage to possess both during her life and after her death. Thus, the husband had the right of "absolute managerial control over all of his wife's property from the time of the marriage ceremony until his death."[104]

Dower was effectively a very limited right. The primary purpose of dower was merely the immediate support of a widow, not her economic independence. The "widow's thirds" entitled the wife only to a life interest in the property; she could not sell or devise it, and at her death it passed to her husband's heirs, not hers. She was not entitled to possession of the marital home, but was merely a tenant and could be, and was often, evicted from her home at her husband's death. At most, she was entitled to money damages of one-third of the purchase price of the home at the husband's death. Women could also waive their rights to dower, and were often forced to do so to facilitate the purchase and transfer of land. Husbands and purchasers routinely ignored dower rights. Property held in equitable estate or corporate form was excluded from dower and thus sheltered from the wife.[105]

Stanton was familiar with the complexities and limitations of dower as her father, as a property and equity lawyer, tried many cases on the issue. Daniel Cady often represented the defendant creditor against the widow, and in the few cases where he represented the widow, he lost.[106]

Stanton thus understood widows as victims of the law. "In this dark hour of grief, the coarse minions of the law gather round the widow's hearthstone, and, in the name of justice, outrage all natural sense of right." She lamented how "the husband has the absolute right to will away his property as he may see fit, . . . leaving his wife . . . dependent on the bounty of her own children."[107] Stanton conveyed the realities of many women, left destitute at their husbands' death, dependent on ne'er-do-well sons, or left to the mercy of creditors. A wife's own money, earned, gifted, or inherited, was not hers even after her husband's death. Stanton exclaimed,

> Go ask the poor widow, childless and alone, driven out from the beautiful home which she had helped to build and decorate, why strangers dwell at her hearthstone, enjoy the shade of trees planted by her hand, drink in the fragrance of her flowers, whilst she must seek some bare and humbler home? Will she tell you she has "all the rights she wants"?[108]

Stanton featured women's experiences as widows to personalize and persuade both women and legislators of the equities of her proposed reforms. "The cases are without number where women, who have lived in ease and elegance, at the death of their husbands have, by will, been reduced to the bare necessities of life."[109] She facetiously applauded the property laws, which recognized a widow as the ward of her "provider," who could leave her in his will the property she helped to earn working "12 to 18 hours out of the 24 for years."[110] She turned the tables on men to illustrate the unfairness. Contemplating the right of a wife to will her own separate property, Stanton sarcastically asked what would become of the happy husband of a millionaire when he became a "tenant for life" and was "cut down in a day" to the use of one-third of his estate, and if he remarried, was "thrown penniless on the cold world?" "Poor man!" Stanton replied. "He would be rich, though, in the *sympathies* of many women who have passed through just such an ordeal."[111]

Stanton's challenge to dower was a symbolic and systemic attack as much as it was a pragmatic demand. Many exceptions and rules of law mitigated the harsh realities of dower. Intestacy law could be avoided altogether by the will of a husband bequeathing property to his wife.[112] And the strict parameters of dower had already begun to recede in colonial times with the expanding commercial economy.[113] Dower, though, provided a context by which to challenge the normative aspects of coverture. Stanton and other nineteenth-century feminists "understood a critique of dower as integrally related to their larger critique of marriage's role in preserving women's unequal status." They saw that "the law's regrettable treatment of widows reflected the basic framework of marriage law and, moreover, that inheritance law reform had the potential to reform the institution of marriage itself."[114] So, for example, when Stanton responded to a report of an Ohio case upholding a proviso in a husband's will forfeiting the wife's inheritance and remitting her to dower if she remarried, she sarcastically compared the principle of the case to the "burning of Hindoo widows on the funeral pile of their husbands."[115] "The civilized man . . . takes a less summary mode of drawing his beloved partner after him; he does it by the deprivation and starvation of the flesh, and the humiliation and mortification of the spirit . . . bequeathing to the wife just enough to keep soul and body together."[116]

More concretely, Stanton challenged the formal inequality of the dower laws. She attacked the laws that provided only a portion for women compared to a larger share for men. "Behold the magnanimity of the law in allowing the widow to retain a life interest in one-third the landed estate, and one-half the personal property" but giving the house and land *all* to the husband had she died first. "How, I ask you, can that be called justice, which makes such a distinction as this between man and woman?"[117] This sex-equality critique offered "a radical vision of equal rights within a reconstructed, nonhierarchical legal family" that challenged the common law world of coverture.[118]

In 1860, the New York legislature equalized the rules of dower and curtesy regarding real property, as Stanton had advanced.[119] This later-generation married women's property act gave the surviving husband or wife with minor children "all the real estate of which the husband or wife died seised, and all the rents, issues and profits thereof during the minority of the youngest child, and one-third thereof during his or natural life." For survivors with no minor children, the law granted a "life estate in one-third of all the real estate." The effect of the law was to increase women's dower rights to include all of the real estate where there were children. It also, however, increased the rights of men in the event of no children, changing a husband's share of the real estate from zero to one-third. These provisions were repealed along with the other marital property changes of 1862.[120] Ultimately, though, Stanton's equality argument prevailed, as New York and other states in the early twentieth century abolished dower in favor of gender-neutral elective share laws that allowed both men and women to elect a one-half share of a spouse's estate.

New York had previously considered a bill enlarging a widow's share of real estate in 1840 when it considered other credit-protective legislation following economic depression.[121] Instead, it, like other states, passed new insurance laws permitting married women to enter insurance contracts on their husbands.[122] The insurance laws provided statutory inroads to the legal fiction of marital unity that accepted the two contractually distinct persons of husband and wife. Insurance evolved to permit husbands to insure their wives' lives, but only through higher rates for coverage of women. Stanton criticized this differential: "Shall we ever get to the end of the absurdities into which men run on the supposed differences in sex." She also criticized the companies' distinctions in coverage. "Believing that women, like cats, have nine lives, they insure us against death, but not accidents." Telling a story about two female railcar companions, Stanton lamented how these dressmakers were swindled by the insurance companies taking their money, which was "too much to lose," and absurdly basing business transactions on the traditional view of women's frailty, and thus high risk of accident. "Are all women to be regarded like a basket of eggs or blown glass ornaments?"[123]

In other contexts, though, Stanton argued that widows deserved special protective legislation. Her arguments seemed to be made in the alternative; if legislatures refused to treat widows equally with widowers, then women were dissimilarly situated and should thus be treated differently. This gendered understanding of dependency seemed more reality than ideal. For widows, she advocated for homestead exemptions. Homestead laws arising in the mid-1800s created exceptions in bankruptcy for the family home to protect it from creditors, though the laws typically only granted the surviving wife a right to reside in the home, and not an alienable interest. These laws were based on family protection and the continuing dependence of the wife.[124] Stanton argued not only that the homestead should be exempted but also that it should be owned by the wife and mother in all cases as their "fixed inheritance." Playing on the conventional wisdom, she argued, "Woman's sphere is home, man has always said, but he has never yet made any provision to secure her in the possession of it. The proverb is a mockery."[125]

Stanton also argued that widows were entitled to special tax exemptions.[126] Continuing her theme of "taxation without representation," she argued that if women were not entitled to vote, they should not be required to pay taxes.[127] She played on the reciprocal relationship between taxing and voting, though theorists by this time articulated public protection, and not suffrage, as the responsive right to the obligation to pay tax.[128] In her national lectures, Stanton featured an Indiana law creating such a widow's exemption. The 1872 law exempted five hundred dollars of property from taxation if the woman's total estate did not exceed one thousand dollars, though Stanton complained that the law was "a dead letter because the women do not know of its existence," and "the officials who collect the taxes do not feel it to be their duty to inform them."[129]

When she learned that the law had been declared unconstitutional by the Indiana Supreme Court, she dissected the opinion in the *Revolution*. The Court struck down the widow exemption as a violation of the state constitutional mandate of "equal taxation," holding that it did not constitute a permissible "charity" exception because it was not based on the purpose of the property, but on the class of the owner.[130] Using classic Aristotelian logic, Stanton challenged the formality of this equal treatment rationale, arguing that it is not equality to treat women the same when they are differently situated. She cited the precedent of other exemptions for types of people, including poor black men, clergy, Indians, and militia. Stanton illustrated the unfairness of the logical extension of these exemptions that expired upon the death of the husband, thereby taxing the widow of the clergy or militiaman for the first time. And she challenged the injustice of the taxation imposed by men without women's participation, exposing their blatant self-interest, like that of sovereigns and nobles before them. "In running over the history of the past it is curious to see the cunning devices of those in power to lay the heavy burdens ever on the shoulders of those classes that cannot help themselves."[131]

Property as Citizenship

This connection among taxation, property, and political rights was part of Stanton's initial philosophy articulated in the Declaration of

Sentiments. In the Declaration, she identified the abuse of power from taxation of single women and widows without a voice in governance. "If single and the owner of property, he has taxed her to support a government which recognizes her only when her property can be made profitable to it." The Declaration made a broad demand for women's status as "citizens" and full members of the community with all civil, economic, and political rights.[132] Citizens, unlike the more general category of "persons," have power and participatory rights in the governance through political action. She challenged the deprivation of "the first right of a citizen, the elective franchise," and demanded women's "immediate admission to all the rights and privileges which belong to them as citizens." These rights included "the right to protect one's person and property; to govern one's self; to have a voice in the law and rulers; to enjoy all the advantages and opportunities of life of which one is capable. This is citizenship in a republic. The natural right to life, liberty, and happiness."[133]

The Declaration of Sentiments "ushered in a new conception of citizenship, for its crucial themes included natural and inalienable rights, suffrage and national citizenship, and legal protection derived from right of contract."[134] Stanton utilized liberal political theories of natural, individual rights, arguing that women, the same as men, were entitled to participation in the public sphere in accordance with rights of self-government.[135] She also appealed to republican political theories of the virtuous citizen working for the collective common good, arguing that women had abilities, as property holders, taxpayers, and morally superior people meriting citizenship.[136]

Women's point of entry into this citizen class, though, was not clear. Citizens were defined by their privileges and obligations of voting, jury service, and military service, all of which excluded women.[137] Women's obligations of citizenship had instead been defined in terms of their family. "From the era of the American Revolution until deep into the present, the substitution of married women's obligations to their husbands and families for their obligations to the state has been a central element in the way Americans have thought about the relation of all women, including unmarried women, to state power."[138] Republican values of political citizenship after the Revolutionary War created the cultural ideology of republican motherhood, which held that women contributed their civic duty through their obligation to their families and in educating and raising citizen sons.[139] This ideology valued women's caregiving, even while it confined women to the private family sphere. Stanton attacked this notion of a "woman-citizen" as something supernatural, a "monster, half-human, half-beast," derived from man's false creation of the image of womanhood sentimentally worshipping her superior virtue yet fearing her emotional and religious nature in the public sphere.[140] Understanding the reciprocal nature of citizenship, Stanton argued that women were ready to assume the duties of citizenship, like jury duty and liability for debts, if only granted the benefits.[141]

Stanton tried to break into this closed circle of citizenship by first latching onto the traditional American basis for granting citizenship rights, property holding.[142] "In the eighteenth century, the liberal individual (male) was defined by owning property, voting, participating in the public sphere."[143] Many states inherited the traditional English system requiring property ownership for voting.[144] Property qualifications were viewed as properly extending suffrage to those "seen as having a vested stake in society" and excluding those "too poor to have a will of their own" and too easily coerced by those who controlled their livelihoods.[145] These property qualifications allowed women, briefly, in New Jersey to vote between 1776 and 1807, because, as the Supreme Court held, for single, propertied women, "the law supposes them to have wills of their own."[146]

Relying on this historical precedent, Stanton argued that women's ownership of property entitled women to the vote, and thus citizenship.[147] "A citizen, says Webster, in the United States is a person native or naturalized who has the privilege of exercising the elective franchise in the qualifications which enable him to vote for senators and to purchase, hold real estate."[148] She endorsed the property connection, arguing, "There is no principle of equity more universally admitted than that the owner of property shall have a word to say in its use."[149] Quoting Benjamin Franklin, she said, "If a man's property can be taken from him without his consent, he is a slave."[150]

Stanton also tried to break into citizenship by linking suffrage to taxation.[151] Echoing the American sentiment from the Revolutionary War, she decried the "tyranny of taxation without representation." Stanton later developed this theme in an 1873 speech delivered to the Rochester Women Taxpayers' Association and a later draft lecture, "Taxation," focusing on the basic idea that "Webster's defines 'tax' as a 'sum of money assessed on the person or property of a citizen.'"[152] She emphasized the citizenship link: "Thus in taxing women the state pays them the compliment of recognizing in them the dignity of citizenship."

> On what principles of justice are there large numbers of men allowed to vote without paying taxes, while the women are compelled to pay taxes without voting? Whatever property the state protects should I think contribute its proportion to the state's support. Hence as loyal law-abiding citizens we are willing to pay our share for the support of the state. But as our taxes are increased not in proportion as many other classes, and many kinds of property are exempt, we have a reason to complain of this injustice and to insist that women as large property holders throughout the United States should have a vote on this question.[153]

Stanton's taxation arguments had popular appeal and were easily adopted by women's rights advocates.[154] Several famous protests by women refusing to pay their taxes were "frequently and widely recounted" by the women's movement.[155] These protestors included eighty-year-old sisters, Julia and Abby Smith, who had their cows seized and sold at auction to pay the taxes, and abolitionist Abby Kelley Foster and her husband Stephen Foster, who refused to pay taxes until Abby, and all women, could vote.[156] "Popular narratives, valuing as they did the Boston Tea Party, continued to convey that civic authority was related to democratic control of taxation."[157] These connections between property and taxation voting were partially successful in obtaining women's right to vote in school or municipal elections, though they enfranchised only relatively well-to-do women.[158] But the arguments failed to achieve Stanton's greater purpose of establishing women's full status of citizenship.

After the Civil War, the resulting constitutionalism of the Civil Rights Amendments provided alternative legal arguments to add to these political rationales for voting. Stanton returned to one of the demands from the Declaration of Sentiments, insisting that women be given "immediate admission to all the rights and privileges which belong to them as citizens of the United States."[159] The Fourteenth Amendment, enacted in 1868, seemed to grant exactly this by guaranteeing that "all persons" are "citizens" against whom states cannot abridge "the privileges and immunities of citizenship." In 1869, Missouri reformer Virginia Minor and her attorney husband, Francis Minor, devised an argument for woman's suffrage based on the plain language of the newly enacted privileges and immunities clause.[160] Stanton quickly adopted Minor's argument, appreciating that the Fourteenth Amendment provided the textual hook women needed. She called the amendment the "title deed" to woman suffrage and dismissed arguments about the framers' intent, citing the legal maxim that "with or without intent, a law stands as it is written."[161] This textual argument became the foundation of Stanton's NWSA legislative and judicial campaigns of "the New Departure" as hundreds of women, including Susan B. Anthony, civilly disobeyed the law by voting under the claimed authority of the privileges and immunities clause.[162]

Stanton, however, extended the legal argument beyond mere textualism. She "proposed a dynamic model of constitutional interpretation designed to keep the principles of the text current with present social conditions and needs." Legal scholar Adam Winkler has argued that Stanton theorized in what was then a "radically different way of understanding constitutional interpretation," by arguing that the Constitution should develop in a dynamic way to meet the ever-changing understanding of society. This idea of a changing, dynamic "living Constitution" would become "the dominant mode of constitutional construction in the twentieth century." Stanton's use of the method not only foreshadowed modern critiques of originalism, but according to Winkler, secured her place as "its most important innovator."[163] Stanton described the fundamental law as "the organic law of the land" that should be "so framed and construed" as to emphasize the progressive development of individual rights.[164] She argued in her speech to the Joint Committees of the District of Columbia, considering women's suffrage in D.C., that "[a]s history shows . . . each step in civilization has been a steady approximation to our democratic theory, securing larger liberties to the people."[165] She gave the example of men's suffrage, which had evolved from rights only for propertied white men, then expanded to universal white male suffrage, including laborers, and then extended to black men. In another example, she cited the legal developments of the married women's property acts that evolved from a new understanding of women's civil rights departing from coverture. "Woman has not been standing still, but has been gradually advancing to an equal place with the man by her side."[166]

In January 1872, appearing before the Senate Judiciary Committee in support of woman's suffrage, Stanton "added a stinging condemnation of the dominant method of constitutional interpretation, originalism, which was proving to be the primary stumbling block for suffrage reform."

> Though the world has been steadily advancing in political science, and step by step in recognizing the rights of new classes, yet we stand to-day talking of precedents, authorities, laws, and constitutions, as if each generation were not better able to judge of its wants than the one that preceded it. If we are to be governed in all things by the men of the eighteenth century, and the twentieth by the nineteenth, and so on, the world will be always governed by dead men.[167]

Stanton argued for an evolutionary understanding of the entire Constitution from 1789 to 1870, arguing that the meaning of the privileges and immunities clause, contained originally in Article IV, had changed.[168]

Stanton needed to depart from the traditional legal constitutional interpretation of originalism because the framers of the Fourteenth Amendment clearly did not intend to include the right to vote in its guarantees. This legislative intent was recent history and familiar to all, especially Stanton's congressional audience, many of whom were the framers themselves.[169] Their primary intent had been to grant civil, legal rights to freed slaves; they explicitly did not include the right to vote, which was envisioned separately as a political compromise in the Fifteenth Amendment granting suffrage to black men.[170] The national citizenship of the Fourteenth Amendment was defined not by the vote, but as the reciprocal obligation of allegiance by the individual to the nation in exchange for protection by the state.[171]

The U.S. Supreme Court agreed, rejecting Stanton and Minor's claim of a constitutional right to vote. In *Minor v. Happersett*, the Court easily recognized women as citizens.[172] As John Bingham, the primary drafter of the Fourteenth Amendment, had explained in a Senate report several years before, there was "no longer any reason to doubt that all persons" born or naturalized in the United States were citizens as declared by the amendment.[173] But that was a conclusion without significance, for the catch was that citizens did not automatically have the right to vote. That had been the feminists' assumption: that voting was the distinguishing privilege of a citizen, and why they focused their goal on establishing women as full citizens.[174] Stanton attacked Bingham's report and its implication that "women are not 'citizens,' but 'members' of the nation!—mere appendages to the State, the Church and the home." She snarked, "If this, indeed, be woman's normal condition, may God grant us a wiser, nobler type of manhood as our prefix than John Bingham, of Ohio."[175]

The Supreme Court in *Minor* agreed that voting was not a privilege of national citizenship protected by the Fourteenth Amendment, but was instead a political right discretionarily granted by the state.[176] The Court defined "privileges and immunities" by reference to its antecedent in Article IV of the Constitution and the intent of the founders, which did not include the vote as a privilege of citizenship. The republicanism of the founders included a belief in virtual representation by which only an elite few property owners were qualified to govern with political rights of voting. The Court applied the traditional originalist interpretation of the intent of the framers, both constitutional and amendment, refusing to engage Stanton's dynamic interpretation.

Undeterred, Stanton continued to press for what she thought was self-evident, even as she simultaneously pursued alternative political strategies like a new Sixteenth Amendment for women's suffrage. "By every principle of fair interpretation we need no amendment, no new definitions of the terms 'people,' 'persons,' 'citizens,' no additional power conferred on Congress" to enable Congress to grant women suffrage.[177] She continued to believe that the text of the Fourteenth Amendment, properly interpreted, should grant women the right to vote. Her argument, however, "was still too radical for its time."[178]

The Death-Blow to Coverture

In speaking of the first New York property reform many years later, Stanton said, "This was the death-blow to the old Blackstone code for married women in this country, and ever since legislation has been slowly, but steadily, advancing toward their complete equality."[179] "This was the first recognition of a wife as an individual."[180] One of the sponsors of the New York laws agreed, writing for the *History of Woman*

Suffrage that "we meant to strike a hard blow and if possible shake the old system of laws to their foundations, and leave it to other times and wiser councils to perfect a new system."[181] Stanton used the married women's property reform symbolically to mark the creation of women's legal identity, as it turned "the femme covert into a living, breathing woman." By beginning to bring married women's existence into the law out of the invisibility of coverture, the reforms instituted a radical shift in legal agency for women. For Stanton, equality for women required both the eradication of barriers to women's opportunity and radical systemic changes in law and society.

Nineteenth-century feminists used the marital property reforms "to exploit the sexual politics resonating from the metaphor of the wife submerged in the husband as dynamically as possible." They were not primarily concerned with "the complexities of New York equity or the minutiae of slowly changing statutes." Instead, they emphasized "the legal fiction of marital unity as symbolic of women's political, economic, and social subservience. Any equation in which one plus one equaled one by virtue of the woman's invisibility was a vivid symbol of male dominion in a cultural as well as a legal context."[182]

Stanton thus "transformed a relatively uncontroversial matter of law reform into a controversial matter of political right, bringing to the foreground of debate the legitimacy of the patriarchal prerogatives coverture embodied."[183] Stanton appreciated the fundamental importance of property in the American legal and political system. From the beginning of her advocacy, she realized that "so weighty is the influence of Property in modern society, that we cannot reasonably look for the emancipation of one sex or the elevation of the other, while Woman occupies her present position in regard to property—a mere dependent in too many cases on the bounty and care of man."[184] The resulting married women's property acts provided some of this change, and thus are appropriately viewed today as the beginning of the equality movement for women's rights. While "initiated to meet legal and commercial needs, the earliest acts stimulated public awareness of married women's common law disabilities and encouraged the development of the women's movement. Given an issue around which to coalesce, the women's movement pressed legislatures to respond at least minimally to their increasingly radical demands, including the demand for suffrage."[185]

2

"The Pivot of the Marriage Relation"

I do not know that the world is quite willing or ready to discuss the question of marriage. . . . It is in vain to look for the elevation of woman, so long as she is degraded in marriage. . . . The right idea of marriage is at the foundation of all reforms. . . . I feel this whole question of woman's rights turns on the pivot of the marriage relation, and sooner or later it will be the question for discussion.
—Elizabeth Cady Stanton to Susan B. Anthony, Mar. 1, [1852]

Dabbling on the periphery of women's marital rights in property reform was not enough for Stanton. Her broader vision demanded a transformation of the entire system of marriage. Calling for engagement with the bigger question, she asked, "[H]ow can we discuss all the laws and conditions of marriage, without perceiving its essential essence, end, and aim? . . . [I]s it possible to discuss all the laws of a relation and not touch the relation itself?"[1] For Stanton, the core of the marriage relation itself had to be the focus of the radical change.

Stanton's first goal was to establish that the institution of marriage was a problem. Woman, she argued, was the "victim of the institution" of marriage, "finding herself equally degraded in each and every phase."[2] Marriage victimized women, not benefited them. She was working against the prevailing sentimental ideology of the Victorian marriage as a romantic ideal of protection and reverence for the delicate, child-like wife. Stanton recast marriage as a confinement, a state of bondage analogous to slavery. She emphasized the ordained headship of man, and his hierarchical marital role as master and the wife's reciprocal obligation to obey him and take his name. She challenged the erasure of women's legal and social status and rights in marriage and their transmission to the husband. Such "man marriage," she claimed, was made by and for men—by male lawmakers and religious leaders who ascribed power and legal right to themselves for their own benefit.[3] Marriage, as accurately understood, was little more than a trap for women, and should thus be entered only carefully and deliberately. Stanton thus endorsed laws to increase the minimum marital age, mandate licensure procedures, prohibit common law marriage, and ban breach of promise actions to enforce marriage.

Stanton's second goal was to offer a solution that would transform marriage into a relation respecting women's equal individuality. Her proposal was to conceptualize marriage legally as a contract, rather than a sacrament or status, which would allow freedom to designate the terms and the termination of the marriage.[4] Socially, she advocated an egalitarian vision of marriage as a union of soul mates that fully respected the freedom of each individual as they worked together as partners in the joint enterprise of the family. This transformational vision of marriage required little state regulation, permitting free divorce and other restrictions on choice of marital partner. Stanton believed in the theoretical ideal of free love, resulting "whenever compulsion and restraint, whether of the law or of a dogmatic and oppressive public opinion, are removed."[5]

So when her friend Frederick Douglass remarried to Helen Pitts, a white woman, she sent her personal congratulations and support for his subversive act. She noted that

> there's much hostile criticism on your condescension in marrying a white woman. After all the terrible battles and political upheavals we have had in expurgating our Constitutions of that odious adjective "white" it is really remarkable that you of all men should have stooped to do it honor. The "white" feature of this contract is bad enough, but "the woman" is still worse.

Stanton commented on the gender implications of the controversy, in which his "large circle of admiring friends protest" against him risking his legacy as a black civil rights leader on white interests, especially those of a mere woman.[6] Stanton wanted to draft a public announcement of support for Douglass from both her and Anthony and invite him to speak at the next women's rights convention. Anthony

Statue, Stanton and Frederick Douglass, National Women's Rights Park. *Courtesy Tracy Thomas.*

refused, concerned with the potential backlash on "the subject of amalgamation" against the growing consensus on women's suffrage. Anthony wrote to Stanton, "I do hope you won't put your foot into the question of intermarriage of the races. It has no place on our platform, any more than the question of no marriage at all, or of polygamy, and so far as I can prevent it, shall not be brought there." She pleaded, do not "throw around that marriage the halo of a pure and lofty duty to break down race lines."[7] For Stanton had publicly supported interracial marriage before, attending legislative hearings in Boston to repeal colonial miscegenation laws and printing an editorial in her newspaper in support of interracial marriage.[8] But this time, she backed down.

Despite the suggestion that marriage was not a proper issue of women's rights, for Stanton, it was central to her vision of equality. Changing the marriage relation, she wrote early in the movement, "is at the foundation of all reforms."[9] Her conviction of the importance of the marriage issue and its core effect on establishing legal and social gender subordination came from her own frustrating experience in marriage. Stanton's own marriage failed to live up to her theoretical ideal of the true partnership. She said very little about her husband in her autobiography and writings, and he said even less of her.[10] Stanton was a strong advocate of free divorce, but she never chose that option for herself. Instead, she recounted late in life only that she had "been true to one relation over fifty years, by example as well as precept," and that she and Henry "lived together, without more than the usual matrimonial friction, for nearly half a century."[11] Except that they didn't. The two lived most of their years physically apart, in a de facto separation. Henry contributed little to the family financially or emotionally.[12] While Elizabeth embraced her individual freedom, she resented carrying the burdens of childcare and household management alone, and regretted the loss of the ideal partnership she so desired. In contrast to the marriages of other women's rights reformers, in Elizabeth's "there was no shared political or reform activity." Henry did not involve his wife in his work, and he ignored her work, oblivious to or perhaps envious of her growing notoriety.[13] The two worked at cross purposes, she derailing his political campaigns and he belittling her early editorial attempts.[14] Out of this experience, however, came Stanton's critique of marriage and her recognition of the need to elevate marriage reform to a core tenet of the women's rights agenda.

Marriage as Slavery

Stanton's first step was to expose the problematic nature of marriage for women's equality. To illustrate her point, Stanton drew upon the slavery metaphor, familiar to reformers and reform audiences.[15] Slavery imagery recast marriage by revealing the degradation and injustice of the existing marital relationship. In the Declaration of Sentiments, Stanton objected that "in the covenant of marriage, she [woman] is compelled to promise obedience to her husband, he becoming, to all intents and purposes, her master—the law giving him power to deprive her of her liberty." Writing to the 1850 Ohio Women's Convention, Stanton repeated, "A married woman has no legal existence; she has no more absolute rights than a slave on a Southern plantation. She takes the name of her master, holds nothing, owns nothing, can bring no action in her own name."[16]

The slavery metaphor grew naturally from feminists' early ties with the abolitionist movement. The argument had been previously made by other women reformers like abolitionist Sarah Grimké.[17] Proslavery defenders in the late 1830s made the analogy to legitimize slavery, comparing it to marriage as two hierarchies mandated by God and nature. As historian Nancy Cott explains, "both marriage and slavery were systems of domination and subordination—or more favorably, of protection and dependence—based on assumptions about inequalities between the parties involved." The relationship between marriage and slavery as two of the legal domestic relations was a concern in early drafts of the Thirteenth Amendment providing that "all persons are equal before the law, so that no person can hold another as a slave." Some senators opposed this language for its potential to regulate all of domestic relations, concerned that "before the law a woman would be equal to a man, . . . A wife would be equal to her husband and as free as her husband before the law." The final amendment read simply that "[n]either slavery nor involuntary servitude . . . shall exist within the United States."[18]

The slave metaphor helped to articulate the abstract critiques of patriarchal marriage and captured women's genuine outrage at marital servitude.[19] The comparison between slaves and middle-class women might seem "melodramatic and self-aggrandizing," Stanton acknowledged. "[W]hen we contrast the condition of the most fortunate women at the North with the living death colored men endure everywhere, there seems to be a selfishness in our present position."[20] She explained, however, that "in comparing the woman with the negro we but assert ourselves subjects of law. . . . The difference in the slavery of the negro and woman is that of the mouse in the cat's paw, and the bird in a cage, equally hopeless for happiness. One perishes by violence, the other through repression."[21] It was not that women's daily experiences were the same as those of a slave in bondage, but "structurally, conceptually, and legally the relations of husband to wife, and master to slave, were parallel."[22]

Stanton emphasized this slavery idea in her letter to the Seventh National Woman's Rights Convention in 1856, trying to illustrate for women the problematic nature of marriage as it existed:

How can she [woman] endure our present marriage relations by which woman's life, health, and happiness are held so cheap, that she herself feels that God has given her no charter of rights, no individuality of her own. I answer, she patiently bears all this because in her blindness she sees no way of escape. Her bondage, though it differs from that of the negro slave, frets and chafes her just the same. She too sighs and groans in her chains; and lives but in the hope of better things to come.[23]

Stanton also used slavery imagery to debunk the existing sentimental idea of marriage as protection.[24] "The laws for married women in some states are exactly parallel with those of the slave code on the southern plantations. Husbands, as well as slaveholders, have availed themselves of this absolute power of the old common law."[25] "Woman loses infinitely more than she gains, by the kind of protection now imposed; for, much as she loves and honors true and noble men, life and liberty are dearer far to her than even the legalized slavery of an indissoluble tie."[26] She appreciated that "it is an unpleasant truth to most men (for no one likes to own himself a tyrant), to admit that they hold women in the same adverse servitude as slaves were held."[27] Nonetheless, it is "just as impossible for men to understand the slavery of the women in their own households as it was for slaveholders to understand that of the African race on their plantations."[28]

Stanton emphasized the husband's absolute control over the wife's person. "Can she be said to have a right to liberty, when another citizen may have the legal custody of her person; the right to shut her up and administer moderate chastisement; to decide when and how she shall live, and what are the necessary means for her support?" Under the law, she explained, a husband "can forbid all persons harboring or trusting her on his account" and "deprive her of all social intercourse with her nearest and dearest friends."[29] And so when an English court rejected the existence of any common law right of a husband to "seize, imprison and chastise" his wife, Stanton called it "the greatest legal decision of the century" for using "broad principles of justice" to affirm "the personal rights of married women" and declare "all those old statutes obsolete that make wives the bond slaves of their husbands."[30]

The slavery analogue provided the solution as well as the framework for the marriage problem. Stanton explained, "[W]e decide the whole question of slavery by settling the sacred rights of the individual" and "asserting that man can not hold property in man." Similarly, the question of women's rights was remedied by settling the rights of wives, by recognizing "their individual existence—their full equality as human beings with all others," and not merely by seeking to improve their conditions.[31]

> If you go to a southern plantation and speak to a slave of his right to property, to the elective franchise, to a thorough education, his response will be a vacant stare . . . [T]he great idea of his right to himself, of his personal dignity, must first take possession of his soul, then will he demand equality in everything. . . . I repeat, the center and circumference of woman's rights is just what the slave's are. Personal freedom is the first right to be proclaimed, that does not and cannot belong to the relation of wife.[32]

After the Civil War, antislavery rhetoric was an even "more powerful political tool" as it gained legal status as the motivation for new constitutional amendments. The slavery metaphor thus "gave feminists an immediate and powerful concept and a language of personal independence that resonated in the dominant culture."[33]

Obey Your Husbands

Stanton argued that women, like slaves, were taught "subjection to white men: 'Servants obey your masters,' 'wives obey your husbands.'"[34] She objected to the "interpretation of the Bible, making man the head of woman, and its forms of marriage, by which she is given away as an article of merchandize, and made to vow obedience as a slave to a master."[35] Playing out the slavery analogy, Stanton proposed that "all these reverend gentlemen who insist on these humiliating ceremonies; that place all wives in the light of slaves, should be impeached in the Supreme Court of the United States, for a direct and positive violation of the Thirteenth Amendment" and its prohibition against slavery and involuntary servitude.[36]

The Declaration of Sentiments focused on this vow of obedience, and it was a topic for discussion early in the woman's rights movement, at the

Rochester convention immediately following Seneca Falls. Those men and women in attendance easily reconciled to the idea of "equal wages for equal work" raised by the discussion of the inequities of the laboring classes and the distinctions between seamstresses and tailors. "But the gentlemen seemed more disturbed as to the effect of equality in the family" and the abandonment of the "old idea of a divinely ordained head" of the husband. One man asked, "[W]hen the two heads disagree, who must decide? There is no Lord Chancellor to whom to apply, and does not St. Paul strictly enjoin obedience to husbands, and that man shall be head of the woman?" Lucretia Mott replied that Quakers, who excluded the marital vow of obedience, had no difficulty and "had never known any mode of decision except an appeal to reason." Stanton emphasized that in many cases women already were the head of the family "to all intents and purposes" as determined by "the strongest will or the superior intellect."[37]

Stanton expanded her response to the biblical view of obedience in a letter to the editor of the Seneca County paper. "Methinks I hear some women say, We must obey our Husbands!! Who says so. Why the Bible. No you have not rightly read your Bible." Stanton placed the injunction "wives obey your husbands" in the same category with "Honor the King." She believed "no one worthy of being called master, but God himself."[38] Stanton also discounted these commands as merely coming from a fallible man, Paul. "We must not make God responsible for all" the writers of the Epistles as "Paul, himself, admitted that he spoke sometimes by permission and sometimes by commission." Mott agreed that the bachelor Saint Paul, who commanded all believers not to marry, was hardly an authoritative source for guidance on marital relations.[39]

Stanton fixated on the ceremonial promise of a wife to obey her husband as evidence of the slave-like relationship of marriage.[40] She objected to the "humiliating act in giving the bride away."

> She is given in marriage like an article of merchandise. . . . and she that is given never dreams that she herself has the most sacred right to her own person. Such a ceremony is a solemn mockery of one of our most sacred social institutions. The rights of humanity are more grossly outraged at the altar than at the auction block of the slaveholder; because there, no superiority of mind or position, no physical or intellectual beauty or

greatness can secure to their possessor the least recognition of her individual rights, her social equality.[41]

The obedience vow, Stanton said, may have once matched the idea of marriage as women's subjection, "but with the equal relations the sexes are assuming to-day, we need a new ceremony more in harmony with the times in which we live."[42]

Stanton refused to make such a promise to obey her husband in her own marriage ceremony. She persuaded the minister to leave out the word "obey" because she "obstinately refused to obey one with whom I supposed I was entering into an equal relation."[43] This defiance was for Stanton a point of great pride that she repeated frequently, elevating it to a subversive boycott of existing gender hierarchies.[44] The waiver, however, may have been her husband's idea, based on the example of his friend Theodore Weld in his marriage to abolitionist Angelina Grimké, which followed the Quaker ceremony omitting the vow of obedience.[45] Stanton called for all women similarly to rebel. "Let all brides who have any true dignity or self-respect, repudiate 'obey' and the giving away scene."[46] She noted with favor friends who followed her advice and expressed contempt for those who did not.[47]

Stanton repeatedly mentioned with favor the Methodist church's decision in 1864 to omit the word "obey" from its ceremony.[48] This, she said, was "a brave blow at the old idea of woman's subjection in marriage."[49] She questioned whether "the reverend fathers see the deep significance and far-reaching consequence of the act."[50] Opponents did in fact appreciate the significance, as one bishop later complained that "the recognized authority of the husband to rule the wife, and the recognized duty of the wife to obey that authority is no longer deemed expedient or necessary."[51] In response, Stanton answered, "[Y]es, that is what we have been working for."

Mrs. Henry

Stanton elaborated on another slave-like badge of marriage, the social custom of marital names. "The slave was Cuffy Davis, or Cuffy Lee, just whose Cuffy he might chance to be. The woman is Mrs. Jones, Brown, or Smith, just whose Mrs. she may chance to be. The individuality of both classes is buried in the master."[52] At the Rochester woman's rights convention in August 1848, Stanton highlighted the importance of an individual name.

> When a slave escapes from a Southern plantation, he at once takes a name as the first step in liberty—the first assertion of individual identity. A woman's dignity is equally involved in a life-long name, to mark her individuality. We can not overestimate the demoralizing effect on woman herself, to say nothing of society at large, for her to consent thus to merge her existence so wholly in that of another.[53]

For Stanton, the touchstone of coverture in the loss of a woman's legal identity at marriage was reflected and reinforced in the custom of a wife's marital name.[54] The custom originated from the effects of coverture and the incorporation of the wife's legal identity into that of the husband, and from the legal requirements that a married woman sue, be sued, and execute documents through her husband.[55] Stanton attacked the custom by which "she is nameless, for a woman has no name! She is Mrs. John or James, Peter or Paul just as she changes masters; like the southern slave, she takes the name of her owner." "[S]he has so little self-respect that she does not see the insult of the custom."[56] Stanton emphasized the importance of a woman's name. "Many people consider this a very small matter; but it is the symbol of the most cursed monopoly on this footstool; a monopoly by man of all the rights, the life, liberty, and happiness of one half of the human family—all womankind."[57]

Stanton insisted upon the use of what she considered her own full name, Elizabeth Cady Stanton, rather than the customary social address of "Mrs. Henry B. Stanton."[58] The idea to reject the social custom was originally suggested to her by Theodore Weld.[59]

> Soon after my marriage, Theodore Weld said to me: Do not allow any of your correspondents to insult you by addressing your letters "Mrs. Henry B. Stanton." I have followed his advice. . . . Furthermore, I have talked this matter over with my husband and he says it would be quite *outré* for us to appear in the papers with either titles or men's names.[60]

Elizabeth crafted her marital name deliberately and after careful thought, to symbolize her principled belief in self-sovereignty within marriage. As she explained in a letter to a friend, "I have very serious objections, . . . to being called Henry. There is a great deal in a name. It often signifies much and may involve a great principle." She again drew the analogy to slavery. "Ask our colored brethren if there is nothing in a name? . . . And why are our colored brethren nameless, unless they take the name of their master? Simply because they have no independent existence. They are mere chattels, with no civil or social rights." The same was true, she said, with women. "The custom of calling women Mrs. John and Mrs. Tom, and colored men Sambo and Zip Coon, is founded on the principle that white men are lords of all. I cannot acknowledge this principle as just, therefore, I cannot bear the name of another."[61]

For several decades, Stanton tried to persuade other women to adopt the custom of using their full name. She argued, "[T]here is a moral influence in a dignified name, representing a life-long individual character." "I conjure every woman to write her full name, and if married retain her maiden name, using the husband's simply as an affix for convenience as a family name."[62] She discounted the custom of using initials and persuaded friends not to represent themselves "by letters, like spools of thread and barrels of flour." She rejected using nicknames like "Susie, Kittie, Libbie, instead of Susan, Katherine, Elizabeth," noting that a "boy would be laughed to scorn who should show himself to be registered Jimmy, Johnny or Dickey." Her recommended convention emphasized a woman's formal first name and maiden name, clearly identifying her gender and her assumption of a public role. Other contemporary woman's rights advocates followed Stanton's protocol of using the full three-part name, including Antoinette Brown Blackwell, Harriet Beecher Stowe, Abby Kelley Foster, Angelina Grimké Weld, Charlotte Perkins Gilman, and Carrie Chapman Catt.

When fellow women's rights advocate Lucy Stone retained her maiden name, Stanton celebrated. "Nothing has been done in the woman's rights movement for some time that so rejoiced my heart as the announcement by you of a woman's right to her name."[63] Lucy Stone and her husband, Henry Blackwell, famously entered a public prenuptial agreement disavowing the patriarchal laws of marriage and creating their own marriage contract. Stanton trumpeted Stone's rebellion against marital law. "Lucy Stone struck a bold blow at the old institution when she accepted the civil obligation of the marriage relation under protest, repudiating the name, even—of her legal husband—so sacredly did she hold her individual sovereignty against all human laws and customs."[64] Though Stone and Stanton later became rivals, leading different suffrage organizations, Stanton continued to admire Stone's radical action of using her marital name. Women who retained their birth names came to be known as "Lucy Stoners." An article in the *Revolution* proclaimed, "Let all women do like 'Lucy Stone,' honor her own name, and then keep it. As men are liable to disgrace their names, and run away from their clinging vines, it is better for every woman to maintain an individual existence and a life-long name to represent it."[65] In a letter read at Lucy Stone's memorial in 1894, Stanton lauded, "Lucy Stone did a brave thing in keeping her name, and it is strange that so few women follow her example. It seems so pre-eminently proper that every individual should have a life-long name, especially when one has made her own distinguished."[66]

Stanton's well-known preference and sensitivity to the issue of her marital name invited misuses by those who sought to attack her in political maneuvers. For example, in 1860 she and Wendell Phillips engaged in a heated debate over divorce at the Tenth National Woman's Rights Convention.[67] After the convention, Phillips sent Stanton a letter addressed to "Mrs. H. B. Stanton." Elizabeth responded with an acerbic letter. "Only think of it—one of the champions of freedom denying to woman, at this late day, her own name." Stanton continued, "[D]id you pen that, or was it done by your private secretary, a perfumed young man who never heard that women and negroes are beginning to repudiate the name of their masters and claiming a right to a life-long name of their own? But how shall I preach to you the new gospel of individual sovereignty?" Her letter triggered a further insulting reply from Phillips on how he could not possibly be expected to remember any girls' first names and that he could not for the life of him be sure whether she was "Lizzie Cady or Susie—or whatnot" (although he had known her for more than twenty years) and so thereafter he would call her "Mrs. Elizabeth Cady."[68]

In another example in 1867, Stanton angered a former supporter of the woman's rights movement, *New York Tribune* editor and future presidential candidate Horace Greeley, by highlighting the fact that his wife had signed the petition for woman's suffrage that Greeley's own newspaper had condemned. Greeley wrote in response,

You are always so desirous in public to appear under your own rather than your husband's name, why did you in this case substitute "Mrs. Horace Greeley" for "Mary Cheney Greeley" which was really on the petition? You know why. Well, I have given strict orders at the *Tribune* office that you and your cause are to be tabooed in the future, and if it is necessary to mention your name, you will be referred to as "Mrs. Henry B. Stanton!"[69]

The Attack on Marriage

As Stanton's personal frustrations increased, her attack on marriage grew more emphatic.[70] A speech dedicated to the topic of marriage in 1857 was perhaps her most shocking. Speaking to the Quaker Friends, Stanton's "Paper on Marriage" delivered a scathing critique of marriage and a call to abandon the institution altogether. She argued, we "now clearly see that the most fatal step a woman can take, the most false of *all earthly relations,* is that under our present legal marriage institution." "The Quaker complacently refers you to his marriage ceremony, as one of *equality.* But I shall believe he walks in the *spirit* of that compact when I shall cease to see in his household the exhausted wife, the mother of a troop of sickly children." Continuing, she said, "Let no woman enter a relation where, by public sentiment, Church, and State, she at once becomes outlawed, civilly dead; where she can have no right to her own person, children, or property; into a relation declared by all our pulpits to be one of subjection and unquestioned obedience."[71]

Escalating, she protested "against this wholesale system of murder and prostitution" that killed women's identity and individuality for the sake of men's lust. She alleged that women had "outgrown" the authority of marriage and "long to be relieved from the crushing power with which it holds both man and woman, blighting and withering the most noble and susceptible natures." She demanded, "let us cast it aside with other false institutions of the past." "What we now demand," she said, "is, the reorganization of our social institutions. *Marriage* is the question before us. The Woman Movement has brought us to that point."[72]

The speech hinted at veiled criticism of Henry and her own marriage. Women must promise to "*cleave* to *that one man* as *long* as he lives; no matter what his transformation or her development may be." "The pleasure, the happiness, the well-being of the woman is not of the slightest consideration; the will of the husband is the absolute law of her life." "In his career of glory and fame, has man ever paused to consider the subtle causes of woman's weakness and degradation?" Have even the best men, she complained, "ever felt the least compunction of conscience" for the "hopeless life of the self-sacrificing wife, the mother of six, eight, or ten children? . . . Victims all, to the lust and selfishness of those to whom they looked for care and support—dead, or suffering life, with the excessive cares and anxieties of maternity!"[73]

When Stanton was finally able to attend a national woman's rights convention again in 1860, she focused on the issues of marriage and divorce. In her second of two addresses at the Tenth Convention in New York City, she "delivered an all-out attack on the institution of marriage itself."[74] Marriage, she asserted, was not a sacred, permanent relation, but rather "legalized prostitution" as women were forced into marriage, sexual relations, and continual childbirth with tyrannical or drunken men with "the power and legal right to hand down their natures to other beings." "The best interests of the individual, the family, the State, the nation, cry out against these legalized marriages of force and endurance."[75] Stanton adopted the phrase "legalized prostitution" to shock her audience out of their passive acceptance of the sentimentality of marriage.[76] "Whatever the 'social position' of a 'mistress' may be, the 'legal position' of a wife is more dependent and degrading than any other condition of womanhood can possibly be."[77]

Many leaders of the women's rights movement, both women and men, shied away from attacking marriage.[78] They argued that the laws on marriage bore equally on men and women, and thus were not properly an issue for the movement focused primarily on suffrage.[79] Stanton disagreed with the premise that the marriage laws applied equally. She argued that while "man, too, suffers in a false marriage relation, yet what can his suffering be compared with what every woman experiences. . . . A man in marrying gives up no right; but a woman, every right, even the most sacred of all—the right to her own person."[80]

Stanton emphatically argued that "marriage and divorce are not 'side issues' to-day; they are the kernel of the question." Those "philosophical thinkers," who explored "the surface wrongs of women, work, wages, property rights, suffrage," discovered "that the fundamental error, from which all these abuses spring, is the present social relation of the sexes, in which, by law and gospel, man is made head, woman subject." Pointing out the potential self-interest, she observed, "the side issues of which these various gentlemen complain so much, invariably strike at their social authority; hence they prefer to keep the guns turned on the State."[81]

Stanton insisted that "the true relation of the sexes is the momentous question at this stage of our civilization." "Our low ideas of marriage, as set forth in our creeds and codes, making man master, woman slave, one to command and one to obey, are demoralizing all our most sacred sentiments and affections, and making the most holy relation in Nature one of antagonism and aversion."[82] "When men begin to look at this marriage question from a woman's standpoint, they will see the fundamental falsehood in all those creeds, codes and customs, that make this any other than an equal relation, with equal rights, duties, and privileges, making the same moral code for both sexes."[83]

"Man Marriage"

As Stanton's advocacy continued, she reframed her feminist critique of marriage into a demand for legal reform "of an entire revision of your whole code on marriage and divorce."[84] Developed in the pages of the *Revolution*, this critique was encapsulated into what she called her theory of "Man Marriage," that marriage was made by and for the sole benefit of men.[85] "The laws governing this institution were made by men, are administered by men, and all to their own advantage."[86] Marriage, Stanton argued, was simply an arrangement contrived by men for their own pleasure. "Nearly every man feels that his wife is his property, whose first duty, under all circumstances, is to gratify his passions, without the least reference to her own health and happiness, or the welfare of their offspring." Woman was nothing more than the "toy of man," created to service his physical lust, with no regard for her own happiness.[87] "Thus far we have had the man marriage, and nothing more. From the beginning, man has had the whole and sole regulation of the matter. He has spoken in Scripture, and he has spoken in law. As an individual, . . . and as a judge and legislator, he still holds the entire control."[88]

Stanton's man-marriage critique emphasized women's absence from the lawmaking process by which the laws of marriage had been created.[89]

"Now, it must strike every careful thinker that an immense difference rests in the fact that man has made the laws, cunningly and selfishly, for his own purpose."[90] She highlighted the exclusive men-only process of lawmaking.[91] "One class never did legislate for another with justice and equality."[92] Women, without access to power in the church, courts, or elections, had no way to redress the false legislation, and thus had been victimized by the man marriage. "The creeds and codes and customs which govern the present institution" had never been consented to by women due to their exclusion from the law-making process.[93]

Stanton's man-marriage critique also focused on the substantive inequality of the marriage laws under which men gained all the benefit, women all the disability.[94] "On what principle does one party in this partnership sacrifice everything, and the other nothing?" She detailed the specific laws of marriage, citing the legal treatise writers and the black letter law to illustrate the lopsided bargain. "From Coke down to Kent, who can cite one clause of the marriage contract where woman has the advantage?"[95] "The contract of marriage is by no means equal." She listed examples of the different marital laws of age, contract, property, wages, and moral and legal liability.[96] "Do not the above citations clearly prove inequality? Is not the very letter and spirit of the marriage contract based in the idea of the supremacy of man as the keeper of woman's virtue, her sole protection and support?"[97] And she objected to the legal vocabulary of marriage, which defined marriage as inequality in concepts of "marital power," "marital rights," "dominion and control," "obedience and restraint," and the word "marital" itself, which derived from the Latin word for husband, "maris."[98]

Stanton emphasized the broader implications of coverture that created man marriage by merging the existence of the woman into that of the husband. "The man gives up nothing that he before possessed; he is a man still; while the legal existence of the woman is suspended during marriage, and henceforth she is known but in and through the husband. She is nameless, purseless, childless."[99] To illustrate the degradation of this law, Stanton switched genders; suppose the law of coverture said the husband and wife were one, "and that one the wife." "There is not a man in this nation, who knowing what the laws are, but would repudiate for himself a relation that would so wholly merge his individual existence in that of another human being."[100] "No sensible man would put his head into a noose that stripped him of personal and property rights, of children, wages, name, moral responsibility and the right of locomotion." Would "Frederick Douglass, a voter, a property holder, a free man, in the State of New York" before the war, have gone down to Georgia to live "where a black man had no rights that any one was bound to respect?"[101]

Stanton's man-marriage critique then dove into the religious foundations of marriage doctrine, grounded in the idea of the headship of man. Stanton attacked the idea that the Bible, the Constitution, or other edicts could make man head of woman. She objected to the depiction of "man in every creed and code, represented as the great central power of the universe,—the head of the family—whom woman is bound to 'obey.'"[102] "Hitherto we have had the 'white male' interpretation of the Bible, making it wise and just and good to enslave the black man to his avarice, and the woman to his lust."[103] She rejected this "'family unit' in which the husband is endowed with absolute power and the wife made a mere subject," arguing that this is not "'God's ordinance' but 'man's contrivance' to get all power into his own hands."[104] "None of the inspired women of the Bible ever made the declaration of man's headship, and we doubt if the 50,000 drunkards' wives in this state would consent that their husbands should be." She stressed, "[T]his fundamental falsehood, that man is in any sense woman's head or hands, must be thoroughly analyzed and disposed of, for in this assumption the whole question is involved."[105]

One vocal supporter of the biblical view of the husband's headship of the marriage was the otherwise liberal Reverend Newman Hall. Hall was involved in his own marital troubles when his much younger wife refused to have sexual relations with him and took up smoking, hunting, and a twenty-year-old lover. A decade later he was granted a divorce by an English court on grounds that his wife failed to obey her husband by stopping smoking and performing her "first duty of a wife," which was to satisfy his sexual needs. Stanton challenged Hall's alleged divine command. "This doctrine of man being woman's head, emanated from the brain of mortal. It has no higher authority and is most destructive and demoralizing in its tendencies." She argued that "the relation of husbands and wives bears no resemblance to that of Christ and the church." Since no husbands "are like their Divine Master," the only hope was "in the rebellion of woman against the dynasty of sensualism, selfishness and violence, that man has inaugurated."[106]

"We Are All Free Lovers"

Stanton's critique of marriage led to accusations that she believed in "free love." The pejorative "free love" label implied promiscuous sexual relations, and it was thrown at women's rights advocates to discredit them by portraying them as fringe radicals.[107] Stanton was annoyed by this attack. "Free love is the greatest of all bugbears to Woman's Rights. So far as I am concerned I have always been too busy to think about such a thing, and have never found time to love more than one man."[108] Yet she endorsed the basic principles. "You ask me if I believe in 'free love.' If by 'free love' you mean promiscuity, I do not. I believe in monogamic marriage."[109] But, she continued, "If by 'free love' you mean woman's right to give her body to the man she loves and no other, to become a mother or not as her desire, judgment, and convenience may dictate, in fine, to be the absolute sovereign of herself, then I do believe in freedom of love; and the next step of civilization will bring woman to this freedom." She argued, "whenever compulsion and restraint, whether of the law or of a dogmatic and oppressive public opinion, are removed, whatever results will be free love."[110] Embracing the label, she exclaimed, "[I]f it is 'free love' for the bride at the altar to insist that the law shall make her the peer of the groom by her side, then let those who are fighting the battle of woman's freedom inscribe 'free love' on their banners."[111]

The free love theory was more complex than the political meme. Free love was a movement crystallizing in the 1850s advocating the elimination of traditional marriage and state regulation of marriage. Marriage ruined love, free lovers argued, and created emotional possessiveness and "psychological enslavement." One of the movement's leading female advocates, Mary Gove Nichols, attacked marriage's forcing of involuntary intercourse and pregnancy for women and the requisite need to flee bad, sexually abusive marriages.[112] Free lovers claimed they were not advocating "free lust" or sexual promiscuity, but rather adopting theories of sexuality respecting individual choice and enjoyment of sex that adapted to meet the personal needs of the individual rather than trapping people in "soul crushing bondage." The earliest forms of the free love movement developed in utopian communities like Berlin, Ohio, and Oneida, New York, that prohibited monogamous marriage. Later in the century, the free love movement expanded its civil libertarian focus in advocating against the Comstock anti-obscenity laws and government control of sexual relations and contraception.[113] The nuance of the free love movement, though, was lost on the public, and it was typically portrayed as a fringe movement advocating serial promiscuity.

Free love's intersection with the feminist movement was primarily a negative one brought on by the involvement of Victoria Woodhull. Woodhull was "a self-taught woman from the wrong side of the tracks," depicted as both a radical social thinker and a promiscuous con-woman. Her unconventional lifestyle of divorce, blended family living with both her husband and her ex-husband, and famous paramours detracted from her work as a speaker, newspaper editor of her paper, *Woodhull and Claflin's Weekly*, stockbroker (trading on inside information from Cornelius Vanderbilt), and the first woman to run for president of the United States. She broke into reform circles and women's suffrage leadership in 1870 by her appearance before the congressional judiciary committee, presenting a new argument that women were already enfranchised by the Fourteenth and the Fifteenth Amendments. She indicted marriage for ruining women's lives, and she spoke of her hatred of marriage and the need for sexual passion.[114] "Only a handful of feminists stood by Woodhull," and one was Stanton, who admired her. Stanton wrote, "Victoria Woodhull has done a work for woman that none of us could have done. She has faced and dared men to call her the names that make women shudder, while she chucked principle, like medicine, down their throats. . . . In the annals of emancipation [her] name . . . will have its own high place as a deliverer."[115] Woodhull's affiliation with women's suffrage, however, was politically devastating to the movement as it fueled perceptions that women's rights were deviant.

Stanton shared many similar positions with the free lovers that preceded her affiliation with and support of Victoria Woodhull.[116] Like the free lovers, Stanton early in her advocacy espoused the foundational premises of individual sovereignty, self-ownership, and the oppressive nature of marriage for women. She supported many of the same specific positions on no-fault divorce, voluntary motherhood, marriage as a contract, and the necessity of divorce so women could leave abusive marriages.[117] Stanton corresponded with Mary Gove Nichols in the early 1850s during the height of Nichols's notoriety and thus was probably familiar with her free love theories.[118] In an editorial in the *Revolution*

"GET THEE BEHIND ME, (MRS.) SATAN!"—[See Page 143.]

Wife (with heavy burden). "I'd rather Travel the hardest Path of Matrimony than follow your Footsteps."

Victoria Woodhull and free love. "Get Thee behind Me, (Mrs.) Satan!" cartoon, Thomas Nast, *Harper's Weekly*, Feb. 17, 1872. *Library of Congress.*

in 1868, Stanton endorsed the shocking claim made by free love advocate Francis Barry that "to be a 'mistress' is less dishonorable than to be a 'wife,'" because a mistress could leave her degradation and was paid compensation, whereas a wife was held in her degradation and forced by her husband to "perform his drudgery, submit to his blows, and (worse) live the uncomplaining victim of his rapacity."[119]

Stanton was always attuned, however, to the "public lightning rod" of the term "free love" and the inability of the media and audiences to discern the nuances of her argument, and thus limited her free love arguments to more liberal audiences.[120] She gave one influential speech on the topic of free love to an audience of radical reformers in New York City.[121] In the speech, she embraced "a vision of emancipation that includes free love and social reconstruction." Stanton portrayed free love as progress, "a step forward," evolving from the basic, but necessary, questions of suffrage to social equality to scientific understanding to aesthetic virtue. She began by admitting that her claims in the prior lecture and other speeches that marriage reforms would not "destroy but would simply improve and perfect marriage" were not completely true. "But stop! I will not be guilty of false pretenses. I will not skulk under the portentous ambiguity in the meaning of the term." Instead, she asserted,

> marriage in some sense will be disturbed, will be abrogated in fine by the progress of reform, in the only sense indeed in which it is defined in the dictionary and in the law book, and in what it is understood by 99/100 of the whole people. Marriage I mean as a compulsory bond enforced by the law and rendered perpetual by that means.[122]

Stanton pled her case for individual freedom and self-sovereignty in marriage and love. She challenged the "element of legal compulsion" that "distinguishes marriage from those natural and free adjustments which the sentiment of love would spontaneously organize for itself." She challenged even the best marriages such as those of prominent women's rights reformers (likely Lucy Stone and Henry Blackwell) as establishing the right of ownership over each other, even though grounded in equality.[123] This arrangement, though, "abdicated their own individual sovereignty, sinking it in the vortex of marriage." What is wanted, she argued, is "[f]reedom, freedom from all unnecessary entanglements and compulsions, freedom from binding obligations inviting impossibilities, freedom to repair mistakes, and to express the manifoldness of our own natures and to progress or to advance to higher planes of development."[124]

Free love, she said, "well, yes, that is what I mean." "Nothing short of unlimited freedom of divorce, freedom to initiate at the option of the parties new amatory relationships, love put above marriage, and in a word the obnoxious doctrine of Free Love." She was against compulsion, and "regulation of the most sacred relation of human hearts." She viewed the exclusive, lifetime mating of one woman and one man "just as much free love as the most unlimited variety or promiscuity." "It is indeed," she said, "of the essence of freedom that it does not attempt to prescribe what the result shall be," trusting to the enlightenment, conscience, influence, or "good taste of the parties." That meant granting others that same freedom of choice, even when they exercised such freedom in a way deemed wrong. "Some people will and do make a bad use of their freedom." Free love simply meant freedom of choice in personal relationships. "And if I mistake not, this and just this is what is meant and all that is meant by the intelligent advocates of free love." Thus, she concluded, "We are one and all free lovers at heart although we may not have thought so."[125]

Writing for the magazine the *Free Parliament*, Stanton explained that the result of the free-love critique of marriage required "a complete revision of all these laws." It required that "the wife's individuality be as fully recognized by law as that of the husband." Again, she took on the accusatory mantle of the free love label. "If it is 'free love' for the bride at the altar to insist that the law shall make her the peer of the groom by her side, then let those who are fighting the battle of woman's freedom inscribe 'free love' on their banners."[126]

Stanton dismissed attempts to use free love to tarnish the mission of woman's rights. "This hue-and-cry of Free Love," she said, is merely "the cry of the day," just as other words had been used to try to discount women, like "blue-stockings" for women writers and "strong-minded," which, it turned out, "we rather liked." She pointed the finger back at her accusers. "Our sires and our sons are, strange to say, the most disturbed on this question of free love." She said that "every man who pens one single line about free love is guilty of the vilest hypocrisy," given that man had already tried for himself every form of the relation of the sexes accruing to his benefit, including monogamy, polygamy, divorce, and wholesale concubinage. All that free love was about, Stanton argued, was women asserting their rights to break from unclean and unholy ties like abusive marriages. The free love she advocated was to "trust both men and women with the same freedom in their social relations."[127]

The Mormon Monster

In the late nineteenth century, the fervor over Mormon polygamy gave Stanton another opportunity to expand her critique of marriage. The antipolygamy crusades late in the century involved federal legislators and conservative female moralists raging against the barbaric "Mormon Monster" of polygamy. The Mormon church officially adopted polygamy in 1852, after moving to the Utah territory and founding the state of Deseret to escape persecution in New York and Missouri. The principle of celestial or plural marriage held that the saints were to build heaven-like marriages here on earth like the Old Testament patriarchs Abraham and Solomon. Women could only enter the priesthood, and thus heaven, through marriage, and thus men had the religious duty to ensure the salvation of multiple women. Mormon founder Joseph Smith allegedly had fifty-five wives, and Utah leader Brigham Young had thirty-three wives.[128]

The issue reached crisis as Utah officially sought statehood. Threatened by the Mormon theocracy in the proposed state of Utah, church control of lucrative economic interests after the expansion of the railroads, and the moral panic over the threat to the family, the public and its leaders vehemently opposed polygamy and the "patriarchal degradation of women." Congress passed a series of increasingly more punitive laws, designed to destroy polygamy and the Mormon church governance.[129] The sanctions targeted women, voiding their marriages, rendering their children illegitimate, denying their newly granted right to vote, and prosecuting them for bigamy and cohabitation.[130] Federal prosecution of polygamist George Reynolds was upheld by the Supreme Court determining that religious freedom protected only beliefs, not actions, like plural marriages, "which were in violation of social duties or subversive of good order."[131] Utah eventually capitulated, entering the union as a state in 1896 after disavowing polygamy and Mormon church control. [132]

Stanton entered this debate in support of the Mormon women and their right to vote. She visited the Mormons, intrigued by the women's grant of suffrage in 1870.[133] She and Anthony spoke on suffrage, and she delivered her "Marriage and Maternity" lecture to women only in the Tabernacle, discussing physiological issues of women's bodies, choice in childbearing, and maternal power.[134] She recalled also discussing with them a recent decision by the Supreme Court declaring the first wife and her children as the only legal heirs.[135] Stanton welcomed Mormon women on the national stage, inviting them to NWSA meetings and allowing them to serve on the board, thereby further alienating the conservative American suffrage group.[136]

But Stanton could not embrace Mormon women's claim that polygamy offered them advantages of autonomy and family. She understood the argument that polygamy might be less "censurable than the practice of keeping mistresses by married men, which prevails in many places outside of Utah,"[137] but she could not countenance any religion that held that "woman is only sure of heaven by being tied to some man."[138] Mormonism, like all religions, Stanton said, made women "the divinely ordained subjects of man."[139] "Men write Bibles and translate them from their own stand point; they make constitutions and statutes in their own interest, and then claim that they, being in direct communication with the Most High, speak by special inspiration." Religious leaders like Moses, Paul, Luther, and Brigham Young "have all taught the same doctrine of subjection of women, whether in monogamic or polygamic relations." She argued that "it is of but little consequence how these systems vary, so long as the fundamental principle of man's superiority and headship remains the same." "The religious sentiment of all women is prostituted in the same way in monagamic systems throughout the civilized world."[140] The Mormon community was shocked by Stanton's radicalism, as the *Salt Lake Herald* proclaimed "Stanton's view of true marriage based upon equals to be a form of 'freelovism' that was 'simply absurd.'"[141]

Nor, however, could Stanton embrace the "female evangelism" of the antipolygamy moral crusades sanctifying and sentimentalizing monogamous marriage.[142] To Stanton, these patronizing views of political men and moralistic women seeking to "protect women" hypocritically ignored women's subordination within the similarly patriarchal form of monogamatic marriage.[143] "However much the different systems of marriage had differed," Stanton said, "they all agreed on one point, and that was the uniform subjection of women."[144]

The divinely ordained inferiority and subjugation of women was the same idea taught in every form of religion, in every age, and the same idea of English common law and the foundation of American jurisprudence. The basic idea, she said, was the same in all cases: "man's right to decide woman's position, in whatever way seemeth good to himself."[145]

Women, she argued, should all be of the same mind, "at least on one point, that we were still far from having reached the ideal position of women in marriage, however satisfied man might be with his various experiments."[146] She urged crusaders to stop focusing on the minor issue of polygamy "instead of utterly and completely repudiating the idea of [woman's] 'divinely ordained subjection.'"[147] A bigger systemic change was required. "If we had done our duty, as a nation, towards women in the inauguration of this government and recognized their equality in every relation in life, we should have changed the status of womanhood on the whole face of the earth, by this time, and there would have been no material to be found for a Mormon experiment."[148]

Marriage as Contract

Stanton thus critiqued marriage in all its extant forms as victimizing women. "Man has experimented, philosophized, sermonized and legislated in the barter and sale of women 6,000 years, in every possible phase of polygamic and monogamic marriage, and no marriage at all, and the mothers of the race have been victims alike in all conditions."[149] Stanton's solution was to redefine marriage as a true contract of equal partners. This required legal reconstruction as well as altered individual behaviors.

By the end of the second half of the nineteenth century, the basic idea of marriage as a contract was being challenged by the backlash of family reformers claiming that this contract idea based on personal individualism threatened moral values and the fabric of society. Their solution was to return to a sacramental understanding of marriage as an institution created for society rather than the individual.[150] Stanton quickly and forcefully debunked the revived idea of marriage as a religious sacrament. The religious origins of marriage, she pointed out, were polygamy. The church's elevation of marriage as a sacrament, she claimed, was based on "false teachings" designed to control and subordinate women.[151] Marriage "was so consecrated to bring to bear upon womankind a religious element which . . . should weigh to maintain the subserviency to which she had, during centuries, been made to succumb."[152] American law generally rejected religious control of civil life and doing so for marriage went against the basic political principles of American governance. Thus, she concluded, "The less latitude the Church has in our temporal affairs, the better."[153]

Stanton offered what has been called a "transformative" analysis to move marriage back "from covenant to contract" and then to a contract of equality.[154] Stanton attacked the peculiar nature of the marriage contract as the "grossest absurdities and contradictions." Stanton argued, "If you regard marriage as a civil contract, then let it be subject to the same laws which control all other contracts. Do not make it a kind of half-human, half-divine, institution which you may build up but cannot regulate."[155] Marriage, she argued, should operate like any other commercial contract. "If it is a mere legal contract, then should it be subject to the restraints and privileges of all other contracts," with the usual legal rules for formation and termination.[156] "Why is it that all contracts, covenants, agreements, and partnerships are left wholly at the discretion of the parties, except that which, of all others, is considered most holy and important, both for the individual and the race?"[157] The contract construct provided the external legal structure to remodel the marriage relationship on the basis of the individual freedom of the parties, with "equal and reciprocal duties."[158] Marriage should be "a contract made by equal parties to lead an equal life, with equal restraints and privileges on either side."[159]

Stanton envisioned a limited role of the state in regulating marriage, as with other contracts.[160] At times she appeared to favor no state regulation of private marriage, similar to the theoretical ideas of the free love movement.[161] "The true family," she argued, "needs no laws or ordinances to bind it together; the Spiritual Union no force to make it enduring; no cement but that which love and friendship ever produce."[162] At other times she clarified that she "recognized the wisdom of laws governing the marriage relation," adding that "any person of common sense must see the necessity of laws."[163] What she opposed was the compulsion of the marriage laws, either religious or civil, that forced women into marriages and trapped them there.[164] As a mere human institution, the state could legislate to recognize marriage, but not to create or sanctify it.[165]

Stanton's legal theory of marriage as a regular contract led her to advocate for more stringent marriage formation laws, but easier divorce laws.[166] These views seemed contradictory from the perspective of other reformers concerned with government regulation or moral reform. But neither of these was Stanton's concern.[167] Her primary focus was on the dangers of marriage for women. Thus laws that provided safeguards restricting the entry of marriage but laws facilitating easy access to divorce were fully consistent with Stanton's feminist goal of keeping women out of marriage. Stanton's foundational belief was that the existing construct of marriage created a trap for women, ensnaring them in permanent servitude of degradation and denial of legal rights from which they could not escape.[168] Given the restrictions of coverture for women, the limitation of married women's domestic sphere, and significant problems of intemperance and domestic abuse, Stanton preferred that the laws not so easily create or maintain marriages.

Stanton objected to the young age of marriage under the common law that allowed a girl of twelve and a boy of fourteen to consent to marriage.[169] The legal ages had been based on the sexual practices of people in a feudal agrarian society, beginning early and desiring many children, and the physiological point at which girls could conceive. "A boy cannot contract for an acre of land, or a horse, until he is twenty-one, but he may contract for a wife, at fourteen."[170] She challenged the New York legislators, "upon what principle of civil jurisprudence do you permit the boy of fourteen and the girl of twelve, in violation of every natural law, to make a contract more momentous in importance than any other, and then hold them to it . . . ?"[171] She argued that "[a] contract, to be valid in law, must be formed between parties of mature age, with an honest intention in said parties to do what they agree."[172]

For Stanton, the proposals to raise the common law marital age to fifteen for girls and eighteen for boys did not go far enough. For her, the right age of marriage was twenty-five. "On what principle, I would ask, should the party on whom all the inevitable hardships of marriage must fall, be the younger to enter the relation? Girls do not get their full growth until twenty-five, and are wholly unfit at fifteen for the trials of maternity." "What knowledge can a girl of fifteen have of the great problems of social life, of the character of a husband, of the friendship and love of which the true marriage should be an outgrowth?" Instead, Stanton argued, women should be "kept in colleges as their brothers are until twenty-five, studying science and philosophy," rather than commencing "the study of man at sixteen."[173] Twenty-five was closer to her own experience, married at twenty-four and a half while Henry was thirty-four. She also cited the French law requiring that the man be twenty-five (but the woman only twenty-one), unless the parents of both parties consented to marriage at an earlier age.[174]

Stanton was also concerned about the burdens on teenage mothers from young marriages. "Both mother and child are enfeebled in such premature relations, and the girl robbed of all freedom and sentiment just as she awakes to the sweetest dreams of life."[175] In an article for the *Revolution*, "About Marrying Too Young," Stanton focused on the disabilities of teenage mothers. "Girls do not reach their maturity until twenty-five, yet at sixteen they are wives and mothers all over the land, robbed of all the rights and freedom of childhood in marriage; crippled in growth and development."[176] She focused on negative effects of teenage pregnancy in which "a vigorous and healthy womanhood" is "sapped," "perverted," and "overtaxed" by early and constant childbirth.

Stanton's advocacy of marriage as a civil contract also led her to advocate the elimination of common law marriage. This placed her in strange company, as other opponents of common law marriage were religious reformers, favoring the sacramental nature of marriage. Common law marriage, or informal or "irregular" marriage, arose out of circumstances of the parties living together as husband and wife, but without the required procedures or solemnization of a ceremony. It applied the "implied in fact" doctrine of contract law in which the circumstances and behaviors of the parties create the contract in the absence of an express oral or written contract. In the nineteenth century, courts generally accepted common law marriages for supporting the social institution of marriage, and in many cases, to allow women to collect pensions, intestacy shares, and divorce settlements.[177]

Stanton, though, with her lens of seeing marriage as a trap for women, objected to the casual creation of so oppressive a relation and demanded more caution.[178] She took this position, even though the doctrine of common law marriage was most commonly asserted by women needing financial support after the death or desertion of a partner.[179] Stanton stuck to her systemic approach of ensuring marriage as a voluntary, equal contract. "While this contract may be formed so ignorantly, thoughtlessly, and irreverently . . . , the whole power of law, religion, and public sentiment are now about to be summoned to enforce its continuance, without regard to the happiness or misery of the parties."[180] Unlike other civil contracts that are ended by mutual agreement of the parties or failure to comply with the conditions of the contract, Stanton said, in "the marriage contract which the State allows to be formed so thoughtlessly, ignorantly, irreverently, the parties have no control whatever, though ofttimes in its formation and continuance all laws of decency and common sense are set at defiance; as forced marriages, mock marriages, suits for breach of promise, and divorce cases, all illustrate."[181]

Stanton challenged the "looseness of the laws" and the "absence of all form and dignity" for creating a common law marriage.[182] "Nothing could be more reckless than our present system, when merely to be seen walking together may be taken as evidence of intent to marry and going through the ceremony in jest may seal the contract."[183] She contrasted the legal formalities required to establish a contract for land with the lack of such procedural protections for establishing marriage. "A legal contract for a section of land requires that the parties be of age and of sound mind; that there be no flaw in the title, no liens or mortgages thereon not specified; and that the agreement be in writing, with the names of parties and witnesses duly affixed, stamped with the seal of the state, and recorded in the office of the county clerk." A legal marriage, however, in most states, "may be contracted between a boy of fourteen and a girl of twelve, without the consent of parents or guardians, without publication of banns, without witnesses, without even the signatures of the parties, the presence of a priest, or of any officer of the state."[184]

Stanton would have instead required strict compliance with the necessary legal procedures to establish a civil marriage. She recommended what she understood to be the practice required by French law: the publication of banns, the ceremony performed by a public official in the presence of four witnesses, and the recording of the marriage in two special registers. Banns were public notices publicizing the intended marriage to the family and community to solicit any objections. States abandoned banns toward the end of the century, adopting licensure as the predominant form of administration, emphasizing bureaucracy rather than the public notice function.[185]

All of Stanton's theorization of marriage as a contract was meant to preserve women's freedom in that relation. The U.S. Supreme Court, however, rejected the construct of marriage as a contract in 1888 in *Maynard v. Hill* by conclusively holding it to be a status, which remains the law today. The Court recognized the accepted judicial understanding of marriage as part contract in that it required the necessary consent between the parties and was distinguished from a religious sacrament. However, it was also more than a mere contract because by operation of law it created a status of a social relation and a "public institution." Marriage, the Court held, creates "the most important relation in life, as having more to do with the morals and civilization of a people than any other institution." "It is an institution, in the maintenance of which in its purity the public is deeply interested, for it is the foundation of the family and of society, without which there would be neither civilization nor progress."[186] The Court thus sided with family reformers who contrary to Stanton argued for a public rather than individual conception of marriage. The result, however, ironically validated the legislative divorce in the Maynard case since marriage as a status did not implicate federal constitutional prohibitions on impairment of contract.

Marriage of Equals

The alternative ideal Stanton offered was one of egalitarian, companionate marriage. "There is one kind of marriage that has not been tried, and that is a contract made by equal parties to lead an equal life."[187] The "true relation" should be based on the complete equality of partners, where "the man and woman stand equal in dignity, honor and rights." There would be no "subjection except to principle; no sacrifice but of the

soul to God . . . [T]he Spiritual Union [needs] no force to make it enduring; no cement but that which love and friendship ever produce."[188]

Stanton argued for a transformation of marriage from its economic,
physical construct to a companionate, spiritual form. "In a true relation," she explained, "the chief object is the loving companionship of
man and woman, their capacity for mutual help and happiness, and for
the development of all that is noblest in each other."[189] This soul-mate
ideal prioritized the spiritual connection of the parties, thereby foster-
ing women's full intellectual and educational development. "Only those
marriages that are harmonious, where the parties are really companions
for each other, are in the highest sense, joined together by God."[190] Stanton explained,

> My philosophy of life, love, and marriage is quite different from that of
> many people. I regard them all with reference to individual develop-
> ment. . . . A true conjugal union is the highest kind of love,—divine,
> creative in the realm of thought as well as in the material world. I have
> great faith in nature's promptings and the sincere love of young men and
> women for each other.[191]

Stanton criticized the status quo that regarded "marriage too much
as a physical union, wholly in its material bearings, and from the man's
standpoint."[192] Stanton exposed marriage as immoral for being merely a
"physical union" for every man to "gratify his passions" with the recip-
rocating subordination of woman as a "pecuniary necessity" for women's
self-support. "I do not believe in a man having a wife for breeding purposes," but no "affinity for spiritual and intellectual intercourse. Soul
union should precede and exalt physical union. Without sentiment, affection, imagination, what better would we be in procreation than the
beasts?"[193] The physical relation should be the "consummation merely
of a spiritual or intellectual sympathy, respect and friendship," rather
than constituting "all there is of marriage" in far too many cases.

> It is a low idea of sex to suppose it merely physical. Those that have
> known the joys of a true love and friendship, feel that there is sex in soul
> as well as body. The higher orders of being are drawn together by the
> sexual attractions of mind and spirit, just as the lower are by those of pas-

sion. Yes, there is a marriage of souls as well as bodies, and it is this true union humanity sighs for to-day.[194]

Stanton was decidedly opposed to marriages coerced for reasons of economics or privilege. Many young women at the time married much older men.[195] Stanton strongly opposed this practice "of that large class of men and women who marry for wealth, position, mere sensual gratification, without any real attraction or religious sense of loyalty toward one another."[196] "With the elevation of woman, we shall indeed have most radical changes in our social life. Independent and self-supporting, she will not marry for bread and a home, and thus desecrate that holy relation."[197] "You all know our marriage is, in many cases, a mere outward lie, impelled by custom, policy, interest, necessity; founded not even in friendship, to say nothing of love; with every possible inequality of condition and development." In some cases, she argued, a man marries a woman for money, which is then quickly given over to creditors. In other cases, the bride may be the "victim of a father's pride or a mother's ambition, betrayed into a worldly union for wealth, or family, or fame."[198] "When womanhood is as dignified and independent as manhood, in and of itself, and labor equally honorable for both, women will not marry to escape the odium of being called old maids or to live by the bounty of another."[199]

Stanton later used the controversy over the English poet Lord Byron's marriage to illustrate the problems of economic marriage. Harriet Beecher Stowe, then famous for her antislavery novel, *Uncle Tom's Cabin*, wrote a notorious 1869 exposé for the nation's top magazine, the *Atlantic Monthly*, entitled "The True Story of Lady Byron's Life," which "has quite plausibly been described as 'the most sensational magazine article of the nineteenth century.'" Under the pretext of writing literary criticism of the poet's work, Stowe defended Lady Byron, who had been attacked by the public for abandoning her husband, and defamed by her husband for his lost love and unhappy life. After Lady Byron's death, Stowe revealed salacious details allegedly learned at Lady Byron's deathbed of the poet's incestuous affair with his half-sister and their resulting child. "From the height at which he might have been happy as the husband of a noble woman, he fell into the depths of a secret adulterous intrigue with a blood relation, so near in consanguinity that discovery must have been utter ruin and expulsion from civilized society."[200]

Stanton picked up on Stowe's feminist insight as to the degrading nature of marriage. "The true relation of the sexes is the momentous question at this stage of our civilization," Stanton said, "and Mrs. Stowe has galvanized the world to its consideration." To Stanton, the Byron case was an example of the "hideous, disgusting slavery in which the women of every class and clime ever have been and are held to-day" and the resulting "abominations of our social life." Lord and Lady Byron's real sin, Stanton said, was that they married for ambition: he for money, she for a title. Out of this "spiritual incest" could come only "discord, falsehood, desertion, disgrace." The present noise and "bluster of the press," Stanton suggested, was due to "this unveiling of man as woman's natural protector." Uncovering the abuse, cruelty, and miseries of married life may be shocking, but "to be criticised by the entire press of the nation may be the strongest evidence that a blow has been struck in the right direction."[201]

Stanton took her opposition to economic marriage to its legal conclusion by advocating for the elimination of breach of promise actions brought to recover for the harm from broken engagements. Breach of promise actions created common law rights for men, and only men, usually fathers and brothers, to institute actions for damages to recover for harm to reputation and economic losses from the continued care of a woman after a broken promise of marriage.[202] Stanton's objection to breach of promise suits was grounded in their commodification of women and reinforcing effect of depicting marriage as an economic transaction for the purchase of women. "There is no stronger proof of the degradation and demoralization of our American womanhood," she exclaimed, "than the frequent cases in our courts 'for breach of promise.'" "We fully believe these prosecutions are in every case instigated by male relatives and designing lawyers." To avoid this socially reinforcing effect, Stanton recommended keeping these cases out of the courts. She thought that women would not "expose their private experiences in our courts and public journals, unless prompted to that step by the material logic of some male brain."[203]

In part, Stanton's objection to the breach of promise actions was to the "looseness" of the system, which, like informal marriage law, too easily recognized marriages. She criticized judicial decisions from New York, Massachusetts, and Kentucky holding that a promise of marriage need not be made in express terms. These courts determined that facts like "frequent visits, conversation aside, expressions of attachment, some presents offered, walks taken together, etc., are sufficient circumstances on which to rely in proving the existence of a marriage engagement."[204] She rejected any laws that forced parties into marriage without clear intent.

Stanton also criticized women for their role in these actions. She objected to women blackmailing men under these legal guises and forcing marriage for economic gain. "This has come to be a trade among an unprincipled order of women who seek by artifices more or less ingenious to attract men of wealth." She also, though, objected to the double moral standard underlying breach of promise suits, reinforced by female society, that concluded loss of reputation and value of the women, but not the men, from a broken engagement and extramarital sex. Telling one story of a "pretty young girl, a member of the Presbyterian church who, outside the conventional rules, has become the mother of a child," Stanton chastised society women who ostracized the girl as Hester Prynne is ostracized in *The Scarlet Letter*.[205] She appreciated that "money brings many blessings," but her advice to this young mother was to "banish the ignoble father, . . . spurn his gold, take her baby to her heart and arms," and learn "self-dependence and self-support." A response in the *Revolution* agreed in principle, but emphasized the practical value of breach of promise damages for a woman who has been rejected by society and is unable to support herself or her child.[206]

Disavowing the economic marriage, Stanton called for an "equal partnership, intended for the equal advantage and happiness of both parties."[207] "Man will gain as much as woman by an equal companionship in the nearest and holiest relations of life."[208] A "true marriage" required "equality, self-respect, independence." That required the health and happiness of each individual. Quoting Ralph Waldo Emerson (who was quoting Margaret Fuller), she said, "[W]e must first have units before we can have unions."[209] Stanton argued that women needed to be economically self-supporting and understanding of "the science of life" and "the laws of reproduction."[210] "When women have their own property and business, they will choose and not be chosen; they will marry the men they love, or not at all; and where there is love between the parents, children will ever find care and protection.[211] She predicted that "until men and women view each other as equals. . . . marriage will be, in most cases, a long, hard struggle to make the best of a bad bargain."[212] Repeating this idea in her "Address at the Decade Meeting on Marriage and Divorce," Stanton emphasized, "When husbands and wives do not own each other as property, but are bound together only by affection, marriage will be a life-long friendship, and not a heavy yoke from which both may sometimes long for deliverance."[213]

Stanton argued that marriage "concerns man and woman equally, and its corner-stone must be laid in the freedom and equality of both parties." Playing into the dominant belief in the sacredness of marriage, Stanton argued that marriage was "intended by God for the greater freedom and happiness of both parties—whatever therefore conflicts with woman's happiness is not legitimate to that relation." However, she added, "woman has yet to learn that she has a right to be happy in and of herself; that she has a right to the free use, improvement, and development of all her faculties, for her own benefit and pleasure."[214] Citing Mozart, Beethoven, Mendelssohn, philosophers, and poets, Stanton said that "the great and good in all ages have felt these yearnings for the higher, truer marriage." "Religion and common sense alike teach that the true ends of marriage are solace, help, the spiritual growth of both parties, and intellectual and moral companionship." "Blessed are they who love for that alone, who, in a true spiritual union, find an element of the permanent, that like myrrh and frankincense, sweetens and glorifies life, makes gods of men and women and paradise on earth."[215] She gave examples of people fitting her theory of equal partnership, like John Stuart Mill, the English author of the women's rights book, *The Subjection of Women*, and his wife, Harriet.[216] And she gave examples of marriages of famous men who failed to meet this standard, including Benjamin Franklin, Henry Clay, and U.S. Supreme Court Chief Justice Oliver Ellsworth, who all abandoned home for lengths of time for work and fame in national governance, leaving their wives behind with the farms, children, and bills.

Finally, Stanton called upon women to proactively create this equality in marriage. "Self-respect is the first step in securing the respect of others."[217] "The content of the women," she said, "is much like that of black men in the old days of slavery. The great thing women do lack is a proper self-respect."[218] She called for women to abandon their "submissive spirit" in their own marriages, citing the example of her friend Louise, who finally challenged her husband's refusal to replace a broken stove by buying the stove herself.[219] "We do not blame man for his injustice to woman, no more than our baby for upsetting the inkstand on a valuable manuscript, they are alike ignorant of what they have done. So long as woman supposed herself made for no higher purpose than to be the toy or drudge of man, how could man possibly know any better himself?"[220]

Stanton argued not to abandon marriage, but rather to radically reconstruct it to incorporate feminist norms. She was, however, suspicious of the limitations and restrictions of the legal relationship of marriage for women, and thus cautioned women about entering the relation. "Our troubles do not arise so much from marriage in itself, for that seems to be the natural state of the human family, and there is no doubt more happiness in marriage than out of it."[221] "We can trust the laws of the universe" as to conjugal love, she sarcastically remarked, "even if the speeches and resolutions of a woman's rights convention seem to conflict with them."[222] When asked whether she thought marriage was a success, she answered, "Yes as much of a success as any other human institution. Like government and religion it is an outgrowth of ourselves, imperfect in our present stage of development, but improving as individual men and women grow in knowledge and wisdom." Her prescription for happy marriages was "to educate men and women into a clear idea of individual rights; the exact limit of their own and the vital point where they begin to infringe on the rights of another."[223]

3

"Divorce Is Not the Foe of Marriage"

*Divorce is not the foe of marriage. Adultery, intemperance, li-
centiousness are its foes. One might as well speak of medicine
as the foe of health.*

—Elizabeth Cady Stanton, "The Need of Liberal
Divorce Laws," 1884

The "marriage question," as it was called in the nineteenth century,
was less about marriage and all about divorce. America inherited the
divorceless legal tradition of England derived from canon law, prohibiting divorce but allowing separation and annulment. A few colonies and
states experimented with divorce, slowly expanding the fault grounds
for divorce by the middle of the nineteenth century, with a few states
adopting broad grounds for any misconduct or cause.[1] Legislatures
were guided by legal concepts of individualism and contract theory, and
influenced by temperance arguments for the protection of women. As
the country grew through expansion, immigration, and industrialization, divorce increased. Numbers went from 9,937 in 1867, the first year
a national census on divorce was taken, to 33,461 in 1890 and to 167,105
by 1920.[2] The moral outcry was loud, as clergy and moral reformers predicted the deterioration of the family and the downfall of society.

Stanton was at the forefront of the very public debate on divorce. She
viewed divorce as an important issue of women's rights because it freed
women from marriage, where their legal status was denied and their
personal freedoms curtailed. Viewing marriage as a trap, she was sup-
portive of any legal means for women to escape, including no-fault or
"easy divorce."[3] Taking this a step further, Stanton argued that women
had a duty, an obligation to divorce, in cases of domestic violence and
intemperance, to protect themselves and their children.[4]

Divorce had been seen historically and biblically as a way for men
to "put away their wives," but Stanton reframed it as a legal remedy for

women. She "single-handedly shifted the age-old idea of divorce as a male prerogative to a right demanded by women on humanitarian grounds."[5] Women needed divorce, Stanton argued, to escape domestic violence, abuse, poverty, and simple unhappiness. "Liberal divorce laws for oppressed wives," Stanton proclaimed, "are what Canada was for Southern slaves."[6] The majority of divorces, over two-thirds, were filed by women—a key fact for Stanton proving the importance of this issue for women and the propriety of including it within the women's rights platform.[7] Divorce was not a morality crisis, but simply a consequence of women's assertion of rights. "This is woman's transition period, from slavery to freedom, and all the social upheavings, before which the wisest and bravest stand appalled, are but necessary incidents in her progress to equality."[8] Divorce provided the self-help remedy that let women enforce their own rights and expectations of marriage, with the secondary effect of transforming marriage into a more egalitarian structure.[9]

Stanton's tenaciousness on divorce, however, alienated colleagues and divided the women's rights movement. Her vocal support of divorce outraged reformers, increased opposition to women's rights, and contributed to the split in the organized women's movement. Stanton remained undeterred, convinced of the necessity of divorce to women's full equality. As the eighty-year-old Stanton recalled, "[S]o bitter was the opposition to divorce for any cause that but few dared to take part in the discussion." But, she said, "I was always courageous in saying what I saw to be true, for the simple reason that I never dreamed of opposition. What seemed to me to be right I thought must be equally plain to all other rational beings."[10]

Temperance and Duty

Stanton inserted herself in the thick of the divorce debate both in New York and on the larger national stage. For two centuries, from 1787 until 1967, her home state of New York permitted divorce only for adultery; it was one of the strictest states in the country.[11] Stanton leveraged her leadership in the emerging temperance movement to advance the idea of divorce as a necessity for women's protection against alcohol-induced violence. The temperance movement, formed in the 1830s, relied on moral suasion and, later, aggressive demonstrations to prohibit the sale of alcohol, resulting in the short-lived Eighteenth Amendment in 1919. Women activists quickly transformed the movement by organizing female societies, relying on "traditional concepts of women's sphere, the home, to promote social reform and political activism" for prohibition and, later, suffrage.[12] Stanton briefly led the New York women's temperance organization in the early 1850s. Under her guidance, "the temperance movement became the first American reform campaign to depict for the public the cruelty of domestic violence." Stanton's proposed solution, however, was more radical than prohibition of alcohol; what she demanded was free divorce.[13]

Divorce and domestic violence were a part of Stanton's initial formulation of a women's rights agenda, articulated in the Declaration of Sentiments' litany of women's wrongs. She criticized the existing divorce laws, made "wholly without regard to women's happiness." And she rejected the law that gave the husband "power to deprive [woman] of her liberty, and to administer chastisement."[14] The old English common law had permitted "domestic chastisement" or physical punishment of a wife by the husband, much as a parent might spank a child. The popular understanding of this law, called "the rule of thumb," was that a husband could beat his wife with a stick, as long as the stick was no thicker than his thumb. Early American treatise writers questioned the legitimacy of this common law rule. Courts formally disavowed such a rule, yet domestic violence continued in practice, and courts did little in response.

Stanton's solution to domestic violence was divorce. She first wrote of her support for divorce in 1850 in a short article aptly titled "Divorce," published under the pseudonym "Sun Flower" in the women's temperance newspaper, the *Lily*. At this time, a New York legislative committee had proposed a bill to expand divorce beyond the cause of adultery to include desertion, imprisonment, drunkenness, and insanity.[15] Stanton brought this to her readers' attention and gave it her vote. "I see there is a bill before the Legislature providing some new doors, through which unhappy prisoners may escape from the bonds of an ill assorted marriage. . . . I hope that bill may pass." She strongly endorsed divorce in the context of intemperance and abuse. "The Legislature, so far from placing any barrier in the way of a woman wishing to leave a drunken husband, ought to pass laws, compelling her to do so." Divorce, she suggested, would be woman's duty in such circumstances. Going further, Stanton proposed a broader right to no-fault divorce.[16] "If, as at present, all can freely and *thoughtlessly* enter into the married state, they should be allowed to come as freely and *thoughtfully* out again."[17]

To personalize her legalistic arguments and garner empathy for the reform, Stanton often added a story about her girlhood friend, who was "a victim of one of those unfortunate unions, called marriage." She recalled that her "feelings had been stirred to their depths very early in life by the sufferings of a dear friend of mine, at whose wedding I was one of the bridesmaids. In listening to the facts in her case, my mind was fully made up as to the wisdom of a liberal divorce law."[18] She said the friends "read Milton's essays on divorce together and were thoroughly convinced as to the right and duty not only of separation, but of absolute divorce." This friend, Stanton said, was "married ostensibly to a gentleman, but in reality to a brute." The day after their marriage, "their splendid home," worth sixty thousand dollars, given to them by the bride's father, was in the hands of the husband's creditors. "He stole her jewels, clothes—everything she had." He told the "young and trusting girl but one short month his wife that he married her for her money, that those letters that she had read and re-read and kissed and cherished, were written by another," and asked her to seek fresh supplies of money from her father.[19]

Stanton advised her friend to leave her husband. But her parents would not take her back. "A year later she appeared, thinly clad, with a baby in her arms, at my door." As Stanton melodramatically retold the incident, "When she told the story of her wrongs to me—the abuse to which she was subject, and the dread in which she lived, I impulsively urged her to fly from such a monster and villain, as she would before the hot breath of a ferocious beast of the wilderness." In one version of the story, Stanton said she "hastened to court with her fugitive friend and heroically plead [sic] her cause before the assembled judges." In another version, Stanton said she "went to Albany, where my father, Daniel Cady, was a Judge. I talked to him and Chancellor Kent about the case" but was told nothing could be done "to free the woman from the brute." The story ends either with her friend emotionally thanking Stanton for giving her the courage to escape her bondage, or with Stanton reporting that "fortunately the man dropped dead."[20] This story, Stanton said, and others like it she told, were not chosen "themes for rhetorical flourish as, . . . pathetic touches of the speaker's eloquence," but evidence of real social degradation requiring not that "we passively shed tears" but rather demand rights of separation and escape.[21]

Stanton gained a platform for her divorce ideas when she became president of the newly organized New York State Woman's Temperance Society in 1852. Stanton, now partnered with Susan B. Anthony, formed the women's group because of outrage at the prohibition on women speaking in the general male temperance societies, similar to what women had experienced in the abolition movement.[22] She spent much of her short tenure with the organization defending that right to female leadership. "We have been obliged to preach woman's rights, because many, instead of listening to what we had to say on temperance, have questioned the right of a woman to speak on any subject."[23] Once she became president of the temperance organization, she used the opportunity to speak about divorce, arguing that it was not only permissible but required in situations of alcoholism and domestic violence. She clashed with the conservative members of the temperance group, further alientating the male leaders opposed to women's public role.

Stanton was fighting against the deeply entrenched social norm that divorce was a religious sin. The prevailing religious view was that Christian women should embrace their drunken husbands and try to reform them, or otherwise sacrifice themselves for the good of the family.[24] "Alas! how many excellent women have dragged out a weary existence in such a partnership, from mistaken ideas of duty—from a false sense of religious obligation?" "The drunkard's wife sits crushed and hopeless—fearing to break the chains that grate on her naked heart—she dies, the victim of a false public sentiment—while the Priest and the Law Giver coolly look on, and pronounce all very good."[25] Instead, Stanton called for the creation of a "new public sentiment in regard to the marriage obligations of Drunkards' wives." She envisioned a higher standard of virtue and true womanhood that did not bestow praises "on those wives who have loved and lived on, in filth, poverty and rags, the wretched companion of a drunkard's sorrow" and mother of his children. "It is not in Conventions, dear Friends, that our best work begins. The radical reform must start in our homes, in our nurseries, in ourselves."[26]

Inverting the accepted teachings, Stanton argued that *staying* in a marriage with an alcoholic husband was the sin. Women in such situations, she asserted, had the moral duty to leave the marriage. Initially, Stanton connected this moral duty to a mother's obligation to protect her children. In a speech shortly after Seneca Falls, she indicted women's passive acceptance of abuse. "Oh! women how sadly you have learned your duty to your children, to your own heart, to the God that gave you that holy love for them when you stand silent witnesses to the cruel infliction of blows and strips from angry Fathers on the trembling forms of helpless infancy." To the contrary, she argued, "It is a mother's sacred duty to shield her children from violence from whatever source it may come, it is her duty to resist oppression wherever she may find it at home or abroad, by every moral power within her reach."[27] She dramatically illustrated the harm to children from a violent marital relationship. "Call that sacred, where innocent children, trembling with fear, fly to the corners and dark places of the house, to hide from the wrath of drunken, brutal fathers, but forgetting their past sufferings, rush out again at the mother's frantic screams, 'Help! oh, help!'" She continued, "Behold the agonies of those young hearts, as they see the only being on earth they love, dragged about the room by the hair of her head, kicked and pounded, and left half dead and bleeding on the floor!"[28]

Given this moral duty, Stanton then argued that the law should permit divorce for drunkenness.[29] Speaking to the second Women's Temperance Convention in Rochester in April 1852, Stanton, four months pregnant and wearing bloomers, explained her pro-divorce position.[30] Taking on the "pious horror at the idea of separating man and wife," Stanton instead argued that it was a sin for a woman to continue to consent to be the wife of a drunkard and a sin to produce children with him. "[A]ny woman sacrifices her claims to virtue and nobility, who consents to live in the relation of wife with any man whom she has ceased to love and respect."[31] At another temperance convention several months later, Stanton repeated, "[I]t has been left for Woman to preach the doctrine of Divorce—a doctrine which is to strike the most effective blow at the sin of drunkenness."[32] True reform, she argued, required not only preventive measures of eliminating the existing evil of alcohol but also the "far higher duty" of protecting against recurrence by the more fundamental and long-lasting reform of divorce.[33]

Stanton's moral appeal to the women's temperance reformers in framing divorce as a moral duty spoke the language of many of the conservative women in the group. Even then, the temperance women resisted, including some, like Clarina Nichols, who had been divorced themselves.[34] Frustrated, Stanton made plans to present divorce more directly, couching it as her individual position, rather than that of the society. "I have as good a right to infuse what we choose of the radical principle into the proceedings of the society, as the miserable time serving conservatives have to infuse their principles of policy and expediency."[35] At the statewide temperance convention in June 1852, the women's society was overruled by conservative clergymen objecting to the women's public participation. Stanton's radical demand for divorce was thus instead read by Anthony to the large seceding group meeting outside the official meeting, with Anthony seconding the right to divorce on grounds of drunkenness.[36]

Anthony renewed Stanton's divorce resolution again at an October meeting of the women's society.[37] The convention took place in Stanton's hometown of Seneca Falls, but still she could not attend since she was expecting to give birth to her fifth child any day. Her resolution, presented by Anthony, stated "that if it be a violation of scripture for man to put asunder those whom God has joined together, it is equally a violation of holy writ for man, by his unjust laws, to hold together those whom God has never joined." In support of the resolution, Anthony argued against the familiar objection to the ground of habitual drunkenness for divorce as contrary to the Bible, asking rhetorically, "[S]hould a woman be bound to live with a man that daily threatens to murder herself and children, until actual murder was committed?" There was "spirited discussion" in opposition to the divorce resolution, with the objectors emphasizing the proper remedy of separation and endorsing legal reform to award all of the property and custody of the children to the wife. There should always be hope for reform of the husband, they said, "and a home and a heart should be ready for him if he should ever regain the dignity of his manhood."[38] Despite these objections, the resolution passed by a small majority.

Stanton's advocacy of divorce within the temperance community occurred as the New York legislature considered proposals to expand the grounds for divorce.[39] In January 1853, the women's temperance organization presented the legislature with petitions of twenty-eight thousand names supporting a "Maine Law" prohibiting the sale of alcohol. In a corresponding written address to the New York legislature, read to the assembly by Anthony, Stanton advocated for the Maine Law, but argued that it was more important that the body pass a law on divorce. "But above all, we conjure you not to let this session pass, without giving us a law making drunkenness a just cause of divorce." "Such a law," she argued, "would be far greater in its permanent results than the Maine Law." Even without all intoxicating drinks, she asserted, men still retain their animal natures. "But back up the Maine Law by the more important one on Divorce and you make a permanent reform in so regulating your laws on marriage that the pure and noble of our sex may be sustained by the power of Government in dissolving all union with gross and vicious natures." Further, she reasoned, "it would create a strong public sentiment against drunkenness for you to declare, that, in your opinion, it is a crime so enormous, as to furnish just cause for the separation of man and wife." Anthony reported that Stanton's "paragraph on Divorce is calling down the condemnation of our pious presses . . . horrified at the idea of allowing the wife of a bloated drunkard, to be released."[40]

Still Stanton persisted, defending the focus on the "important subject of divorce."[41] The idea of divorce, however, proved too outrageous for the conservative temperance society. After the June 1853 meeting, Stanton was voted out as president.[42] The defeat didn't bother Stanton in the least. She was weary of conventions and overwhelmed with housekeeping and the birth of her fifth child. Stanton wrote to Anthony that she was not "plunged in grief," but rather satisfied with what she had done. "I accomplished at Rochester all I desired by having the divorce question brought up." "Waste no powder on the Woman's State Temperance Society," she continued. "We have other and bigger fish to fry."[43]

Outside the confines of the temperance organization, Stanton continued to advance the idea of divorce as necessary protection for women.[44] She snuck divorce into her comprehensive 1854 address to the New York legislature, avoiding the use of the "D" word. Stanton made a legalistic appeal based on marriage as a contract and the existing contractual law granting "the full right to dissolve all partnerships and contracts for any reason, at the will and option of the parties themselves." She repeated her equitable arguments in support of the desperate drunkard's wife, developing a more sophisticated analysis understanding the power and control of domestic violence. Stanton decried the husband's common law "right to whip his wife with a rod not larger than his thumb, to shut her up in a room, and administer whatever moderate chastisement he may deem necessary to insure obedience to his wishes, and . . . deprive her of all social intercourse with her nearest and dearest friends."[45] In other writings, she appealed to men as parents and lawmakers, asking, "What father could rest at his home at night, knowing that his lovely daughter was at the mercy of a strong man, drunk with wine and passion, and that, do what he might, he was backed up by law and public sentiment?"[46]

People responded sympathetically to this imagery of the abused wife that fit within the conventional ideology of women's need for protection. The pitiful figure of the abused wife "presented the most vivid and compelling case for divorce." Legislators could understand the need for divorce as a "self-defense, a measure of last resort to counter the physical violence leveled at women by drunken and abusive husbands."[47] Stanton recalled how in New York, "there had been several aggravated cases of cruelty to wives among the Dutch aristocracy, so that strong influences in favor of the [divorce] bill had been brought to bear on the legislature."[48] On the popular level, too, people began to accept the need for divorce for abuse.[49] States quietly added statutory grounds for divorce based on cruelty and habitual drunkenness, solidifying divorce as an acceptable legal solution, or at least, the lesser of two evils.[50]

Others pressed for more aggressive criminal and tort remedies for domestic violence. Civil claims by wives against their husbands were blocked by marital immunity against suing one's spouse, and evolving judicial concepts of marital privacy rationalized governmental noninterference in marriages.[51] Lucy Stone unsuccessfully lobbied for protective legislation, similar to a bill passed in England, to grant battered wives the right to obtain protection orders, support, and custody.[52] She then began to favor legislation for criminal punishment of wife beaters by whipping post.[53] By the late nineteenth century, wife beating became a law-and-order issue as part of a bigger movement against violent crime, and a handful of states passed laws to punish wife beating by public flogging. An American Bar Association committee seriously considered the proposal as a potentially strong deterrent to wife beating, but ultimately rejected it as inhumane, ineffective, and humiliating to the man.[54]

Stanton briefly weighed in on the topic in an 1899 editorial, "Wife-Beaters." She said that while she had "always advocated humane treatment for ordinary criminals in our jails and prisons," she found that "a man who could beat his wife in the presence of his children, belongs to an exceptional class and calls for exceptional treatment." A man, she said, should be held to the same level of self-control toward his wife as the law (of assault and battery) required toward another man—even more so for a wife, she argued, since another man possessed equal status of legal right and personal strength, but those were "advantages a wife does not possess, as the husband owns her and has the right to administer moderate chastisement, according to the old common law of England, its influence not yet wholly obliterated from judicial decisions and the statutes of the several States." Less than a year later, though, the *Woman's Journal* reported that Stanton did not approve of recommendations of New York magistrates to punish wife beaters by flogging, saying instead that "the real cure for wife-beating is to be found not in disciplining an occasional brute, but in teaching men to respect women."[55]

Making the Case

The social issue of domestic abuse gave Stanton the toehold she needed to make her more radical demand for free, no-fault divorce. Moving beyond her temperance work, she presented her full analytical case in support of divorce before a crowd of one thousand people at the Tenth National Woman's Rights Convention in New York City in May 1860.[56] Stanton had newly committed herself to active public advocacy, freed from some of the daily demands of domestic management as her youngest child, Bob, turned one. As she wrote to Anthony, "I may add that I am well, and full of steam, that the house is all cleaned for summer; that every spare moment I seize my pen, and that, in a word, I am now ready to do what is to be done."[57] On the first day of the Tenth Convention, Stanton repeated her address to the New York legislature from the previous February on expanded married women's rights to property and earnings. On the second day, she shocked her suffrage audience with a speech unveiling strong support for divorce.[58] The divorce speech established Stanton as a leading national voice on the issue, but convinced few reformers and angered many.

In spring 1860, divorce was dominant in the public discourse. The New York legislature was again considering a divorce bill expanding fault grounds. The front pages of the *New York Tribune* featured a three-month debate provoked by this legislation and led by editor Horace Greeley and socialist Robert Dale Owen. Greeley was a strong opponent of divorce and its alleged elevation of selfish individualism over the good of the community. The debates resurrected earlier divorce debates Greeley had featured in 1852 with free lover Stephen Pearl Andrews and Henry James Sr.[59]

Stanton inserted herself into this debate in the Tenth Convention speech, saying, "[L]et us hope that all wisdom does not live, and will not die, with Horace Greeley."[60] With her usual wit, Stanton confronted the reticence to discuss divorce. "This question of divorce, they tell us, is hedged about with difficulties; that it cannot be approached with the ordinary rules of logic and common sense," as it was too holy, too sacred. Jokingly she said that while men might find it difficult to reason and "ratiocinate" about divorce, women were fortunately endowed with mere "woman's intuitions" and moral instinct, enabling them to see the right and wrong of the question.[61]

Stanton began her address to the convention by emphasizing the instrumentality of law, but exposing its inherent fallibility of male bias. She challenged the common law and "the whole system of jurisprudence" based on man's idea of right. Since man was fallible, she argued, "[W]e must look for many and gross blunders in the application of its general principles to individual cases." Introducing her "man marriage" argument, she said that for divorce, "man has had the whole and sole regulation of the matter. He has spoken in Scripture, and he has spoken in law. As an individual, he has decided the time and cause for putting away a wife; and as a judge and legislator, he still holds the entire control."[62] Since woman was excluded from this lawmaking process, the laws failed to protect or include her interests. Thus far in the debate over divorce, "just one-half of the ground has been surveyed, and that half but by one of the parties, and that party certainly *not* the most interested in the matter." In all the transactions of marriage and divorce throughout time, woman has been excluded from consideration, as "if she had had no part nor lot in the whole matter." Without complete assessment, the resulting divorce law created unworkable situations that went against human nature, making "laws that man cannot and will not obey," serving "to bring all law into contempt." Such laws were easily avoided as "those who wish to evade them have only to go into another State to accomplish what they desire."[63]

Stanton then challenged the accepted notion that divorce was a public harm. Divorce, she said, might be a personal problem, "a calamity, but not ever, perhaps never, a crime."[64] In the mid-nineteenth century, the law conceptualized divorce as a crime, a harm against society. The state allowed an action to be "prosecuted" against the wrongdoer who committed a "fault" against the social institution of marriage.[65] Stanton later elaborated on this point, questioning the legal construct of viewing divorce "as quasi criminal" by "limiting the causes of divorce to physical defects or delinquencies," making the proceedings public, and "punishing the guilty party in the suit." The real crime, she said "against both the individual and the state" was compelling discordant marriages to continue. "No, no; the enemy of marriage, of the State, of society, is not liberal divorce laws, but the unhealthy atmosphere that exists in the home itself. A legislative act cannot make a unit of a divided family." Instead, the key consideration for policy and law was the individual's right to happiness. "The best interests of a community never can require the sacrifice of one innocent being—of one sacred right."[66]

Stanton then endorsed expanded fault bases for divorce and unveiled her radical support for no-fault divorce. Citing the New York legislature's attempt to extend divorce beyond adultery, she supported those proposals with the melodramatic stories of her abused bridesmaid friend, drunkards' wives and children cowering in the corner, and startling newspaper accounts of murdered spouses.[67] But Stanton then made the radical analytical leap of arguing for no-fault divorce simply upon the will of the party. Factually, she empathized with the many unhappy, "miserable people" who had fallen into the pit of "wretched matches" and were now required by the statutory laws "to stay there, and pay the life-long penalty of having fallen in." Legally, she introduced her argument of marriage as a contract and its ability to be terminated at will. Marriage was merely a human institution, a "mere outward tie" entered into for reasons both good and bad, and in no case requiring adherence to a sacred ideal of divinity.

Stanton then addressed the fundamental counterargument that separation adequately solved the problem of discordant marriages. De facto physical separation of the estranged parties had long been an accepted practice, with husbands deserting their families or by women simply returning to their father's house.[68] And legal separation was available on some limited grounds in equity courts, following ecclesiastical practice. Some feminists advocated greater laws of separation to provide for maintenance and custody for women in separations, which Stanton supported.[69] But fundamentally, separation remained an unsatisfactory option for Stanton because of its social stigma and enforced solitude. First, separation's social stigma effectively barred women from choosing that option. "[A]s long as you insist on marriage as a Divine institution, as an indissoluble tie," and maintain the present laws against divorce, "you make separation, even, so odious, that the most noble, virtuous and sensitive men and women choose a life of concealed misery, rather than a partial, disgraceful release." Even when women separated "in spite of public sentiment," they ran into the second barrier, the ban on remarriage after separation that condemned them to a life of celibacy and isolation. The inability to remarry, Stanton argued, was harder on women than on men because "marriage is not all of life to man." Man has other resources for occupation, business, politics, and friendship, whereas women were directed to marriage as the "sole object in life." Stanton protested the resulting denial of women's sexuality. "Would you drive her to a nunnery; and shall she be a nun indeed?"[70]

Antoinette Brown Blackwell, the first ordained woman minister and college graduate of Oberlin, spoke against Stanton. She began by saying that there were more than two sides to the divorce debate, that there were three or even more sides than just the positions of Stanton and Greeley. While she asserted that "all divorce is naturally and morally impossible," her arguments proposed a middle ground between spiritual ideal and legal practicality. Blackwell theorized marriage as permanent, as a sacred, covenant-like relation more indissoluble than Stanton's marriage contract or outward tie. But Blackwell tolerated and even encouraged divorce where necessary. She argued that legal divorce was appropriate whenever a woman was unjustly subjugated in marriage, citing examples of marital rape and drunkenness. A wife, she said, had a right to claim her own sovereignty, and where that individual right was denied by the husband, the wife should go to a state where she could be granted a legal divorce. The catch, however, was that Blackwell denied women the right to remarry. Drawing on her religious perspective, Blackwell asserted that after divorce, a wife retained the responsibility to work for her husband's redemption and salvation, though not by his side, "no, that would be wrong." Ernestine Rose quickly rejected Blackwell's "sermon on the ideal of marriage" and argued that in an imperfect world, real women and men needed the option of divorce. She supported expanded fault grounds for divorce for "other crimes" like cruelty, desertion, habitual intemperance, and other vices, stopping short of endorsing Stanton's no-fault position.[71]

Abolitionist reformer Wendell Phillips challenged Stanton as to the propriety of including divorce in the women's rights convention. He went so far as to rule her address out of order and moved to strike it from the convention record. Phillips argued that divorce was the same issue for both men and women, and thus did not require attention from those focused on women's inequality. He was also concerned that the divorce issue would "open a gulf into which our distinct movement will be plunged," diverting political success toward suffrage. William Lloyd Garrison said he agreed with Phillips, but admitted that marriage and other issues were included on the antislavery platform as relevant. Following Anthony's speech asserting the right to discuss marriage and divorce, Phillips's motion was defeated, thus preserving the record of Stanton's remarks.[72]

The newspapers went crazy over Stanton's divorce resolutions. The New York *Evening Post* warned that readers "will be disgusted with this new dogma" that equates marriage with a business contract and its "exceedingly loose view" that would allow women to seek divorce whenever marriage became "distasteful." The paper called it "suicidal" for women to propose abolishing marriage because marriage laws had been written expressly to protect women. The *Tribune* called the new doctrine of "marriage as a business" "simply shocking" and was appalled "that a modest woman should say" the things Stanton said. The *New York Observer* called the meeting "infidel and licentious" and was shocked that resolutions "which no true woman could listen to without turning scarlet, were unblushingly read and advocated by a person in woman's attire, named in the programme as Mrs. Elizabeth Cady Stanton." Such resolutions, they charged, "would turn the world into one vast brothel." Stanton's colleague, Parker Pillsbury, laughed at the media outrage. Writing to Stanton, he said, "[W]hat a pretty kettle of hot water you tumbled into at New York! Your marriage and divorce speeches and resolutions you must have learned in the school of a Wollstonecraft. . . . You broke the very heart of the portly *Evening Post* and nearly drove the *Tribune* to the grave."[73]

Stanton defended herself and her pro-divorce position in an editorial in Greeley's *Tribune*.[74] She ignored the criticisms of impropriety and instead directed her arguments to rebutting Phillips's contentions from the convention that the laws of marriage and divorce "rested equally on man and woman." Previewing what would become her stock speeches on "Man Marriage" and "Marriage and Divorce," Stanton detailed the substantive inequalities of the specific laws of marriage, coverture, and divorce and deconstructed the male bias of the lawmaking process. Phillips was not convinced and refused to reconcile with Stanton for "lugging onto our platform that noisy alien 'M & Divorce.'" He responded with insult, beginning to address his colleague intentionally as "Mrs. H. B. Stanton" despite her known objection to the practice.[75]

Stanton's stubborn insistence on advancing divorce fueled and sustained the organizational split between the conservative and radical wings of the woman's movement. The women's suffrage movement broke into Stanton's New York–based National organization and Stone's Boston-based American organization, as divorce entrenched their estrangement over the Fifteenth Amendment and personal slights.[76] Stone and Blackwell feared that Stanton's public stance on divorce would "taint the quest for the ballot and lose the suffrage movement critical support." Years earlier, Stone had written privately to Stanton of her support for the right to divorce, particularly for drunkenness, but had said that she thought those issues belonged in a separate women's convention; but now she was not willing to support divorce publicly in any way.[77] By late 1870, Stanton's continued prioritization of divorce in her newspaper, public lectures, and women's rights meetings solidified the conservative women's refusal to merge and their efforts to create a separate, national organization to lead the woman's suffrage movement.

Freed by organizational constraints, Stanton accelerated her advocacy of divorce as a core woman's right and not an irrelevant "side issue."[78] She reminded critics from "the Boston Society" that the social wrongs of women "occupied altogether the larger place" in early debates of the women's rights movements and that suffrage had then seemed the more outrageous demand.[79] Stanton took on the "masculine writer" and male editors at the *Woman's Journal*, who all "seem to have the same yard-stick for measuring the height, depth, the length and breadth, of the woman's rights movement" by claiming that "women should play on one string; that . . . they should sing suffrage songs, and nothing more; no solos on 'side issues,' especially on marriage, divorce or other social op-pressions." So-called side issues, Stanton said, like divorce, education, and infanticide, were properly part of the women's rights movement, just as social and civil side issues were included as proper targets of the anti-slavery movement, including "the negro pew, the Jim Crow car, colored schools," and antimiscegenation laws.[80]

Still angry at the perceived betrayal by former allies, Stanton took on the reformer establishment itself. "Of all 'white male' leaders on this woman question, the New England Abolitionists are the most danger-ous, because the women look up to them as gods, trusting that they will do for them what they did for the slaves on the southern plantation." But, she said, what they forget is that in women's rights reform, "men are themselves the slaveholders, who made the creeds, the codes, the con-ventionalisms, for the women of their households." Continuing to press her point even deeper, she said, "[T]he side issues of which these various gentlemen complain so much, invariably strike at their social author-ity." And thus it was clear why men preferred to "keep the guns turned on the State," rather than address "the flag of rebellion" raised at their own fireside.[81] Though "cowards and knaves turn from the subject and try to suppress the discussion," Stanton reasserted that the momentous problem of the day was "the true social relation of man and woman."[82]

Antidivorce feminists thought they had won when finances forced Stanton and Anthony to sell the *Revolution* in early 1870 to new editor Laura Curtis Bullard, who changed the paper's masthead to the antidi-vorce quote "what therefore God hath joined together, let not man put asunder." Conservatives took this as an announcement that the women's rights paper would drop its controversial position on the marriage ques-tion. Woman's rights supporter Lillie Devereux Blake was glad of what appeared to be a shift in the paper's position on divorce, as she wrote in an essay entitled "The Divorce Question." She said it had "been a source of regret to me ever since I joined the Woman Suffrage party, that so many of the advocates of that measure are advocates also of greater liberty of divorce." She endorsed the new motto, saying that every true and Christian woman should hold to the church's conservative doctrines that "there should be no divorce except for that offence which utterly breaks and annuls the marriage vow," adultery. However, Bullard subsequently stated the paper's radical support of divorce, clarifying that the motto meant, as Stanton had said, that marriages should only continue where the mutual love of the parties demonstrated that God had truly joined them. "Man," Bullard explained, "has bound in wedlock many women God has not joined together. Indeed, it is difficult for a close observer not to come to the conclusion that marriage, as it now exists, is a curse to society and to the human race; it is a source, far more frequently, of misery than of happiness."[83]

Thirty years later, Stanton recalled the controversy over her Tenth Convention discussion of divorce. She remembered the "severe criticisms" from the press and how "enemies were unsparing in their denunciations, and friends ridiculed the whole proceeding." Stanton joked, "[S]o alarming were the comments on what had been said, that I began to feel that I had inadvertently taken out the underpinning from the whole social system." Which, of course, was in fact what she had intended. But after the excitement died down, Stanton noted, "[T]he earth seemed to turn on its axis as usual, women were given in marriage, . . . and family life to all appearances was as stable as usual."[84]

"The Laws of Divorce Are Quite Unequal"

Stanton refused to be drawn into the morality debate, refocusing the divorce question legalistically on the existing inequalities of the law and its underlying moral standard. She used an invitation to address the New York legislative judiciary committee in February 1861 to advance these arguments. The committee was considering a divorce bill to add desertion and cruel and inhumane treatment to the existing ground of adultery for divorce. Stanton supported the bill, seeking the tangible result she had been advocating for abused wives, but she was not content in that limited solution. Instead she said, "I come not before you, gentlemen, at this time, to plead simply the importance of divorce in cases specified in your bill, but the justice of an entire revision of your whole code of laws on marriage and divorce." "How," she asked, "can we go before the Legislatures of our respective States, and demand new laws, or no laws, on divorce, until we have some idea of what the true relation is?"[85]

Stanton eased into her argument by first defending her right to speak publicly on "such delicate subjects as marriage and divorce." She said, "may I not, without the charge of indelicacy, speak in a mixed assembly of Christian men and women, of wrongs which my daughter may to-morrow suffer in your courts?" She cited again her bridesmaid friend's experience and how she came around to an interest in the subject of divorce. Given these real experiences of women in marriages and the courts, Stanton argued, it was important for a woman to speak on the topic, and the exclusion of women in legislatures and the courts necessitated her speaking here. Stanton addressed the legislature's demonstrated political reluctance to enact divorce laws, pointing out the existing negative realities. "What have we now?" but "separation and divorce cases in all your courts; men disposing of their wives in every possible way; by neglect, cruelty, tyranny, excess, poison, and imprisonment in insane asylums." Arguing for the rule of law, she recommended that the lawmakers "give the parties greater latitude, rather than drive either to extreme measures, or crime" and to grant that power equally to women.[86]

Continuing in her address on the divorce bill, Stanton included her critique of man marriage, her theory of marriage as a contract, and then added arguments about the inequalities of the law. "The laws on divorce are quite as unequal as those on marriage; yes, far more so. The advantages seem to be all on one side, and the penalties on the other." Arguing like a lawyer, she detailed the procedural disadvantages in bringing a lawsuit for divorce, as women were denied standing to file a claim or access to marital funds to finance the suit. "[I]n a majority of the states she is still compelled to sue in the name of another, as she has no means of paying costs, even though she may have brought her thousands into the partnership." Stanton also detailed the economic inequalities of legal remedies. "If the husband be the guilty party, he still retains a greater part of the property! If the wife be the guilty party, she goes out of the partnership penniless." She addressed the inadequacy of alimony of monetary payments to the wife pending resolution of the lawsuit, and elsewhere accepted women's equal responsibility to pay alimony to husbands. "There are many women who would be glad to give their husbands alimony, or any other money, if they would only sail for parts unknown, never, never to return."[87]

Stanton then addressed the substance of the divorce laws as unequal. Harkening back to her point first made in the Declaration of Sentiments, she derided the laws that framed the proper causes for divorce only on grounds of interest to men. The divorce laws facilitated divorce for men by including grounds of interest to men, namely, adultery, but excluding grounds like cruelty, intemperance, and desertion that motivated women to divorce. She mocked the law that granted divorce for adultery and physical impotency, reflecting a male preoccupation with sexual privilege in marriage.[88] In support, she quoted Milton, who said, "[O]f all insulting mockeries of heavenly truth and holy law, none can be greater than that physical impotency is cause sufficient for divorce, while no amount of mental or moral or spiritual imbecility is ever to be pleaded in support of such a demand."[89] Stanton argued that these mental or emotional harms were more familiar in the gendered experiences of women, deserted, abused, or subordinated by their husbands, and thus necessitated additional legal grounds that made divorce equally available to women. As examples of this type of equal access law, Stanton cited cases from Michigan and Illinois where Supreme Court judges decided that divorce statutes for "cruelty and abuse" comprehended "more than simply physical cruelty, such as kicking, pummeling, pinching" and also included "those humiliations of the spirit occasioned by indifference, contempt and aversion."[90]

Even the limited existing divorce laws were unequal because they applied a gendered standard of adultery for divorce.[91] Stanton explained that the treatise writers all "take the ground that man and woman are not to be judged by the same moral code." Many jurists "are of opinion that the adultery of the husband ought not to be noticed or made subject to the same animadversions as that of the wife, because it is not evidence of such entire depravity, nor equally injurious in its effects upon the morals and good order, and happiness of domestic life." She said that legal theorists insisted that the cases of husband and wife in adultery "ought to be distinguished, and that the violation of the marriage vow, on the part of the wife, is the most mischievous, and the prosecution ought to be confined to the offense on her part." The analogous English law of adultery, which had been codified in the first judicial divorce statute in 1857, incorporated this dual standard. A wife's adultery was sufficient for a divorce, but a husband's misconduct required aggravated adultery, adultery plus some additional offense like cruelty, incest, or desertion.[92] Women's misconduct was considered worse because it violated the social sexual mores for women and legally complicated the heritance lineage based on paternity.[93]

After her address in New York, Stanton went deeper in this critique of the inequalities of adultery and divorce to undermine the normative assumptions of the law based on the double moral standard. She demanded that legislators "blot out this infamous code from their statute books" of unequal divorce laws and "establish one code of morals for man and woman."[94] Instead, the dual moral standard was perpetuated by these laws and by the related social mores, as depicted in Nathaniel Hawthorne's novel, *The Scarlet Letter*, which she cited as an example where women are shunned as a result of adultery while men are immunized and empowered. From her earliest advocacy, Stanton had attacked this dual morality, decrying in the Declaration of Sentiments that man "has created a false public sentiment, by giving to the world a different code of morals for men and women, by which moral delinquencies which exclude women from society, are not only tolerated but deemed of little account in man."[95] The law of divorce, adultery, infanticide, and prostitution all created a higher standard of absolute intolerance for women, thereby regulating women's sexuality. Men were not held to this same standard, as the law accepted men's indiscretions of extramarital and unwed sexual intercourse with little social stigma or legal responsibility for actions. The assumption was that "boys will be boys," that men's animalistic and sexualized natures understandably drove them to commit certain acts. Instead, the Declaration's resolutions demanded equality between men and women in the amount of virtue required in the social state, and that "the same transgressions should be visited with equal severity."

Stanton's solution to this "false code of morals" was not to raise men to some higher bar, but to stop penalizing women for failing to demonstrate this separate perfection of purity. Stanton shared some beliefs with the social purity reformers, who were committed to moral reform of prostitution and male licentiousness and to equal moral standards elevating the male sexual norm. But unlike the social purity crusaders, Stanton did not think the solution was to make men more pure. In "Patriotism and Chastity," Stanton defended Irish leader Charles Parnell, whose political legitimacy was challenged by adultery charges against him in the O'Shea divorce suit alleging his longstanding affair with Mrs. O'Shea and paternity of three of her children. Stanton's point was not to excuse his adulterous behavior, but to blame the double moral standard of law and religion that educated men to public virtues rather than the domestic virtue of chastity that was woman's "crowning glory." Stanton revealed in her diary her frustration with the "little set of social purity people down on my article who do not choose to understand it." They did not understand that she agreed with them on the dual "false standards of morals," but would solve the problem not by hounding men to some higher, pure standard, but by deconstructing the moral standard as applied to women. She questioned why "unlimited license in marriage" producing a family of twelve children and an invalid wife "casts no shadow" on moral judgment, but "a happy, healthy mother and child outside the bonds of legal wedlock . . . are ostracized by the community as unchaste."[96]

To illustrate her point about the double moral standard and the divorce laws, Stanton tried to capitalize on the notorious Beecher-Tilton trial in 1874. The trial itself raised the issue of the double standard when nationally respected preacher and moralist Henry Ward Beecher was accused of adultery with his parishioner Elizabeth Tilton, wife of his protégé and friend, journalist and editor Theodore Tilton. The scandalous case of prominent, religious people engaged in sexual escapades and alleged domestic abuse dominated the headlines, from the pretense of a church investigation to the 112-day civil trial by Tilton against Beecher for his wife's alienation of affection and criminal conversation. The trial ended in a hung jury, because the jury was unable to discern which of the two men was lying. Elizabeth Tilton was barred by the marital privilege from testifying in court or participating as a party, since the law framed the dispute as one compensating the husband for his lost property rights in his wife. Stanton called for the repeal of the statute barring marital testimony, and indicted the entire case in which Elizabeth was a pawn. "Dragged into court by the quarrels of men, by laws made by men, accused of falsehood, cowardice, dishonor, adultery, ridiculed, scarified, and condemned by the press of the nation and yet not allowed one word in her own defence. Such is the dignity the law confers on the wife." Four years after the trial, Elizabeth admitted the adultery in a public letter. Beecher continually denied the charges, claiming emotional but not sexual intimacy with Elizabeth in his role of pastoral counselor, and that she aggressively "thrust her affections on him unsought." Most of the public believed him.[97]

Stanton's ability to make full use of this case was compromised by the accusations hurled at her. She was accused of knowing and/or lying about the affair, of gossiping about the details to Victoria Woodhull for publication in her newspaper, of her close friendship with Theodore Tilton, and of a radical women's rights agenda, all which diminished her credibility and linked her name with the specter of free love.[98] Nevertheless, Stanton could not let the opportunity pass without using the case to make her points about women's rights. Stanton explained that the public's obsession with the case was not due to prurient interests but to the importance of the social question of marriage. She warned early in the controversy of the importance of an equal application of the moral code. "The true social code, whatever it is, must be the same for both sexes." After the trial, she asserted that one beneficial effect of the case that had "so tediously nauseated the whole country" was to equalize the moral code, "making the standard of tolerated and reputable behavior of women and men equal." The problem the case so clearly illustrated to Stanton was a need to review the divorce laws. "To compel unhappy husbands and wives, by law and public sentiment, to live together, and to teach them that it is their religious duty to accept their conditions" would only produce "social earthquakes" like Beecher-Tilton. Stanton's lesson, however, was lost on the public. "Instead of helping to liberalize public opinion on the marriage question, the Beecher scandal . . . contributed to the conservative reaction against divorce."[99]

Easy Divorce

Stanton's focus on the inequalities of divorce, however, did not detract from her ultimate goal of free divorce. In advocating for what we now call no-fault divorce, Stanton drew accusations of support for "easy divorce." But she rejected the immoral implications. "You speak of me as an advocate of 'easy divorce.' I hate and repudiate that phrase, and the promiscuous relations it seems to indicate."[100]

Stanton, though, quite clearly and publicly endorsed free divorce. She was explicit in stating her position: "I firmly believe in divorce." "No obstacle," she said, "should be put in the way of divorce by mutual consent or agreement of the parties, any more than that there should be compulsory marriage."[101] She explained, "I think divorce at the will of the parties is not only right, but that it is a sin against nature, the family, the State, for a man or woman to live together in the marriage relation in continual antagonism, indifference, disgust."[102]Her position was that "any constitution, compact or covenant between human beings, that failed to produce or promote human happiness, could not, in the nature of things, be of any force or authority;—and it would be not only a right, but a duty, to abolish it." And as Stanton saw it, divorce was not only permissible but an entitlement of an individual right, "the just right of every woman" necessary for social equality.[103]

To counter the conventional wisdom of the indissolubility of marriage, Stanton traced the history of divorce. In the beginning, she said, divorce was the husband's individual prerogative, until the Catholic Church ordained marriage as a sacrament and thus indissoluble. The whole matter, she said, "rested in the hand of the individual man, who took or put away his wife at his pleasure, where it remained, for centuries alike under the Mosaic and Christian dispensation, until by a Papal act of encroachment, the power and arbitrament of divorce were rested [sic] from the master of the family, and marriage became a sacrament of the Church." However, she noted, the right of woman to put away a husband, be he ever so impure, is never hinted at in sacred history.[104] Stanton, following Martin Luther and other Reformation writers, impeached the church's corrupt motivations for this change, "perceiving the great revenue and high authority it would give them" to control and charge for annulments. But Stanton went further, indicting the church's ban on all divorce as a pretext to control women. "All this talk about the indissoluble tie and the sacredness of marriage, irrespective of the character and habits of the husband, is for its effect on woman." She elaborated, "[S]he never could have been held the pliant tool she is to-day but for the subjugation of her religious nature to the idea that in whatever condition she found herself as man's subject, that condition was ordained of Heaven." Stanton asserted that without church interference with divorce, women would have developed their own individual agency. "But for these false teachings of the church, multitudes of women through the centuries, would have risen up in their native purity and dignity and sundered with their own hands the unholy ties that bound them to disease, vice and crime, in unclean marriage relations."[105]

Stanton grounded her argument for free divorce in religious theory, summarizing her approach as "the Protestant rather than Catholic ground," which held "divorce expedient and right 'at the will of the parties,' as in freedom only can they find their true relations." Stanton explained that "one of the prominent features of the reformation was the demand of its leaders for free divorce." She cited their motivations as "the interests of morality, in view of the licentiousness of Catholic Europe," a reference here to Martin Luther's harsh criticism of the Catholic practice of acknowledging marriage impediments, for a price, that could be used to obtain church annulments.[106] Stanton's religious arguments drew heavily, and sometimes verbatim, from the theories of Puritan John Milton, the author of the poem *Paradise Lost*.[107]

Milton, writing in 1643, endorsed divorce at the will of the parties, though his theories became more popular in the nineteenth century than during his lifetime. Milton asserted the right of private divorce without any authority of the church or government.[108] He may have been searching for a solution to his own problems, for at the time he first wrote of divorce, the thirty-five-year-old Milton was estranged from his seventeen-year-old bride, who abandoned him after one month of marriage and returned to her father's house. They reconciled two years later, but Milton continued to write additional tracts on divorce. He expanded the proper grounds for divorce to include "that indisposition, unfitness, or contrariety of mind, arising from a cause in nature unchangeable, hindering and ever likely to hinder, the main benefits of conjugal society, which are solace and peace."[109] Such divorce for incompatibility, he argued, was especially appropriate when there were no children to the marriage and both parties consented. Sounding like Martin Luther, Milton argued that biblical commands were spiritual, not legal. "It is not the outward continuing of marriage that keeps whole that covenant, but whatsoever does most according to peace and love."[110]

Milton's divorce tracts, written during the English Civil War, drew an analogy between the political right to rebel and separate from an unjust government and the right to separate from an unsatisfactory marriage. In a provision Stanton often quoted, Milton said,

> Those who marry intend as little to conspire their own ruin, as those who swear allegiance, and as a whole people is *to an ill government,* so is one man or woman *to an ill marriage.* If a whole people, against any authority, covenant or statute, many by the sovereign edict of charity, save not only their lives, but honest liberties, from unworthy bondage, as well may a married party, against any private covenant, which he or she never entered, *to his or her mischief,* be redeemed from unsupportable disturbances, to honest peace, and just contentment.[111]

As a Protestant reformer, he rejected the canon law of "the popes of Rome" and their corrupt incentives of "great revenue and high authority" over princes that divested the right "which God from the beginning had entrusted to the husband." "The absolute and final hindering of divorce," he asserted, "cannot belong to any civil or earthly power, against the will and consent of both parties, or of the husband alone." He admitted a role for the civil magistrates to referee, if need be, on differences of "dowries, jointures," and other property issues.

To adopt Milton's reasoning, Stanton had to reframe his core points under a feminist lens. Milton's theories created a right of divorce in only the husband, by either unilateral or mutual consent. While he was perhaps ahead of his time in identifying some mutuality of husband and wife, he still asserted the sole patriarchal right of the husband.[112] Stanton ignored this assertion of male prerogative and instead translated Milton's arguments as gender neutral. She grabbed onto Milton's assertion that marriage was not a covenant or sacrament, but merely a common civil contract. This paralleled her legal arguments about marriage as a civil contract, which like any generic legal contract could be terminated freely by the will of the parties. Milton's understanding of divorce as a private right matched her own view of divorce as an individual right and freedom. And she embraced his alternative interpretation of the familiar Matthew passage against divorce. Milton debunked the passage so reified by the canon law that said "what God hath joined let no man put asunder," deconstructing the premise of "what God has joined" to say that God has *not* joined unfitness, wrath, perpetual loneliness, or discord, and thus man and law should not "unite what God and nature have not joined together." Stanton explained that reading the marriage service did not signify that God had joined a couple, but "only those marriages that are harmonious, where the parties are really companions for each other, are in the highest sense made by God."[113]

Stanton's support for free divorce correlated to her ideal of enforcing egalitarian marriage. As she explained, "to-day the only hope for the purification of manners and morals is in free divorce; in elevating the ideal of marriage so that it shall consist of the spiritual as well as the physical element." In Stanton's ideal, the only true grounds for marriage were "companionship and conscientious parenthood." Where those were missing, and the relation "brings out the worst characteristics of each party, or if the home atmosphere is unwholesome for children," she argued that the marriage was already practically annulled. Continuing, she argued that since "incompatibility of temper defeats the two great objects of marriage, it should be the primal cause for divorce." She then connected the individual right to the greater societal interest. In cases "where unfitness exists, it would be for the interest of society for the state to step in . . . and insist on annulling the contract, instead of impeding a separation." For, "if the real object of marriage is defeated, it is for the interest of the State, as well as the individual concerned, to see that all pernicious unions be legally dissolved." While many argued that the indissolubility of marriage was absolutely necessary to the happiness of the family, the purity of society, and the good of the state, Stanton turned that on its head. "But to my mind," she said, "so important is *unity in marriage*, so dependent upon this the usefulness of the home, the good of society, the solidarity of the State; so lamentable the consequences invariably resulting from *disunity in marriage*, that every encouragement to divorce ought to be given."[114]

Stanton appreciated a role for the law in divorce, not in restricting the individual choice to divorce for incompatibility but to redress the economic consequences. "The question of Divorce, like Marriage, should be settled as to its most sacred relations, by the parties themselves, neither the State nor the Church having any right to intermeddle therein." Like the Quaker marriage, which the parties conduct themselves, Stanton envisioned a similar approach to divorce in which the parties simply declared after living together for several years that they found themselves "still unsuited to each other and incapable of making a happy home." However, she added, "as to the property and children, they must be viewed and regulated as a civil contract." As a contract, the agreement, if breached, required legal process to redress economic consequences and potential losses. "Any person of common sense must see the necessity of laws regulating the duties of parents to their children and to each other, the right of property, inheritance, support, alimony, etc., all important for the welfare of the State as well as the family." Such a process would ensure that "the union should be dissolved with at least as much deliberation and publicity as it was formed." Yet Stanton also endorsed private ordering by which the parties could sort out these legal consequences for themselves. "Reasonable men and women could arrange all the preliminaries, often even the division of property and guardianship of children, quite as satisfactorily as it could be done in the courts." Stanton thus presented a framework for not only tolerating divorce but making it respectable and "recognized by society as a duty as well as a right" in which the law facilitated the private decisions of the married partners.[115]

The Woman's *Dred Scott* Decision

In spring 1870, the public obsession over the McFarland-Richardson trial presented Stanton with a new opportunity to air her arguments for divorce. The trial of Daniel McFarland for the murder of his ex-wife's lover was a notorious trial providing national exposure to the problems of divorce. On November 25, 1869, McFarland lay in wait at the *New York Tribune* newspaper office, where he shot point-blank famous Civil War correspondent Albert Richardson. Richardson lingered several days, during which he married McFarland's ex-wife, Abby, in a deathbed wedding allowing her to inherit his property and care for his three children. The courtroom melodrama and media circus dominated the front-page news during the five-week trial as daily transcriptions of the sensationalized trial were printed in the papers. After a two-hour deliberation, the jury acquitted McFarland on grounds of temporary insanity.[116] Stanton provocatively called the case the "woman's Dred Scott decision." Her invocation of the U.S. Supreme Court case, *Dred*

Scott v. Sandford, and its holding that a slave remained his master's property even when residing in a free territory, drove home the point that a wife was merely "a species of property" that "could not be alienated by cruelty and abuse."[117]

The underlying truth about the McFarlands' disastrous marriage challenged the Victorian sentimentalities of rational men and guardian angels. Married at age nineteen to a man twice her age, Abby soon discovered Daniel McFarland's false claims to sophistication and wealth, his financial scams, and his inability to support the family. More shockingly, she discovered his "very fitful and passionate" temper and his alcoholism. Abby described how her husband was "unspeakably cruel" to her, with violent outbursts, rages, thrown objects, and threatened assault. Abby separated from McFarland many times during their ten-year marriage to live with her father, but she always returned. She became the sole support for her family, now including two young boys, through her work as an actress and author. McFarland continued to devolve into the depths of alcoholism and abuse, and she finally left him in February 1867 in a separation brokered by her father and close friends.[118]

McFarland refused to accept the agreement. He raided Abby's apartment, discovering a love letter from Richardson. He stalked the couple on the street, shooting Richardson in the leg. He filed for custody of his children, harassing Abby with depositions until she agreed to his custody of the eldest of their two sons, which her lawyers counseled would likely happen under the law anyway given her alleged adultery. McFarland then sued Richardson for alienating his wife's affections. Richardson responded by publishing his side of the story in an editorial. When McFarland refused to let Abby visit her son, she finally decided to "take legal steps to get free" from her husband. She moved to Indiana, where sixteen months later she obtained a divorce on grounds of cruelty and was awarded legal custody of her younger son, though she requested custody of both children.[119] One month after the divorce, McFarland shot Richardson.

The jury, though, never heard Abby's side of the story. Her testimony and supporting witness evidence were barred by the marital privilege rule that prohibited a wife from testifying against her husband, since under coverture the two were one. The Indiana divorce was not recognized by New York as valid, and thus the McFarlands were still consid-

"First Day of the McFarland Trial," *Harper's Weekly*, April 23, 1870. *Library of Congress.*

ered married.[120] The key evidence at trial offered by the defense was a litany of love letters from Richardson and letters from Abby's friends encouraging her to leave her husband. The prosecution failed to object, oblivious to how these letters, "so full of feminist support for a woman to leave her husband, would be perceived by the family men on the jury."[121] The defense bolstered its case with medical expert testimony as to the latest neuroscience, now considered absurdities, of "cerebral exhaustion" and "cerebral congestion" explaining McFarland's temporary insanity directed at just one person on one occasion. The expert relied on the quack scientific evidence of a dynamograph machine that measured a man's power over his will by tracing the defendant's ability to hold a pen in his hand still.[122]

Defense counsel's eight-hour closing argument emphasized gendered notions of a husband's patriarchal right to protect his wife and home as justification for the murder. The defense was limited to arguing temporary insanity, since the provocation defense was not available as Mc-Farland could not be acting in "the heat of passion" because he had not reacted immediately after seeing the two in a compromised position. It was two years after discovering the affair, and thus now the defense had to argue that he was temporarily insane, acting out of love to protect his wife and children and the family home.[123] The defense cited two other infamous cases, of Congressman Sickles and General Cole, where men had been acquitted for shooting their wives' lover based on this "unwritten law" of permission for a man to defend his home and rescue his wife.[124] Counsel cited every possible biblical passage of patriarchal authority. "There is no absolute equality in the Bible between man and wife. . . . [M]an was made for God and woman for man; . . . woman is the weaker vessel, and is meant to be under the protection of the stronger vessel, man; and . . . any attempt from any quarter to interfere with that supremacy," even with the consent of the woman, is an infraction of the husband's rights. And then he made it personal, instructing the jury, "You are to reflect in your action the value you place upon your own hearths and the affection with which you regard your own firesides." The jury acquitted McFarland after less than two hours of deliberation.[125]

Stanton was outraged by the verdict and its larger implications for women's rights. After the shooting, Stanton came out publicly in support of Abby. "You ask what I think of the Richardson affair. I rejoice over every slave that escapes from a discordant marriage." "My opinion," she said, "is, that a woman has a right to choose between a base, petty tyrant and a noble, magnanimous man." "What folly to talk of McFarland's devotion to his wife!" His cowardly assault "under the plea of protection, is like the kindness of the eagle to the lamb he carries to his eyrie, on the barren rocks." [126] When the verdict was issued on May 10, 1870, Stanton was ensconced in organizational meetings defending against motions to dissolve her one-year-old National suffrage organization and merge with the rival American group as the "Union Woman's Suffrage Society." After defending her separate organization, Stanton switched to the "far more important" issue of a woman's right to "be set free—the absolute sovereign of her own person, her own affections, and her own home." Stanton argued that "shooting paramours," and "wives running to Indiana, and Connecticut, like slaves to their Canada" should rouse the indignation of every woman against "the whole idea on which all these prosecutions are based—man's right of property in woman."[127]

The next week, Stanton organized a mass meeting to protest the verdict and its "indictment against American womanhood."[128] Stanton was warned to "be very cautious and guarded" on "the very difficult topic" of the McFarland trial because of the risk of "undermining the family state" and the moral law of marriage.[129] Of course, this was exactly Stanton's intent. Speaking to a packed audience of two thousand professional and reform women at Apollo Hall, Stanton delivered a fiery indictment of the gendered social and legal problems exemplified by the case.[130] She repeated the speech and the protest a few weeks later in Brooklyn.[131]

Stanton opened by dismissing the shadow of free love. "Ladies, I have sometimes been accused of free-love proclivities. My answer to that accusation is that I've lived thirty years with one man, and expect to live with him to the end, and I'll let my life speak for me." These meetings, Stanton roared, "to protest against the unjust decision in our courts, the scurrility of the press, the popular idea of marriage" should be the handwriting on the wall that women will no longer sit silently by. "The deep interest of the entire nation in the McFarland trial," she said, was because "the trial indirectly involves the solution of the momentous questions of marriage and divorce, questions that underlie our whole social, religious and political life." The *New York Tribune* discounted her speech as "the demands of the shrieking sisterhood" for "free divorce."[132] Stanton dismissed the rants of the papers, including the *Sun*, where her husband worked, "and its editorial staff" as mere male temper tantrums that would soon pass, as she well knew, having brought up five sons.[133]

Stanton sympathized with the circumstances of poverty and abuse, having read Abby's published account of the marriage in the newspapers.[134] However, she noted, "[S]ympathy as a civil agent is vague and powerless until caught and chained in logical irrefragable propositions and coined into State law." Direct legal change was required. First, reform of the law of temporary insanity was needed to require confinement in an asylum. Stanton was outraged that McFarland went free, and remained the legal guardian of his son. "What a travesty of justice and common sense that while declaring a man too insane to be held responsible for taking the life of another, he might still be capable of directing the life and education of a child."[135]

Second, Stanton renewed her call for divorce reform. "Let the women of this State," she called, "rise in mass and say they will no longer tolerate statutes that hold pure, virtuous women indissolubly bound to gross, vicious men, whom they loathe and abhor." She argued for change to the New York divorce law to include fault grounds for desertion and cruelty, and no-fault grounds of indifference. She appealed to her audience as mothers to become interested in divorce reform. "When the calendars of our courts are crowded with divorce cases, and sad details of private life" paraded in public papers, and when there are so many divorce cases in one year, "we who have sons and daughters growing up to be happy or miserable in their relations have a deep interest in finding the cause of all this social confusion, and suggesting some remedy."[136] At the meeting's conclusion, the group endorsed resolutions calling for women to be self-supporting, for them to exercise care in the formation of marriage, and for the governor to imprison McFarland in an asylum.[137] Stanton explained that the governor had no power to incarcerate McFarland, and that the proper legal avenue was to appeal to the legislature to change the law of the insanity defense.[138] She did not want to see the man hung, as she was against capital punishment, but argued that a woman, "had she escaped the gallows—would have been lodged in a mad-house."[139]

Stanton got the opportunity to apply her theory of gendered punishment for criminal defendants in the subsequent trial of Laura Fair. Fair's case was another notorious trial, and the sensationalized story dominated national newspapers, trumping reports of the presidential race and the Franco-Prussian war. Fair, a thirty-three-year-old "seductive blonde," shot her married lover point-blank in November 1870. She lurked in the shadows as he met his wife and children on the San Francisco ferry and then killed him with a newly purchased revolver. During their seven-year cohabitation, her lover had promised to divorce his wife, but instead reunited with his family.

At trial, the prosecution focused on the lurid story of free love and characterized Fair as an assertive, "manly" businesswoman. Fair was a "strong-minded woman" with a bad reputation as an unchaste woman with four prior marriages. The defense claimed temporary insanity from dysmenorrhea.[140] Doctors testified that her behavior was incontestable proof that women's biological cycle limited their abilities and created grave instability. Fair was declared guilty and sentenced to death. The judge was congratulated on his "manly" handling of the trial.

While the appeal was pending, Stanton arrived in San Francisco on her lyceum tour. Stanton came to Fair's defense, meeting with her in prison, delivering lectures on the trial, and granting interviews to the newspapers. She presented Fair's case as the untoward result of a gendered system of double moral standards and an all-male legal system—the same arguments she had made a few years earlier in defense of another woman, Hester Vaughn, sentenced to death for the murder of her child.[141] Fair, she argued, was

> tried for violations of laws to which she has never given her consent, by a Judge in whom she has had no choice, by a jury of foreigners, not her own peers in either country, education, or sex, by a public sentiment that makes one code of morals for man, and another for woman, and with no voice in the election of the sheriff who is to perform the last devilish deed.

Analogizing to the other cases of paramour shootings, Stanton demanded, "Give Laura Fair the benefit of the doubts and legal subterfuges that Sickles, Cole, and McFarland enjoyed in Courts of their peers, and I am content."[142]

The newspapers, however, countered that Fair's trial was fully consistent with those cases, as in all, it was the paramour who was indicted. "The truth is that the San Francisco jury, in convicting Mrs. Fair, acted upon the same principle as did the New York jury in acquitting Mr. McFarland." Both, the paper asserted, "expressed . . . their judgment that no mercy should be shown to the person, whether man or woman, who violates the sanctity of the marriage. Indeed, if Mrs. Fair had been killed by Mrs. Crittenden [the wife], instead of killing Mr. Crittenden, the act would doubtless have been approved by a jury."[143]

Stanton also made the lawyer-like argument that a "well-settled point of criminal law" had been violated by the admission of bad-character evidence designed "to make her appear as black as possible." The prosecution melodramatically had asked each witness about Fair's "reputation for chastity." The California Supreme Court agreed with Stanton's assessment and overturned the conviction for failure to exclude reputation evidence of character. It also found procedural error in the out-of-order closing arguments denying the defense the last word to the jury.[144] After a second trial, Fair was found not guilty on the basis of insanity. Fair latched on to Stanton's feminist critique of the case, adopting it as her own on a short-lived lecture tour.[145]

Newspapers were "astonished" at Stanton's support for Fair, which they found "simply outrageous." "What is meant by Cady Stanton's sympathy with the 'beautiful woman' who pursued her affinity, even to the foot of the gallows? If this does not mean FREE LOVE, what does it mean?" Stanton responded calmly and logically that attempts to link woman's suffrage to Laura Fair were absurd. Laura Fair was the result of the double standard, "the product of man's moral code and not of the suffrage movement."[146] Women's rights advocates, however, distanced themselves from Stanton and Fair, concerned that the scandalous affair detracted from the issues of suffrage.[147]

"Speaking Wisdom to the Popular Ear"

Bored and betrayed by organizational reform politics, Stanton sought a larger audience. She took her message to the national stage to speak directly to the people on the Lyceum Tour. The Lyceum national speaking circuit featured Stanton as a speaker, and she traveled west to Chicago, Iowa, Wisconsin, Utah, California, and other locales for twelve years. After the McFarland outrage, Stanton committed to focusing her national lecture tour on the subjects of marriage and divorce.

Planning for the tour schedule to begin in fall 1870, Stanton revealed to a reporter that she planned to make divorce and marriage reform the centerpiece of her platform. "My whole soul is in it; therefore, it will be my best."[148] She spent the summer after the McFarland protest writing and perfecting her legalistic analysis, elaborating on ideas of free divorce she had previously raised. She promised to "speak wisdom to the popular ear," "less sensation than the presentation of truths" and "less pleasing of the popular ear than awakening the popular heart."[149] Stanton knew she was a maverick on the divorce question, but unencumbered by organizational or editorial ties, she now felt even greater freedom to speak out on the subject. She was confident that in twenty years, the public would eventually catch up to her on divorce, just as they had taken as long to accept her position on suffrage.[150]

Stanton debuted her planned "Marriage and Divorce" lecture to the public in Washington, D.C., with "occasional flashes of wit and sarcasm," and repeated it the next week at the second Decade Celebration of the woman's rights movement in New York City.[151] Stanton would feature this lengthy two-hour lecture, in whole or in part, on her national tour for the next eleven years.[152] Stanton began with the premise that the social revolution of women's equality in marriage and divorce was "greater than any political or religious revolution that the world has ever seen, because it goes deep down to the very foundations of society." She said this social question was of "greater magnitude" than suffrage because, she optimistically stated, "it looks as if the suffrage battle was nearly fought and won," citing the new women's voting laws in Wyoming and Utah. Her thesis for this lecture was that "how to marry is the primal question to what justifies divorce, and to know how to do the first wisely would, in most cases, obviate the necessity of the other at all." Thus, she devoted part of the lecture to discussing how to improve marriage. Strategies included adopting safeguards for entering marriage, transforming marriage to a true egalitarian relation, securing women's collegiate education, pecuniary independence, and control of motherhood, and ensuring divorce.[153]

Turning to divorce, Stanton carefully rebutted the popular objections to liberal divorce.[154] First, it was said that to make divorce respectable would "break up all family relations." Stanton countered that divorce would be irrelevant to those in happy, egalitarian relations, and could incentivize greater kindness if there was an option to divorce. Second, it was argued that divorce would allow fickle men to "take a new wife every Christmas, if they could legally rid themselves in season of the old one." Women, including progressive women, had long articulated the fear that men would manipulate freer divorce laws to discard their wives at will in exchange for younger, more attractive ones.[155] As the *Chicago Tribune* asked, "Is Mrs. Stanton quite sure that freedom of divorce for no other cause than the mere desire to exchange an old husband or wife for a new one, is among the coveted boons that women crave?" Continuing, it asked, "[D]oes she consider in how many instances the chief problem of life, that of support, binds the wife to the husband, and in how few instances it binds the husband to the wife?" Instead, the paper concluded, "the system of 'easy divorce,' which Mrs. Stanton extols" simply gave "every vagabond husband a change of wives as often as he likes."[156]

Stanton responded that the "centripetal force" of strong love weighed against this fear, but that in any case, such men could already do these things by adultery, divorce, or prostitution. More important, she argued, is that with a change to a new regime in which women worked and were educated to self-support, they would not "clutch at every offer of marriage, like the drowning man at the floating straw." Opponents of liberal divorce, however, feared that people would not exercise deliberation in choosing marriage wisely. Stanton quickly dismissed this objection, finding that people already entered marriage carelessly, as evidenced by common law marriage. Since people currently entered marriages in haste, it was far better to have legal divorces "than discord or erratic relations outside of law."[157]

Stanton next addressed the argument of divorce opponents that the best interests of the children required an indissoluble union. She disagreed, pointing out instead the harm to children from remaining in unhappy marital families. While one of the objects of marriage was appropriately the care and training of children, she said, "[T]hey cannot be well born in unhappy, antagonistic relations." Children trapped in abusive situations might face poverty, crime, or imprisonment. For others, she noted the "demoralizing influence on children when trained in an atmosphere of discord and dissatisfaction, such as a false marriage relation inevitably creates." "No amount of care and education can ever compensate," she argued, "for the morbid conditions of its organization, resulting from coldness, indifference, or disgust in the parents for one another. Stanton cited Milton and his argument about the harm to children raised in unhappy marriages and "the misfortune of being trained in the atmosphere of a household where love is not the law, but where discord and bitterness abound; stamping their demoniac features on the moral nature." She suggested instead that two people "who, like oil and water never seem to move in the same currents" could separate and raise their children through a "pleasant friendship" in which they could agree on matters of the children. Moreover, Stanton concluded, "[A] wise mother would be able to train her children far better alone, than subject to the abuse and interference of a vicious, besotted man; or, the reverse."[158]

Finally, Stanton took on the objection to divorce that the Bible condemned it. Stanton quipped, "[W[hen those who are opposed to all reforms can find no other argument, their last resort is to the Bible. It has been interpreted to favor intemperance, slavery, capital punishment, and the subjection of women," and, now, divorce. Instead, she argued, a "multitude of passages can be quoted" from the Bible showing the practice of divorce. In the Old Testament, men took and put away their wives at pleasure, and divorce was universally recognized as a right. In the New Testament, Paul permitted divorce for desertion, and Luther, Calvin, and Milton all allowed divorce. "As the Bible sanctions divorce and polygamy, in the practice of the chosen people, and is full of contradictions, and the canon law has been pliable in the hands of ecclesiastics," it would simplify the discussion of divorce to confine it "wholly to the civil law." Concluding, Stanton expressed her frustration with the literal reliance upon a single sentence of the Bible that ignored the spiritual context of marriage. "The relation that should be the most beautiful, one which must make every home, where it really exists, a temple and a school as well, is sacrificed to a book which demands that we shall on that point throw away the experience of thousands of years, and compress ourselves to a rite of barbarism."[159]

Stanton reported that "[w]omen respond to this divorce speech as they never did to suffrage."[160] Thousands of men and women in all parts of the country heard Stanton repeat this lecture and her new ideas of egalitarian marriage and free divorce. While women gravitated to Stanton's words, the press did not. But Stanton didn't care, as she wrote to Anthony after a Michigan lecture. "The women gladly hear the new gospel so let the press howl."[161] Reporters covering the lyceum tour favorably complimented Stanton as motherly, wise, dignified, and articulate. But they could not accept her theories of easy divorce. While they might concede divorce in a compelling case of domestic abuse, the mainstream press could not agree that society would be better off with free divorce.[162]

Conservative feminists were not convinced by Stanton's rebuttal. While many remained morally opposed to divorce in principle, they also focused on the problems of economic survival after divorce. Women were concerned about what happened after divorce—how they would support themselves with no marital property or husband's income and whether they would lose custody of their children.[163] As Lillie Devereux Blake concluded, "[M]en are, and probably always will be, the money-earners of the world, the higher duties of maternity, the sacred care of home, preventing women from competing with them with full chances of success, and rendering wives dependent upon their husbands certainly during the childbearing period." If a wife became "a mere companion of the hour," this "license would be at once used to repudiate those wives who were no longer pleasing, and we should have in society the miserable spectacle of hundreds of women who had worn out their youth in the bearing of children" to be turned out in midlife to "earn their own support by some wretched drudgery, to starve or to die."[164]

The rival *Woman's Journal* also "found Stanton's rhetoric naïve and disingenuous in its assumption that free divorce would primarily benefit women." Editor Lucy Stone and her followers argued that "freedom" for a divorced mother of six was not independence, but rather abandonment and desperation. "For how many mothers under the circumstances could afford to sweep grandly out and set up housekeeping on their own?" Free divorce was practically just "the freedom of unworthy men to leave their wives and children to starve." Stone's American Woman's Suffrage Association affirmed, "[W]e believe in *marriage for life*, and deprecate all this loose, pestiferous talk in favor of easy divorce."[165] However, some of its members, like Mary Livermore, eventually came around to divorce on expanded fault grounds like drunkenness and cruelty. Sounding like Stanton, Livermore wrote, "[I]t is at variance with the best interests of society, and lowers the ideal of marriage, for such persons to be compelled to live in marital relations."[166]

Stanton's answer to the economic concerns was for each woman to develop her own pecuniary independence and self-support through education and employment, both during and after marriage. This simplistic solution, however, belied the realities of women's limited access to training, job opportunities, living wages, or childcare. Stanton's point, however, was that it was important for women to take the first step of freedom and obtain at least "a quit-claim deed to themselves."[167] She, perhaps better than anyone, appreciated that divorce was only one piece of the complex puzzle of legal and social reform necessary for women's full equality and autonomy to be achieved. And she advocated those changes to property and custody laws that would grant women the much-needed family rights. But she would not be deterred from her belief that divorce was still a critical step of the process.

Backlash and Domestic Warfare

Stanton's divorce tour arguing for no-fault divorce to end the "perpetual domestic warfare" of unhappy marriages stood in stark contrast to the social conservatism sweeping the country in the late nineteenth century. Her continued support for divorce in the face of this social backlash sounded increasingly more outrageous and radical to these conservative audiences. Still Stanton persisted, determined to fight against what she viewed as the threat to women's agency in marriage, enforced by the veto power of divorce. The family savers and moralists of the late nineteenth century railed against the immorality of divorce and the downfall of families. This conservatism, fueled by the antipolygamy crusades, social purity reforms against vice and obscenity, and the emerging social science of protecting children and juveniles, focused on preserving and restoring the sanctity of the family. Social and legal policy retreated from notions of private freedom in consensual family relations and moved toward the need for public, government regulation of the family as the institutional foundation of a moral society. This backlash halted divorce liberalization and reversed course toward restricting divorce access as states repealed prior permissive divorce laws and increased residency requirements.

Stanton instead resurrected the idea of individual freedom, viewing the family savers as a threat to women's rights under the veil of the revered family. "The best interests of a community never can require the sacrifice of one innocent being, of one sacred right." Instead, she tried to bring to the forefront of the policy discussions the continued relevance and importance of women as individuals in the family. "In the settlement, then, of any question," she proclaimed, "we must simply consider the highest good of the individual. It is the inalienable right of all to be happy." To prove her theory of individual sovereignty, she relied on the "great doctrine of Christianity" and its primary "right of individual conscience and judgment" to which all other interests of state, church, society, and family were secondary. Stanton then questioned the idea that the individual and society were mutually exclusive, arguing instead that "the highest good and happiness of the individual and society, lie in the same direction."[168]

Opposition to divorce, however, grew louder. In the last decades of the nineteenth century, an organized effort by conservatives emerged to repudiate easy divorce. The movement began in Connecticut, led initially by conservative clergy and President Timothy Dwight of Yale University. The legislature resisted the demand for repeal, but did authorize a legislative committee to investigate the divorce situation. The resulting study produced statistics that were "highly disquieting to the moralists," since they revealed a significant increase in the number of divorces in Connecticut in the short time of fifteen years, from 544 (1849–1852) to 1,253 (1861–1864).[169]

The organized divorce opposition was then spearheaded by Theodore Woolsey, Dwight's successor as Yale president. In 1867, he published a series of articles on divorce, which were later collected into a book published in 1869. Woolsey placed the blame for the increase in the divorce rate "squarely on the divorce laws" rather than on other possible demographic and economic changes like immigration, westward expansion, industrialization, or the diminishing influence of the church. He set out nine principles for the formation of a good divorce law. Two related to adultery: prohibiting the adulterer from remarrying the partner of his or her crime and making adultery an automatic criminal offense following the divorce. He endorsed the historic distinction making adultery by the wife a greater offense. "The crime is the same," he said, except that it "is justly regarded as a greater advance in wickedness" for women because the harm done to society is greater. Two other principles favored the innocent injured partner, granting a greater share of property and awarding custody of the children. Woolsey sought to deter divorce by laws that used legal separation as a temporary measure, required magistrates to attempt to reconcile parties, and imposed a waiting period before a blameworthy partner could remarry. Finally, Woolsey advocated uniformity of state laws and the elimination of judicial discretion in awarding divorces.[170]

Stanton responded to Woolsey in the pages of the *Revolution*. "No, no, President Woolsey," she argued, public morals cannot be improved by compelling men and women to live in constant antagonism. The laws would not produce the desired moral result, because such laws, intended as "a check on the vicious, have no effect on them, but bear heavily on the virtuous." Arguing the individual-right point, she emphasized that "there is nothing more demoralizing to the individual than a marriage without love and attraction." Turning to a legalistic point, she argued the rule of law, that "nothing more surely undermines respect for all law than legislation on those subjects that human legislation cannot regulate."[171]

Governor Jewell of Connecticut, however, was persuaded to seek repeal of the state's liberal divorce law. Jewell proposed to eliminate the general clause that allowed divorce "for any such misconduct as permanently destroys the happiness of the petitioner, and defeats the purposes of the marriage relation." The problem, he said, was too many divorces and divorces from out of state. The state in the last year had seen 4,734 marriages but 478 divorces, as "discontented people came here from other States to take advantage of what is called our liberal legislation, to obtain divorces which would be denied them at home." Echoing Woolsey, the governor stated that the causes of divorce were too numerous and that "too wide a discretion is given the courts." He concluded, "As the sacredness of the marriage relation lies at the foundation of civilized society, is [sic] should be carefully guarded." Stanton responded to the governor's proposal, homing in on a key point of his address: "the singular fact that the majority of the applications for divorce were made by women." She said since Connecticut had "been a Canada for fugitive wives from the yoke of matrimony, pray keep that little State like an oasis in the desert, sacred to save wives," at least until women had the right to vote and say whether they were ready to make marriage an indissoluble tie.[172]

The problem of too many divorces was said to be caused by the lack of uniform laws and the problem of migratory divorces. In migratory divorces, petitioners like Abby McFarland temporarily migrated to other states where they could take advantage of the relatively liberal laws and shorter residency requirements of other states. Conservatives claimed that these state idiosyncrasies that opened up a state to all people essentially imposed easy divorce upon all the states. Other states were often more attractive—not just the states like Indiana that had easier grounds of cruelty or general misconduct but also states with short residency requirements. While most eastern states required one year of residency before divorce, other state requirements were shorter, like the Dakotas' three months, Wyoming and Idaho's six months, Indiana's simple "bona fide residence," and Utah's "resident or wishes to become one." The location of the divorce mills changed quickly as locals resisted the immoral

label, and easy states moved from Pennsylvania in the early century expanding west to Indiana, Ohio, Chicago, Utah, South Dakota, and eventually the mecca of Nevada.[173]

Stanton tried to dismiss the anxious concerns over migratory divorce.
She joked, "I had heard such a hue and cry about Indiana's divorce laws
that I was quite surprised to find the mass of men and women living
in the same harmonious, faithful relations as in my native state, where
divorces are unhonored and unknown."[174] Reacting to a report of another proposal to modify the Illinois divorce laws to forbid divorce for
any cause, Stanton fell back on her standard argument about the importance of divorce to protect women and give them a voice in their own
governance. "[L]et the divorce code alone," she said, "until the women
of the state have the right to vote, and then we shall find out if virtuous,
refined, educated women desire to be indissolubly bound to men who
are gamblers and drunkards" and other ill-sorted men.[175]

The divorce opponents, however, were not so easily dismissed. Opposition was pressed by clergy, social reformers, and temperance women
to curtail the divorce trade and supposed affiliated vice. In addition to
the perceived migratory problem, by 1870, the "official law and the law
in action were radically different."[176] In practice, parties and lawyers
colluded in sham proceedings, lying about affairs or cruel treatment to
procure what was otherwise an agreed-upon divorce. There was clearly
a popular demand for divorce, and that's what concerned opponents.
States developed a "sudden passion for statistics" to show the obvious
trends toward a rise in both the absolute numbers of divorces and the
ratio of divorces to marriages. These studies, combined with the vocal
opposition, worked, and states began to turn back their liberal divorce
laws. Indiana repealed its omnibus clause in 1873, extended its residency
requirement to two years, and forbade a plaintiff to remarry for two
years when the divorce was obtained through notice to the defendant by
publication. After a brief divorce boom from 1875 to 1878, triggered by
the expanding railroad, Utah abolished its omnibus clause and added a
one-year residency requirement. Connecticut, too, eventually conceded
and repealed its notorious general misconduct clause in 1878.[177]

After this success in Connecticut, divorce reformers expanded their
efforts. Headed by Woolsey, they founded the New England Divorce Reform League in 1881 (later renamed the National Divorce Reform League

and then the National League for Protection of the Family). The league, comprised of representatives of all the leading Christian churches, pushed for the standardization and tightening of divorce laws. In 1884, it proposed a federal marriage amendment to give Congress the express power to enact national divorce legislation. This marriage amendment would be continuously proposed over the next sixty years, though without success.[178] The league proposed a national commission for uniform standards, which finally convened in 1890 and evolved into the uniform commission responsible for enacting uniform laws of commerce, trusts, and many other areas of the law. Its advocacy produced successful results against divorce in the 1880s: Maine abolished its previous omnibus clause and restricted the remarriage of both parties; Vermont stiffened its residency requirements and restricted the defendant's right to remarry; and even South Dakota succumbed to the opposition condemning "consecutive polygamy" and lengthened its residency requirement to six months (one year if notice was not by personal service).[179] Congress appropriated funds to study the issue of marriage and divorce, producing the first national census. The study showed a stark 157 percent increase in divorce nationally from 1867 to 1886, and the next decade's census showed total divorces increasing nationally from 9,937 in 1867 to 25,535 divorces in 1886. The study, however, also concluded that migratory divorce was not a major cause of this increase. The commissioner of labor, Carroll Wright, previously an opponent of divorce, came to support it after immersing himself in the study of the details of the miseries, abuse, and unhappiness that led partners to divorce.[180]

Early on in this reactionary period, Stanton seemed to concede the need for a uniform state law. "We need a national law or no law on this question," she stated. Stanton the lawyer appreciated the problems of conflicting divorce laws, extra-territorial effect, and evasion of the law.[181] Without uniform laws, Stanton noted, "a man or woman who could be legally married in Connecticut might be convicted of bigamy in New York."[182] The bigger problem was that "this dodging from one State to another, so common to-day, to secure freedom, is educating our people into contempt for all law." But Stanton the feminist later changed her view when she realized that the uniform law movement was a pretext for repeal and restriction of divorce rights. "If a national divorce law were enacted it would be framed by the judges and bishops of the

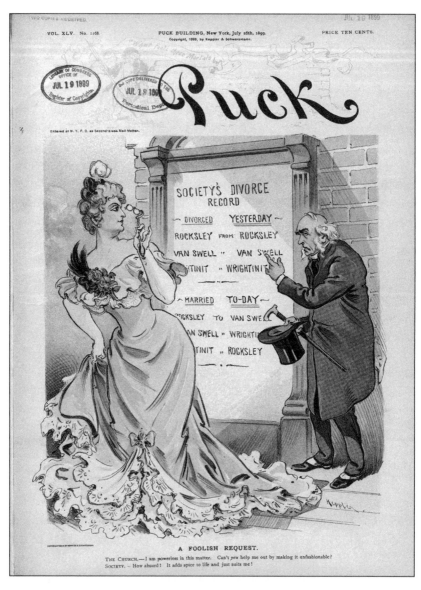

"A Foolish Request" cartoon, *Puck*, July 2, 1899. *Library of Congress.*

land," both conservative classes seeking to "make all the free States more narrow." Stanton emphatically declared that "such a law would unquestionably not be in the interest of women." It would be of no consequence to a man, "because he can get along very well as things are at present" by simply leaving his wife, being endowed with control of property and earning ability. "Unhappy husbands have many ways of mitigating their miseries, which are not open to wives, who are financial dependents, and burdened with children." Women could not just walk away in de facto divorce, but needed legal divorce to restore their rights as single women to earn and hold property, and be legal custodians of their children.[183]

After a break from the divorce debate while she visited two of her children in England and France, the eighty-year-old Stanton renewed her efforts to resist proposals for uniform divorce laws. Her goal was to emphasize how such laws were a threat to women's rights and ability to divorce.[184] Her article "The Need of Liberal Divorce Laws" for the prestigious journal the *North American Review* rebutted the arguments of Judge Noah Davis (prosecutor in the McFarland trial) for a uniform law restricting divorce. Stanton challenged the assertion that divorce historically had been restricted, citing to historical evidence of divorce in the American colonies, by Protestant reform, and the liberal laws of some states in the early nineteenth century. She focused her arguments on the importance of divorce for women, tracing the recent history of liberal divorce laws adopted on women's behalf. "Finding the marriage relation theoretically a condition of slavery, and practically so when tyrannical husbands chose to avail themselves of their legal rights, women early began to ask release from their yoke of bondage." And the law responded: "[H]ere and there, humane legislators, roused with a sense of woman's wrongs, began to open the door of escape through liberal divorce laws." Women were reluctant at first to divorce, Stanton said, weighed down by religion and public sentiment, but with newer knowledge of the true marriage, they began to understand the degradation of "remaining with unworthy and unloved partners." Given that "the vast majority of applications for divorce" were made by women, Stanton rejected "the specious plea of protection" from the divorce reformers demanding "more stringent laws for women's protection!"[185]

Stanton then directly challenged the pretext of the law, intended not for uniformity but for restriction of divorce to the narrowest ground. It was clear to her that since the suggestion for a national divorce law "comes uniformly from those who consider the present divorce laws too liberal, we may infer that the proposed National Law is to place the whole question on a narrower basis, rendering null and void the laws that have been passed in a broader spirit." Of course, she noted, "the widest possible law would not make divorce obligatory on anyone," while a restrictive one would compel many to continue living in "uncongenial relations."[186] Stanton was quite concerned that the uniform law movement advocated not for the "progressively freer laws of divorce that the true American sovereign of the West will surely demand" but instead for the South Carolina ideal of prohibiting all divorce.[187] South Carolina boasted that it had not granted a divorce since the time of the Revolution, but Stanton revealed by "judicial evidence the disastrous effect" and the "meretricious connections" produced by the lack of a divorce law. The South Carolina legislature had to regulate by statute the proportion of property that a married man could give to his concubine. The state courts heard cases like *Jelineau v. Jelineau* adjudicating maintenance and support arising when a wife sought to separate from her husband because he had compelled her to live together with his female slave and concubine.[188] Stanton's point was that restrictions on divorce do not create the idealized marital unity envisioned, and can result in other legal and moral perversions.

Stanton wrote to her daughter Harriot and acknowledged the attacks her divorce article drew. "My divorce article in the North American Review, for which, by the way, I was paid sixty dollars, has called down on me most merciless criticism by the religious press." She reported the slew of accusations against her as "a traitor to her sex," "infidelity," and "free love," but dismissed them as "full of hypocrisy." She counseled her daughter, and probably herself, too, that "the less notice we can learn to take of ill-natured remarks, the better. Life is too precious when one lives for a great purpose to allow one's thoughts to be diverted from worthy themes and one's time to be occupied with the petty dissensions of the ordinary run of people." On a positive note, she mentioned that she had received "several letters from New York lawyers praising my effort," and one comment by a judge to her son Bob, also a lawyer, that "your mother has laid Judge Davis out stiff and stark."[189]

As the marriage amendment efforts escalated, Stanton added structural arguments to her opposition, challenging federalist action. Her legalistic arguments emphasized the threat to democratic state experimentation of a federal law, which would deny the more flexible localities the opportunity to try "different laws under varying circumstances, and thus learn their comparative merits." Since there was such divergence of opinion as to the availability and grounds for divorce, Stanton argued, it was too early for a national uniform law.[190] Her example was public education, for, she said, just think "if the matter had to be settled at Washington! The whole nation might find itself pledged to a scheme that a few years would prove wholly impracticable."[191] She argued that a federal amendment confined states into a constitutional straightjacket that denied respect to more liberal states with "a broader spirit of inclusiveness."[192] This states-rights position, however, contrasted starkly with her approach for women's suffrage, where she dismissed the experimental state approach as inefficient and ineffective, demanding instead federal constitutional amendment.[193] Her anticlerical arguments resurrected her opposition to church control of familial rights, deriding the Episcopal-led divorce reform movement and the attempts to reclaim church jurisdiction over divorce. Stanton quipped, "The less latitude the Church has in our temporal affairs the better."[194]

Running throughout Stanton's opposition to the marriage amendment was the absence of woman's voice in the lawmaking process.[195] "In justice to the daughters of this republic there should be no such final settlement of this question as a constitutional amendment involves until woman has a direct voice in the legislation of the country." If there was to be a national law, Stanton said, "I want women to have an equal voice in its adjudication." "Thus far," she said, "we have had the man's idea exclusively. Now let us see what the united thought of men and women could suggest by way of improvement." Other women's rights reformers by now agreed with Stanton in opposing a national law of divorce that would narrow the existing fault grounds for divorce without women's voice. "Whatever legislation may be undertaken, whether by concerted State action or through a national constitutional amendment, concerns both sexes equally, and both should have equal influence in directing it." Echoing Stanton, they argued, "men have made the laws of marriage and divorce, and women have never been consulted as to their wisdom, or their adaptability to women's own circumstances, or their approval of them."[196] When divorce reformers and clergy tried to use this connec tion between suffrage women and divorce to defame both movements, Stanton reminded them that history had seen divorce with Milton, Henry VIII, and Napoleon long before the women's suffrage movement had been born.

Keeping the Debate Going

In 1890, reflecting back on her advocacy of the transformation of marriage and divorce, Stanton recalled, "[W]hat I said on divorce thirty-seven years ago seems quite in line with what many say now." "The trouble," she said, "was not in what I said, but that I said it too soon, before the people were ready to hear it." Still, she hoped, "[I]t may be that I helped them to get ready; who knows?"[197]

In the month before her death, Stanton engaged in a written symposium in William Hearst's newspaper, the *New York American*, on the question of how to solve "the divorce evil, the great national disgrace, and preserve the purity of the American home." Stanton opened the symposium with an article recycling her arguments from her prior articles, "The Need of Liberal Divorce Laws" and "Divorce versus Domestic Warfare."[198] She repeated her theories that divorce was not the foe of marriage, that individual interests should not be sacrificed to society, that no-fault divorce should be available on the parties' terms, that federalism could produce restrictive laws stifling experimentation, and that women should have a voice in the ecclesiastical and legal debates on the issue. A week later she followed up with a letter to the editor. "I have read all the contributions so far printed in your grand symposium on Divorce, and though several proposed a national divorce law, not one has suggested that any woman should help in drafting such a law."[199] She submitted two more articles. She first responded specifically to an article by an Episcopal bishop who used biblical arguments to assert that the husband and wife are one flesh, and thus the wife should not be allowed to divorce on any ground whatsoever, except maybe desertion. Stanton retorted, "I agree with exactly one sentence of the Bishop—'Most women will object to this article.'" She said, "I decline to accept Hebrew Mythology as a guide in twentieth-century science. . . . More and more intelligent people embrace truth as it is revealed to-day by human reason."[200] In the final article, published three days after her death, Stanton renewed her arguments for divorce from the Tenth Convention, coming full circle back to her first thorough debate on the issue.[201] She reminded her audience that marriage is a human institution, that women like her bridesmaid friend endured harsh realities without it, that separation is no solution, and that John Milton provides the theological support for no-fault divorce.

Stanton's promise of a free, no-fault right of women to divorce would be delayed, stymied by renewed moral conservatism and manipulation of the fault-based system sufficient to accomplish the desired end. It would not be until the 1970s that no-fault divorce based on the incompatibility of the parties, as Stanton recommended, became the prevailing law in virtually every state.

4

The "Incidental Relation" of Mother

The woman is greater than the wife or the mother; and in consenting to take upon herself these relations, she should never sacrifice one iota of her individuality to any senseless conventionalisms, or false codes of feminine delicacy and refinement.

—Letter from Mrs. Stanton to Seventh National Woman's Rights Convention, Nov. 24, 1856

Stanton continued to demand women's freedom in marriage by focusing on a woman's right to choose motherhood. In a time when motherhood defined all women culturally and legally, Stanton challenged the entrenched norm dictating that women's primary role in life was that of mother. Womanhood, she said, was the "first consideration" of women's own happiness: wifehood and motherhood secondary, "mere incidents of their lives."[1] Stanton continually emphasized that woman, "as an equal factor in civilization," was entitled to "use all her faculties for her own safety and happiness" because of the "individuality of each human soul" and "the right of individual conscience and judgment" inherent in citizenship. These paramount individual rights were not to be subordinated, as philosophers argued, to the necessities of woman's "incidental relations" of mother and wife, for not all women assumed these roles, and men's duties and rights were not determined by their relation as father.[2] This improper subordination of women's individual rights to motherhood, however, resulted from enforced motherhood and the laws that supported it. Stanton identified the problems of women's lack of reproductive control and men's sexual privilege as victimization and oppression, not natural or ordained relations. Her solution was to give woman alone the right to choose and control procreation. She demanded that the law recognize a woman's right to bodily autonomy and self-determination in sexual relations, a radical contribution to the developing feminism.[3]

The "sovereign right to her own person," as Stanton articulated it, was a wife's cognizable right to counter the husband's common law conjugal right. It was a right of sexual refusal and abstinence. The nineteenth-century woman's movement shared Stanton's critique of the male sexual prerogative in marriage and endorsed this alternative ideology of "voluntary motherhood" establishing a wife's right to refuse sexual relations. Women were entitled to this gendered, unilateral control over reproduction because of their individual right to bodily autonomy, for they alone bore the consequences of maternity to their physical health and freedom from pregnancy and the obligations of childcare. Stanton encouraged women to exercise this right of sovereignty in their own marriages to produce fewer but healthier children under an "enlightened motherhood" theory of maternity. This contradicted the social conservatism of the late nineteenth century, which demanded that white, middle-class women fulfill their duty to produce more children "to preserve the race" against threats from increased immigration and racial diversity.

Women's growing awareness of the oppression of forced maternity led to an increase in the practice of abortion by the mid-nineteenth century. The increase triggered moral outrage, public debate, and legislative reforms resulting in the criminalization of early-term abortions for the first time. Stanton joined the discussion on her own terms, eschewing the moralization and refocusing the debate on the underlying issues of women's legal and social victimization. She attacked the double standards of sexuality that tolerated male licentiousness, but imposed all costs of extramarital sex on women, from the social shunning of unwed mothers to the crimes of prostitution and infanticide. Stanton used the context of infanticide to make more sweeping criticisms of the structural defects of the legal system that excluded women at every level—as lawmakers, judges, juries, lawyers, and witnesses. Stanton demanded the participation of women in all aspects of the legal process to remedy the unjust prosecution of desperate acts like infanticide and the resulting injustice of judgment without mercy.

Involuntary Motherhood

The terms of marriage in the nineteenth century included the husband's prerogative to control sexual relations. A husband had the power to demand sexual intercourse, while the wife had the duty to submit. The law justified the husband's sexual right to his wife's body under a theory of initial consent to the marriage. Drawing from the political theory of consent of the governed, the justification was that the woman's consent to marriage was irrevocable consent to all sexual relations at any time.[4] This was a status-based rule, operating automatically for all marriages regardless of individual choice or dissent. The laws of marriage, divorce, and rape endorsed the husband's sexual privilege. In divorce cases, courts refused to grant wives' petitions for cruelty based on forced marital sex, finding that "copulation itself was in the exercise of the marital right," and a usual and expected part of marriage.[5] At the extreme, this marital consent theory excused marital rape. Rape by definition could not be perpetrated against one's wife. As English treatise writer Sir Matthew Hale explained the common law, "[T]he husband cannot be guilty of a rape committed by himself upon his lawful wife, for by their mutual matrimonial consent and contract the wife hath given up herself in this kind unto her husband, which she cannot retract."[6]

Feminists uniformly rejected this legally sanctioned violence of forced sex and maternity. They instead advocated for "voluntary motherhood," giving the wife the unilateral right to refuse sexual relations—to abstain periodically or permanently unless she desired procreation.[7] There was wide consensus among women reformers on this issue, including the radical free lovers, the feminist suffragists, and conservative moral reformers. "On no question did the feminists agree so clearly as on . . . 'voluntary motherhood' . . . incorporating both a political critique of the status quo, as *involuntary motherhood,* and a solution."[8] "Their priority was women's right to say no to men."[9] These women proposed a radical reversal of the entrenched norms of marital power by granting women, and not men, the sole right to dictate the terms of marital sex.

Stanton voiced her strong rejection of this male sexual privilege and identified it as a source of women's oppression. Writing to Anthony in 1853 about marriage as a key site of subordination, Stanton argued, "[M]an in his lust has regulated long enough this whole question of sexual intercourse. Now let the mother of mankind, whose prerogative it is to set bounds to his indulgence, rouse up and give this whole matter a thorough, fearless examination."[10] A few years later, she featured forced maternity in her "Paper on Marriage," directed to a Quaker audience.

Have the best Christian men in this nation ever felt the least compunction of conscience, as they have contemplated, year by year, the droop-
ing form, the pale cheek, the sunken eye, the joyless, hopeless life of the
self-sacrificing wife, the mother of six, eight or ten children? . . . *Victims
all*, to the lust and selfishness of those to whom they looked for care and
support—*dead,* or *suffering life*, with the excessive cares and anxieties of
maternity![11]

"All things," she argued, "are inverted, disorganized, so long as the
mother of the race is subjected to man—so long as all her holy intuitions of virtue, purity, chastity, are sacrificed to the lust and selfishness
of man."[12]

Other women reformers shared Stanton's indictment of male lust
at women's expense, including abolitionist and early feminist Sarah
Grimké.[13] In an 1856 essay, "Marriage," Grimké expressed her visceral
reaction to the way man subordinated women to his own passion by
the principle of superior rights.[14] Her critique stemmed from first-hand
observations of the difficult, successive pregnancies of her sister, Angelina Grimké Weld, and the resulting disability that caused Angelina to
abandon public abolition and women's rights work. "Man seems to feel
that Marriage gives him the control of Woman's person just as the Law
gives him the control of her property."

Has she not been continually forced into a motherhood which she ab-
horred, because she knew that her children were *not* the offspring of Love
but of Lust? Has she not in unnumbered instances felt in the deepest
recesses of her soul, that she was used to minister to Passion, not voluntarily to receive from her husband the chaste expression of his *love*?

Grimké empathized with the shattered sentimentality of marriage
in which women "entered the marriage relation in all purity and innocence expecting to realize completion of their own halfness, the round-
ing out of their own being," but "too soon discovered that they were
unpaid housekeepers and nurses, and still worse, chattels personal to
be used and abused at the will of a master." "How many so called wives,"
she challenged, "rise in the morning oppressed with a sense of degradation from the fact that their chastity has been violated, their holiest in-

stincts disregarded, and themselves humbled under an oppressive sense of their own pollution, and that, too, a thousand times harder to bear, because so called husband has been the perpetrator of the unnatural crime." The solution, she argued, was "a right on the part of woman to decide *when* she shall become a mother, how often and under what circumstances."[15]

The feminists advocating voluntary motherhood developed a structural attack on forced marital sex, looking beyond the individual behavior of husbands to the law and economics of marriage. Their phrase "legalized prostitution" encapsulated the idea of the legally prescribed exchange of sex for money in the dependency of marriage. "Is marriage sacred," Stanton asked rhetorically, "where a woman consents to live in legalized prostitution! her whole soul revolting at such gross association!"[16] Feminists challenged the basis of marriage, which essentially was an economic transaction that rendered women socially and financially dependent upon their husbands. The wife, like a street prostitute, was forced to submit to unwanted sex in exchange for monetary support. "If marriage was to rise above 'legalized prostitution,'" Stanton argued, wives "needed personal freedom more than a legal right to control marital intercourse." Freedom came only with economic independence and economic profession, providing the necessary alternative to marriage.[17]

Mainstream popular literature picked up on the criticisms of involuntary motherhood, but rejected the feminists' structural insights. Women's magazines, novels, and popular guides to women's health incorporated the feminist ideas of involuntary motherhood as legalized prostitution and agreed that women should control their husbands' sexual access. However, these prescriptive writers focused on the solution of changing men's individual behavior by appealing to "manly self-restraint" and men's own self-interest. They persuaded men that they would be happier if their wives were happier, and wives would be happier if given respite from insistent demands for unwanted sex and pregnancy. This view played into the convention of the husband's superior power, encouraging his benevolent use of it, rather than adopting the feminist demand for a wife's prioritized right to make the decision herself.[18]

"Sovereign of Her Own Person"

The most radical idea of the voluntary motherhood movement was a woman's "right to her own person." By this, the women's rights advocates meant the right to bodily autonomy and individual control of their bodies for sex and procreation. They prioritized this right, claiming it as "a subject which lies deeper down into woman's wrongs than any other."[19] As free love advocate Mary Gove Nichols wrote, "[W]oman's one, single, and supreme right and the one which includes all others, is her right to herself."[20] Stanton corresponded with Nichols in the early 1850s and agreed with her that "the right to control one's body was the preeminent personal and political right."[21]

Stanton wrote publicly in 1855 to emphasize the centrality of the issue of sexual autonomy to women's rights, "the battleground where our independence must be fought and won."[22] The vast majority of women, she said, regarded the present marital arrangements "with deep and settled disgust." While rights to vote and hold property were important, "the sacred right of a woman to her own person, to all her God-given powers of body and soul," was a great social and human right "before which all others sink into utter insignificance." She focused on the idea that "to the mother of the race, and to her alone, belonged the right to say when a new being should be brought into the world." Has man, she asked, "in the gratification of his blind passions, ever paused to think whether it was with joy and gladness that she gave up ten or twenty years of the heyday of her existence to all the cares and sufferings of excessive maternity?"[23]

Lucy Stone begged Stanton to address the issue of "a wife's right to her own body" at the Seventh National Woman's Rights Convention.[24] Stone wrote, "I very much wish that a wife's right to her own body should be pushed at our next convention. It does seem to me that you are the one to do it." Stone, though, prudish even by Victorian standards and sensitive to public rejection, refused to address the issue herself.[25] Stanton obliged, writing a short letter to the convention, though it arrived too late to be discussed. Stanton called women to "a proper self-respect" and decried the marriage in which a woman accepted "herself as a mere machine, a tool for men's pleasure."[26] Elsewhere, she elaborated on what she

meant by a woman "owning her own body." By this she meant, "[A]s opposed to the old common law of England, I deny the husband's right . . .
to burden her with the hardships of reproduction . . . I deny man's right
to seek gratification of his sexual nature at the expense of undermining
the well being of the woman and her offspring."[27]

The *New York Times* attacked this assertion of a woman's right of
self-ownership, dismissing women's claims of abuse from involuntary
motherhood.[28] The paper revealed what it assumed was the shocking
proposition that "the Woman's Rights movement leads directly and rapidly in the same direction, viz. to Free Love, that extreme section of it
we mean which claims to rest upon the absolute and indefeasible right
of woman to equality in all respects with man and to a complete sovereignty over her own person and conduct." Sarah Grimké responded to
the attack by affirmatively embracing the charge: yes, she said, "[T]his
exposition of the *principles* of the Woman's Rights movement I heartily
accept. We do claim the absolute and indefeasible right of woman to an
equality in all respects with man and to a complete sovereignty over her
own person and conduct." Human rights, she asserted, are universal,
not based upon sex, color, capacity, or condition, and "none but des-
pots will deny to woman that supreme sovereignty over her own person
and conduct which Law concedes to man." "Yet," she said, "the Times is
horror-struck at the idea of a woman's claiming '*A supreme sovereignty
over her own person and conduct.*' Is it not time that she should? Has not
man proved himself unworthy of the power which he assumes over her
person and conduct?"[29]

Stanton "understood a woman's right to control her person as the
foundational right upon which political and economic equality needed
to rest if they were to have any value."[30] Writing to Anthony, she argued,
"[W]hen we talk of woman's rights, is not the right to her person, to her
happiness, to her life, the first on the list?"[31] Stanton's solution was for
women to have the sole and absolute right to refuse marital sexual intercourse. This restructured the existing law of irrevocable consent to the
marital contract and shifted the privilege of determining sexual relations
to women. This was "an intensely gender-specific argument" for a right
intended for women only, because they were the ones solely responsible
for the physical demands of maternity itself and the caring and raising
of children. Stanton, as the mother of seven children, experienced the

social reality that imposed the work of raising children exclusively on women.[32] She thus vividly understood "that women needed to have full control over marital intercourse so that they could determine how many children they would raise and when."[33]

Other feminists agreed with both Stanton's view of the sovereign right to self-determination and her justification for that unilateral right stemming from women's exclusive responsibility for bearing and raising children.[34] "The law of motherhood should be entirely under woman's control, . . . and that woman must first of all be held as having a right to herself."[35] As Grimké wrote, "[S]urely as upon her alone devolves the necessity of nurturing unto the fullness of life the being within her and after it is born, of nursing and tending it thro' helpless infancy and capricious childhood, often under the pressure of miserable health, she *ought* to have the right of controlling all preliminaries." She described the "burden on woman by the care of many children following in quick succession" and its resulting "unnatural tug upon her constitution." She added, "[I]f man had all these burdens to bear, would not *he* declare that common sense and common justice confer this right upon him."[36]

In the following decades, Stanton's speeches and lectures aimed to convince women of their "right to their own person" and the "preservation of their own womanhood." "Let us remember," she repeated, "that womanhood is the great fact, wifehood and motherhood its incidents."[37] Must the heyday of her existence be wholly devoted to the one animal function of bearing children? Shall there be no limit to this but woman's capacity to endure the fearful strain on her life?"[38] In her "Marriage and Maternity" lecture, Stanton advised women that bearing children was not their sole duty and purpose, as they had been told. "We must educate our daughters," she said, "first—to regard their own lives and bodies and the laws which govern them."[39] She argued that "the preservation of their own womanhood was the one prime object of their lives."[40] Instead, she said, "[A]s it is now, we look up to wives and mothers, and down on womanhood. This is wrong." Stanton said she revered single women like "Susan B. Anthony and [sculptor] Harriet Hosmer who have done great things in the world without having borne children."[41] She continued, "[W]e must educate our girls that they are independent; that in the society of the refined they may be happy; that they may live peaceful, glorious lives, and take high seats in Heaven, without ever seeing a man."[42]

Enlightened Motherhood

Stanton extended her advocacy of voluntary motherhood into the idea of "enlightened motherhood." Enlightened motherhood added to the rhetoric of individual rights a second argument about the eugenic consequences of unwanted pregnancies. It articulated a concern for the greater human race by controlling pregnancy to produce fewer children, but children of "superior quality."[43] Stanton emphasized the impact of unwanted and unhealthy pregnancies on the mental and physical health of the child, arguing that women should aim "to have one good kind of child" rather than many and should endeavor to produce "lions not jackasses."[44]

As historians have explained, "This concern with eugenics was characteristic of nearly all feminists of the late nineteenth century."[45] Feminists used eugenic arguments to bolster their credibility as to reproductive control and "conquer conservative and religious scruples about reproduction."[46] Women had been told it was their duty to the human race and the greater social good to produce multiple children. By co-opting this rhetoric about the greater good of the human race, feminists identified a social benefit from women's restriction of procreation. The newly articulated eugenics theory provided a scientific basis for that argument.

The early eugenicists focused on individual environmental changes that could be made to develop the health of children, such as enhancing the physical and mental conditions of the mother during pregnancy.[47] Influenced by the new evolutionary theories, eugenics was used by many social reformers to buttress their arguments that improvement of the human condition was possible.[48] As it evolved, eugenics began to include a fear about the decline of the white race due to social, political, and economic threats from an expanding class of immigrants. Later in the twentieth century, eugenics became more invidious as it legally sanctioned the involuntary sterilization of criminals, the mentally disabled, and poor, black mothers. But the thought "originally was primarily directed at the elimination of idiocy, criminality, and drunkenness" as isolated character traits on the theory that such undesirable qualities were hereditary.[49] "Feminists assumed the inheritability of acquired characteristics and contended that a husband's licentiousness and a wife's unhappiness about her impending maternity would be transmitted to their child before birth, forever diminishing the child's capabilities and prospects."[50]

Stanton repeatedly warned of the eugenic consequences of forced maternity. "So long as children are conceived in weariness and disgust," she claimed, "you must not look for high-toned men and women capable of accomplishing any great and noble achievement."[51] Adapting a familiar biblical passage, she argued, "Truly are the sins of the father visited upon the children. God, in his wisdom, has so linked together the whole human family, that any violence done at one end of the chain is felt throughout its length."[52] "Men and brethren look into your asylums for the blind, the deaf and dumb, the idiot, the imbecile, the deformed, the insane . . . and there behold the terrible retributions of your violence on woman!"[53] She wove this message into her temperance speeches as well, linking enlightened motherhood with the consequences of living with alcoholism and domestic violence. "Live with him as a friend, . . . but for woman's sake, for humanity's sake, be not his wife—bring no children to that blighted, dreary, desolate hearth."[54]

Stanton melodramatically presented this issue of enlightened motherhood in her letter to the Seventh National Woman's Rights Convention. She argued that polluted marital relations produced "the shocking monstrosities of . . . deformed and crippled offspring," "miserable progeny conceived in disgust and brought forth in agony." Asylums, abortion, and crippled children, she said, exemplified to "what a depth of degradation the women of this Republic have fallen, how false they have been to the holy instincts of their nature, to the sacred trust given them by God as the mothers of the race." Women, Stanton argued, had a higher duty to control and deliberate in reproduction, not simply propagate. Her solution was to "let Christians and moralists pause in their efforts at reform and let some scholar teach them how to apply the laws of science to human life."

To her readers in the *Revolution*, Stanton emphasized the need to base the fundamentals of social and family life "on science and philosophy by educating women into the idea that to bear noble children to noble men with sound bodies and sound minds, is a worthy work and one that brings its own happiness and reward." But, she continued, "to fill the world with idiots, lunatics, criminals, the blind, the deaf, the dumb," and to "spend one's days nursing muling, puling, limp-backed, hydroce-phalic abortions of humanity, is not a work worth a Christian woman, but a sin against herself, the state, and a gross violation of the immutable laws of God."[55]

Stanton's solution was what she called "conscientious parenthood"—deliberate and physiologically based reproduction.[56] "Let us but use as much care and forethought in producing the highest order of intelligence, as we do in raising a cabbage or a calf, and in a few generations we shall reap an abundant harvest of giants, scholars and Christians."[57] "Woman must be made to feel that the transmitting of immortal life is a most solemn responsible act and never should be allowed, except when the parents are in the highest condition of mind and body."[58] She emphasized the importance of a woman's intentional choice. "If in such a family, children are born, it is by the wish and will of the mother, conceived with a holy purpose, stamped with a high and noble nature, and welcomed to the earth with rapture and hope; where each new creation is the product of love, friendship, passion, and sentiment."[59]

Stanton directly engaged with the issue of enlightened motherhood at a conference of the newly formed First Woman's Congress of the Association for the Advancement of Woman in New York City in October 1873. The conference was organized by conservative woman's rights reformer and Stanton rival Julia Ward Howe.[60] Stanton attended the Woman's Congress to speak on the topic of the coeducation of the sexes, but the topic at the meeting turned to enlightened motherhood and the notion that women should engage in more deliberate and healthful pregnancies.[61] The speeches opened with strong condemnation of infant mortality rates, pleaded for women to improve their knowledge and physical condition during pregnancy, and demanded that men practice sexual self-control so that healthier babies were born.[62] One speaker, Elizabeth Lovering, made what the newspapers called "a tricky case." "No child should be brought into the world which was not the product of a perfect love," she said, because "the damage to the race from the birth of children, the product of an overburdened and unwilling motherhood, or of an exhausted vitality on the part of either of the parents, was incalculable."[63]

Stanton responded to this argument during the discussion. She asserted that the character of the child was formed before birth, and she made eugenics-type arguments against bringing "deformed" children into the world. Stanton said, "It is not the right and duty of every man and woman to be fathers and mothers, for it is the ante-natal conditions that determine the character of the race." She contradicted the prevailing idea of (white) women's duty to bear children to preserve the human race, renewed by the nativist concerns from increasing immigration and lower native birth rates. "I want to have women to think on these things. They must not take the teaching of men, that have taught women their whole duty was to multiply and replenish the earth. This was a mistake; we have too many children already." She analogized to an artist who would not spend all her efforts "filling a gallery full of distorted statues and everything crooked about them," yet the proliferation of pregnancies was "filling the world with men and women with crooked legs and crooked brains and everything crooked about them altogether." In explicit language, Stanton continued: "Every woman knows we are bringing into the world moral monstrosities. When physical monstrosities are born the physician thinks it is perfectly just to put them out of the world."[64]

The conservative Julia Ward Howe was shocked, and quickly attempted to distance herself and the convention from the implications of Stanton's remarks. Howe said that she "was deeply mortified if any sanction of infanticide should go forth from that meeting" and that she "was fearful that the impression might go abroad that the Woman's Congress favored infanticide based upon Stanton's remarks."[65] Later, in her diary, Howe wrote,

> Sparred with Mrs. Stanton, who excused infanticide on the grounds that women did not want to bring moral monsters into the world, and said that these acts were regulated by natural law. I differed from her strongly, asserting that the moral law of man's being was paramount to the mechanical tendencies, quoted as natural laws, and that infanticide was usually a crime of gross selfishness, though under some circumstances, the struggle against it must be agonizing. Nature has a dark horror of the act, I think.[66]

At the conference, Stanton sarcastically retorted that "she had not the least idea that the majority of the audience thought that she favored infanticide. She had merely stated what was an acknowledged fact in the world and always would be until women had the full and entire control of their own person."[67] Stanton continued to say that if a woman was grand enough to bring into the world a dozen children, by all means let her do so.[68] But absent that, "[I]f a woman with weak, sickly constitution is married to a drunken and profligate husband the fewer the children she brings into the world the better."[69]

Of course, Stanton considered herself grand enough to be such an enlightened mother. Though she had many children, she always publicly presented these pregnancies as intentional and controlled. In her "Marriage and Maternity" lecture, she boasted of her healthy and easy pregnancies resulting from exercise, open air, the Graham diet of wheat and restricted sugar, comfortable dress, naps, and mental stimulation. "The night before the birth of the child I walked three miles," gave birth "without a particle of pain," and then came down and dined with the family the same day.[70] Stanton publicized her births, at a time when such things were not spoken of, flying flags from her house announcing the births, white for the girls and red for the boys.[71]

However, to control this careful narrative of pregnancy as health rather than disability, Stanton hid evidence of her own difficulty in her last pregnancy. Pregnant at age forty-three with her seventh child, Bob, Stanton at the last minute canceled an important speaking engagement before the Boston Fraternity Lecture course. She had been the first woman invited to present at this prestigious program. Stanton lied about her exhaustion and sickly pregnancy prohibiting travel, preferring instead to offer the frivolous excuse that she had lost her trunk on a recent trip with the notes and proper clothes for the lecture. Organizers were shocked, and pleaded with her to appear as announced, even if for a few minutes "for the cause of women." Stanton refused. She confided to her cousin, Elizabeth Miller, that she had made the engagement in good faith, expecting that she would have felt "well and heroic" in the fifth month of pregnancy as she always had, but that this time was different. But the consequences of such an admission of disability, Stanton felt, were too important to admit. She explained, "[A]s the maternal difficulty has always been one of the arguments against woman entering public life, I did not like the idea that I, who had a hundred times declared that difficulty to be absurd,

Elizabeth Cady Stanton with Harriot, 1856. *Library of Congress.*

should illustrate in my own person the contrary thesis. It was all too humiliating to be disclosed." Several months later, baby Robert was born, weighing twelve and one-fourth pounds, after a difficult delivery.[72]

"The Science of Life"

Wide support for voluntary motherhood among women reformers and feminists did not, however, mean that these women endorsed contraception. Methods of birth control were known from ancient Egyptian times, with rudimentary condoms, douches, diaphragms, and pessaries available, though many were derived from poisonous substances and incorrect science. Technical advances in 1844 with the patenting of vulcanized rubber allowed mass production of condoms, and at mid-century advertisements for contraceptives appeared in most mainstream newspapers.[73] Several books on birth control had been written, including utopian Robert Dale Owen's *Moral Physiology* (1831), Dr. Charles Knowlton's *Fruits of Philosophy* (1832), and Dr. Edward Bliss Foote's *Medical Common Sense* (1864). Foote also operated a clinic distributing information and patented devices to his patients until his arrest in 1876. Women's health advocates began to preach on physiology, or the "science of life," informing women of the details of sex, menstruation, and reproduction.[74]

Stanton preached this new sexual physiology to women in "Marriage and Maternity." She reported to friends that this "new gospel of fewer children" was "gladly received." "What radical thoughts I then and there put into their heads as they feel untrammeled, these thoughts are permanently lodged there! That is all I ask."[75] Her lectures uniquely for women only taught "the laws of life and health" and advised them "to learn and practice the true laws of generation."[76] Stanton endorsed the theories of Dr. John Cowan and his book on sexual physiology, *The Science of a New Life*. "I have read Dr. Cowan's work, and made it my text-book in lectures, 'to woman alone,' for several years," she wrote. Cowan detailed male and female anatomy and the biological functioning of sex and reproduction, believing that "knowledge must precede virtue." He credited the many legitimate reasons women desired to prevent pregnancies, but cautioned that while "all manner and means are and have been used" to accomplish prevention, most as a rule caused physical or spiritual harm to the individual. He detailed the options for "the prevention of conception," including withdrawal, condoms, sponges, syringes, and the rhythm method. Condoms, he noted were effectual, but not pleasurable to the male. Sponges or rubber barriers, he stated, were widely used, but not reliable because often inserted incorrectly. Syringes with powders were "damaging to the vitality of the part" and unreliable. Cowan's conclusion was that continence (abstinence) was the only appropriate method to prevent conception.[77]

Audiences, however, questioned Stanton as to the practical realities of accomplishing prevention by this, or any other, means. In San Francisco, as reported by a male journalist who allegedly snuck into the women-only lecture in female disguise, one woman asked, "How can we follow your advice and keep from having children?" Stanton answered on two fronts: structural and personal. First, she said, "[W]oman's perfect independence is the answer to that query. Woman must at all times be the sovereign of her own person." When asked a follow-up question by a second woman, "What are we to do when men don't agree with us?" Stanton gave a second suggestion, based on her support of the social purity idea of a single sexual standard and systemic reduction in the sexualization of women. She replied that men could be educated as to voluntary motherhood, that their passions could be controlled, and that women should stop stimulating men's passions with dress, dance, and fashion with bare arms and bare necks. One lady then "asked a question which hinted at prevention by other than legitimate means." The paper reported that "Mrs. Stanton promptly replied that such views of the matter were too degrading and disgusting to touch upon, and must be classified in the category of crime alongside infanticide."[78] Apparently Stanton, or perhaps the reporter, did not want to go on the record as supporting abortion, by then illegal in many states.

Stanton's personal views on birth control are not clear. Biographers have concluded that her "writing was ambivalent on the subject of birth control." "Some indicate that she was ignorant of contemporary methods of contraception, others indicate that she was aware of and approved of birth control, but did not practice it."[79] The evidence of Stanton's large family of eight pregnancies (one miscarriage) in seventeen years, and her private frustration with this frequent childbearing, suggests that she did not use birth control or practice abstinence, even with her husband's lengthy absences from home.[80] As she reminisced in her diary, "I knew no better than to have seven children in quick succession."[81] This was not Stanton's obedience to her wifely duty, however, but rather an embracing of her own sexuality. "In contrast to many of her contemporaries, Stanton was aware of women's sexuality, and she agreed with an 1853 phrenological analysis of herself as 'able to enjoy the connubial relationship in a high degree.'"[82] In another diary entry, she criticized a Walt Whitman poem for ignoring women's sexuality. "He speaks as if the female must be forced to the creative act, apparently ignorant of the fact that a healthy woman has as much passion as a man, that she needs nothing stronger than the law of attraction to draw her to the male."[83]

Stanton's public recommendation of abstinence, rather than birth control, was the common thinking among reformers at the time. Feminists in the nineteenth century opposed birth control as harmful, conducive to promiscuity, and contrary to broader demands for women's empowerment.[84] They feared the promiscuity contraception would facilitate by granting men license to engage more freely in extramarital sex and prostitution. To separate sex from reproduction did not help women, as it merely allowed men to further indulge their sexual proclivities and family irresponsibility. Contraception also contradicted the systemic goals of the women's rights movement to empower women generally. While the movement sought freedom from excessive pregnancies and childbearing, it also sought respect and authority for motherhood and freedom from male sexual tyranny. "Abstinence helped women strengthen their ability to say no to their husbands' sexual demands, . . . while contraception . . . would have weakened it." The solution to both the problem of unwanted pregnancies and sexual tyranny was abstinence and a single sexual moral standard restraining both women's and men's sexual impulses. Nineteenth-century feminists "wanted to help women avoid pregnancy for physical or psychological reasons," but not for the reason of permitting women to "engage freely and often in sexual intercourse" without the possibility of pregnancy.[85]

From a modern perspective, "a principle of voluntary motherhood that rejects the practice of contraception seems so theoretical as to have little real impact." But as historian Linda Gordon explains, the breakthrough of the voluntary motherhood movement was in its acceptance of women's sexuality and women's unilateral right to control it. "To suggest, as these feminists did, that women might have the capacity to be sexual subjects rather than objects, feeling impulses of their own, tended to weaken the claim that the maternal instinct was always dominant." Voluntary motherhood was the radical theoretical foundation of the right of reproductive control; more specific strategies of birth control and abortion were adopted later as means by which to execute this fundamental right.[86]

In the nineteenth century, however, the public discussion and dissemination of birth control information became illegal when it was banned as obscenity under the 1873 federal Comstock Law. The Comstock Law, named for moral purity crusader Anthony Comstock, prohibited the sale, offer, publication, possession, advertisement, or other distribution of any obscene writing, picture, instrument, or drug and any of these intended "for the prevention of conception or procuring abortion." States passed related "Little Comstock Laws" prohibiting other distribution and manufacturing of contraception and birth control information.[87] In addition to these obscenity laws, medical professionals and moral reformers condemned the "unnatural" and sinful limitation of family size and the "race-suicide" it threatened for the white middle class. Yet people continued to practice family planning by some means, as the average number of children per family declined over the century from 7.04 in 1800 to 3.56 by 1900.[88]

Stanton hinted at her opposition to this ban on discussing birth control.[89] In the early 1880s, while in England visiting her daughter Harriot, Stanton met the free thinker and radical Annie Besant. Besant had been convicted in 1877 of obscenity for publishing Knowlton's *Fruits of Philosophy* detailing methods of contraception. The "Knowlton trial" triggered the founding of the Malthusian League in Britain, building on the ideas of Thomas Malthus regarding overpopulation and now promoting birth control to redress the overpopulation and its related poverty and social problems.[90] Stanton seemed to agree with this theory in recounting her meeting with Besant in her diary.[91] "My sense of justice was severely tried by all I heard of the persecutions of Mrs. Besant and Mr. Bradlaugh for their publications on the right and duty of parents to limit population." "Who can contemplate," she continued, "the sad condition of multitudes of young children in the Old World whose fate is to be brought up in ignorance and vice—a swarming, seething mass which nobody owns—without seeing the need of free discussion of the philosophical principles that underlie these tangled social problems?" Her view stood in contrast to that of her colleague Matilda Joslyn Gage, who in response to the Knowlton trial, condemned Besant's endorsement of contraception, while supporting the broader concept that the "law of motherhood should be entirely under woman's control."[92]

Feminist endorsement of contraception would not come until the early twentieth century, after Stanton's time. Socialist and nurse Margaret Sanger coined the term "birth control" in 1916 and established a clinic in Brooklyn, New York, to provide information about contraception to working-class women. She was arrested and convicted of violating the New York Comstock Law. On appeal, the court upheld the conviction, but found that physicians and pharmacists were exempted by the law, thus permitting medical professionals to distribute birth control information and contraception for "the purposes of preventing disease." Sanger's case thus medicalized birth control, a result that practically ended the ban on contraception, while also removing such procreative decisions solely from women's autonomy.[93]

The Campaign against Abortion

In the absence of legal and effective contraception, abortion, and even infanticide, were practiced in the nineteenth century. By 1850, there was a demonstrable increase in abortions facilitated by advertisements for abortion medicines and services, and by the growing use of the practice by married couples as birth control. This triggered moral and legal outrage resulting in a public campaign to criminalize abortion, which became a "mass political issue in America" in the late 1860s. The campaign, led by the male medical profession, overtook feminists' advocacy of voluntary motherhood and indicted women's attempts to obtain control of procreative decisions.[94]

Stanton joined in at the periphery of this debate, drawn by its attack on women. She did not engage with the moral question of abortion, but instead utilized the public attention to reframe the issue as one of women's rights more generally. She gravitated to the related, but more shocking issue of infanticide, expressing empathy for women defendants and criticism of the discriminatory legal system that convicted them. The male-dominated abortion debate provided the toehold for Stanton to get an audience for her radical ideas about women's legal and social equality, which questioned the absence of women in the legal process as well as the gendered sexual moral standard. As she had in other contexts, Stanton revealed her aptitude for capitalizing on the media's attention to keep her agenda of the broader "woman question" front and center.

Abortion had not always been publicly condemned. At common law in America, abortion was legal prior to quickening, which occurs at around four months, when fetal movement can be felt. Abortion was morally tolerated, though publicly invisible, as an "often-regrettable necessity" for poor, young, unmarried women who had been seduced. Early laws prohibited late-term abortions or targeted medical malpractice and poisonous medicines that harmed women. By midcentury, however, abortion had increased as middle-class, married people used abortion as birth control. Abortion became more visible as newspapers ran barely disguised advertisements for "French" and "Portuguese" medicines ("French" meaning contraception and "Portuguese" being code for abortion) and physician services to "restore the natural return of menses." The prevalence of abortion raised it to a public concern, fueled by nativist fears that immigrants would replace white Americans through the birth rate. The medical profession instigated the efforts for legal reform, supported by sensationalist journalism, which produced new laws that criminalized abortion at any time in every state by the turn of the century. This anti-abortion campaign was infused with anti-woman sentiments, fearful of women's growing social power and reasserting patriarchal control and women's maternal submission.[95]

The lobbying effort to criminalize abortion was spearheaded by the medical profession. In 1859, the American Medical Association (AMA) issued a resolution condemning abortion as an "unwarrantable destruction of human life." The doctors had scientific, ethical, and professional motivations for leading the charge against abortion. Practically, as doctors professionalized, the new "regulars"—male medical school graduates—sought to drive out the competing local practitioners, the untrained "irregulars"—mostly female midwives—who had monopolized obstetrical and gynecological care. Women, though, became the targeted evil. Horatio Storer, one of the first male gynecologists and the leading anti-abortion crusader of the AMA, wrote that "[t]he true wife" does not seek "undue power in public life, . . . undue control in domestic affairs, . . . or privileges not her own."[96] The AMA's 1871 *Report on Criminal Abortion* denounced the married woman who aborted a pregnancy: "She becomes unmindful of the course marked out for her by Providence, she overlooks the duties imposed on her by the marriage contract. She yields to the pleasures—but shrinks from the pains and responsibilities of maternity." The AMA campaign succeeded in convincing the public and the politicians that abortion, and women, were a threat to the social order and male authority.[97]

The campaign expressly took on the feminists and their claim of reproductive control. Nineteenth-century feminists did not publicly support abortion, just as they did not endorse legalized birth control. Abortion, like contraception, only increased male sexual license, and threatened physical harm to women from poisonous substances and surgical malpractice.[98] The physicians' campaign, however, distorted the feminists' reproductive-rights metaphor of legalized prostitution to claim that these women heretically endorsed prostitution by advocating that "man's natural sexual urges were allowed expression in marriage without reproductive consequence." Dr. H. S. Pomeroy took on Stanton directly in his book, *The Ethics of Marriage*. "There are lecturers to 'ladies only' who profess to be actuated simply by good-will toward their unfortunate sisters, who yet call woman's highest and holiest privilege by the name of slavery, and a law to protect the family from the first step toward extinction, tyranny." "There are apostles of woman's rights," he continued, who "arouse women to claim privileges now denied them. . . . And there are those who teach that their married sisters may save time and vitality for high and noble pursuits by 'electing' how few children shall be born to them."[99] Storer added that "if each woman were allowed to judge for herself in this matter, her decision upon the abstract question would be too sure to be warped by personal considerations, and those of the moment. Woman's mind is prone to depression, and indeed, to temporary actual derangement, under the stimulus of uterine excitation." Women were thus mentally incapable of making the procreative decision.[100]

The media supported the physicians' lobbying campaign, inflamed by sensational journalism. The newspapers published editorials against the "frightfully prevalent" "social evil" of "child murder," commenting that "the murder of infants is a common thing among American women." One editorial lamented that "thousands of human beings are thus murdered before they have seen the light of this world." The papers printed stories recounting the horrific details of women dying from abortions in squalid conditions and exposés on the underground abortion trade in New York City.[101] The remedy, they declared, was in the prohibition and criminalization of abortion. These mainstream papers, however, were complicit in the escalation of the abortion practice as they accepted lucrative abortion advertisements soliciting such business and selling medicinals for abortion.[102] They stopped publishing such ads only when prohibited by law, first by New York state law and then by the federal Comstock anti-obscenity law.[103]

New York, Stanton's home state, was at the forefront of this debate and evolution of the law of abortion. Early revisions of the code in 1828 and 1845 were designed to protect women from malpractice and criminalize a larger practice of behavior, but practically had little effect due to the high prosecutorial burden of proving beyond a reasonable doubt that a woman was "pregnant" and had the "intent thereby to procure a miscarriage."[104] The Medical Society of the State of New York renewed legal reform lobbying in 1867, to "arrest this flagrant corruption of morality among women, who ought to be and unquestionably are the conservators of morals and of virtue" and prohibit newspaper ads as "highly detrimental to public health and morals."[105] In 1868, the New York legislature banned advertisements for any "article or medicine for the prevention of conception or procuring of abortion."[106] Another law in 1869 made abortion at any time, including prior to quickening, illegal and removed the prosecutors' burden of proving pregnancy, and revisions in 1872 further strengthened its prohibitions and penalties.[107]

In the midst of this public and legislative frenzy over abortion in New York, Stanton began her new women's rights newspaper, the *Revolution*.[108] Starting in January 1868, the paper was drawn into the fray, designed as it was to engage its readers with all topics of the day. The paper published a few submissions opposing abortion and calling for stricter prohibitions.[109] Its financier, George Francis Train, registered his disgust of abortion, attacking the "French habits, French customs, poisonous drugs, and a false life, combined with the terrible demoralizing effect of the speculum and the lancet—the one poisoning the system, the other destroying chastity as well as maternity"—which failed to "maintain law and virtue" or "respect our manhood."[110] The *Revolution* also printed articles from feminist voices reacting to the anti-abortion campaign's demonization of women.[111] These writers, including Matilda Joslyn Gage, were "highly sympathetic to the reasons why women sought abortions" and placed the moral blame on men who refused to control their sexual demands.[112] "This crime," Gage wrote, of what the papers called "child murder," lies at the door of the male sex.[113] Another writer pointed to the larger class issues and "antagonism" underlying the abortion problem. "When the conditions of society are so false that mothers kill their own children, the trouble lies deeper down than 'Restellism.'" "Prohibitory laws and the imprisonments of the Madames Restell do not remedy drunkenness or child murder; they do not touch the case."[114]

"Restellism," the epithet for abortion, derived from the most famous practitioner of abortion from 1836 to 1878, Madame Restell (Ann

Lohman). Madame Restell flaunted a very public existence, living in a palatial mansion on Fifth Avenue in New York City and operating her practice out of her home. In addition, she sold products through the newspapers and mails. Lohman was arrested many times, but was convicted finally in 1878 following a sting operation by Anthony Comstock. She committed suicide after she lost her appeals.[115]

Stanton's male coeditor, Parker Pillsbury, also wrote several articles on abortion in the *Revolution*, revealing his moral opposition but rejecting criminal regulation. Pillsbury's moral stance against abortion was consistent with his religious belief of perfectionism and his background as a former Congregationalist minister and zealous abolitionist.[116] In the *Revolution*, he expressed his abhorrence of the "evil" crime of "foeticide" and "killing the unborn," and his concern over "the frightful increase" in abortion. He attacked those who encouraged the practice of abortion, "that very evil in all its horrible enormity and extent." He berated those like Madame Restell who profited from abortion, "those who make it a profession and grow enormously rich in the murderous business; and yet walk unblushingly, and ride most magnificently on Broadway in broad day, and receive both the gratitude and gold of those who employ them."[117]

In another *Revolution* editorial entitled "Quack Medicines," Pillsbury condemned the mainstream and religious newspapers for supporting Restellism by publishing advertisements for abortion and contraceptive medicines. He criticized them for accepting the "advertisements of professional murderers, who commit infanticide for pay," simply because the advertising patronage paid "far better than any other."[118] The *Revolution*, he said, refused to publish such "gross personalities and quack advertisements." The paper did, though, print ads for female physicians for services of an "accoucheuse" (midwife) who devoted "special attention to female disease."[119] Like the other feminist writers in the *Revolution*, Pillsbury blamed men for the unwanted pregnancies. His proposed solutions were women's empowerment and foundling hospitals run by the state that would care for the children given up for adoption.[120]

Stanton weighed in briefly in her editorial "Infanticide and Prostitution."[121] The short blurb written during the *Revolution*'s second month of operation responded to the sensationalist attacks on women in the mainstream press just as the New York legislature considered a restrictive new abortion law. She began by reprinting an excerpt from the *New York Tribune* in which that paper concluded that "the murder of infants is a common thing among American women." The *Tribune* lamented "child murder," claiming that "the murder of children, either before or after birth, has become so frightfully prevalent that physicians, who have given careful and intelligent study to the subject, have declared that were it not for immigration the white population of the United States would actually fall off!" Stanton also excerpted an article from the *New York Sun* on the "social evil statistics" of prostitution, showing how she linked together these issues as related to male licentiousness.

Stanton dismissed the moral and religious outrage directed against women. "Let us no longer weep, whine and pray over all these abominations." Instead, she cut to the underlying systemic cause of these social concerns. "We believe the cause of all these abuses lies in the degradation of woman." The only remedy, she said, was "the education and enfranchisement of woman." Stanton wrote that she was not surprised that women "do everything to avoid maternity" because maternity is presented religiously as a curse, and women "through ignorance of the science of life and health find it so." The blame instead belonged to men. "Strike the chains from your women; for as long as they are slaves to man's lust, man will be the slave of his own passions." Stanton called for the remedy of "enlightened conscientiousness" and "for every thinking man" to change things in his own household by facilitating intentional and healthful procreation.

Stanton, however, wrote nothing further on the issue. Instead, she became obsessed with the notorious trial of Hester Vaughn, sentenced to death for infanticide. The Vaughn case engaged these questions about the sexual double standard and women's reproductive control while providing the additional opportunity for Stanton to challenge the greater systemic problems of a legal system that professed to dispense justice for women without women's participation in the process.[122]

Defending Hester Vaughn

Stanton became embroiled in the case of Hester Vaughn, an eighteen-year-old, unwed English immigrant sentenced to "be hanged by the neck until she is dead," for allegedly killing her newborn infant. Vaughn worked as a domestic servant, and when she became pregnant either by rape or seduction, was forced out on the streets. She rented a room in a tenement house and there, in the dead of winter, with no heat or water, she gave birth alone. Three days later she was found in her room next to the dead infant. She was denied the right to testify at her own trial and convicted by an all-male jury. The judge sentenced her to death despite her "excellent face," "because you have no idea how rapidly the crime of infanticide is increasing. Some woman must be made an example of."[123] Stanton took on Vaughn's public defense in the pages of the *Revolution*, using it to voice her criticisms of a gendered social and legal system.[124]

Stanton called for women to come together in defense of Vaughn and "make her case your own."[125] The Working Woman's Association (WWA) responded to the call to take up the cause of Hester Vaughn.[126] The WWA was a women's labor union formed in September 1868 by Susan B. Anthony, initially comprised of skilled female typesetters demanding equal pay, but then becoming a short-lived professional association of women journalists, physicians, and teachers. During the height of the WWA's activism, the group searched for an issue or cause to elevate female workers, leery of suffrage with its negative connotations of "strong-minded women" with short hair and bloomers. Its investigative committee, led by journalist Eleanor Kirk, settled on petitioning for Vaughn's pardon and release. The WWA sent a delegation to interview Vaughn in Philadelphia, raised money, and passed resolutions challenging her conviction and condemning the death penalty.[127] Stanton and her cousin Elizabeth Smith Miller traveled to present the WWA's resolutions to Pennsylvania governor Geary, who resented their interference as New Yorkers, but promised he would not sign Vaughn's death warrant.[128] Stanton with Miller went on to visit Vaughn. She noted that "on seeing the poor girl, our interest in her greatly intensified, and we felt more than ever convinced of her innocence." Stanton complained to the guards of the mice and cockroaches that had bitten Vaughn, and received the curt reply from the guard that "a prison is not a hotel." Stanton relayed this encounter in her paper, calling for empathy and assistance to help end the suffering of people imprisoned.[129] The *Revolution*'s public defense of Vaughn triggered a backlash by the mainstream papers condemning the women's labor organization for tangling with issues like infanticide and capital punishment.[130]

Stanton developed legal critiques of the Vaughn case based on the insufficiency of the evidence and the ineffective assistance of counsel. Arguing like a criminal defense lawyer, Stanton claimed that "every lawyer accustomed to examine evidence must see the strong points for doubt as to her guilt." Citing the preeminent English treatise on criminal law, she noted that intentional infanticide is difficult to establish, as "newborn infants are easily killed by cold and starvation." The evidence in the Vaughn case fit this alternative explanation as she was alone in a cold room in the depth of winter for several days after the birth, "long enough, without any violence, for a child to die, with either cold or starvation." Feminist supporter and physician Dr. Clemence Lozier offered another explanation for the baby's death: puerperal mania and blindness caused by the birth. This temporary insanity made Vaughn unaware of her actions, and in her delirium, she may have lain on the baby after its birth. Moreover, Lozier noted, there was no evidence that the premature eight-month-old baby had in fact been born alive because no routine coroner's inquest had been made.[131]

Stanton argued that "there was so much room for doubt in the case that if she had been properly defended, the jury would either have acquitted her, or disagreed," either way resulting in her release. The ineffective assistance of counsel claim attacked the inadequacy of Vaughn's lawyer. He had failed to visit her in prison or consult with her regarding a defense, and he spoke with her only in open court. He failed to raise any defense about the stillbirth of the child, the lack of witnesses, or the potential postpartum delirium and accident. Vaughn had paid him her last thirty dollars. Stanton and the working women criticized what they called "the $30 defence" with references to the betrayal of Jesus by Judas Iscariot for thirty pieces of silver.[132]

The Vaughn case also gave Stanton the opportunity to renew her longstanding critique of the legal process and women's right to a "trial by a jury of her peers."[133] Under English common law adopted in the United States, women were excluded from juries because of "the defect of sex" making them incompetent and in need of protection from the depravity of the courts.[134] One exception during colonial times was for women to serve on a "jury of matrons" convened to determine issues of paternity, abortion, infanticide, and other cases involving verification of pregnancy, which is where Stanton's critique found grounding.[135] She argued that women should be included on juries to provide the necessary mercy required for justice. Women, she argued, who "had known the depth of a mother's love and the misery of a lover's falsehood," would understand the social norms and double standards, the limited economic and social options for unwed mothers, and the betrayal of a suitor as mitigating factors. "Shall the frenzied mother, who, to save herself and child from exposure and disgrace, ended the life that had but just begun, be dragged before" a tribunal of all men to answer for her crime? she asked. "How can man enter into the feelings of that mother? How can he judge of the mighty agonies of soul that impelled her to such an outrage of maternal instincts?"[136] Stanton criticized the bias of these all-male juries, analogizing to the technical English law of peremptory challenges for dismissal of biased jurors because of class.[137] As with peasants and nobility, Stanton said, men cannot make and execute just laws for women "because in each case, the one in power fails to apply the immutable principles of right to any grade but his own."[138]

Infanticide for Stanton starkly illustrated the male privilege of the law, enacted and enforced without women. The laws legislated and adjudicated by men penalized only the woman in the illicit relation, while exonerating the male perpetrator. While "the erring girl of eighteen may be tried and hung for the crime of infanticide, he who betrayed her trust may sit in the jury-box or on the bench, with no true women to pity or protect." "What a holocaust of women and children we offer annually to the barbarous customs of our present type of civilization, to the unjust laws that make crimes for women that are not crimes for men!" "Men," she claimed, "have made the laws cunningly, for their own protection; ignorantly, for they can never weigh the sorrows and sufferings of their victims." "The imprisonment of his victim and the death of his child, detract not a tithe from his standing and complacency. His peers made the law, and shall law-makers set nets for those of their own rank?" No women were there in defense, even as lawyers. "While they punish us for the violation of law, drag us into their courts to be tried not by our peers, but by judges, jurors, lawyers, all men, they close their law schools against us." The solution was for women to "study the laws under which they live, that they may defend the unfortunate of their sex in our courts" and for law schools to open their doors to girls "who have brains to understand the science of jurisprudence and hearts big enough to demand justice for the humblest of God's children."[139]

In spring 1869, the governor quietly pardoned Vaughn on the condition that she return immediately to England.[140] When the supporters learned of her release, they expected to meet her at the train station with donation money in hand. Vaughn never appeared. In August 1869, Dr. Susan Smith sent a letter to the *New York World* confirming that Vaughn had returned safely to England and excerpted a letter that she had received from Vaughn asking for the money her supporters had collected.[141] Hester Vaughn was never heard of again.

5

Raising "Our Girls"

*But the great work before us is the proper education of those
just coming on the stage. Begin with girls of this day, and in
twenty years we can revolutionize this nation.*
— Letter from Mrs. Elizabeth Cady Stanton to the Woman's
Rights Convention in Akron, Ohio, May 28 and 29, 1851

The final piece of the family law puzzle for Stanton was women's status
as mothers. She worked to transform the existing social and legal structure of maternity from one of subordination into one of power. This
meant endowing mothers with legal rights to custody of children and
authority in the home, displacing the absolute common law prerogative
of fathers. It required reconstructing gender roles from early childhood
by educating girls equally with boys and teaching them "masculine"
virtues of physical strength, courage, intellect, and self-sufficiency
through employment. She took this message of feminist parenting to the
masses in her "Our Girls" lyceum speech, using her motherly persona to
softly convey her radical message of reconstructing gender. Ultimately,
for Stanton, transforming maternity meant taking on the entrenched
religious doctrines that supported gender subordination by challenging church interpretations of longstanding biblical principles. These
heretical departures from accepted religious and social norms proved
too extreme for the public and other reformers. Stanton was ostracized
from the women's rights movement by a younger generation of more
conservative suffragists focused narrowly on the vote. She would not
be silenced, however, believing that transforming religious beliefs about
gender was the final battle necessary to eradicate the separate spheres
ideology of women's inferiority.

Stanton drew heavily on cultural feminist principles in advocating
maternal rights. She trumpeted women's superior differences as mothers, including their instinctual wisdom and procreative power. "Moth-

ers are second only to God," for their power to both create and nurture the next generation. Drawing on positivist theory, Stanton argued that the public sphere required restoration of balance and social equilibrium by the elevation of the distinctive "feminine element." These views provided common ground with social feminists and temperance women similarly focused on recognizing women's moral superiority as mothers. This conservative maternalism revered and sentimentalized the home and worked toward reforming men to assume their proper moral headship of the family. Stanton capitalized on this maternalist thinking to accomplish her desired ends for voting and maternal rights.[1] However, her maternal feminism strongly rejected any ideas of confining women to a domestic role with the reassertion of paternal authority and women's loss of individual and family autonomy.[2] Maternalism justified power, not limitation, and an equal role for women in the public sphere of work and political control.[3] Stanton's vision rejected all semblance of separate spheres, demanding integration of public and private roles and reciprocal obligations and rights for both men and women in all spheres.[4]

Separate Spheres

During the nineteenth century, the metaphor of "separate spheres" described the social and economic power division between men and women. Public life and private life were segregated into separate worlds by gender, with men dominant in the public world of work and governance, and women relegated to the domestic role. Women were "protected" in their homes, where their important role as citizens was that of "republican motherhood" with the responsibility for inculcating morality.[5] Some reformers advocated the separate spheres ideology in order to elevate women's rights within that sphere, for example, advancing higher education in female seminaries, separate collegiate training in home economics, or temperance reform and extension of women's morality into the public sphere through the vote.[6]

The perceived threat to this domestic sphere was a primary objection to women's rights. Activists like Stanton commonly heard the complaint of "what about the babies?"[7] Rather than accepting the juxtaposition of motherhood and feminism, Stanton appealed to the traditional ideology of republican motherhood by agreeing with the importance of mothering. "The fountain rises no higher than its source," and thus the source, mothers, needed to be empowered and elevated.[8] Mothering was important, Stanton agreed, and thus evidenced the rightful power of women, not their subservience. She boasted of her own superior mothering skills as evidence that feminism need not detract from mothering. She often gave practical advice about raising babies, disavowing conventional wisdom based on superstition and quack remedies like Mrs. Winslow's Soothing Syrup (morphine) to quiet babies. Developing her own maternal gravitas helped persuade traditional women and men that motherhood was not threatened by feminist reforms.[9]

From the beginning, however, Stanton challenged the accepted social structure of gender. In the Declaration of Sentiments, she stated that "woman has too long rested satisfied in the circumscribed limits which corrupt customs and a perverted application of the Scriptures have marked out for her, and . . . it is time she should move in the enlarged sphere which her great Creator has assigned her." It identified as one of man's wrongs to women the creation of separate spheres, in which man "has usurped the prerogative of Jehovah himself, claiming it as his right to assign for her a sphere of action, when that belongs to her conscience and her God." And it concluded "that all laws which prevent woman from occupying such a station in society as her conscience shall dictate, or which place her in a position inferior to that of man, are contrary to the great precept of nature, and therefore of no force or authority."[10]

Deconstructing the separate spheres ideology, Stanton identified three key problems: it limited women's action, it designated women as inferior, and it usurped their personal right of choice. Stanton emphasized women's "inalienable rights" to choose their own sphere of action rather than be limited, as man ordained. "If God has assigned a sphere to man and one to woman, we claim the right to judge ourselves of his design in reference to *us*, and we accord to man this privilege." She asserted that "there is no such thing as a sphere for a sex." Rather, "[E]very man has a different sphere, and one in which he may shine, and it is the same with every woman." And, she noted, "the same woman may have a different sphere at different times," citing Angelina Grimké Weld and Lucretia Mott as examples of women who alternated between the public work of abolition and the domestic work of family.[11] Only woman can decide for herself, "they who have taken their gauge of womanhood from their own native strength and dignity—they who have learned for themselves the will of God concerning them." Natural rights, not men, determined law, as men perverted God's will to subordinate women for their own purposes, as shown by customs of harems, foot binding, and widow's funeral pyres.[12] "Divine Nature," she said, "is a woman and understands all our wants and needs too well to put us in the limits usually prescribed by custom."[13] Claims of moral, intellectual, and physical inferiority, Stanton explained, were merely the result of women's prior limitation of action and not justification for such limitation.

By the 1870s, Stanton took her critique of the separate spheres to the masses, integrating some key ideas into her "Home Life" lecture.[14] Hidden within interior design advice about natural light, hardwood floors, and a second kitchen for laundry were subversive ideas for transformative change of the domestic sphere in which women abdicated their sole responsibility for housework. Stanton's bias was clear—she hated housework. She shared that "after being a housekeeper over forty years," she saw the difficulty of the "isolated household" and how women "waste their lives in domestic service" rather than paid employment at the sacrifice of individual happiness and development.[15] Referencing the work of French social utopian philosopher Charles Fourier and his criticism of the "isolated household," Stanton elaborated on how bearing the sole responsibility for housekeeping was, for the mother, overwhelming, inefficient, and soul numbing. Fourier, popularized in America in the 1840s, believed that the isolated household denied women economic and sexual independence and also that in terms of labor, "[T]he work of a single household sentenced woman to domestic drudgery, an inefficient, piecemeal approach that could be improved through communalizing domestic labor."[16]

Stanton renewed these philosophical ideas in "Home Life," painting a picture of the daily "gauntlet" of the homemaker, inundated with constant demands where "paterfamilias and every child immediately wants something," be it lost hats, missing boots, or a loose button, blaming all such calamities on the mother. "The wife, with grace, self-control, uttering no forcible expletives, tries to fill every deadly breach." At the end of the day "the school children and the man of business appear on the scene once more. And now comes dinner with its chance pitfalls, and the evening lessons to be learned for next day." Then "she who has been nurse, chamber maid, coachman, cook all day must now turn Professor of the rudiments of all branches of learning."[17] Stanton added, "[I]f to do anything beyond cooking meat and bearing children is unsexing woman," as women's rights opponents accused, "pray let her be unsexed, for that is a sphere too small to satisfy any human being."[18] Stanton's own solution was to hire a housekeeper, Quaker Amelia Willard, who remained with the family for thirty years.[19]

Stanton recommended several alternatives to "reorganize the home" to remedy women's isolation in the domestic sphere: enlisting fathers, joining associations, or residing in apartment houses. The first solution was that fathers should take on domestic responsibilities. Parents, she said, should be "co-leaders" in the home, a "wiser division of labor between Father and Mother than custom now requires." "If they propose to have children, the responsible duties of parents should be equally shared as far as possible."[20] "We would have them stay there, educate their children, provide well for their physical wants, and share in each other's daily trials and cares."[21] A second option would be for women to consider the Fourieran idea of living in cooperative households or utopian associations with shared resources, like her friends the Grimké-Welds. Stanton considered moving to the Raritan Bay Union in New Jersey, but doubted she would have enough money or that Henry would go.[22] Writing to Paulina Davis, she observed, "[A]ll our talk about woman's rights is mere moonshine so long as we are bound by the present social system" of women's designated segregation in the home.[23]

Third, she proposed apartment house living, conceived as having individualized living units, with central kitchens and nurseries staffed by specialists.[24] Foreshadowing arguments later popularized by feminist Charlotte Perkins Gilman in her critique of domestic mythology and economic inefficiency of the home, Stanton endorsed the idea of apartment living with its "scientific, sanitary, and labor-saving improvements" and its ability to reduce "the drudgery of housekeeping and homemaking to a minimum." She dismissed "frightened moralists" who feared the apartment house would lead to "the deterioration of the American home life" and the "breaking up of the privacy and sanctity of the home."[25]

Ultimately, Stanton's goal was to dismantle the separate spheres framework and integrate the spheres for both men and women. Her vision was that partners' "life work" would be "side by side." "Men should take more interest in their homes and women more in the state." "The family needs a father's thought and wisdom, and the nation needs a mother's love and care." The continued "divorce of spheres," Stanton warned, threatened fatal consequences for society at large. For an outer world of stern justice untempered by mercy makes victims of the weak, while a family of sweet mercy without justice creates tyrants of the young. Eliminating separate spheres ideology, and integrating men and women fully into all aspects of work and family life, Stanton argued, was thus the path to both social reform and women's equality.[26]

Maternal Preferences to Custody

Stanton exposed the emptiness of the separate spheres ideal for women in its lack of concrete rights for the revered mother, even as related to the domestic sphere.

> The mother must have an equal right to her children; to the home that shelters them, to the joint earnings of the co-partnership; to be the sole guardian and protector of the family and estate at the death of the husband, as the father is when left a widower. If home is the sphere of women, do make them queens in their sphere and not slaves and dependents.[27]

But that was not how the law worked.

Under English common law, the father had the unquestioned legal right to custody and guardianship of children. "Moored in the medieval equation of legal rights with property," children were considered the property of the father, "dependent . . . assets of estates in which fathers had a vested right" to labor and services in exchange for the duty of support. The mother, Blackstone explained, "was entitled to no power, but only to reverence and respect."[28]

The father's custodial prerogative included the absolute right to designate guardians for the children and bind them out as apprentices. Most American states followed the longstanding English law that a father could unilaterally establish a guardianship "by deed executed in his lifetime, or by last will and testament in writing [to] dispose of the custody of his minor children," which was "good and effective against all and every person claiming the custody and tuition of such children."[29]

While mothers exercised practical authority over their children during marriage, from a legal point of view, they were "considered as agents for their husbands, having no legal authority of their own." After a father's death, a mother was the guardian only if the father did not appoint another guardian. The mother also lost her guardianship if she remarried, as her obligation to her new husband was said to supersede any obligation to her child. The common law allowed for separate guardians of the person and the estate of the child, and in colonial America fathers frequently appointed a male guardian to control the child's monies until the age of twenty-one, even where the mother retained physical custody.[30]

Stanton attacked this common law patriarchal theory of the father's absolute power to child custody in the Declaration of Sentiments. She charged man with unjustly framing the laws of separation and guardianship "to be wholly regardless of the happiness of women—the law, in all cases, going upon the false supposition of the supremacy of man, and giving all power into his hands."[31] She raised the issue of custody again a few years later to the Second Women's Temperance Convention, encouraging them to petition the legislature[32]—which she then did herself, featuring the demand for maternal custody rights in her 1854 written address to the New York legislature.[33] Invited to lobby for the proposed married women's property act, Stanton expanded her discussion to demand a complete "new code of laws" redressing all of women's legal disabilities under coverture, including the denial of custody and guardianship of children. Judge Hertell's original 1836 proposal for marital property rights in New York had included custody, and thus custody and property were interlinked in legislative considerations of married women's rights.[34]

Stanton appealed to the cult of motherhood to make her case. "There is no human love so generous, strong and steadfast as that of the mother for her child; yet behold how cruel and ruthless are your laws touching this most sacred relation." She continued, "Nature has clearly made the mother the guardian of the child; but man, in his inordinate love of power, does continually set nature and nature's laws at open defiance." She criticized the father's ability to apprentice his child, to "bind him out to a trade or labor, without the mother's consent—yea, in direct opposition to her most earnest entreaties, her prayers and tears." Stanton noted examples of the "abuse of this absolute power," in fathers binding children to gamesters, rum sellers, or brothels in order to cancel their debts. She attacked the New York guardianship law that granted every father the right by "deed or last will" to "dispose of the custody and tuition of such child during its minority." By this law, Stanton decried, "the father, about to die, may bind out all his children wherever and to whomsoever he may see fit, and thus, in fact, will away the guardianship of all his children from the mother." Thus, she concluded, "by your laws, the child is the absolute property of the father, wholly at his disposal in life or at death."[35]

Stanton emphasized the injustice of the law that, in case of separation, "gives the children to the father; no matter what his character or condition," even in extreme cases of domestic abuse. Even if women left their abusive husbands, custody remained with the father. "All these have been robbed of their children, who are in the custody of the husband, under the care of his relatives, whilst the mothers are permitted to see them but at stated intervals." Such a result was dangerous, Stanton argued, "as the condition of the child always follows that of the mother, and as by the abuse of your laws the father may beat the mother, so may he the child." Yet "a mother's love can be no protection to a child; she cannot appeal to you to save it from a father's cruelty, for the laws take no cognizance of the mother's most grievous wrongs."[36]

Stanton's lobbying efforts were successful, if short lived. An 1854 Assembly committee report proposed to grant the mother a veto over the father's absolute guardianship rights.[37] Stanton renewed her demand again in 1860 before the New York legislature, emphasizing the injustice of this denial of basic natural rights to the mother.[38] By the time Stanton gave her delayed speech, the legislature had already passed a revised married women's property act expanding women's parental rights, which awaited the governor's signature. The new law provided that "[e]very married woman is hereby constituted and declared to be the joint guardian of her children, with her husband, with equal powers, rights and duties in regard to them, with the husband."[39] The courts, however, interpreted this statute narrowly, holding that it did not create any legal right in the mother, but simply a joint right with the father during marriage, operating under coverture and thus leaving the common law of paternal prerogative intact.[40]

Two years later, the New York legislature repealed the guardianship statute altogether.[41] The revised law of 1862 revoked the language of joint guardianship and provided only that the father must obtain the mother's consent before appointing a testamentary guardian or indenturing the child as an apprentice. Women's rights activists, distracted by war efforts, had not continued to pressure the legislature. As Stanton noted in later speaking to the 1876 American Centennial celebration, despite "years of untiring effort" to obtain guarantees of property and custody, they were "repealed in States where we supposed all was safe." She noted the larger implications of petitioning on the basis of appeal to benevolent favor. "Thus have our most sacred rights been made the football of legislative caprice, proving that a power which grants as a privilege what by nature is a right, may withhold the same as a penalty when deeming it necessary for its own perpetuation."[42] New York would, however, reinstate the 1860 joint guardianship law thirty years later, allegedly influenced by efforts of social feminist groups advocating better child protection against neglectful fathers.[43]

In custody, feminists found "a particularly effective issue" because "few areas of coverture were more directly at odds with the cult of domesticity than the father's common law right of guardianship." The accepted sanctity of motherhood called into question the continuance of a paternal prerogative and thus affiliated both feminists and maternalists, while helping to advance feminists' larger purpose of granting women legal status in the family.[44] Feminists also appealed to what seemed to them to be the illogical legal result that an unmarried woman had full, and sole, legal right to her child while a married mother had none.[45] As an 1877 convention protest decried, "The laws treat married women as criminals by taking from them all legal control of their children, while those born outside of marriage belong absolutely to the mothers."[46] Yet there was still a reluctance to grant mothers explicit legal rights.[47] The fear was that if women were granted too many rights, nothing would keep them from leaving their husbands and the family would be destroyed.[48]

These maternal parenting rights, however, developed informally through the common law judicial decisions.[49] By midcentury, courts had moved away from the absolutism of paternal power with respect to maternal custody after a divorce or separation. The evolution of the law of child custody began early in the nineteenth century, when American judges rejected the absolute property concept of the father's ownership in the child, guided by earlier English precedent.[50] They "abandoned the hierarchical concept of the family that had dominated English common law and colonial practice," while concurrently displaying a "new faith in women's innate proclivities for child rearing and in developmental notions of childhood." As a New York court explained in 1840, the law of custody had evolved from the absolute grant of right in the father to a law "placing the parents on an equality as to the future custody of the children." The law focused on the "best interests of the child," directing the court to exercise its discretion to "make such order as between the parties, for the custody, care and education of the children of the marriage, as may seem necessary and proper."[51] This was a significant shift, as "traditional paternalistic custody rules and practices disappeared," replaced by a new standard of judicial discretion. The new best interest standard focused on parental fitness and fault of the spouse in causing the separation, which matched the social norms of the republican family and maternal expertise.[52]

Mothers thus gained the ability to obtain legal custody of their children. This partial legal capacity, however, was limited in practice as courts held on to a patriarchal sense of the father's control of the family and its dependents.[53] The courts clung to the traditional view that "it can hardly be doubted that the father is entitled to the custody of his infant children" and that "where . . . differences unfortunately exist between the parents, the right of the father is preferred to that of the mother," unless he has forfeited that right by misconduct. An article in the *Revolution* gave another example of a decision by the respected jurist Justice Cardozo, who as a state court judge ordered the temporary placement of a child with a "lady friend" of the father, removing it from the mother. When the mother hysterically chased the child out of the courtroom, Cardozo reversed his decision and allowed the child to remain with the mother during the pending litigation. The attorney submitting this report commented on the injustice of the decision and of a law that allowed the judge to "tear a child from its mother's arms and consign it to a strange woman, at the will of a husband who has voluntarily parted with his wife, because of *his superior* rights."[54]

At this same time in many states, the best interest standard developed further into a maternal preference. The change was triggered by reform in English law and Parliament's passage of the Infant Custody

Bill of 1839. The bill was a result of intense lobbying efforts from Caroline Norton, well known in feminist circles for the injustice of her case of marital separation. Norton, the daughter of a prominent English political family and author of popular fiction stories, separated from her violently abusive husband. The law allowed only the husband the right to initiate divorce, and Norton's spouse failed to prove her alleged adultery with the prime minister. In the separation, however, he retained custody of their four children and ownership of all earnings from his wife's books. The new Infant Custody Bill granted mothers the right to petition for custody of children under age seven and seek access to children under sixteen, thus altering the common law paternal custody right. However, Norton's husband evaded the new law by taking the children to Scotland, where one child died without seeing his mother again.[55]

American courts began to adopt rules recognizing mothers' priority in custody of young children by judicial rule and in some states by statute. This "tender years presumption" evolved to usually grant custody to the mother under the principle that a child of "tender years" under seven should be placed with mother as the more naturally nurturing parent.[56] As a Philadelphia court explained in a widely publicized case, "the reputation of a father may be stainless as crystal, he may not be afflicted with the slightest mental, moral, or physical disqualification from superintending the general welfare of the infant . . . and yet the interest of the child may imperatively demand the denial of the father's right, and its continuance with the mother." Understanding that the father would engage a third-party relative or servant to raise the child, the court held, while

> not doubting that parental anxiety would seek for and obtain the best substitute which could be procured, every instinct of humanity unerringly proclaims that no substitute can supply the place of her, whose watchfulness over the sleeping cradle or waking moments of her offspring is prompted by deeper and holier feelings than the most liberal allowance of a nurse's wages could possibly stimulate.[57]

Courts, however, continued to exercise their discretion, even under the tender years presumption, and denied custody to mothers engaged in "immoral" activity like adultery, divorce, or antireligion, or when mothers lacked the economic ability to support the child.[58]

Stanton believed too in this superior biological and experiential ability of women to parent children and its basis for mother's preferential rights. "The love of children," she stated, "is not strong in most men, and they feel but little responsibility in regard to them. See how readily they turn off young sons to shift for themselves, and unless the law compelled them to support their illegitimate children, they would never give them a second thought."[59] Stanton discounted the father's real interest in custody disputes, appreciating the strategic wrangling of litigation.

> Where the mother is capable of training the children, a sensible father would leave them to her care, rather than place them in the hands of a stranger. But where divorce is not respectable, men who have no paternal feeling will often hold the child, not so much for its good, or his own affection, as to punish the wife for disgracing him.

The tender years presumption turned out to be a "double-edged sword for women." It achieved concrete legal rights for women, but by reinforcing stereotypes of gender. The precedent thus limited the ability to extend these legal gains to other civil rights or translate the advances into greater gender reform. In addition, it simply substituted judicial discretion for the husband's; it still gave no legal right to the mother. Stanton noted in 1900 that "in thirty-seven States to-day a married mother has no right to her own children," and she encouraged the conservative Mothers' Congress to add the issue of custody to its agenda.[60]

"Our Young Girls"

Securing women's legal custodial rights was only part of Stanton's intended reform. She had a more ambitious strategy of reconstructing the way gender roles were socially established. Stanton was convinced that permanent cultural change required a reeducation of gender roles at the grassroots level, retraining the next generation of children in new gender expectations. "The only hope of a radical reform in social life, lies in the education of children, their development is the starting point of the philosopher." She argued that "for a Revolution in the whole life of the race," a new type of womanhood was required. Otherwise, each generation continued to learn by observing its own parental role models, thereby perpetuating the "same feudal hierarchy of the saintly and moral mother subject to the authority and brute force of the father."[61]

To eliminate this gender hierarchy of male power and female subordination, Stanton proposed to teach girls "masculine" virtues and boys "feminine" virtues. Girls would be empowered to independence, while boys would be socialized without male privilege.[62] Instead, under the status quo, girls were socialized to be "ladylike," delicate, concerned with fashion, and "afraid alike of a thunder-storm and a mouse." Boys were taught that they were entitled to education, advancement, and superiority over girls. To counter this ingrained socialization, Stanton proposed to teach girls from a young age to be courageous, educated, and self-supporting—and to teach them alongside boys to eliminate the idea of privilege and a separate degraded class.[63]

Stanton's ideas for this resocialization of gender emerged from her own frustrating experience with the limitations of her sex. She previewed these thoughts in the early 1850s, writing to conventions and presenting them at her Seneca Falls "conversationals." She revealed her own regrets and ennui from the false socialization of girls as she was raised, training them only for marriage and home. She lamented the utter "vacuity" of girls' lives, "without aim, object, plan or design" or profession. Autobiographically, she lamented the case of the school girl who wins prizes in math and language yet is unable to obtain further college education or profession because she was not a boy.[64] Over a decade later, Stanton developed these ideas about changing the socialization of girls into articles for the *Revolution* entitled "Our Young Girls" and "The Coming Girl," and later expanded and featured them in her most popular lyceum speech, "Our Girls."[65] Stanton's deliberate choice of the word "girls" was intended to convey empowerment as she rejected the use of the conventional term "young ladies" and its connotations of fragility, fear, and need for protection.

Stanton's "Our Girls" thesis, simplified for her lecture audiences, was that mothers should teach their girls to be "healthy, wealthy and wise."[66] This nonthreatening rhyme fit with the motherly persona she emphasized on the circuit of empathy and caring based on her own experiences as a mother of seven children, which softened her "wholesale

OPERA HOUSE, MASSILLON.

ELIZABETH CADY STANTON.

Saturday Evening, Feb'y 6, 1875.

LECTURE, "OUR GIRLS."

"Our Girls" poster, 1875.

attack on traditional gender roles." What she was arguing, however, was that the traditional masculine virtues of physical strength, autonomy, courage, and independence belonged to women. Girls should be healthy, physically strong; wealthy, engaged in professional market work; and wise, educated equally with boys to a profession and political role. On the surface, "Our Girls" was a practical, entertaining, and inspirational talk about parenting by a mother who offered commonsense advice. "At a deeper level, however, 'Our Girls' was a bold attack" on traditional gender roles, which encouraged mothers to examine their own degradation.[67]

Stanton's first point in "Our Girls" was that women should strive for physical health, rejecting the status quo of women's presumed weakness. Women's inferior physical size and strength was often used to rationalize their subjugation, as Stanton addressed in her speech on women's rights just after Seneca Falls.[68] Moreover, women themselves accepted this cultural norm of delicacy and timidity with their tight-corseted waists, sickness, and invalidity. "Nine tenths of American women are invalids, and an increasing number of our girls go annually to the insane asylum."[69] Stanton instead recommended a new type of womanhood of strong physical health. Beginning in youth, girls should run free with the boys, climb trees, skate, swim, "wash their brothers' faces in the snow, and beat them in a race on yonder pond."[70] Girls needed exercise, not warnings about getting their dresses dirty.[71] She rejected the main conventional activity for girls, needlework, as a "one-eyed demon of destruction."[72] She advocated a game of billiards and horseback riding for young women rather than "an anxious hour over a cook-stove."[73] And she embraced the new sport of bicycling for women, ignoring medical experts who warned that cycling would deplete women's reproductive health and cause cancer, and conservatives who feared cycling would make women more "manly."[74]

Stanton raised her own children just as she recommended. The girls were raised the same as the boys, all allowed to run free and play. Stanton converted her Seneca Falls barn into a gymnasium where the children could play during the long New York winters.[75] She encouraged daily exercise, walks in the sunshine, nutritious food like "tender beefsteak" and not peanuts, and "plenty of sleep."[76] She once told a story of a father, clearly Henry, who pontificated that his girls should be raised like boys, until he saw his daughter climbing high in a tree. Stanton recounted: he cried out, "my daughter, do not go any higher." "Why not?" said she. "Bob goes to the top; I have two legs as he," and on she went. Stanton told how she "promptly called his attention to the effect of such remarks, and added, 'Fortunately your daughter's confidence in herself is stronger than her reverence for your authority, and she takes her rights.'"[77]

In advocating physical health for girls, Stanton cited to the work of Dr. Diocletian Lewis, a temperance leader and the noted founder of physical education.[78] She liked how Lewis was "rapidly changing our ideas of feminine beauty" with his endorsement of "large waists and strong arms of the girls under his training."[79] Lewis established public gyms in Boston and developed physical education at the girls' school he ran from 1864 to 1867. In 1871, he published a book, *Our Girls*, advocating in conversational style his advice to girls on dress, health, work, and exercise. He counseled on "the importance of soap," recommended "naked sunshine baths," and extolled the virtues of "the waists of jolly grandmothers." He had diet advice as well. "Are you too fat?" "Eat less food, with a larger proportion of meat; rise early in the morning and exercise much." Or, "are you too thin?" Then sleep more and eat lots of oatmeal and cereal with sugar.[80] Stanton chimed in with her own diet advice. "Eat regularly three times a day; don't be munching candies, peanuts, and other like things between meals; let your digestive organs have some rest."[81]

Like Lewis's advice, Stanton's "Our Girls" theory of physical health included an indictment of fashion and the beauty myth of feminine dress.[82] Fashionable dress sent the wrong message, of frailty, flirtation, and artificial beauty. Cosmetics enforced this false appearance, and threatened harm with white lead. True beauty, she said, "depends far more on the culture of the intellect, the tastes, sentiments, and affections of the soul, on an earnest unselfish life purpose to leave the world better than you find it, than the color of the hair, eyes, or complexion." [83] Other fashion physically harmed women, from high heels to chignons to tight corsets disrupting digestion, bruising ribs, and impeding exercise and deep breathing.

Stanton had embraced dress reform in the early 1850s, adopting the Bloomer dress for convenience and feminist statement.[84] The Bloomer dress was named for Stanton's Seneca Falls neighbor and *Lily* editor Amelia Bloomer, who published articles advocating the "Turkish dress" of long, loose pants tight at the ankles, with a mid-calf-length dress.[85] The costume, however, attracted widespread public ridicule, revealing how threatening dress reform was to the very image of gender. The Bloomer became a symbol of feminism that stirred up "the public's deepest fears about femininity, masculinity, and the division of labor."[86] Tired of the distraction from other important issues, Stanton abandoned the Bloomer dress. Her cousin Gerrit Smith, however, disagreed with her, arguing in a public letter that dress reform was the most pragmatic and attainable of women's rights. He encouraged her and all women to reject the absurd conventional dress and "its symbol of false doctrines and degradation" that imprisons and cripples.[87] Stanton agreed, but knowing how dress detracted from the broader agenda, reminded Smith that there were many more important rights at stake.[88]

Elizabeth Cady Stanton in Bloomer costume, 1851.

In "Our Girls" Stanton "struck at the deeper, root causes of gender discrimination in child rearing and education" by examining the psychological impact of gender subordination.[89] While young girls might be free to play with the boys, they soon learned as boys prepared for higher education and vocation that "one sex was made to clutch the stars, the other but to kiss the dust." Watch awhile, Stanton said, and you will see these noisy, happy, healthy girls grow pale, sad, listless, and unsatisfied, for "they have awakened to the fact that they belong to an ostracized, a degraded class; that to fulfil their *man-appointed sphere* they are to have no individual character, freedom, life, purpose, fame or immortality. They are simply to revolve round one man, to live only for him." They are never to know the "freedom and dignity that one secures in self-dependence and self-support." "The hope of marriage, all we offer girls, is not enough to feed an immortal mind. . . . [T]he more fire and genius a girl has, with no outlets for her powers, the more complete is her misery." Fires that might have glowed with "living words of eloquence in courts of justice, in the pulpit, or on the stage" are instead consuming their victims in insane asylums, domestic discontent, and vain pursuits of pleasure and fashion.[90]

Stanton emphasized how segregated and inferior education produced this negative societal effect of entrenching male privilege. "What adds to the girl's humiliation, is the fact that the boy finds out that to him alone the world is free, to be, to do, to dare all that he can." The whole world supports him and urges him on, while he sees that girls are not encouraged in the same way, blocked instead by law and custom. "In these artificial distinctions boys learn their first lessons of contempt for all womankind," Stanton said. "They naturally infer that they are themselves endowed with some superior powers, to match their superior privilege." Stanton charged that "custom has made this type of boy, and now these boys perpetuate the custom." They make the creeds, the codes, and the constitutions, while woman is nothing but "an appendage to lordly man."[91]

This result of privilege and subordination, Stanton said, must change. "Our daughters are nouns—not adjectives," she said.[92] They were active subjects in their own right, not "appendages made to qualify somebody else." Stanton thus demanded that society give "the girl the same sense of dignity, of self-respect, of freedom that the boy has."[93] "Take down your fences everywhere for sex, throw your time-worn theories to the winds, and let your daughters feel that they too have a right to the universe; that their home is the world and their duties wherever they find food for thought or work to do." This required teaching girls to reject the prejudice of public sentiment and showing them "how worthless and rotten a thing it is." "It is a settled axiom with me that public sentiment is utterly false on every subject," Stanton said, and yet what a tyrant it was, especially over woman, educated that it was "her highest ambition to be approved."[94]

While audiences flocked to Stanton's "Our Girls" message, journalists reminded readers of the dangerously radical message of her lecture. A reporter for the Dubuque, Iowa, paper expressed the conventional view that society rejected Stanton's subversive proposal for gender reversal. "We do not love a 'manly woman,' neither can we endure a 'womanly man,' and in the popular acceptation of woman's rights we don't believe." The writer elaborated. "A true woman despises femininity in man and as a natural sequence a true man ought to detest masculinity in a woman." He then took a dig at Stanton. "For a man to reflect softness and delicacy instead of strength and courage is no less out of place than for a woman to assume masculinity and seek out clear notoriety in the lecture room." The editorial concluded with a reminder of woman's proper place. "Our impression is that woman shines most brightly at home; the domestic circle should be her pride; her family her chief desire."[95] Yet despite this early rejection of her idea of gender osmosis, Stanton continued her "Our Girls" message, and developed a companion piece fleshing out the second part of the equation, changing the definition of masculinity.

"Our Boys"

Stanton expanded her plan of recreating gender through parenting by developing a parallel theory for educating boys. Boys needed "feminine virtues" of morality, grace, and manners, just as much as girls needed the masculine virtues.[96] In her "feminist perspective on child-rearing," Stanton rejected the harsh discipline and religious indoctrination of patriarchal culture and endorsed experimental models of more liberal approaches" of practical training, scientific inquiry, and compulsory education. These ideas "challenged prevailing social and religious norms and envisioned a new, more progressive democratic culture." As a skeptical local newspaper noted, her advice on "the management and training of boys" might appear "rational," but it differed "materially from views held by the mass of professing Christian parents."[97]

Stanton's ideas about educating boys, like those about educating girls, developed early during the height of her parenting years. Writing in the *Lily* in the early 1850s in her "Letters to Mothers" series, she explored the question of "what shall be done with the boys," "who are coarse, rude and vicious, and roam the streets by day and night disturbing the quiet of our town. They annoy us in our homes by breaking our windows, fences and trees; in public meetings by their noise and laughter; in the streets by their disrespect and vulgarity." Stanton identified the problem as boys "hav[ing] nothing to do" and being "under no restraint." It was the mother's obligation, she said, to keep them in at night and contribute to their higher development by interesting them in playing organized games, reading books, and drawing pictures around the evening table.

She also recommended that the boys learn to do their own sewing "with a neat little instrument called scissors." "In this way the boys doing their own mending, and the father, when he returns from his office or store doing his, the mother can have some time to the improvement of herself and children" and play games with the children like chess, conundrums, and "puss in the corner," as Stanton did herself.[98]

Yet, despite Stanton's depiction of herself as the omnipotent mother, her own boys were terrors. She told stories of their mischief and her stress in trying to deal with them while also accomplishing her work. She wrote to Anthony of how she was staying up late at night to finish the requested 1854 address to the New York legislature, but was stymied by the boys and their escapades.[99] "Yesterday one of the boys shot an arrow into my baby's eye. The eye is safe, but oh! my fright when I saw the blood come and the organ swell, and witnessed her suffering! What an escape! Imagine if I had been in Rochester when this happened!" In another story, one son made a life preserver of corks and "tested its virtues on a brother about eighteen months old." "Accompanied by a troop of expectant boys, the baby was drawn in his carriage to the banks of the Seneca, stripped, the string of corks tied under his arms, and set afloat in the river, the philosopher and his satellites in a row-boat, watching the experiment." The child, allegedly, splashed as if it was his morning bath, but "he was as blue as indigo, and as cold as a frog when rescued by his anxious mother." Another time, that same "victimized infant was seen by a passing friend, seated on the chimney, on the highest peak of the house," placed there by the older boys. Stanton recounted how the older boys locked the youngest in the smokehouse. And in yet another episode, she wrote to a friend of how Bob was "at present unfortunately in the throwing-stone dispensation. I pay for many more broken glasses than is at all desirable considering my resources."[100] As adults, only Neil showed signs of some of this mischief, with his involvement in the custom bribery scandal and shady dealings in Reconstruction. Three sons, Henry, Gat, and Bob, practiced law often "with more causes than effects." Theodore was the only son to develop along Stanton's ideal of masculinity. He moved to France, where he married and was politically active, writing *The Woman Question in Europe*.[101]

Stanton drew on these personal experiences to establish her credibility in proposing the changes in parenting developed in her "Our Boys" lecture, introduced in 1875. "Having five boys of my own," she said, "I have had some experience in the perverse ways of these sons of Adam." As with "Our Girls," Stanton used "entertaining stories, motherly advice, and a patriotic celebration" to soften the edges of her radical social critique of gender and "vision of revolutionary change in the socialization and education of young boys." She rejected the conventional wisdom of raising boys with strictness, somber discipline, religious fear, punishment, and hard physical labor. Alternatively, she proposed that boys be raised with kindness, entertainment, emotion, and education. She discussed three successful reform experiments that she said illustrated the wisdom of this approach. These were a wealthy French industrialist's housing and educating boys with daycare, kindergarten, practical training, and libraries; a young female schoolteacher from Buffalo who "feminized" the boys by cultivating kindness, etiquette, and the "polite" arts of music and conversation; and a Brooklyn pastor whose church-based social club of a shooting gallery and library of popular books saved troubled boys. Stanton endorsed billiards, card games, gymnasiums, and keeping public parks and venues open on Sunday to entertain the boys of all classes.[102] This socialization also included teaching boys sexual responsibility and the importance of abstaining from fatherhood until they were financially able to support children. She noted "the importance of giving our sons and daughters some lessons on this divine passion, that they may keep it pure, undimmed for one worthy of such centered affection." "Though young people," she said, "pride themselves on their multiplied love experiences, yet there is no greater misfortune."[103] Stanton's alternative vision also advocated compulsory public education for the masses. Boys of both wealthy and working classes should be taught together in the new kindergartens and then in the same upper-level curriculum in practical, experiential knowledge of science and hands-on experimentation. "Capitalists should remember want breeds discontent, and discontent revolution. Our people should be educated, and should possess inviolable homesteads," she said.[104]

"A Purse of Her Own"

Stanton's "Our Girls" arguments that girls should be taught to be "wealthy and wise" were part of her larger agenda of economic independence as a core of women's equality. "The coming girl" of the next generation must be educated and engaged in market work. "There must be a money value upon her time."[105] Stanton gave her daughter Maggie the same advice while she was in college. "Fit yourself to be a good teacher or professor so that you can have money of your own and not be obliged to depend on any man for every breath you draw."[106] Economic autonomy, what Stanton called "a purse of their own," was critical for all women.[107] She tried to explain to women how "a right over my *subsistence,* is a power over all my thoughts and actions," and thus a reason to resist dependency.[108] Self-support was the individual transformative act by which each woman could shift the gender power in her own life, while also contributing to the broader shift in gendered power.[109]

First, women required higher education for a trade or profession. As she protested in the Declaration of Sentiments, man "has denied her the facilities for obtaining a thorough education—all colleges being closed against her," and "he has monopolized nearly all the profitable employments, and from those she is permitted to follow, she receives but a scanty remuneration. He closes against her all the avenues to wealth and distinction, which he considers most honorable to himself. As a teacher of theology, medicine, or law, she is not known." Historically, girls had not been educated. In colonial times they were not educated at all, and later were educated only through primary school or with some private schooling at home.[110] As Stanton chronicled, "Girls always had fewer privileges than boys. When free schools were first established they were not allowed to enter. Their education was limited to the 'dame' schools, where they were taught to patch quilts, dress dolls, work a sample with the alphabet and numerals, and also to study the catechism and spelling book." She recounted how "great efforts were made to keep them in their appropriate sphere. More advanced classes were permitted to study addition, subtraction, multiplication and division, but fractions and interest were considered too intricate for their delicate brains."[111] Stanton recalled the time when "not a college in the land admitted women, and even Oberlin, the first to open its doors, did not grant them the same privileges as to men students."[112] Although by 1879 approximately half of the nation's colleges were coeducational, women were not admitted to the standard "male curriculum," but instead relegated to programs in home economics or female training.[113] Other female seminaries for women taught some academic courses, but were mostly finishing schools teaching dance, art, and music. These schools rationalized higher education as important for women to be competent mothers and wives. Stanton attended Emma Willard's seminary, considered one of the more progressive for the time, but she hated it, and resented her father's refusal to send her to college despite her outstanding academic performance and ambition.[114]

In her speech, "The Co-Education of the Sexes," Stanton summed up the main objection to coed college education for women, which was the supposed danger to their moral purity and health. It was claimed that the sexes were different and thus required different education; women would lower the grade of scholarship and morals; girls had not sufficient strength of mind and body; it would make boys effeminate, less brave and manly; and boys and girls could not study together as they would be constantly flirting. Medical experts warned that collegiate education, especially math and science, endangered women's reproductive health and that their nervous systems would be disturbed by the impossible "effort to cram mathematics into the female mind" and the demonstrably smaller brain. These experts, including the president of Harvard College, claimed that college for women was "dangerous," "impracticable," "at variance with the ordinances of God," and "destructive of the health, morals, and manners of our girls."[115]

Stanton rejected all of these claims. She pointed out that coeducation had already been happening and was a demonstrable success. Elementary schools, country schools, normal schools for teachers, western universities, and colleges like Michigan and Cornell had experimented in coeducation and shown only that good moral behavior survived and that girls in fact elevated the scholarship, earning top prizes and being more conscientious in study. Real friendships took the place of flirtation, building the foundation, Stanton argued, for better, and later, marriages. The real problem was that "'inferiority' is what these gentlemen really mean when they talk of a 'difference in sex.'" Of course there was a difference in sex, she said, whether moral, spiritual, vegetable, or animal; that was the biological fact. "But this difference in the sexes is too subtle, and as yet too little understood to attempt to shape all the conditions of life with reference to it." What mattered was that the same faculties and power of mind were common to both sexes, and that was what was relevant to education. She advocated for the elite schools of the East like Harvard, Yale, and Columbia to open their doors to girls: "It is important for the girls now knocking at the doors of these venerable institutions to know that they have a right inside." While opponents feared that coeducation would "undermine the whole foundation of our social edifice," that was exactly what Stanton intended.[116]

The second step for women establishing a purse of their own was work. Stanton viewed work as important for economic survival, intellectual actualization, and social power.[117] It would be better, she argued, for parents to "teach their daughters trades and professions, and thus have them prepared to battle successfully for themselves, than to leave them dependent."[118] Women should be trained as store clerks, postal workers, printers, railroad conductors, steamship captains, photographers, telegraph operators, and carriage drivers.[119]

Of course, women already worked, as Stanton noted. Women worked in family businesses in taverns and mercantiles, and laboring women worked in factories. Over 50 percent of African American women worked outside the home, often as domestic servants.[120] Women like Susan Anthony became teachers, drawn by the intellectual work and tolerated by society, who saw the profession as an extension of the republican motherhood ideal of women educating young sons.[121] Other women, Stanton noted, worked in public capacities doing charitable work in prisons, tenements, and hospitals, though, she remarked, "somehow women's duties are always gratuitous," volunteered rather than compensated.[122] She also noted the disconnect between this breadwinner ideology and the reality of many working-class women, the "thirty thousand sewing women in New York City" who could not simply "sit in the shade to be delicate and helpless" while cheering on their men with "soft smiles."[123] The question, she said, "is not what advantage you and I, who have friends, education and position, shall secure for ourselves; but what shall we do for those who are perishing for work and wages."[124] "It is your duty and mine," she said, "and our interest, too, to open new avenues for work and wages to this class of women."[125]

Stanton also demanded the right of women to equal pay. She appreciated both the financial burden to individual women from unequal pay and the class-wide gendering of female employments that reduced the market compensation.[126] Teachers presented the classic problem and consequences of unequal pay. "What is the reason," Stanton asked, "that to-day the majority of the teachers in all our schools are women?" "Is it because women are better teachers than men? Not at all—simply because they teach at half-price." And why were so few able and ambitious men found "in that most important of all professions" as the educators of the nation? Only one reason: "[W]oman, by her cheap labor, has driven man out and degraded that profession."[127] She demanded equal wages for female typesetters and a higher minimum wage for domestic workers, who were mostly women.[128] One reporter doubted that Stanton's prescription for equal pay was reasonable. "Mrs. S. may make the opportunities equal, but she can't regulate wages, and legislatures of women couldn't do that; the law of demand and supply will take care of that."[129] When legislatures did propose instead to limit women's wages by restricting them from certain industries on protectionist grounds, Stanton objected. She appealed to the Thirty-First Woman's Rights Convention to protest this "crusade by men as a piece of arrant hypocrisy," arguing that none of these industries were "more trying to health and womanly refinement than standing at the wash tub, the ironing board or over the cooking stove all day" or scrubbing floors or washing clothes in the depth of winter and that they operated only to impose "lower wages than she could earn in the popular industries side by side with man in the world of work."[130]

Stanton's solution to women's equality grounded in work was resisted even by those sympathetic to her more formalistic reforms. An Iowa reporter excoriated her attempts to challenge the gendered order. He thought Stanton should "stick to the facts" of formal legal reform, doing "much good by exposing glaring injustices and absurdities in jug-handle laws" and urging that "all the artificial tight-lacing of a social, business and political sort [be] cast off from women's ribs." He thought her ill advised to challenge the "fact of sex and special functions in life" as "if they were mere arbitrary laws and contrivances of man," as it would only "upset the natural scheme and lead [to] a hermaphrodite career." For, the reporter concluded, "after all is said and done, . . . there remains the inevitable fact of sex. Man, like the rest of nature, is dual, and there must be a division of labor. While there are Amazons among women, men were meant to be the protectors and providers." Women "were meant to keep the home and raise the children. That is the general rule." While he did not begrudge "to woman a single place or privilege that man takes," including the right to teach, preach, navigate, plead, practice medicine, edit, build railroads, or manufacture, he thought that "such optimists as Mrs. S raise false hopes, and confuse facts and relations." Given family relationships, "practically, not one married woman in 1,000, perhaps not one in 10,000, will ever do these things *if* she is a mother, *if* she keeps a place that can be called a home—no more than there will be one husband in 1,000 or 10,000 that will nurse children or keep house and mend clothes." For if "instinct and taste and necessity do not prevent her, the competition of the wages will." What employer, he asked, would offer women equal wages knowing the possible "contingencies" of pregnancy, childcare, and menstruation? "Her body is, up to an uncertain age, surrounded with a Zodiac of 12 monthly signs; being a wife she is liable to become a mother (unless she commits sexual crimes, which the 'advanced' reformed woman will not do)." In the evolutionary survival of the fittest in wage competition, women would lose out.[131]

Stanton's proposal for women's paid work thus clashed with engrained norms of the male provider. Man was defined by his public work, woman defined by her work and protection in the home.[132] Stanton's proposal shattered this accepted gender ideology. This custom against women working, Stanton said, was a result not of their own inability but of men's pride. "This sentiment is not based on chivalry for woman, for wives are permitted to do all kinds of menial service in their homes. But on man's pride. It is considered a blow at their dignity and efficiency as business men to have their wives receive money for work in the outside world."[133] It was time to accept dignity and ambition in women as equally important. "Work is worship" for men, and should similarly be an expected obligation and a respected vocation for women.[134] "Women who work must be regarded as honorable as men who work. Now a woman who works is dropped from society. I hope the time is coming when a woman who has nothing to do will be regarded with the contempt that an idle young man now is."[135] And women's ambition and career should not trigger the type of social humiliation and ridicule women currently face. "Not a woman who has found an occupation outside of domestic life has escaped injustice, however small, done her simply because of her sex."[136] In claiming a career, a woman "meets a dozen obstacles where a man does one," in both the usual battles for "bread and life" and the additional burden of "these artificial barriers of law and custom."[137] Stanton's daughters fulfilled her vision of women aspiring to a professional career. They both attended Vassar, a single-sex college that contradicted Stanton's ideals—but their tuition was paid by their Stanton aunts. Maggie became a physical education teacher. Harriot was frustrated that she could not attend Cornell, where she could have studied economics, history, and math, but she did become a civil engineer and later feminist and labor activist, following in her mother's steps.[138]

Stanton continued to return to her core argument that women's pecuniary independence was critical to their ability, and right, to self-sufficiency. She offered a reality check, reminding women that most of them would have to support themselves at some point in their lives. "The theory is that each woman will have some strong right arm to lean upon, but the facts are otherwise. . . . Husbands may die or become bankrupt, and their wives should be able to support themselves."[139] The sentimental imagery of the oak and vine "as representing the true relation of man and woman," she said, "melts into thin air before the facts of life." The oak, the father of the family, is often struck down, while the mother is left to support herself and her children.[140] Without work, she melodramatically argued, want may drive women to walk the streets as prostitutes if they are not taught to earn a living.

Stanton later featured this idea of the necessity of women's self-dependence in what would become one of her most famous addresses, "The Solitude of Self."[141] Scholars have suggested that this speech, introduced very late in Stanton's life, was an evolution of thought—but it was nothing new.[142] The importance of women's self-dependency was always evident in Stanton's feminist advocacy. From her earliest iteration of "Our Girls" in 1853, she discussed each woman's solitude, need for self-reliance, and risk of dependency.[143] "Fathers, Brothers, Husbands die, banks fail, houses are consumed with fire, friends prove treacherous, creditors grasping and debtors dishonest." In such circumstances, "the skill and cunning of a girl's own brains and hands are the only friends that are ever with her, the only sure means of self protection and support."[144] By the early 1890s, Stanton made this theme of self-sufficiency the primary focus of her "Solitude of Self" address, frustrated by women's continued resistance to their own empowerment. In her speeches to the annual women's rights convention and before the congressional

suffrage committee, Stanton directed her remarks to the continued social expectation of women's dependence and isolation in the domestic
sphere. She appealed to women to prepare themselves to navigate their
own way through the "fierce storms of life." Each person, she said, comes
into the world alone and leaves the world alone, as husbands leave and
children marry.[145] Each woman, Stanton argued, must be able to pull
herself through, armed with the economic resources of education, work,
and the vote.

"A Change of Employments"

Stanton's goal was not just for women to work, but to work in positions
of power. "Money is power," she said. "Now, man will not, of course,
help along a cause that he blindly supposes hostile to his own interests.
So, what money we have, we must make; and the question is, how are
we to get this last essential requisite?"[146] Her answer was "by a change
of employments." "The mass of women in this country support themselves, and although they work a lifelong, and, as a general thing, sixteen
hours out of the twenty-four, but very few have, by their own industry, amassed fortunes. And why? Because the employments they have
chosen are unprofitable, slavish, and destructive." From seamstresses to
teachers, women had been permitted only occupations with scant remuneration.[147] Instead, she commanded women to take "what belongs to
us" and "take possession of all those profitable posts, where the duties
are light, which have heretofore been monopolized by man."[148] In particular, she recommended law, medicine, theology, and academia as
the preferred professions of power.[149] In her ideal, women would not
merely join these professions, but improve them. Speaking to a graduat-
ing class of women physicians, she said, "I hope women are not to enter
this profession as men, merely to follow in their footsteps and echo their
opinions, but to bring the feminine element into this science, which, in
its greater tenderness, caution, and affection," will expand into wellness
and hygiene rather than only systems of therapeutics.[150]

Stanton often encouraged women to become lawyers. This may have
been her own personal ambition, given her work and training with her
father, and her knowledge and advocacy of legal reform. She recommended women to the legal profession, for "if the elevating, purifying

influence of woman is needed anywhere, it is in our courts of justice, especially in those cases involving the interests of her own sex."[151] Stanton directed fathers to teach their daughters their own profession, particularly the profession of law, as she wished her own father had done. "What possible objection is there in educating your daughters for that profession?" she said. "If woman has the gift of eloquence, could man plead as well as she all those cases in which the interests and disappointments of her sex are so deeply involved? How can man weigh all the nice causes by which she is outraged and undone?" She appealed to men's business interests, arguing that "your daughters of ordinary capacity could attend to your office and financial business and they would feel a far deeper interest in all your affairs than any mere stranger possibly could." And she appealed to them as fathers.

> Would not the reading of Blackstone and Kent's commentaries enlarge their minds quite as much as the yellow covered literature of the day? Would not daily talks with sensible men, with bankers, farmers and merchants, on statute law, land titles, bonds and mortgages, for which they might receive a fee of $5 of $10, be quite as profitable as a three hour's chat with a dandy, on high life, its fashions and follies?[152]

The law, however, did not support Stanton's prescription for women lawyers. In 1873, the U.S. Supreme Court in *Bradwell v. Illinois* denied Myra Bradwell's right to be admitted to the Illinois bar to practice law.[153] Bradwell had trained in law in her husband's practice, passed the bar examination with high honors, and edited the *Chicago Legal Times*, obtaining a public grant to issue authoritative recordings and analyses of the courts. The state bar refused to admit her to practice, which the Illinois Supreme Court upheld. The U.S. Supreme Court agreed, interpreting the privilege and immunities clause of the newly enacted Fourteenth Amendment as not protecting the right to work as a privilege of national citizenship. A concurrence by Justice Bradley, however, made it clear that the decision was in large part about women's rights, as several justices who had found a right to work in the *Slaughter-House Cases* announced the day before denied that right as applied to women. In the now infamous passage by Justice Bradley, he reaffirmed the separate spheres ideology, coverture, and the incapacity of women:

The civil law, as well as nature herself, has always recognized a wide difference in the respective spheres and destinies of man and woman. Man is, or should be, woman's protector and defender. The natural and proper timidity and delicacy which belongs to the female sex evidently unfits it for many of the occupations of civil life. The constitution of the family organization, which is founded in the divine ordinance, as well as in the nature of things, indicates the domestic sphere as that which properly belongs to the domain and functions of womanhood. The harmony, not to say identity, of interest and views which belong, or should belong, to the family institution is repugnant to the idea of a woman adopting a distinct and independent career from that of her husband. So firmly fixed was this sentiment in the founders of the common law that it became a maxim of that system of jurisprudence that a woman had no legal existence separate from her husband, who was regarded as her head and representative in the social state; and, notwithstanding some recent modifications of this civil status, many of the special rules of law flowing from and dependent upon this cardinal principle still exist in full force in most States. One of these is, that a married woman is incapable, without her husband's consent, of making contracts which shall be binding on her or him. This very incapacity was one circumstance which the Supreme Court of Illinois deemed important in rendering a married woman incompetent fully to perform the duties and trusts that belong to the office of an attorney and counsellor.

The paramount destiny and mission of woman are to fulfil the noble and benign offices of wife and mother. This is the law of the Creator. And the rules of civil society must be adapted to the general constitution of things, and cannot be based upon exceptional cases.[154]

And so, Stanton explained, "Myra Bradwell is denied the right to practice law in the state of Illinois because she is a married woman. I wonder if she thinks the roots of this decision are based deep down in love."[155]

The *Bradwell* case had reverberating consequences, reaffirming as it did married women's confinement to the domestic sphere. The result of this suit taught women that "the methods for earning their daily bread, in the trades and professions, the use of their powers of mind and body, could be defined, permitted or denied for the citizen by State authorities."[156] The judicial resurrection of coverture outraged Stanton and other activists and halted their planned legal advancement under the new civil rights amendment. They had thought such separate spheres thinking was gone, since by the time of the decision, five states and the District of Columbia had admitted women to the practice of law.[157] But states and the U.S. Supreme Court continued to deny women lawyers the right to practice.[158]

Extirpating the Roots of Gender

As Stanton entered her seventies and eighties, she became more firmly emphatic about the need to transform the underlying sexist norms permeating society. Surface reforms of laws of property, marriage, and divorce were necessary, but they did little to go to the roots of women's subordination. While the rest of the woman's rights movement narrowed in on the single issue of suffrage, Stanton broadened her agenda, examining the deep-seated causes of beliefs in women's inferiority in religion. These religious beliefs not only influenced laws and governance; they convinced women themselves of their own subjugation, explaining women's apathy and resistance to the women's rights movement. "With such lessons taught in the Bible and echoed and re-echoed on each returning Sabbath day in every pulpit in the land, how can woman escape the feeling that the injustice and oppression she suffers are of divine ordination?" "From the inauguration of the movement for woman's emancipation the Bible has been used to hold her in the 'divinely ordained sphere.'"[159] Stanton challenged women's "blind faith in accepted authorities" of religion by deconstructing the Bible and religious doctrine to reveal male bias and privilege, and reconstructing religion to read women and their experiences into a new gospel of "justice, equality and liberty for woman."[160]

In mining the bias of the accepted religious doctrines of gender, Stanton drew on the ideas of her feminist foremothers, Quakers Lucretia Mott and Sarah Grimké, who had questioned conventional interpretations of the Bible and called for women to interpret the Bible for themselves.[161] Some of these ideas made it into the Declaration of Sentiments, reflecting Mott's influence. Stanton's own background lacked a close affiliation with religion. She was raised in the strict Scotch Presbyterian Church, had a brief evangelical experience as a teenager, attended Episcopal services, and affiliated with Free Thought.[162] Stanton often stated a personal belief in a divine being of both God and Christ Jesus.[163] But near the end of her life, Stanton wrote that she hoped women would base their faith not on religion, but on "science and reason, where I found for myself at last that peace and comfort I could never find in the Bible and church."[164]

Initially, Stanton, like prior feminist thinkers, focused on debunking the creation story, which was the heart of patriarchy.[165] The story of Adam and Eve, and Eve's alleged responsibility for original sin, was continually cited as evidence of divine command for women's subordination.[166] In what Stanton called the allegorical myth, Eve is created second, from the rib of Adam, to be his "helpmeet." She brings sin into the world by succumbing to the snake's temptation to eat of the tree of knowledge, and then manipulates Adam to similarly sin, thus causing the fall of all humankind into an imperfect world.[167] Eve's punishment is the curse of pain in childbirth and subordination to Adam. "The idea of being a mere helpmeet to somebody," Stanton said, "has been so sedulously drilled into most women that an individual life, aim, purpose, ambition is not considered even by the majority."[168]

Stanton instead relied on the first of two Old Testament versions of creation as controlling. She quoted the first text to appear in the Bible in which it is said, "God made man in his own image, *male and female* made he them, and gave *them* dominion over all lower forms of life."[169] This reading conveyed to Stanton the gender duality of God, "a plain declaration of the existence of the feminine element in the God head," both male and female simultaneously created and both granted dominion over the world. "It is exact equality in origin, destiny and power."[170] This version reconciled with the "nature, science and experience" of the animal kingdom and new evolutionary theories recognizing the importance of maternity to procreation and production of the human race. It was reinforced, Stanton said, by the apostle Paul's New Testament words, "In Christ there is neither male nor female, neither Jew nor Greek, neither bond nor free but all are one in Christ Jesus."[171]

Elevating the significance of the feminine embodiment of God, Stanton embraced ideas of the Trinity represented by God the Father, God the Mother and Holy Spirit, and Jesus the Child. "All the evils that have resulted from dignifying one sex and degrading the other may be traced to this central error, a belief in a trinity of *masculine* gods from which the *feminine* element is wholly eliminated." Understanding the feminine as part of the Trinity, Stanton said, was more in harmony with the biblical description of the duality of the Godhead and the divine family, and also eliminated a core source of religious reification of men and subordination of women.[172] Together, Stanton argued, drawing on positivist theory, "[T]he masculine and feminine elements, exactly equal, balancing each other, are as essential to the maintenance of the equilibrium of the moral universe, as the positive and negative electricity, the north and south magnetism, the centripetal and centrifugal forces in the world of matter."[173]

Stanton further deconstructed the Eve story to debunk the myth of the curse of maternity. "One of the greatest obstacles in the way of the advancement of our girls to-day, is this old idea of 'the curse pronounced on Woman in the beginning,' preached in the pulpit, echoed in the parlor and the press."[174] "We have been taught that woman is the special object of God's wrath and curse; that the fact of motherhood so far from being her highest glory and exaltation, is her deepest sorrow and humiliation. One can hardly measure the depressing effect of this one false idea forever pressed on woman's soul; out of this ignorance of the science of life come all these absurd theories of the natural weakness and disabilities of woman."[175] She pointed out the contradiction of the church in extolling Mary, the mother of Jesus, while subjugating all other mothers. The worst part was that women believed it themselves. "I am pained" that a woman "entertains the monstrous idea that maternity is a curse and must ever be a period of danger, sorrow, and humiliation."[176]

"So far from motherhood being a 'weakness' it is an added power to mind and body alike."[177] Women's maternal ability, Stanton said, proved "woman's individual existence, power, conscience, judgment, not as a 'helpmeet' merely, but an independent, creative will power."[178] "When woman, by the observance of the laws of life and health, is restored to her normal condition, maternity will not be a period of weakness, but added power."[179] Instead, women needed to be taught a "higher gospel that by obedience to natural law she might secure uninterrupted health and happiness for herself and mould future generations to her will."[180]

After the exhausting decade of lyceum tours and writing the *History of Woman Suffrage*, Stanton spent much of the 1880s in England staying

Elizabeth Cady Stanton with Harriot and Nora, 1888. *Library of Congress.*

with Harriot. During what Stanton described as a turning point in her advocacy, she renewed her emphasis on the religious undercurrents of women's oppression. In a sermon to a London Free Thought church, she delivered one speech on the topic "Has the Christian Religion Done Aught for Woman," which would form the basis for her religious critique for the next two decades.[181] Stanton refuted the popular argument that Christianity benefited women by elevating them to a higher level of reverence or moral superiority than did so-called heathen societies.[182] Stanton rejected this supposition, showing that the entrenched patriarchy of Christianity degraded women in the same fashion. Stanton traced the historical origins and perversions of canon law, arguing that it displaced more egalitarian regimes in Egypt and Rome and produced the extremes of witch burnings, polygamy, celibacy—all based on an abhorrence and subjugation of women. "Women have ever been the chief victims in the persecutions of the Church amid all its awful tragedies, and on them have fallen the heaviest penalties of the canon law."[183]

Stanton's target now more heretically was the church itself, and its supporting priesthood and doctrines she identified as perpetuating the core of gender subordination. Thirty years earlier, she had appeased reformers fearing her anticlericalism, saying, "[W]e do not attack the Church; we defend ourselves merely against its attacks," reminding audiences how the Bible had been misused to endorse slavery, war, and intemperance.[184] But by now she clearly was attacking the church "as the greatest stumbling block to women's complete emancipation" and demanded that women "have no fellowship with churches" that deny them equality.[185] Churches took women's money and membership, but denied them leadership and ordination, and all the while pontificated from the pulpit on women's divine inferiority. "Your worst enemies still, in sacred vestments, minister at your altars. They still preach the monstrous doctrine of your inferiority and subordination, a doctrine that poisons the very foundation of our social life." Stanton was careful to distinguish the false doctrines of the church and priesthood from the core teachings of Jesus, which, she argued, taught only "complete" and "exact equality" of all humankind though those ideas had been "too far in advance of his age to mould its public opinion."[186]

In these writings and speeches, Stanton explicitly drew the connection between religion and social and legal inequality for women. "Whenever, during the struggle of the last forty years, we have demanded a new liberty these triune powers [state, church, and home] have rallied in opposition" citing "God's law and divine ordination." "Wherever the canon law has touched civil law or social customs it has undermined all freedom and respect for woman."[187] "In this age of the world, when statute laws and constitutions are being moulded to the people's will, it may be more in harmony with the spirit of the age to reconsider the 'Injunctions' of this Presbytery than to ignore the fundamental idea of Protestantism, the right of individual conscience and judgment."[188] Women's individual right to lead was in fact recognized in early Christianity, Stanton noted, alluding to Mary Magdalene, Joanna, Susanna, Priscilla, Thecla, and Junia. "During the first four hundred years of the Christian Church women were the chosen companions of Christ, and his followers as preachers, elders, deacons, officiating in all the sacraments, yet these facts are carefully excluded from all English translations of the scriptures." Given this, it was time for women of the nineteenth century to translate the Bible for themselves. "It is just here that our chief work for woman lies to-day, to free her from the theological bondage that is crippling all her powers." "Not until they make an organized resistance against the withering influence of the canon law, will they rid themselves of the moral disabilities growing out of the theologies of our times."[189] Stanton convinced NWSA to pass resolutions to this effect, but that only further incited evangelical ministers against the cause of women's rights.[190] Stanton pleaded with NWSA to organize action against the church.

> *Dear Friends,*—My convictions from year to year have been steadily growing stronger that, before we can secure woman's emancipation from the slavery and superstitions of the past, we have an important work to do in the Church. Hence, I would suggest in our plan of work for the coming year that we now begin the same vigorous agitation in the Church that we have kept up in the State for the last forty years. As the canon law, with all the subtle influences that grow out of it, is more responsible for woman's slavery to-day than the civil code, with the progressive legislation of the last half-century, we have an interest in tracing to their origin the lessons taught to woman in the churches.[191]

In the early 1890s, Stanton added to her historical argument of the perversions of the church by offering an alternative to this ordained gender structure of "the matriarchate." She incorporated this theory of maternal power into addresses to national conventions, writings on Wyoming's new grant of women's suffrage, and other essays on women's rights.[192] Stanton drew on emerging anthropological theories of matriarchal societies, prehistoric cultures like the Amazons, Iroquois, and others in which women ruled as the creative force, wielding power and peaceful governance. The theory of matriarchy was a popular idea that emerged in the late nineteenth century, originating with Swiss lawyer and jurist Johann Jakob Bachofen and advanced by Marxist thinker Friedrich Engels and others.[193] The theory of a matriarchal prehistory held that earlier societies existed in which women controlled government and property, created the first families, developed agriculture, and were worshipped as goddesses because of their reproductive and caregiving abilities. A "patriarchy cataclysm" disrupted the peace, harmony, and ecological balance of these matriarchal systems with intervening wars and weapon development, after which patriarchy evolved as the superior social structure and provided survival and advancement.[194]

Stanton wrote from England in 1890 that she had "been reading the whole year to glean these facts" about the matriarchate by studying British scholars.[195] She was likely also influenced by her colleague, Matilda Joslyn Gage, who was developing similar theories about religion and matriarchy, later published in her magnum opus, *Woman, Church, and State*.[196] Stanton, like Gage, appropriated the anthropological matriarchal theories of the nineteenth century for her own feminist purposes. Because these theories had been developed to justify the converse, the superiority of patriarchy. They held that society had evolved from the unsophisticated, chaotic matriarchal systems into ordered and aggressive systems grounded in patriarchy. Stanton, interpreting the theory through her feminist lens, concluded that the matriarchate provided historical evidence of women's ability and superior powers and the negative influence of the destructive forces of male aggression and patriarchy. "Thus, instead of being a 'disability,' as unthinking writers are pleased to call it, maternity has been the all-inspiring motive or force that impelled the first steps" toward "the birth of civilization." Matriarchal theory was attractive because it freed women's rights advocates from the "charge of their critics that male dominance was biological and eternal, and therefore inevitable and unchangeable." Stanton used this evidence not to advocate a return to female supremacy, but rather as evidence of women's capabilities sufficient to support an "Amphiarchate," a shared power between women and men in the "as yet untried experiment of complete equality."[197] Second-wave feminists of the late twentieth century resurrected these ideas of the matriarchate bolstered by archeological finds of prehistoric fertility goddesses and a strong current of feminism seeking support for alternative gender structures of power.[198]

Stanton, frustrated by the clergy's increased conservatism on women's issues, and the growing religiosity of the women's movement, accelerated her "ideological assault on religious orthodoxy."[199] At her eightieth birthday celebration in 1895 honoring her half-century of service to the woman's movement, she bypassed polite remarks of thanks and instead delivered her thundering indictment of the church to an audience of six thousand.[200] Stanton insisted that the "imperative duty" of the woman's movement "at this hour" was "to demand a thorough revision of creeds and codes, Scriptures and constitutions" that oppressed women in the name of religion.[201] Stanton said that she was "not willing that another generation of children shall be taught the Bible idea of woman's subjection as interpreted by the lessons of the pulpit, and the action of the church."[202] The first step was to show that the Bible was "neither written nor inspired by the Creator of the Universe . . . but that the Bible emanated, in common with all church literature, from the brain of man."[203] For more than two decades, she had been calling for a new translation of the Bible by women who "read, translate and interpret" the Bible for themselves.[204] A revision, she said, would change everything. "[I]t seems from the debate that 'immemorial usage,' 'laws and constitutions' are not the only obstacles, and if 'the Bible, and the religion of the country teach the subordination of woman to man,' all that remains to do then is to have another revision of the Bible."[205] The public scoffed that it was "ridiculous" for women to translate the Bible, and reformers, including women's rights advocates, worried about political fallout. Stanton was unapologetic. "Reformers who are always compromising, have not yet grasped the idea that truth is the only safe ground to stand upon."[206]

Two weeks after the birthday celebration, Stanton published the first volume of her *Woman's Bible*. The time was right, for it was a period of "intense religious concern" precipitated by the advent of evolutionary science, a revised translation of the Bible from the familiar 1611 King James version, and German biblical criticism rejecting literal interpretation.[207] Stanton's *Bible* was not a new translation, but a book of commentaries, excerpting all of the biblical passages pertaining to women, about 10 percent of the Bible, Stanton said, and providing feminist commentary on the passages. The passages were said to have come from the first translation of the Bible by a woman, Julia Smith of the tax protest and cow-selling fame—except that the excerpts are not Smith's language, but instead, that of the King James version.[208] Stanton began the project in earnest in 1886, assisted by her daughter Harriot and English reformer Frances Lord, who helped identify the relevant passages. But further help was not forthcoming, despite Stanton's pleas and drafting of colleagues to her Bible-revising committee, as most wanted to distance themselves from the heretical project. At the end of the day, Stanton wrote most of the commentaries herself, consolidating much of the material from her prior decades of speeches and writings. She reified biblical examples of powerful women, like Ruth and Deborah. At the same type she de-mythologized women like Sarah, Rebekkah, and Rachel, who had been held up by men as the feminine ideal. These women, Stanton said, "il-lustrated only how women who lacked legitimate power and influence were driven to deception and trickery" in a patriarchal society.[209]

"In sharp contrast to the praise and adulation of her birthday tributes, the *Woman's Bible* again made Stanton the object of criticism and scorn, not only among religious leaders and social conservatives, but even among her colleagues in the suffrage movement."[210] Clergy preached sermons denouncing the book as disrespectful and heretical, and news-papers called it "the work of the devil."[211] "By undermining this corner-stone of Victorian culture, Stanton had gone too far. The *Woman's Bible* was seen as a frontal assault on the moral authority of women, and by extension, the moral integrity of the nation."[212] The woman's movement too was shocked by Stanton's attack on the Bible. The movement, now guided by the strong organizational leadership of Susan Anthony, had narrowed in on suffrage as the sole question, buoyed by affiliations with the temperance women, led by Frances Willard. The two hundred thou-sand women of the Woman's Christian Temperance Union significantly expanded the ranks of the ten-thousand-member NAWSA, and the po-litically pragmatic Anthony understood how the consensus helped ad-vanced reform on the vote.[213] Stanton, however, was less interested in political accommodation and focused on keeping the radical feminist challenge alive on a broad scale. Anthony refused to participate in the *Woman's Bible* project, as she was by then on her separate and singular path of suffrage.[214] Anthony did defend Stanton and her *Bible* to the newly merged NAWSA, even as it censored its founder, passing a resolu-tion that the organization had "no official connection with the so-called 'Woman's Bible.'"[215]

Stanton's *Bible* "was one final, great stroke in her battle against in-equality. It was also the ruin of her historical reputation."[216] This her-esy had reverberating political consequences, ostracizing her from the movement she had founded and diminishing her historical legacy even before her death. The new generation of younger suffrage women—conservative, religious, and aligned only on the issue of the vote—rejected Stanton as an old radical. These younger women "sanctified

"The Apotheosis of Suffrage" cartoon, *Washington Post*, Jan. 26, 1896.

Anthony and ignored Stanton, even crediting Anthony with the Seneca Falls convention that she did not attend." "Aunt Susan" became the
grandmother of suffrage as her name was given by Alice Paul to the
Susan B. Anthony Nineteenth Amendment for women's right to vote,
passed in 1920, and the Susan B. Anthony dollar coin honored her as the
founder of women's rights. Subsequent attempts by Stanton's children
Harriot and Theodore to redeem their mother's legacy failed, and in
the long run backfired, as they redacted and rewrote radical ideas in the
papers they chose to save.[217]

Stanton's foray into religion, however, was no mistake. "Like other
'mistakes,'" she wrote, "this too, in due time will be regarded as 'a step
in progress.'"[218] To her, undermining religion finally got at the intran-
sigent foundation of sexism and explained why women continued to
resist women's rights, claiming "I have all the rights I want," and why
laws and institutions refused to change even after fifty years of advocacy on women's rights. The *Woman's Bible* became a bestseller, going
through seven printings and translated into six languages, even though

Stanton financed much of this herself.[219] Stanton thus "accomplished precisely what she set out to accomplish: the *Woman's Bible* attracted extraordinary attention, refocused the debate over women's rights on the root causes of sexist oppression." Politically, it "shook up a movement that Stanton felt had stagnated in its single-minded pursuit of the elective franchise."[220] For as Stanton appreciated, "[I]n taking on law, feminism is taking on a great deal more."[221] Given that "a whole constellation of forces is at work in the establishment and reinforcement of patriarchy, feminists must look beyond the letter of the law and examine the cultural, social, religious, and economic forces behind women's oppression."[222] And that's where Stanton both began and ended.

Conclusion

"Still Many Obstacles"

Although we have opened a pathway to the promised land, and cleared up much of the underbrush of false sentiment, logic and rhetoric, intertwisted and intertwined with law and custom, blocking all avenues in starting, yet there are still many obstacles to be encountered before the rough journey is ended.

—Elizabeth Cady Stanton, Formal Opening of International Council of Women, March 25, 1888

By the end of Stanton's life, family law had changed, even if it did not include all of her proposed reforms. Married women's property acts allowed women to retain their own wages and property acquired separately. Maternal custody rights gave women legal capacity and authority. Divorce was possible on grounds of cruelty to enable women to escape domestic violence. At the same time, other rights for women retracted. The early glimmers of no-fault divorce were abolished. Abortion was outlawed, eliminating women's common law right of choice. The full veil of coverture had been lightened, but not eliminated. Law and society were still threatened by women's rights and heightened fears of the downfall of the family.

From today's vantage point, Stanton's family law reform was a success. Virtually all of her proposals for family reform are now law. No-fault divorce is now available in all states, adopted in the 1970s and recognizing Stanton's insight of the need to provide easy legal redress for parties' continued unhappiness and dysfunction (though Stanton's New York was the lone state that resisted until 2010).[1] States eliminated breach of promise actions and dower, and most abandoned common law marriage.[2] Marital property laws at divorce changed to recognize joint property rights of both partners, incorporating Stanton's theory of the economic partnership of marriage.[3] The legal age of marriage was raised by most states to eighteen, the average age of first marriages rose to twenty-seven for women, and neuroscience confirmed Stanton's insight that twenty-five is the age of full maturity.[4] Domestic violence laws evolved to facilitate separation and divorce, protecting women from this violence. Social practices changed to embrace an alternative custom of marital names, adopting the convention of "Ms.," and the law changed allowing a woman to retain her birth name after marriage.[5] Maternal custody preferences dominated for a century until struck down as unconstitutional sexist presumptions, but courts retained the recognition of the full autonomy of the mother under the best interest standard, albeit laced with persistent gendered assumptions.[6]

Stanton's theories of family law seem so reasonable today because they have become so familiar. As Stanton surmised, it was not that what she said on marriage and divorce was wrong—only that she said it too soon. The backlash, however, has not subsided. Conservative advocates of "family values" decry feminism, no-fault divorce, and working mothers, while fathers' rights groups challenge maternal custody and control.[7] Feminists often shy away from marriage and family issues, even though such issues of work/life balance and reproductive control dominate daily realities and political agendas. Stanton, however, confronted this battle head on, denying that feminism is the antithesis of family. Family, she said, is not a "side issue" to feminism, but rather is "the kernel of the question," the core of women's social and legal equality.

Feminist Reinvention

This revolution of gender equality in the family was slow in coming. Family law reform stagnated in the first half of the twentieth century, bogged down in technical battles over state jurisdiction and interstate recognition.[8] When reform of the family came, it was driven more by lawyers than by feminists. Feminists of the twentieth century were not focused on family law issues. Suffrage continued to be the primary woman's rights issue through the first two decades of the century, finally realized in 1920 through the militant politics and political leadership of Alice Paul and the Nineteenth Amendment's guarantee of women's right to vote. Protection for working-class women laborers became a key issue for many social feminists, following Florence Kelley and her legal work on the famous Brandeis brief in *Muller v. Oregon* that established social science jurisprudence along with women's legal right to be protected in the workplace by maximum-hour laws. Kelley's advocacy coopted Stanton's "mothers of the race" ideas to emphasize women's biological and social difference and need for special legal classification and protective labor laws. Social and labor feminists battled Paul's postsuffrage demand for an Equal Rights Amendment (ERA) focused on an absolute guarantee of formal equality based on women's identity to men.[9] Intervening events of the Great Depression and two world wars diverted further prioritization of women's rights. The 1960s brought the second wave of the feminist movement, rediscovering feminism and reigniting political demand for women's rights. The second-wave feminists prioritized demands for guarantees of equality, equal employment opportunity, and reproductive rights.[10]

The feminists of the 1970s then rediscovered Stanton. Gloria Steinem featured Stanton in her opening remarks to the historic National Women's Conference in Houston, Texas, in November 1977. "If more of us had learned the parallels and origins of the abolitionist and suffragist movements, there might have been less surprise when a new movement called Women's Liberation grew from the politicization of white and black women in the civil rights movement of the 1960s." This lost history led to "many painful years of reinventing the wheel before we re-learned organically what our foremothers had discovered and could have taught us: that a false mythology" was being used to keep women down and in support of cheap household labor. The conference included an Olympian torch relay beginning in Stanton's Seneca Falls and winding to Texas, where Maya Angelou read a poetic redraft of Stanton's Declaration of Sentiments.[11] It provided the framework for numerous proposed reforms, including the National Organization of Women's (NOW) advancement of a joint economic partnership theory of marriage and concrete ideas for homemaker Social Security and vocational retraining.[12] Steinem embraced Stanton's theory of the matriarchate, using it similarly to emphasize the viability of an alternative system of female power.[13]

By this time, women had entered the law as Stanton had hoped. Stanton knew that for the women's rights movement, "one thing is certain, this course will necessarily involve a good deal of litigation, and we shall need lawyers of our own sex, whose intellects, sharpened by their interests, shall be quick to discover the loop-holes of retreat." Women, not men, were needed to press the agenda. "It is quite time that we have these laws revised, by our own sex—for man does not yet feel, that what is unjust for himself, is also unjust for woman. Yes, we must have our own lawyers. . . . We cannot accept man's interpretation of the law."[14] Stanton saw the beginnings of this feminist advocacy, as the first woman lawyer, Arabella Mansfield, was admitted to practice law in Iowa in 1869; the first women, Ada Kepley and Phoebe Couzins, graduated law school; and all-female law schools were established in the Washington College of Law (now American) and the Portia Law School (now New England).[15] But women did not reach the tipping point in the legal profession until the 1970s. Today, women constitute 34 percent of the legal profession, 25 percent of the judiciary, and 20 percent of the legislators: an improvement, but still not an equal or controlling share of the power.[16] Women now serve equally on juries, although it was not until 1975 that the Supreme Court definitively granted women this right, reflecting Stanton's belief that women offered a different perspective, based on "gender and resulting life experience," necessary to justice.[17]

This presence of women in the law made a difference, as Stanton had hoped. Sex equality law was shepherded through by leading feminist law professor, now Supreme Court Justice, Ruth Bader Ginsburg. Her work with the American Civil Liberties Union (ACLU) Women's Rights Project attacked all formal inequalities of sex based on gender stereotypes, often using male plaintiffs to better illustrate the irrationality of sex-based classifications. Ginsburg's goal was to "deconstruct the breadwinner-homemaker system in which men and women were seen as belonging to separate spheres" and to reconstruct gender roles for both men and women, but the Supreme Court was unwilling to be led that far.[18] In the 1970s, the Court interpreted the Equal Protection Clause of the Fourteenth Amendment to prohibit laws that discriminate on the basis of sex, examining such laws with heightened scrutiny to uncover bias and stereotype and striking down formal gender distinctions.[19] This constitutional common law effectively created a right to equality despite the failure of the ERA, passed by Congress in 1972 but not ratified by the states. The Women's Law Fund, founded by lawyer and law professor Jane Picker in 1972, attacked women's inequality in education and employment, beginning with mandatory maternity leaves, which were invalidated by the Court.[20] Feminist legal thinker Catharine MacKinnon then moved beyond formal inequalities to attack systemic causes of women's oppression, namely, the sexualization of women through pornography and sexual abuse. MacKinnon, and other critical legal scholars, focused on deconstructing the "objective" laws to reveal bias and developed the insight that the law is inherently "male" in that it substantively favored men and primarily governed the public sphere.[21]

The dominant issue, however, of political and legal feminism since the 1970s has been abortion. The first legal efforts to challenge the century-old criminal prohibition of abortion began in the late 1950s by, ironically, the medical profession. The physicians, who once led the charge against abortion, now were concerned with the public health crisis of back alley abortions. In 1962, the expert body of the American Law Institute (ALI) proposed therapeutic abortion laws that permitted doctors to perform abortions when physicians determined they were justified by a woman's physical or mental health.[22] The abortion movement converged with feminism in 1969 when NOW leader Betty Friedan came to appreciate abortion as the key to women's ability to control their own lives and place in society. In an influential speech, she said, "[T]here is no freedom, no equality, no full human dignity and personhood possible for women until we assert and demand the control over our own bodies, over our own reproductive process."[23] Departing from the physicians' movement, she said, "There is only one voice that needs to be heard on the question of the final decision as to whether a woman will or will not bear a child, and that is the voice of the woman herself. Her own conscience, her own conscious choice." As Stanton had argued, the right of a woman to be "sovereign of her own person," to control her own body and reproduction, was among the most important of all women's rights.

During this time, the Supreme Court recognized a constitutional right of women to access birth control. Birth control became public with Margaret Sanger's clinics and her founding of Planned Parenthood in 1942, which shifted the image of the organization to one of proactive family-planning education. Statutory prohibitions against contraception remained on the books, however, regulating a moral standard that contradicted actual practice as private doctors gave advice to patients and drug stores sold contraception "under-the-counter."[24] The advent of the birth control pill in 1960 radically changed the technology and certainty of the medical science of contraception. In 1965, the Supreme Court in *Griswold v. Connecticut* invalidated an old state Comstock Law prohibiting the distribution of contraceptive information, holding that the law unconstitutionally intruded upon the right of marital privacy by denying a married woman birth control. The Court extended that reasoning to unmarried women in 1972 in *Eisenstadt v. Baird*, but left intact the state right to restrict distribution to medical professionals.[25]

The next year, the Supreme Court recognized a woman's constitutional right to choose an abortion in the famous case of *Roe v. Wade*.[26] The Court held that the Constitution gave women a right to privacy in their own bodies that could only be burdened by the state with regulation after the first trimester of pregnancy. Thus, the Court effectively reinstituted the common law rule allowing abortion prior to quickening. The rule was now grounded in what Stanton identified as a woman's self-sovereignty and right to her own person. *Roe*, however, did not end the abortion debate. Persistent and vocal political opposition continued by those unwilling to accept the legal compromise of *Roe*. The so-called informed consent laws, like those of Akron, Ohio, invalidated by the Supreme Court in 1983, imposed restrictions on obtaining an abortion such as waiting periods, counseling, mandatory disclosures, and hospital requirements. The cases continued, however, with the Court a decade later limiting *Roe* by permitting abortion restrictions as long as they do not "unduly burden" a woman's constitutional right. In 2007, the Court expanded the legal justification for government restriction of abortion to include the state's interest in protecting women's important role and special bond as mothers and protecting women from making irrational emotional choices. Justice Ginsburg issued a scathing dissent, attacking the majority's rationale of "protecting women" as bias that "reflects ancient notions about women's place in the family and under the Constitution—ideas that have long since been discredited."[27]

During this political renegotiation of *Roe*, Stanton emerged as a figurehead of the anti-abortion movement, resurrected by the pro-life lobbying group, Feminists for Life (FFL), and quickly embraced by conservative politicians and scholars.[28] Founded in 1972 in Columbus,

Ohio, by two women, a homemaker and a professor, the group supports equal opportunity for women in education and employment but opposes abortion for any reason. It gained renewed visibility in the past decade from the prominence of its pro bono counsel, Jane Sullivan, wife of Supreme Court Chief Justice John Roberts, and the popularity of its national spokesperson, actress Patricia Heaton of *Everybody Loves Raymond* and *The Middle* fame.[29]

FFL featured Stanton on its posters, website, and commemorative coffee mugs as a "feminist foremother" to the anti-abortion movement. The group claimed that Stanton was "strongly opposed to abortion" and proactively engaged in anti-abortion activity.[30] It believed Stanton was the perfect spokesperson for the movement because of her motherly persona and because she was a "feisty gal who had seven children and was outspokenly pro-life." Stanton, they said, "condemned abortion in the strongest possible terms" and was "a revolutionary who consistently advocated for the rights of women . . . acceptance of motherhood—and for the protection of children, born and unborn."[31] And it represented in amicus briefs to the U.S. Supreme Court that "Elizabeth Cady Stanton clearly argued that the liberation of women was needed to stop the killing of children before and after birth" and that she expressed "an uncompromising view that abortion is 'child-murder.'"[32]

FFL developed what it calls "the feminist case against abortion."[33] The argument asserts that second-wave feminists of the 1960s "made a drastic about-face" from the original intent of "the now revered feminists of the nineteenth century," who were "strongly opposed to abortion because of their belief in the worth of all humans." It claims that the criminal laws against abortion passed in the late 1800s were the "result of advocacy efforts by feminists who worked in an uneasy alliance with the male-dominated medical profession and the mainstream media." FFL advocates collected historical excerpts in the book *ProLife Feminism*, contending that leading American feminists like Stanton, Susan B. Anthony, and others supported a continued tradition opposing abortion.[34] This narrative of Stanton and other historical feminists resonates because it seemingly challenges the prevailing legal view that feminism and gender equality must include a right to abortion. Scholars of Anthony and Stanton, however, have strongly refuted the claim that either woman proactively spoke against abortion, and FFL admits that

"When we consider that women are treated as property, it is degrading to women that we should treat our children as property to be disposed of as we see fit."

Elizabeth Cady Stanton
Founder of the Women's Movement

Another humorless old biddy for life.

Feminists for Life flyer, c. 2007.

abortion was not an issue to which either gave any time. Still the claim persists. Anthony continues to be featured on the FFL website, her name is used for the pro-life fundraising group, the "Susan B. Anthony List," and her Birthplace Museum in Rochester is owned and managed by the Feminists for Life.[35]

As for Stanton, FFL continues to insist that she was outspoken against abortion. It relies on a few pieces of alleged historical evidence: three articles in the *Revolution*, the absence of abortion advertisements in the paper, and a note in Julia Ward Howe's diary. Of the three editorials, only one can even be attributed to Stanton.[36] The two anonymous editorials were more likely written by Stanton's coeditor, Parker Pillsbury, who was on record as morally opposing abortion and whose other signed writings match these sentiments. Pillsbury also wrote the article that explained the reasoning for the *Revolution*'s policy of refusing abortion advertisements, although Stanton also objected to advertisements for harmful quack medicines and gimmicks that preyed on women consumers.[37] None of these editorials supports the criminalization or regulation of abortion. All endorse the empowerment and elevation of women through legal rights, and Pillsbury supports the idea of government-sponsored foundling hospitals or orphanages.

The Stanton article cited by pro-life advocates, "Infanticide and Prostitution," discussed in chapter 4, reacts to the media's condemnation of abortion and infanticide by defending women against the attack and dismissing the religiosity and moral outrage over abortion.[38] Stanton deflected the moral debate over abortion and redirected public discourse to the systemic exclusions of women from the legal system and the gendered injustice of infanticide prosecutions.[39] Elsewhere, Stanton mentioned the word "abortion" only once in her writings, listing it in 1856 in a letter to the Seventh Convention as one example of the social consequences caused by sexual violence against women and involuntary motherhood.[40] Stanton did not campaign with the physicians or endorse the proposed state regulation of abortion. To the contrary, she expressed outrage at a legal system that would penalize women's conduct rather than grant them self-determination and autonomy.

The final claimed evidence of "pro-life feminism" involving Stanton is a quotation allegedly from her contained in her rival Julia Ward Howe's diary. However, the existence of this document cannot be verified.[41] FFL admitted that it could not locate the letter, "which may never have been written or perhaps has been lost," and promised to stop attributing the quotation to Stanton. Yet the Howe quotation has taken on mythical proportions, featured in pro-life campaign literature, emblazoned on FFL coffee mugs, and embroidered on a quilt donated by FFL to the Seneca Falls History Museum.[42] The quotation resembles Stanton's critique of the male privilege of the guardianship laws, but pro-life advocates see an abortion reference: "When we consider that women are treated as property, it is degrading to women that we should treat our children as property to be disposed of as we see fit." What is verifiable from Howe's diary, as discussed in chapter 4, is that the conservative suffrage leader was "deeply mortified" by Stanton's remarks that seemed to excuse infanticide.[43] Stanton's comments at the First Woman's Congress reaffirmed her commitment to a woman's reproductive control, consistent with the rest of the historical record in which Stanton repeatedly asserted woman's unfettered right to the "sovereignty of her own person." Stanton's position was the antecedent to the modern constitutional right of women to choose an abortion, not the foundation of an anti-abortion movement.

Nevertheless, Stanton's feminist legacy has been embedded in modern anti-abortion advocacy. FFL proposed federal legislation named after her, which Congress introduced in 2005. The "Elizabeth Cady Stanton Pregnant and Parenting Students Services Act," sponsored by Senator Elizabeth Dole (R-NC) and Representative Melissa Hart (R-PA), was designed to provide resources and support for pregnant college students so "they do not feel that abortion is the only answer."[44] The Stanton Act became law as part of the voluminous and complex 2010 healthcare reform. It provides federal grants to states and colleges for students who are pregnant or parenting, including healthcare, family housing, childcare, toys, formula, and counseling.[45] FFL claims that the law reflects shared common ground between anti-abortion advocates and Stanton on eliminating economic and social conditions that force women to seek abortions.[46] Stanton may have agreed on education and empowerment, but her position was clearly the opposite on women's right to self-sovereignty in choosing motherhood against all paternalist regulation and control. Maternity for Stanton was a qualification for power and autonomy, not a basis of weakness and irrationality in need of state protection.[47]

The Persistence of Domesticity

Today's families look different than those of the late nineteenth century. The number of people in married households and the percentage of people who marry are at an all-time low of less than 50 percent, replaced by the rise in single-parent households, cohabitation partners, and same-sex partners.[48] Significantly, people are creating family rela-tionships without traditional marriage as 40 percent of all births now are to unmarried parents.[49] The divorce rate has stabilized after increasing from 1900 to its height in the 1960s and 1970s.[50] Younger people age twenty-five to thirty report desiring equal roles in both home and work, though studies of the "second shift" show that women, even working women, still perform more of the housework and caregiving.[51] These demographic changes are attributed to women's work opportunities, feminism, and the birth control pill.[52] One new important emerging distinction in the family is that of class. More higher-educated and higher-earning partnerships marry; more working-class partners do not. More working-class women have children out of marriage. And more working-class partners follow traditional male breadwinner roles and experience greater divorce.[53]

At the same time, families today look surprisingly similar with respect to the dependence of care. Most women, close to 90 percent, become mothers.[54] Children are dependents requiring adult care.[55] Twenty-five percent of mothers are full-time homemakers, while the majority of mothers in paid employment worked only part-time to accommo-date family responsibilities.[56] "Stereotypes about gender and parenting may be 'outdated'; but the truth is, still, that most primary caretakers are mothers. That holds true even if they work outside the home."[57] The women's lib solution of the 1970s was translated as rejecting motherhood altogether, representing the ultimate feminist choice as that of a single working woman, epitomized by the glamorously intellectual Gloria Steinem. The ERA debates fueled these mommy wars with opponents like Phyllis Schlafly (a lawyer and mother of six herself) arguing that feminists sought to outlaw motherhood. Meanwhile, evangelical doc-trines of complementarianism rose again in mainstream churches, hold-ing that women were created as different. They were intentionally made to be more emotional, less intellectual beings designed for the gift of caring and teaching children, but never for teaching or leading adults.[58] The law did little to change all this. "The groundbreaking sex discrimi-nation cases of the 1970s ended legal distinctions between the duties of husbands and wives but left largely in place both gender norms and substantive rights within marriage, tax, and benefits law that encourage specialization into breadwinning and caregiving roles."[59]

The millennium saw a continuation of the reification of domesticity in the "intensive mothering" model.[60] Motherhood was reinvented as organic and natural with the rise of pioneer woman cooking, home-made baby food, and raising chickens in the backyard. Mommy blogs celebrate motherhood even as mothers post about "the travails of motherhood, commiserating, fuming or laughing about their shared lives."[61] The modern mother is portrayed as anticonsumer, rejecting processed and purchased options for which the mother can do-it-herself. Others criticized this "mommy myth" of the indispensable home mother and its opposition to time-saving options like formula, Target Halloween costumes, and store-bought cupcakes for the PTA bake sale. The complaint is that this organic mothering ideology directs women back to the home into a subordinate and unpaid role in the private sphere. This domestic labor, of course, is volunteered, sacrificially given as the "price of motherhood" with homemakers earning no income, no credit, and no Social Security benefit. Society still relies on the gratuitous, sacrificial work of women to sustain a system of family and childcare. The modern mothering movement, like that of the nineteenth-century maternalists, seeks to elevate it to give women respect and dignity in these otherwise subordinate roles.[62]

This renewed domesticity contrasts with the rise of girl power. Stanton's transformative socialization of girls seems to have stuck, especially in recent times. Her subversive "Solitude of Self" speech of courage and gender noncompliance is now sold as a little gift book at card stores packaged as sentimental words of encouragement for women. Girl power is promoted everywhere in terms of physical strength and workouts, Michelle Obama's arm muscles, Tae Kwon Do defense training, and marathon running. Girls play sports, guaranteed equality by Title IX. Cheerleading is out; lacrosse is in. Girls major in engineering, not home economics. We tell them they can do anything they want, including math, coding, or soccer, even if they have to do it with all-pink gear and Legos. Writers exposed "the Beauty Myth" in the false images of magazines, the harm of parabens and carcinogens in cosmetics, and the double standard of women's aging.[63] Even political conservatives like former vice-presidential candidate Sarah Palin embrace the girl power mantra.[64]

While this girl power ideology has not translated into representation of women in positions of power, like CEOs, there has been an acceptance of women's market work. The second women's liberation movement prioritized market work in the way Stanton had envisioned. Understanding of women's need for a life purpose and educational and professional avenues for ambition was popularized in Betty Friedan's 1963 best-selling book, *The Feminine Mystique*.[65] Friedan, later president of NOW, focused the women's rights group on removing barriers to women's equal employment. Title VII of the Civil Rights Act, passed in 1964, guaranteed that women could not be discriminated against in employment on the basis of sex, though sex was added to the race-based civil rights law only as an afterthought, with virtually no legislative debate.[66] Laws against sexual harassment, invented by women for women, helped create tolerable workplace environments that respected women's role as employees.[67] And Title IX of the Education Acts passed in 1972 guaranteed women equal opportunity in education and, most visibly, in sports.[68]

This pro-work ideology, however, runs smack into the maternal wall when women combine their public role with a role as a parent. "Raised to believe that girls could accomplish anything, these women have reached parenthood, only to find they faced many of the same pay, equity and work-family balance issues that were being fought over decades before."[69] Pregnancy is often the first time women report actionable evidence of sex discrimination. The "maternal wall" blocks women employees from advancement long before they hit the glass ceiling. In the workplace, the ideal worker is defined as male: a body without pregnancy, with immunity from family caregiving, and with unlimited hours for work.[70] Newspapers indict the "opt out moms" who leave the workplace after years of education and opportunity because they can't handle it.[71] The courts are inundated with cases of pregnancy discrimination, pregnancy accommodations, and sex discrimination claims, all arising from continued gendered ideals of workers and women.[72] There were advances. The Pregnancy Discrimination Act of 1978 prohibits discriminatory employment action due to pregnancy, reversing Supreme Court precedent that employment actions taken on the basis of pregnancy were not a form of sex discrimination.[73] The Family Medical Leave Act grants both men and women unpaid leave for the birth of a child or care of any family member.[74] These are attempts to harmonize family and work life, but still, at some point, the system forces women to choose one or the other without adequate systemic and legal supports.

Socially, the battle between market and care work is played out in the "mommy wars" where women are pitted against each other. The lines are drawn in the sand. Feminists versus mothers. Working mothers versus stay-at-home-mothers. Not all mothers buy into this opposition, as some groups, like MomsRising.org, form alliances with traditional feminist groups like NOW on shared issues like family leave.[75] But legal scholars continue the private/public debate, arguing over the proper feminist strategies. Should we work to empower women in their traditional caregiving role? Or work to shift women into socially valued masculine gender performances of paid work and outsourced care work?[76] The first strategy adopts a maternalist feminism focused on supporting women in their right to choose full-time motherhood, with legal protections for homemakers like joint property or exemptions from labor laws.[77] The second strategy emphasizes workplace reforms like equal pay, shorter work weeks, paid leave, and part-time benefits to counteract the "structural impediments" that "prevent people from acting on their egalitarian values, forcing men and women into accommodations" that do not reflect their preferences, like opt-out moms or caregiving dads.[78]

The different assumptions about women's desired homemaking status play out in the context of alimony law reform. Should the outdated theory of alimony, premised on the husband's duty to provide for a wife whom he could not legally divorce, be eliminated to direct women during or at least after marriage to market work and pecuniary independence?[79] Or should the law reflect the realities of women's continued caregiving and the persistence of gendered family expectations and award economic support for women's lost opportunities and investment in others?[80] Or should the law strive for both, reflecting women's work in both the market and the family through theories of shared family enterprise and correlated reform of workplace expectations of the male norm?[81] This last option was Stanton's ideal: that the law encompass an understanding of women's roles and rights as both mother and worker. Her theories advanced maternity as a basis of power, wisdom, and autonomy, even while it encouraged women to profession, employment, and self-support. For Stanton, it was not either family or work, but both—and a demand that the law reflect women's full and equal opportunity on their own terms.

Keeping the "Woman Question" in Family Law

As the law continues to grapple with family conflicts, it is important to keep asking Stanton's "woman question." Rejecting the artificial divide of public and private, deeply rooted in American law, is the key to better resolving gender issues in the family.[82] For today, it is often at the juncture of family and work where legal questions fester. Issues of reproductive rights, pregnancy discrimination, maternal walls, and glass ceilings require a reconciliation of both private and public rights. Stanton's legacy also counsels that we apply feminist methodology to family law analysis. That means questioning and deconstructing objective rules for gender bias and reading women's experiences into the exercise of judicial discretion. Most critically, this means understanding that formal equalities are merely the starting point, as Stanton said. The law must appreciate the differences of women in pregnancy and maternity, as relevant to workplace accommodations, family leave, or healthcare. And we must not fail to include the system.

Legal analysis using Stanton's wisdom must look beyond formal equalities to evaluate the systemic causes of gender inequality and the complicity of the law, state, church, and market, such as the male norm of the ideal worker or the implications of an inadequate childcare system. Most significantly, Stanton offers us a reconstructed family alternative of complete egalitarian partnerships and maternal autonomy. Ever the pragmatist, Stanton wanted more than to critique the system—she wanted to change it. Her legacy proves that feminists over time have demanded equality, dignity, and autonomy for women in the family and have not simply acquiesced to the subordination. Women leaders did what they could from the periphery of power to challenge the status quo and demand alternatives.

For Stanton, the Declaration of Sentiments at Seneca Falls was merely a first step on the long path of women's freedom. "Our successors . . . have a big work before them—much bigger, in fact, than they imagine. We are only the stone that started the ripple, but they are the ripple that is spreading and will eventually cover the whole pond."[83] The "whole pond" included radical reform of the multiple fronts of family, state, church, and law. The family was key to this cultural transformation. It was not an untouchable private sphere where discriminatory views of women could be left to breed. Instead, woman's equality in the family—in the private relationships of marriage and parenting—was paramount to her complete attainment of civil liberty.

ACKNOWLEDGMENTS

After more than a decade on this labor of love, interrupted by the daily demands of work, family, and life, I am grateful that the book has made it to completion. I am indebted to the work of Ann Gordon and her colleagues at Rutgers University for the historical archives of the Elizabeth Cady Stanton and Susan B. Anthony Papers and the ease by which these microfilms and books brought the treasures of women's rights history to my desk. Thanks to Ann as well for her willingness to share Stanton documents and insights. A warm thank you to Coline Jenkins, Elizabeth Cady Stanton's great-great-granddaughter, for her enthusiastic support of this project.

I thank the University of Akron and the University of Akron School of Law for supporting this research through summer fellowships, grants, and sabbaticals. Parts of this book previously appeared in Tracy A. Thomas, "Elizabeth Cady Stanton on the Federal Marriage Amendment," 22 *Constitutional Commentary* 137 (2005); Tracy A. Thomas, "Elizabeth Cady Stanton and the Notion of a Legal Class of Gender," in *Feminist Legal History* (2011); and Tracy A. Thomas, "Misappropriating Women's History in the Law and Politics of Abortion," 36 *Seattle University Law Review* 1 (2012). My appreciation goes out to my colleagues at Akron who supported this research both in spirit and in kind, including Jane Moriarty, the Momus writers' group, and the women's writing retreat gang. Thank you to Deans Dick Aynes and Elizabeth Reilly for mentorship and institutional support. I benefited from the dedication and help of the law librarians and IT personnel at Akron, who assisted on this lengthy project, especially Eli Eubanks. My gratitude goes out to the many research assistants who helped battle the technology and piece the facts together over many years: Betsy Bare Hartscuh, Julie Beadle, Deanna Durbin, Elizabeth Davis, Kerry Hageman, Jessica Knopp, Catherine Loya, James MacDonald, Kristina Melomed, Sara Radcliffe, Ryan Shepler, and Charlotte Sheppard. A special thanks to Jyme Mariani for pushing this through to the finish line. I appreciate those who agreed to read portions of this manuscript: Tracey Jean Boisseau, Brant Lee, and Mary Ziegler, with a special appreciation for my general reader, Bill Funk.

I also want to take this opportunity to acknowledge and celebrate the women in my life who have made all the difference. My mom, Linda, who made me feel invincible against a world that rendered me invisible. My grandmothers, Hazel, for her love of women's biography, and Kaye, for her silent resilience. To Professor Laurie Levenson for giving me my professional jumpstart as a lawyer and academic, and exemplifying true mentorship along the way.

Last, but never least, to my family. To my Dad, who gave me the will to succeed. To Steve, for encouragement and partnership on every level. To Peter, may your passion for history make a difference to how you encounter the world as you venture out on your own. And to Caroline, may you accomplish all that you have dreamed for yourself, unburdened by any limitations of gender.

NOTES

PREFACE

All Stanton sources cited herein can be found in the Stanton and Anthony Microfilm Collection.

1 Felice Batlan, "Engendering Legal History," 30 *Law and Social Inquiry* 823 (2005).

INTRODUCTION

1 Ginzberg, *An American Life*, 10; Kern, 172.

2 Declaration of Sentiments, *Report of the Woman's Rights Convention, Held at Seneca Falls, N.Y., July 19th and 20th, 1848*; ECS, "The Degradation of Disfranchisement," *Boston Investigator*, Apr. 20, 1901, *Microfilm* 41:1038; ECS, "The Degradation of Disfranchisement," address to the NAWSA Twenty-third Annual Convention, *Woman's Tribune*, Mar. 7, 1891; Clark, "Religion," 29–30, 50.

3 "Degradation," 1901; ECS, "National Law for Divorce," Nov. 15, 1899, unidentified newspaper clipping, *Microfilm* 40:227; Griffith, "Marriage," 233.

4 Ginzberg, 120; Griffith, *In Her Own Right*, 125; Gornick, 18; Lutz, 63; ECS, "Shall the World's Fair Be Closed on Sunday," *Woman's Journal*, Feb. 25, 1893; ECS, Hearing, House and Senate Committees on the District of Columbia, Jan. 22, 1870.

5 Griffith, "Marriage," 235; Edward Finch Bullard, "Daniel Cady," 9 *Green Bag* 95, Mar. 1897; HBS, *Random Recollections*, 139; HBS, "Daniel Cady, Biographical Sketch of the Late Judge Cady," *NY Times*, Jan. 25, 1855; "Obituary, Death of Hon. Daniel Cady," *NY Times*, Nov. 3, 1859.

6 ECS, *Eighty Years*, 13–14, 30–32, 46–50; "Our Girls," *Indianapolis Sentinel*, Jan. 19, 1879; ECS, Emma Willard Assoc., Alumnae Questionnaire [1898?], *Microfilm* 39:7; HBS to ECS, June 23, 1842; *Papers*, vol. 1, xxv; Griffith, "Marriage," 237; J. A. Fowler, "The Late Elizabeth Cady Stanton: A Phrenological Interview and Personal Reminiscences of the Great Pioneer Suffragist," *Phrenological Journal and Science of Health* 82 (Mar. 1903); HBS, *Random Recollections*, 147; Griffith, *In Her Own Right*, 8, 14–29; Wellman, 32; author's telephone interview, Coline Jenkins (great-great-granddaughter of ECS), July 17, 2013; Stanton and Blatch, vol. 1, foreword, xiv; DuBois and Smith, *Thinker*, 7–8; Lind, "Symbols, Leaders, Practitioners," 1327, 1338.

7 Ida Husted Harper, "Elizabeth Cady Stanton," *American Monthly Review of Reviews* (Dec. 1902) in Griffith, *In Her Own Right*, xix, 173–75.

8 Address of Mrs. E. C. Stanton at the Tenth National Woman's Rights Convention, May 11, 1860, 65, 71, in *Papers*, vol. 1, 419.

9 Rice, 481, 483.

10 Ginzberg, *An American Life*, 30–41; ECS, *Eighty Years*, 78–79; Rice, 132, 146, 198, 201, 211; Griffith, "Marriage," 234–36; Griffith, *In Her Own Right*, 26–37; *Papers*, vol. 1, xxix, 8; ECS to SBA, April 2, 1852.

11 Advertisement, "Henry B. Stanton. Attorney and Counsellor," in letter HBS to ECS, June 11, 1844.

12 HBS, *Random Recollections*, 141–42; "Henry B. Stanton's Death," *NY Times*, Jan. 15, 1887; *e.g.*, Houston v. City Bank of New Orleans, 47 U.S. 486 (Jan. Term 1848) (bankruptcy); Parker v. Ferguson, 1 Fish. Pat. Rep. 260, 18 F. Cas. 1126, 1 Blatchf. 407 (Cir. Ct. N.D. N.Y. 1849) (patent); Foote v. Silsby, 2 Blatchf. 260, 9 F. Cas. 385 (Cir. Ct. ND NY July 1851) (patent), aff'd Silsby v. Foote, 55 U.S. 218 (1852); Erastus Corning and John F. Winslow v. Peter Burden, 56 U.S. 252 (1853); "Hook-headed Spike," *NY Times*, Dec. 27, 1852; "'The Hook-Headed Spike' Case Decided," *NY Times*, Apr. 17, 1869.

13 Rice, 318; Griffith, *In Her Own Right*, 89; Ginzberg, *An American Life*, 30.

14 ECS to SBA, Apr. 2, 1852.

15 Griffith, "Marriage," 237; ECS, *Eighty Years*, 136.

16 ECS, Letter to the Woman's Rights Convention at Worcester, Oct. 23–24, 1850, 52.

17 Rice, 46, 230, 255; Griffith, *In Her Own Right*, 44, 48–49, 228; Griffith, "Marriage," 237. Stanton may have also miscarried in March 1849. Wellman, 169.

18 ECS, *Eighty Years*, 147–48; Griffith, "Marriage," 238.

19 Wellman, 197.

20 Address of Mrs. Elizabeth Cady Stanton on Woman's Rights, Sept. 1848 (ms.), *Papers*, vol. 1, 94; Wellman, 4, 9, 193; *NY Daily Tribune*, July 19, 1848; HBS to ECS [Sept. 8, 1848].

21 Declaration, 3.

22 ECS, "A Private Letter," *Rev.*, Nov. 10, 1870; Ginzberg, *An American Life*, 61; Clark, "Religion, 30–31"

23 "Private Letter."

24 Isenberg, xviii; Leach, 9; Siegel, "Home," 1073, 1158; Clark, "Religion," 29.

25 Campbell, 51; DuBois, *Feminism and Suffrage*, 24, 191; *HWS*, vol. 1, 124, 163, 215, 375, 517, 472.

26 ECS to SBA, Apr. 2, 1852.

27 ECS, *Eighty Years*, 165.

28 ECS to SBA, Sept. 10, 1855; Griffith, *In Her Own Right*, 88; ECS to SBA, Jan. 24, 1856.

29 Griffith, *In Her Own Right*, 87; ECS to SBA, Nov. 1, 1857.

30 ECS to SBA, July 4, 1858.

31 *Id.* at 8.

32 Griffith, *In Her Own Right*, 106 (citing ECS to SBA, [1861]).

33 Wellman, 221; ECS, *Eighty Years*, 165; SBA to Antoinette Brown Blackwell, Sept. 4, 1858; SBA to ECS, Jan. 16, 1861.

34 Griffith, *In Her Own Right*, 98–99.

35 *HWS*, vol. 2, 50–89; Griffith, *In Her Own Right*, 112; Venet, 103; Eric Foner, *The Fiery Trial: Abraham Lincoln and American Slavery*, 291–92 (New York: Norton, 2010).

36 Rice, 428–62, 470; Testimony, Journal of the Committee on Public Expenditures, U.S. Congress, House of Reps., Report No. 111, 38th Cong. 1863–64 (Washington, D.C.: Gov't Printing Office); Congressional Report, *NY Daily Tribune*, June 16, 1864, 4; HBS, "The New-York Custom-House," *NY Times*, Nov. 6, 1863; Griffith, *In Her Own Right*, 120, 127.

37 Griffith, *In Her Own Right*, 125–30; DuBois, *Suffrage*, 79–104.

38 Earlier women's rights newspapers included the *Lily* (1849–1853) and Pauline Wright Davis's *Una* (1853–1855). Rakow and Kramarae, 7.

39 ECS to SBA, Dec. 28, 1869.

40 ECS to Wendell Phillips, May 25, 1865; Address of ECS, in Proceedings of the First Anniversary of the AERA, May 9, 1867; Thomas, "Sex v. Race, Again," 33.

41 ECS, "Manhood Suffrage," *Rev.,* Dec. 24, 1868; ECS, Address to National Woman Suffrage Convention, Jan. 19, 1869; ECS, Address to Anniversary of the AERA, May 12, 1869; ECS, Anniversary of the NWSA, *Rev.,* May 19, 1870.

42 ECS, "Equal Rights to All!" *Rev.*, Feb. 26, 1868.

43 "Manhood Suffrage"; Mitchell, 128.

44 Suffrage Address, Jan. 1869; ECS, *Eighty Years*, 241–43; ECS, "Letter to Editor," *Woodhull and Claflin's Weekly*, Mar. 4, 1871; ECS to Gerrit Smith, Jan. 1, 1866; *Papers*, vol. 2, xxii–xxiv; DuBois, *Thinker*, 3–4; DuBois, *Feminism and Suffrage*, 61.

45 ECS, "Hartford Convention," *Rev.*, Nov. 11, 1869; "Woman Suffrage," *NY Times*, May 12, 1870; SBA, Remarks to AWSA, Cleveland, Nov. 23, 1870; ECS, "Woman Suffrage Organizations," *Free Parliament*, Dec. 9, 1871; Griffith, *In Her Own Right*, 137–38; Rakow, 49; DuBois, *Feminism and Suffrage*, 165, 190; Tetrault, 35–37.

46 Lutz, 193; Ginzberg, *An American Life*, 143; Griffith, *In Her Own Right*, 169.

47 ECS, "Lyceum Experiences," *Topeka Daily Capital*, June 14, 1885.

48 ECS, *Eighty Years*, 259–60; ECS to Gerrit Smith, Jan. 25, 1870; Griffith, *In Her Own Right*, 163; Hogan and Hogan, 415–19.

49 ECS to Elizabeth Smith Miller, Mar. 1879; ECS to Margaret Stanton, 1872; ECS, "A Basket of Varieties," *Golden Age* (NY), Jan. 6, 1872.

50 ECS to Elizabeth Smith Miller, Sept. 11, 1888.

51 Griffith, *In Her Own Right*, 144, 160–61; Ginzberg, *An American Life*, 152.

52 Tetrault, 112–44.

53 ECS, *Eighty Years*, 352–75; ECS Diary, Stanton and Blatch, vol. 2, 196–213, 235–36; ECS, "Address of Welcome," Formal Opening of the Council, in Report of the International Council of Women, Mar. 25, 1888, 31; Holton, 1112, 1114, 1121–29; Ginzberg, *An American Life*, 68.

54 ECS, *The Woman's Bible* (1895); ECS, "Has Christianity Benefited Woman?" *North American Review* 389, 395 (May 1885); Kern, 100–02.

55 Stansell, *Feminist Promise*, 112–17.

56 Address by ECS, Thirty-first Annual Convention, Feb. 10, 1890; ECS, "The Subjection of Woman" Speech, [1873], in *Papers*, vol. 2, 621.

57 SBA to ECS, before Oct. 26, 1902.

58 Stanton and Blatch.

59 Cott, *Feminism*, 3.

60 *Id.* at 3, 13–14; Offen, 119, 125.

61 Marie-Anne Hubertine Auclert to SBA, Feb. 27, 1888; *HWS*, vol. 3, 899, 952; *Papers*, vol. 4, 299; Report of the International Council of Women, NWSA, Mar. 25–Apr. 1, 1888, 9; ECS, *Eighty Years*, 177.

62 Sue Davis, 219–20; DuBois, *Thinker*, 2, 6, 19.

63 Marshall, 132, 134, 216, 219; Wayne, 32.

64 Cole, 553, 553–54; Fuller, 51, 96; Marshall, 224–30.

65 Wellman, 160; ECS to Elizabeth J. Neall, Nov. 26, 1841; ECS to Elizabeth Pease, Feb. 12, 1842; Sarah Grimké to ECS, Dec. 31, 1842; Lerner, *Grimké Sisters*.

66 Reid, 1123, 1179.

67 *E.g.*, Mrs. Stanton's Suffrage Convention Letter, *Washington Chronicle*, Jan. 28, 1883; *HWS*, vol. 1.

68 Cott, *Feminism*, 4–5; Offen, 135–36; Chamallas, 12; Dowd and Jacobs, 9–11; Thomas and Boisseau, *FLH*, 8–11.

69 Cott, "Comment," 203–5; Siegel, "Home," 105–6; Zillah R. Eisenstein, *The Radical Future of Liberal Feminism* (London: Longman, 1981).

70 *But see* conclusion.

71 Cott, *Feminism*, 19; Clark, "Religion," 34; Offen, 136; Sue Davis, 2.

72 ECS, Address to the Legislature of New-York, Feb. 14, 1854, at 17–18; Declaration, 5.

73 Address on Woman's Rights; Campbell, 52; Clark, "Religion," 31–33.

74 Declaration, 6; ECS, "Subjection" Speech; ECS, Address to the New York State Legislature, Mar. 19, 1860, repeated as Address by Mrs. E. C. Stanton at the Tenth National Woman's Rights Convention, May 10, 1860, *Microfilm* 9:629.

75 ECS, Free Love Speech (ms.), [c.1871], in *Papers*, vol. 2, 392.

76 Miranda McGowan, "Gender Equality: Dimensions of Women's Equal Citizenship," 28 *Constitutional Commentary* 139, 145 (2012).

77 1854 NY Address, 17; Address on Woman's Rights; "Subjection" Speech; "Disenfranchisement"; ECS to SBA, Mar. 1, [1852].

78 Chamallas, 173–219.

79 ECS, "Rev. Joseph Thompson on Woman's Suffrage," *Rev.*, Apr. 22, 1869.

80 1854 NY Address, 17; "Subjection" Speech; ECS, "The Degradation of Woman," *Rev.*, Jan. 15, 1868; ECS, "The Christian Church and Woman," *Index*, Oct. 3, Nov. 6, and Dec. 4, 1884.

81 1854 NY Address, 17; "Rev. Thompson."

82 ECS, "Miss Becker on the Difference in Sex," *Rev.*, Sept. 24, 1868; "Subjection" Speech; ECS, "The Other Side of the Woman Question," 129 *North American Review* 432 (1879); Sue Davis, 154; Hasday, 1373; Kern, 55; Offen, 135; DuBois, "Comment," 95–96; Cott, "Comment," 205.

83 "Other Side," 432.

84 Address on Woman's Rights.

85 "Miss Becker."

86 Address on Woman's Rights; "Manhood Suffrage"; AERA Anniversary Address; "Subjection" Speech.

87 1854 NY Address; "Manhood Suffrage"; Address on Suffrage; Address of Mrs. Stanton, *Chicago Republican*, Feb. 12, 1869; Kern, 56.

88 Hasday, 1377–78, 1384–85.

89 Thomas and Boisseau, *FLH,* 4; Cott, *Bonds,* 1–2, 63–64, 71, 97; Welter, 1.

90 ECS, "Wife," *Lily,* Jan. 1852; Address on Woman's Rights.

91 "Manhood Suffrage"; "Miss Becker"; ECS, "The Pleasures of Age: An Address Delivered by ECS on Her Seventieth Birthday," New York, NY, Nov. 12, 1885; S.F. [ECS], "Man Superior," *Lily,* Apr. 1850; ECS, "Why Must Women Vote," *Lily,* May 1850; ECS, "Rev. Henry Edgar," *Rev.,* June 10, 1869; Kern, 55–57; Sue Davis, 152–53; *Papers,* vol. 2, 183 n. 3.

92 Clark, "Religion," 36.

93 Kern, 55–57; Sue Davis, 152–53.

94 "Miss Becker"; Address on Woman's Rights; ECS, "Progress of the American Woman," 117 *No. Amer. Review* 904 (Dec. 1900).

95 "Miss Becker"; "The Other Side," 432–33; "Progress"; Clark, "Religion," 35.

96 Address on Woman's Rights; "Miss Becker"; Joan Williams, 1267, 1282.

97 ECS, "Social Vice," *NY Sun,* Nov. 30, 1900.

98 Joan Williams, 1266–72.

99 Cott, *Bonds,* 99–100.

100 "Degradation," 1891; Thomas, "Notion," 139.

101 ECS, "Our Defeats and Our Triumphs," NAWSA, 30th Annual Convention, *Woman's Tribune,* Feb. 19, 1898; ; ECS, "Teach Women to Think," *National Citizen and Ballot Box,* Sept. 1880; Address on Woman's Rights; ECS, "I Have All the Rights I Want" [c.1859], *Microfilm* 9:501; ECS, "I Have All the Rights I Want," *Rev.,* Apr. 1, 1869.

102 1854 NY Address, 7; ECS, Address to the New York State Legislature, Mar. 19, 1860, repeated as Address of Mrs. E. C. Stanton at Tenth National Woman's Rights Convention, May 10, 1860, at 34, *Microfilm* 9:629.

103 *HWS,* vol. 1, 15; 1860 NY Address; ECS, "Women Their Own Emancipator," *Woman's Journal,* Aug. 25, 1894.

104 ECS, "The Solitude of Self" to NAWSA Twenty-fourth Convention, Jan. 18, 1892, *Woman's Tribune,* Jan. 23, 1892; ECS, Address, Hearing Before the House Committee on the Judiciary, Jan. 18, 1892; ECS, "The Solitude of Self," *Boston Investigator,* Jan. 12, 1901.

105 "Mrs. Stanton to the Mothers' Congress," *Woman's Journal,* May 26, 1900; Formal Opening, 33.

106 Declaration, 5.

107 *HWS,* vol. 1, 721; Thomas, "Notion," 146–50; Siegel, "Home," 1158.

108 Sue Davis, 71; Harris, 581; Stansell, "Missed," 32; Dowd, 5–6; Newman, 5, 56–64 (1999).

109 DuBois and Smith, *Thinker*, 4.

110 Harris, 585–90; Stansell, "Missed," 32–36; Mitchell, 128.

111 Ann Gordon, "On Account," 111; Sue Davis, 145–47; Thomas, "Sex v. Race, Again," 33–40; *e.g.*, ECS to Phillips, May 25, 1865; ECS, Letter to the National Anti-Slavery Standard, Dec. 26, 1865; ECS, "Letter to the Editor: The Subjection of Woman," *NY Times*, Mar. 7, 1873; Report of the International Council, 48; ECS, "The Worship of God in Man," *Parliament Papers*, 1234 (Sept. 1893).

112 Frontiero v. Richardson, 411 U.S. 677 (1973); Thomas, "Notion," 140–42.

113 "Degradation," *Rev.*, Jan. 15, 1868.

114 ECS, "Address at the Decade Meeting on Marriage and Divorce," in Report of Proceedings of the Twentieth Anniversary, Oct. 20, 1870, *Microfilm* 14:1031, at 61; 1860 NY Address; Address on Woman's Rights; "Degradation," 1891.

115 Fineman, "Feminism," 619–20; Fineman, "Identities," 1713.

116 Address on Woman's Rights.

117 Worcester Letter, 52.

118 Address on Woman's Rights.

119 "National Law."

120 Cott, *Public Vows*, 3.

121 1 William Blackstone, *Commentaries on the Laws of England* 430 (1765) (1979 ed.); see 2 James Kent, *Commentaries on American Law* 74 (3d ed. 1836); Tapping Reeve, *The Law of Baron and Femme, Parent and Child, Guardian and Ward, Master and Servant* (2d ed. 1846).

122 Chused, 71.

123 Basch, *Eyes of the Law*, 17.

124 Grossberg, ix, 12–16; Reid, 1167–71; Warbasse, 28; *e.g.*, Kent; Joel Bishop, *Commentaries on the Law of Marriage and Divorce* (1852 and 1882); James Schouler, *The Law of Domestic Relations* (1870). Joel Bishop apprenticed in Henry Stanton's law office. *Papers*, vol. 1, 50 n. 4.

125 ECS, An Address to the Women of the State of New York, in Proceedings of the Yearly Meeting of Congregational Friends Held at Waterloo, NY, June 3–5, 1850; ECS, "Should Women Vote," *Lily*, July 1850.

126 ECS, "The Christian Church and Woman," *Free Thought Magazine*, Nov. 1896, 673, 681.

127 Reid, 1126–28; ECS, "The Power of the State Legislature," Feb. 18, 1885, *Woman's Tribune*, Apr. 1, 1885.

128 1854 NY Address, 9.

129 Thomas and Boisseau, *FLH*, 4–7; Minor v. Happersett, 88 U.S. 162 (1874); Bradwell v. Illinois, 83 U.S. (16 Wall.) 130 (1872); Ex Parte Lockwood, 154 U.S. 116 (1894).

130 Norton, *Founding Mothers*, 96–137.

131 Thomas and Boisseau, *FLH*, 4; Kerber, *Republic*, 11–12; Address on Woman's Rights.

132 Grossberg, 9–11; Iversen, 14, 100.

133 ECS, "The Need of Liberal Divorce Laws," *No. Amer. Review*, Sept. 1884, 245.

134 Welter, 152–57; "Wife."

135 Declaration; 1854 NY Address; ECS, "How Shall We Solve the Divorce Problem?" *NY American and Journal*, Oct. 13, 1902.

136 "Marriage and Divorce," *NY Tribune*, May 30, 1860; "Address of Elizabeth Cady Stanton on the Divorce Bill, Before the Judiciary Committee of the New York Senate," Feb. 8, 1861; ECS, "Divorce versus Domestic Warfare," *Arena*, Apr. 1890, 563.

137 "'Free Love': Mrs. Stanton on Woman Suffrage and 'Free Love,'" *SF Chronicle*, July 15, 1871.

138 *HWS*, vol. 2, 577.

139 "'Free Love,'" *SF Chronicle*; ECS, "Mrs. Stanton to Mr. Hooker," *Rev.*, Feb. 24, 1870.

140 ECS, "Bible Marriage," *Rev.*, Apr. 2, 1868; "Miss Becker"; "Mrs. Stanton to Mr. Hooker."

141 "'Free Love,'" *SF Chronicle*.

142 Decade Meeting Address, 61; ECS, "Marriage and Divorce," *SF Chronicle*, Aug. 19, 1871; "Free Love," *SF Chronicle*; "The Other Side"; "Bible Marriage."

143 "Free Love," *SF Chronicle*; "Marriage and Divorce," *SF Chronicle*; "Editorial Notes," *Rev.*, Sept. 7, 1871.

144 Decade Meeting Address, 60; "Marriage and Divorce," *Chicago Tribune*, Jan. 26, 1871; "Other Side."

145 *See* Kathleen Kelly Janus, "Finding Common Feminist Ground: The Role of the Next Generation in Shaping Feminist Legal Theory," 20 *Duke J. Gender Law and Policy* 255 (2013).

146 Alfred L. Brophy, "Introducing Applied Legal History," 31 *Law and History Review* 232 (2013).

CHAPTER 1. "WHAT DO YOU WOMEN WANT?"

1 ECS, "Our Defeats and Our Triumphs," NAWSA, 30th Annual Convention, *Woman's Tribune*, Feb. 19, 1898; J. A. Fowler, "The Late Elizabeth Cady Stanton: A Phrenological Interview and Personal Reminiscences of the Great Pioneer Suffragist," *Phrenological Journal and Science of Health* 82 (Mar. 1903).

2 *HWS*, vol. 1, 51–52.

3 Basch, *Eyes of the Law*, 164.

4 ECS, "How Shall We Solve the Divorce Problem?" *NY American and Journal*, Oct. 13, 1902.

5 Warbasse, 28, 39, 42, 82–85, 254, 289.

6 Reid, 1127.

7 Rabkin, 683, 686, 756.

8 ECS, *Eighty Years*, 31–32; "Elizabeth Cady Stanton Dies at Her Home," *NY Times*, Oct. 27, 1902.

9 *E.g.*, Van Epps v. Van Deusen, 4 Paige Ch. 64 (N.Y. Chancery 1833) (defending executor on debt for value of slave girl); Jackson v. Brainard, 5 Cow. 74 (N.Y. Sup. Ct. 1825) (chain of title and adverse possession); Warner v. Van Alstyne, 3 Paige Ch. 513 (Chancery Ct. N.Y. 1832) (equitable lien).

10 "ECS Dies."

11 ECS, *Eighty Years,* 31; "Defeats."

12 ECS, *Eighty Years,* 31–33; ECS, "A Threat Never Executed," *Woman's Tribune,* Aug. 1, 1891.

13 "A Threat Never Executed"; ECS, *Eighty Years,* 31–32; "Defeats," NAWSA.

14 ECS to Paulina Wright Davis, Dec. 6, 1852.

15 Wellman, 165–66.

16 Daniel Cady, Deed to ECS for House at Seneca Falls, June 22, 1847, *Microfilm* 6:635; Will of Daniel Cady, Sept. 13, 1859, in Fulton County Surrogate Court, Johnstown, NY, Will Book 5, pp. 196–98; Quitclaim Deed, Edward and Tryphena Bayard to ECS for Chalk Rights, Farm at Seneca Falls, Jan. 4, 1866, *Microfilm* 11:263.

17 ECS Warranty Deed to John S. Edwards, Apr. 21, 1862, *Microfilm* 10:204; ECS, Discharge of Mortgage to John S. Edwards, Apr. 21, 1864, *Microfilm* 10:761; ECS Warranty Deed to James H. Lay, Mar. 31, 1866, *Microfilm* 11:413.

18 ECS, "Editorial Correspondence," *Rev.,* Oct. 1, 1868.

19 Declaration of Sentiments, *Report of the Woman's Rights Convention, Held at Seneca Falls, N.Y., July 19th and 20th, 1848,* 3.

20 Basch, *Eyes of the Law,* 172; Miller, 152, 164.

21 Siegel, "Home," 1073, 1152.

22 Num. 27:1; ECS, "Teach Women to Think," *National Citizen Ballot Box,* Sept. 1880.

23 Katharine Doob Sakenfeld, "Feminist Biblical Interpretation," 46 *Theology Today* 154, 155–56 (July 1989); Num. 36:1–13.

24 *HWS,* vol. 1, 66–67 (passed by the Senate 23–1 and in the Assembly 93–9).

25 Chused, 1359, 1398–1401 (1983); Rabkin, 694; Siegel, "Home," 1082–83.

26 Basch, *Eyes of the Law,* 70–72; Rabkin, 690–94; e.g., Martin v. Martin, 1 N.Y. 473 (1848); Yale v. Dederer, 18 N.Y. 265 (1858).

27 ECS, "The Married Woman's Property Bill," *Post Express,* Mar. 26, 1896.

28 Basch, *Eyes of the Law,* 114; Rabkin, 690–96.

29 *HWS,* vol. 1, 16, 63–64; "Property Bill"; ECS, "Married Woman's Property Bill of 1848," *Woman's Tribune,* Dec. 4, 1897; "Defeats."

30 Basch, *Eyes of the Law,* 38–39; Rabkin, 719.

31 Basch, *Eyes of the Law,* 115.

32 Rabkin, 726–27.

33 Judge Thomas Herttell, *Remarks Comprising in Substance Judge Herttell's Argument in the House of Assembly in the State of New-York, in the Session of 1837, in Support of the Bill to Restore to Married Women "The Right of Property" as Guaranteed by the Constitution of this State,* 9, 21–23, 57–58 (New York: Henry Durell, 1839).

34 *HWS,* vol. 1, 38; Basch, *Eyes of the Law,* 119; Ginzberg, *Untidy,* 10–12.

35 *NY Assembly Documents,* Petition, Mar. 15, 1848, No. 129, 1–2, in *Documents of the Assembly of the State of New-York, Seventy-first Session* (Albany, NY: Charles Van Benthuysen, 1848).

36 ECS, "Women Their Own Emancipators," *Woman's Journal,* Aug. 25, 1894; ECS, "U.S. Senator Hoar Reminded," *Woman's Tribune,* Aug. 25, 1894; Basch, *Eyes of the Law,* 137; "Property Bill"; "Property Bill of 1848"; "Defeats."

37 "Defeats."

38 E. P. Hurlbut, *Essays on Human Rights and Their Political Guaranties* (New York: Greeley and McElrath, 1845); Wellman, 162; ECS to Elizabeth Smith, Feb. 15, 1843; *HWS*, vol. 1, 38–39; ECS to SBA, Dec. 1, 1843.

39 *NY Assembly Documents*, Feb. 26, 1844, No. 96, 3–6, in *Documents of the Assembly of the State of New-York, Sixty-Seventh Session*, vol. 3 (Albany, NY: Carroll and Cook, 1844).

40 Rabkin, 734-35; Basch, *Eyes of the Law*, 149–55.

41 William G. Bishop and William H. Attree, *Report of the Debates and Proceedings of the Convention for the Revision of the Constitution of the State of New-York, 1846* (Albany, NY: Albany Argus, 1847), 1038–42.

42 Warbasse, 219.

43 Basch, *Eyes of the Law*, 153–55; Wellman, 152.

44 Warbasse, 225.

45 *HWS*, vol. 1, 64; Wellman, 152.

46 Laws of New York, 1848, chap. 200, available at http://www.heinonline.org/.

47 Laws of New York, 1849, chap. 375, available at http://www.heinonline.org/.

48 *HWS*, vol. 1, 63.

49 ECS, "Editorial Correspondence," *Rev.*, Oct. 1, 1868.

50 "Defeats"; Siegel, "Home," 1084.

51 *HWS*, vol. 1, 751–52.

52 Siegel, "Home," 1108–10.

53 Chused, 1400 (citing Rabkin, 125–38; Warbasse, 237–40).

54 *E.g.*, White v. White, 5 Barb 474 (N.Y. S. Ct. 1849); Siegel, "Marital Status," 2138; Basch, *Eyes of the Law*, 200–03.

55 Chused, 1411.

56 Siegel, "Marital Status," 2141–42.

57 ECS, "Legislative Doings," *Lily*, May 1850.

58 Siegel, "Home," 1076, 1095.

59 Proceedings of the Woman's Rights Conventions, Held at Seneca Falls and Rochester, N.Y., July and Aug. 1848; *HWS*, vol. 1, 80.

60 Worcester Letter, 18.

61 ECS, Address to the Legislature of New-York, Feb. 14, 1854, at 19.

62 ECS, Address before the U.S. Senate Special Committee on Woman Suffrage (Feb. 8, 1890), *Woman's Tribune*, Feb. 15, 1890.

63 Siegel, "Home," 1114–15.

64 *Id.* at 1083.

65 *Id.*; Basch, *Eyes of the Law*, 194–95.

66 Siegel, "Home," 1125–27; Address of Mrs. E. C. Stanton at the Tenth National Woman's Rights Convention, May 11, 1860, at 65, 89, in *Papers* vol. 1, 419.

67 ECS to SBA, Jan. 16, 1854.

68 ECS to SBA, Jan. 20, 1854.

69 ECS, "A Threat Never Executed"; Solomon, 354.

70 1854 NY Address, 3.

71 *Id.* at 11.

72 *Id. at* 9–11, 18–19.

73 *HWS*, vol. 1, 613, 616.

74 *Id.*; *NY Assembly Documents*, Mar. 27, 1854, No. 149, 1, *in Documents of the Assembly of the State of New-York, Seventy-Seventh Session* (Albany, NY: Charles Van Benthuysen, 1854).

75 *NY Assembly Documents*, 77th Sess, vol. 4, n. 129 (1854) in *Documents of the Assembly of the State of New-York, Seventy-Seventh Session* (Albany, NY: Charles Van Benthuysen, 1854); *HWS*, vol. 1, 618 n. 6.

76 Siegel, "Home," 1139–40, n. 229.

77 "Defeats"; *HWS*, vol. 1, 619; Basch, *Eyes of the Law,* 190–91; Miller, 161.

78 Siegel, "Home," 1140.

79 *HWS*, vol. 1, 629.

80 Siegel, "Home," 1197.

81 ECS, Appeal to the Women of the Empire State, July 1859.

82 Siegel, "Home," 1143–44; *HWS*, vol. 1, 686–87.

83 SBA to Martha Coffin Wright, Feb. 15, 1860; *HWS*, vol. 1, 678.

84 ECS to SBA, Jan. 25, 1860.

85 *Papers*, vol. 1, 406–8; *Journal of the Assembly of the State of New-York, Eighty-third Session* (Albany, NY: Charles Van Benthuysen, 1860), at 663.

86 Amory Dwight Mayo to ECS, Mar. 19, 1860; ECS, Address to the New York State Legislature, Mar. 19, 1860, repeated as Address of Mrs. E. C. Stanton at Tenth National Woman's Rights Convention, May 10, 1860, at 34, *Microfilm* 9:629; "Mrs. Stanton on Woman's Rights," *National Anti-Slavery Standard*, Mar. 31, 1860; Miller, 156.

87 1860 NY Address.

88 Laws of New York, 1860, chap. 90, sec. 1–3, available at http://www.heinonline. org/.

89 Siegel, "Marital Status," 2145.

90 "Notes from the Capital," *NY Times*, Mar. 21, 1860.

91 Basch, *Eyes of the Law*, 164–65.

92 Laws of New York, 1862, chap. 172, sec. 3, available at http://www.heinonline.org/.

93 Siegel, "Marital Status," 2156–57; see Brooks v. Schwerin, 54 N.Y. 343 (N.Y. Ct. App. 1873).

94 Birkbeck v. Ackroyd, 74 N.Y. 356 (N.Y. Ct. App. 1878).

95 Siegel, "Home," 1084–85.

96 Siegel, "Marital Status," 2154, 2158.

97 ECS, "American and Hindoo Widows," *Rev.*, Apr. 16, 1868; "Woman's Right of Property in Maine," *Rev.*, Aug. 20, 1868; "Woman's Property Rights in Illinois," *Rev.*, Mar. 25, 1869; Parker Pillsbury, "A Wife's Debts and Earnings," *Rev.*, Aug. 5, 1869; "Civil Code of Louisiana," *Rev.*, Sept. 23, 1869; C. I. H. Nichols, "Property Rights of Wives," *Rev.*, Sept. 2, 1869; "The Married Woman's Separate Property Bill

Defeated in Connecticut," *Rev.*, July 7, 1870; S., "Letters from Friends," *Rev.*, July 7, 1870; C. I. H. Nichols, "The Laws of New York," *Rev.*, June 16, 1870; "Widows of Husbands, Dead and Living," *Rev.*, Apr. 14, 1870.

98 "Emancipators"; "Senator Hoar."

99 Rochester Proceedings, Aug. 1848, 15.

100 Basch, *Eyes of the Law*, 176.

101 1854 NY Address, 12.

102 Dubler, "Shadow," 1641, 1660–63, 1670–71.

103 Homer H. Clark Jr., *The Law of Domestic Relations in the United States*, 2d ed. (St. Paul, MN: West, 1988), 288; Warbasse, 279.

104 Hartog, *Man and Wife*, 145.

105 Salmon, 141–46; Hartog, *Man and Wife*, 145–46; Dubler, "Shadow," 1660–63.

106 *E.g.*, Walker v. Schuyler, 10 Wend. 480 (S. Ct. Jud. 1833); Kittle v. Van Dyck, 3 N.Y.Leg.Obs. 126 (Chancery Ct. N.Y. 1843); Kennedy v. Mills, 13 Wend. 553 (S. Ct. Jud. 1835); Jackson ex dem. Clark v. O'Donaghy, 7 Johns. 247 (N.Y. S. Ct. 1810).

107 1854 NY Address, 12.

108 ECS, "I Have All the Rights I Want," 3 [c. 1859], *Microfilm* 6:501; 1854 NY Address, 12.

109 1854 NY Address, 13.

110 "Sister Stanton," *Wash. C. Press*, Feb. 25, 1880.

111 1854 NY Address, 11.

112 Salmon, 141.

113 Basch, *Eyes of the Law*, 85–87.

114 Dubler, "Shadow," 1676.

115 "Hindoo Widows."

116 1854 NY Address, 14.

117 *Id.* at 13.

118 Dubler, "Shadow," 1677–78.

119 Laws of New York, 1860, chap. 90, at 157 (83rd Session) (passed Mar. 20, 1860).

120 Laws of New York, 1862, chap. 172, sec. 2 at 344 (85th Session) (passed April 10, 1862).

121 Basch, *Eyes of the Law*, 122.

122 *Id.* at 137; Mary L. Heen, "From Coverture to Contract: Engendering Insurance on Lives," 23 *Yale Journal of Law and Feminism* 335, 345 (2011).

123 ECS, "Railway Passengers Assurance Company," *Rev.*, Oct. 8, 1868; ECS, "Rev. Joseph Thompson on Woman's Suffrage," *Rev.*, Apr. 22, 1869; ECS, "The Co-education of the Sexes," Papers at the First Woman's Congress of the Association for the Advancement of Woman, Oct. 17, 1873, 39–51, *Microfilm* 17:316.

124 Siegel, "Home," 1172 n. 367.

125 ECS, "Home Life," *Milwaukee Sentinel*, May 21, 1878.

126 "Rev. Thompson."

127 ECS, Taxation Lecture (ms.), 9–10 [1877], *Microfilm* 19:717; ECS, Speech to the Women Taxpayers' Association in Rochester, New York, Oct. 31, 1873, in *Papers*, vol. 3, 4.

128 Kerber, *Ladies*, 113–15; ECS, "An Unjust Decision against the Tax-Paying Women of Indiana," *National Citizen Ballot Box*, Oct. 1880.

129 ECS, Letter to the Editor, reprinted, *National Citizen and Ballot Box*, April 1879.

130 "Unjust Decision"; State ex rel. Tieman v. City of Indianapolis, 69 Ind. 375 (Ind. 1880).

131 Taxation Lecture, 2.

132 Declaration, 3; McClain and Grossman, 1, 8.

133 ECS, "Women Do Not Wish to Vote," *National Bulletin*, Apr. 1894.

134 Isenberg, 32.

135 ECS to SBA, July 4, 1858; ECS, "The Power of the Statute Legislature," *Woman's Tribune*, Mar. 1, 1885.

136 ECS, "A Household of Women," *Woman's Tribune*, Oct. 6, 1900; Mrs. Stanton's Suffrage Convention Letter, *Washington Chronicle*, Jan. 28, 1883; Sue Davis, 2, 19–20.

137 Kerber, *Ladies*, 94; Isenberg, 13.

138 Kerber, *Ladies*, 11.

139 Kerber, *Republic*, 283; Norton, *Liberty's*, 247–49.

140 Isenberg, 198; 1860 NY Address; ECS, "The Degradation of Woman," *Rev.*, Jan. 15, 1868; Miller, 173.

141 ECS, "Editorial Correspondence," *Rev.*, Mar. 17, 1870; "Rev. Thompson."

142 ECS, *Bible and Church Degrade Woman*, 3d ed. (Chicago, IL: H.L. Green, 1899), *Microfilm* 39:651.

143 Clark, "Self-Ownership," 905.

144 Isenberg, 26.

145 Kerber, *Ladies*, 94.

146 Isenberg, 24.

147 Taxpayers' Speech.

148 Taxation Lecture, 15–16.

149 Taxation Lecture, 23h.

150 "Household."

151 Declaration; *Bible and Church*, 1–12.

152 Taxpayers' Speech.

153 Taxation Lecture, 23e–g.

154 Rochester Proceedings, 15.

155 Kerber, *Ladies*, 100–104; Jones, 265, 269.

156 Jones, 269.

157 Kerber, *Ladies*, 113.

158 Jones, 272–73.

159 Declaration, 4.

160 "Francis Minor," *Rev.*, Oct. 21, 1869; "Mrs. Francis Minor," *Rev.*, Oct. 28, 1869; "Fundamental Rights," *Rev.*, Jan. 20, 1870.

161 Argument of Mrs. Stanton before the Judiciary Committee, reprinted as "Woman Suffrage," *Daily Morning Chronicle*, Jan. 13, 1872.

162 Winkler, 1456, 1475–77, 1483; DuBois, "Taking the Law," 23–34.

163 Winkler, 1456–59, 1468, 1480, 1515.

164 ECS, Speech to Joint Committees of D.C., in "The Women in Washington," *Rev.*, Jan. 27, 1870.

165 *Id.*; *HWS*, vol. 2, 411–16.

166 *HWS*, vol. 2, 510.

167 "Woman Suffrage"; *HWS*, vol. 2, 510.

168 Winkler, 1482–83.

169 *Id.*, 1472–74.

170 Jack M. Balkin, "How Social Movements Change (or Fail to Change) the Constitution: The Case of the New Departure," 39 *Suffolk University Law Review* 27, 46 (2005); John Bingham, H.R. Rep. No. 41–22, Report, Committee on the Judiciary, 41st Cong., House of Rep., Jan. 30, 1871.

171 Bingham Report.

172 88 U.S. 162 (1875).

173 Bingham Report.

174 "Rev. Thompson"; *HWS*, vol. 1, 412; see 41st Cong., 3d Session, H.R. Rep. 22, Jan. 30, 1871, by Reps. Loughridge and Butler (pt. 2, minority) (Judiciary Committee) (Minority Report, 9); *HWS*, vol. 2, 594.

175 ECS, Letter to Editor, *Woodhull and Claflin's Weekly*, Mar. 11, 1871.

176 88 U.S. 162 (1875); Slaughter-House Cases, 83 U.S. (16 Wall.) 36 (1872).

177 ECS, "Statement of Mrs. Elizabeth Cady Stanton," hearing before the Senate Select Committee on Woman Suffrage, Apr. 2, 1888, *Microfilm* 26:579.

178 Winkler, 1465.

179 *HWS*, vol. 1, 14, 64; Senate Committee Statement.

180 ECS, "Man Marriage," *Free Parliament*, Nov. 11, 1871.

181 *HWS*, vol. 1, 65.

182 Basch, *Eyes of the Law*, 168–69.

183 Siegel, "Marital Status," 2142.

184 Worcester Letter, 17.

185 Basch, *Eyes of the Law*, 10.

CHAPTER 2. "THE PIVOT OF THE MARRIAGE RELATION"

1 ECS, "Marriage and Divorce, to the Editor," *NY Daily Tribune*, May 30, 1860.

2 *Id.*

3 ECS, "The Man Marriage," *Rev.*, Apr. 8, 1869.

4 ECS, "Side Issues," *Rev.*, Oct. 6, 1870; ECS, "The Kernel of the Question," *Rev.*, Nov. 4, 1869.

5 DuBois, "On Labor," 65.

6 ECS to Frederick Douglass, June 27, 1884; *see* Maria Diedrich, *Love across Color Lines* (New York: Hill and Wang, 1999).

7 SBA to ECS, Jan. 27, 1884; Newman, 4.

8 ECS to Elizabeth J. Neall, Feb. 3, 1843; "Theodore Tilton's Opinion of Anna E. Dickinson," *Rev.*, Nov. 5, 1868.

9 ECS to SBA, Mar. 1, [1852].

10 HBS, *Random Recollections*, 74.

11 ECS, *Eighty Years*, 71; "Mrs. Stanton's Views on Marriage and Divorce," 66 *Nation* 403, May 26, 1898.

12 Griffith, "Marriage", 235, 244; ECS, "Our Mt. Morris Letter," *Democrat and Chronicle*, Feb. 25, 1871; "A Talk with Mrs. Stanton: Her Opinion concerning the Great Scandal Trial," *Sun*, July 17, 1875.

13 Griffith, "Marriage," 236–37; Blanche Glassman Hersh, "A Partnership of Equals: Feminist Marriages in Nineteenth-Century America," *American Man*, Elizabeth Peck and Joseph Peck, eds. (New Jersey: Prentice-Hall, 1980), 187.

14 Rice, 335–36; ECS to SBA, Feb. 15, 1855.

15 ECS, "The Women and the State," *Rev.*, Aug. 19, 1869; "Mrs. Stanton's Address, Anniversary of the NWSA," *Rev.*, May 19, 1870.

16 ECS, Letter to the Convention, in Proceedings of the Ohio Women's Convention, Held at Salem, April 19th and 20th, 1850, *Microfilm* 6:997.

17 Sarah Grimké, *Letters on the Equality of the Sexes, and the Condition of Woman* (Boston: Isaac Knapp, 1838); Reid, 1172–74.

18 Cott, *Public Vows*, 63, 80.

19 *Id.*, 61; Clark, "Bonds," 30–31.

20 ECS, "Editorial Correspondence," *Rev.*, Jan. 28, 1869.

21 ECS, "Man the Usurper," *Rev.*, March 12, 1868.

22 Cott, *Public Vows*, 62–66.

23 Letter from Mrs. Stanton, Nov. 24, 1856, in Proceedings of the Seventh National Woman's Rights Convention, Nov. 25 and 26, 1856, 88, *Microfilm* 8:807.

24 Clark, "Bonds," 47.

25 "The Man Marriage"; ECS, Address to the New York State Legislature, Mar. 19, 1860, repeated as Address of Mrs. E.C. Stanton at Tenth National Woman's Rights Convention, May 10, 1860, at 34, 37, *Microfilm* 9:629; ECS, "Miss Becker on the Difference in Sex," *Rev.*, Sept. 24, 1868.

26 "Marriage and Divorce," *Rev.*, Oct. 29, 1868.

27 "Women and the State."

28 ECS, "A Private Letter," *Rev.*, Nov. 10, 1870.

29 1860 NY Address; 1854 NY Address; Address of Mrs. E.C. Stanton at Tenth National Woman's Rights Convention, May 11, 1860, at 65, in *Papers*, vol. 1, 419.

30 Regina v. Jackson, 1 Queen's Bench 671 (Ct. Appeal 1891); ECS, "Reminiscences, Chap. LXVIII," *Woman's Tribune*, 1892; ECS, "The Lord Chancellor," *Woman's Herald*, Mar. 28, 1891.

31 "Marriage and Divorce," *NY Tribune*; "Women and the State."

32 ECS to SBA, July 20, 1857.

33 Clark, "Bonds," 48.

34 "Women and the State"; ECS and Elizabeth W. McClintock to the Editors, *Seneca County Courier*, after July 23, 1848.

35 "Man Marriage"; ECS, "Reminiscences, Bishop Janes and the Word Obey," *Woman's Tribune*, Nov. 8, 1890.

36 "'Obey' in the Marriage Service, Unconstitutional," *Rev.*, Mar. 24, 1870; ECS, *Eighty Years*, 72.

37 *HWS*, vol. 1, Aug. 2, 1848, 78–79.

38 ECS and McClintock; Address of Mrs. Elizabeth Cady Stanton on Woman's Rights, Sept. 1848 (ms.), *Papers*, vol. 1, 94.

39 ECS and McClintock; *HWS*, vol. 1, 79.

40 "Mrs. E. Cady Stanton on Marriage and Divorce, and Other Things," *Wisconsin State Journal*, Nov. 29, 1870; "Marriage and Divorce," *Rev.*, Oct. 26, 1870; "Marriage and Divorce," *Chicago Tribune*, Jan. 25, 1871.

41 Letter from Mrs. E. C. Stanton, *Sibyl*, Feb. 1, 1857; Mrs. E. C. Stanton, "Paper on Marriage," *Proceedings of the Yearly Meeting of the Friends of Human Progress* 28 (June 7–9, 1857).

42 "'Obey' Unconstitutional."

43 ECS, *Eighty Years*, 71.

44 *Id.* at 71–73; ECS, "Overland Letters," *Rev.*, June 22, 1871; Yalom, 198.

45 Griffith, "Marriage," 235.

46 "'Obey' Unconstitutional."

47 "Overland Letters"; ECS, Letter to the Editor, *National Citizen and Ballot Box*, June 1878; "'Obey' Unconstitutional"; "Bishop Janes."

48 "Man Marriage"; "Bishop Janes"; "Why She Liked Him," *New World*, Mar. 18, 1870; "'Obey' Unconstitutional"; ECS, "Address at the Decade Meeting on Marriage and Divorce," in Report of Proceedings of the Twentieth Anniversary, Oct. 20, 1870, *Microfilm* 14:1031, 66; ECS, *Eighty Years*, 71–73.

49 ECS, "The Subjection of Woman," *NY Times*, Mar. 7, 1873.

50 "Mrs. Stanton's Address, Anniversary of the NWSA."

51 ECS, "The Family Unit," *Index*, Sept. 18, 1884.

52 "Women and the State"; Tenth Convention Address, 37; "Lucy Stone," *Rev.*, April 1, 1869.

53 *HWS*, vol. 1, 80.

54 Griffith, *In Her Own Right*, xix.

55 Una Stannard, *Married Women v. Husbands' Names: The Case for Wives Who Keep Their Own Name*, 1–5 (San Francisco: Germainbooks, 1973).

56 ECS, *Woman's Bible*, 205; Letter to Seventh National Convention, 89.

57 Letter to Seventh National Convention, 89.

58 Banner, 22.

59 Griffith, *In Her Own Right*, 237 n. 20.

60 ECS to Rebecca Eyster, May 1, 1847.

61 *Id.*

62 ECS, "Full Names," *Inter-Ocean*, Nov. 20, 1880.

63 Lutz, 101 (citing ECS Letter to Lucy Stone @ 1855).

64 "Mrs. Stanton's Address, Anniversary of the NWSA."

65 "Lucy Stone"; "Mrs. Stanton's Address, Anniversary of the NWSA."

66 ECS, Proceedings of the Twenty-Sixth Annual Convention of the NAWSA, Feb. 15–20, 1894, in *Woman's Tribune*, Feb. 15, 1894.

67 *See* chapter 3; ECS to Wendell Phillips, Aug. 10, 1860; Wendell Phillips to ECS, Aug. 21, 1860.

68 ECS to Wendell Phillips, Aug. 10, 1860; Wendell Phillips to ECS, Aug. 21, 1860; ECS to Wendell Phillips, Feb. 5, 1861.

69 ECS, "Address in Favor of Universal Suffrage, for the Election of Delegates to the Constitutional Convention," Jan. 23, 1867, *Microfilm* 11:907; ECS, "New York Constitutional Convention in 1867" (ms.) [1894], *Microfilm* 33:69; ECS to Emily Howland, July 10, 1867.

70 Griffith, "Marriage," 244.

71 "Paper on Marriage," 28; ECS, "Mrs. Dall's Fraternity Lecture," *Liberator*, Nov. 16, 1860.

72 "Paper on Marriage," 21–23.

73 *Id.*

74 Ward and Burns, 92.

75 Tenth Convention Address; "Address of Elizabeth Cady Stanton on the Divorce Bill, Before the Judiciary Committee of the New York Senate," Feb. 8, 1861.

76 ECS to SBA, July 20, 1857; Divorce Bill Address, 8.

77 ECS, "Marriages and Mistresses," *Rev.*, Oct. 15, 1868.

78 Clark, "Bonds," 41; Tenth Convention Address; "Marriage and Divorce," *NY Tribune*; ECS, "A Private Letter," *Rev.*, Nov. 10, 1870.

79 "Marriage and Divorce," *NY Daily Tribune*; "Marriages and Mistresses"; Divorce Bill Address.

80 ECS to SBA, July 20, 1857.

81 "Side Issues"; "Kernel."

82 ECS, "The Moral of the Byron Case," *Independent*, Sept. 9, 1869.

83 ECS, "Editorial Correspondence," *Rev.*, Dec. 23, 1869.

84 Divorce Bill Address, 11–12.

85 Tenth Convention Address; Divorce Bill Address; "Marriages and Mistresses"; "The Man Marriage," *Rev.*; ECS, "Man Marriage," *Free Parliament, Golden Sun*, Nov. 11, 1871.

86 "Man Marriage," *Free Parliament*.

87 "The Man Marriage," *Rev.*

88 Tenth Convention Address, 72; "Marriage and Divorce," *Rev.*

89 "Marriages and Mistresses"; "The Man Marriage," *Rev.*

90 "Marriage and Divorce," *NY Daily Tribune*; Divorce Bill Address; ECS, "Marriages and Mistresses."

91 "Man Marriage," *Free Parliament*.

92 "Marriages and Mistresses."

93 "The Man Marriage," *Rev.*

94 "The Man Marriage," *Rev.*; ECS, Divorce Bill Address; "Man Marriage," *Free Parliament*.

95 "Marriage and Divorce," *NY Tribune*; Divorce Bill Address.

96 "Marriages and Mistresses."

97 "Marriage and Divorce," *NY Tribune*.

98 "Marriage and Divorce," *NY Tribune*; Divorce Bill Address.

99 "Marriages and Mistresses"; Divorce Bill Address, 4.

100 "The Man Marriage," *Rev.*; "Miss Becker."

101 "The Man Marriage," *Rev.*; Decade Meeting Address, 76.

102 ECS, "The Woman Question," *Radical*, Sept. 1867, 19; ECS, "St. Paul on Duties of Wives," *Rev.*, Aug. 6, 1868.

103 "The Man Marriage," *Rev.*

104 "Family Unit."

105 ECS, "The Head of the Family," *Rev.*, Aug. 1869; Decade Meeting Address.

106 ECS, "Rev. Newman Hall," *Rev.*, Jan. 21, 1869; "The Newman Hall Suite: Conduct of a Wayward Woman," *NY Times*, Aug. 13, 1879, 2; "A London Preacher's Suit for Divorce," *NY Times*, Aug. 15, 1879, 1.

107 "Family Unit."

108 "'Free Love': Mrs. Stanton on Woman Suffrage and 'Free Love,'" *SF Chronicle*, July 15, 1871.

109 ECS to Elizabeth Miller, Aug. 11, 1880.

110 ECS, Free Love Speech (ms.), [c.1871], in *Papers*, vol. 2, 392; DuBois, "On Labor," 65.

111 "Man Marriage," *Free Parliament*.

112 Thomas Low Nichols and Mary S. Gove Nichols, *Marriage: Its History, Character, and Results*, 201 (New York: T.L. Nichols, 1854); DuBois, "Feminism and Free Love"; Passet, 21–38.

113 Cott, *Public Vows*, 68; DuBois, "Feminism and Free Love."

114 Barbara Goldsmith, *Other Powers: The Age of Suffrage, Spiritualism, and the Scandalous Victoria Woodhull* (New York: Knopf, 1998); DuBois, "Feminism and Free Love."

115 "Elizabeth Cady Stanton on Woman," *Newark Sunday Call*, Jan. 2, 1876.

116 DuBois, "On Labor," 257, 263.

117 Ann Braude, *Radical Spirits: Spiritualism and Women's Rights in Nineteenth-Century America* (Bloomington: Indiana University Press, 2001); DuBois, "Feminism and Free Love."

118 DuBois, "Feminism and Free Love"; M. S. Gove Nichols to ECS, Aug. 21, 1851; ECS to Nichols, Aug. 21, 1852; ECS to Nichols, Aug. 31, 1852.

119 "Marriages and Mistresses."

120 *Id.*; DuBois, "On Labor," 264; Clark, "Bonds," 43.

121 Free Love Speech; DuBois, "On Labor," 264.

122 Free Love Speech, see second translation in *Microfilm* 15:862.

123 DuBois, "On Labor," 264–65.

124 *Id.*

125 Free Love Speech.

126 "Man Marriage," *Free Parliament.*

127 "'Free Love,'" *SF Chronicle.*

128 Iversen, 12 n. 9; Sarah Gordon, *Mormon Question*, 22–29; Cott, *Public Vows*, 105.

129 Morrill Act, 1862; Poland Act, 1874; Edmunds Act, 1882; Edmunds-Tucker Act, 1887.

130 Iversen, 22, 39 n. 9; Sarah Gordon, *Mormon Question*, 111–12; Cott, *Public Vows*, 72–73, 113.

131 98 U.S.145, 165–66 (1878).

132 Sarah Gordon, *Mormon Question*, 151–55; Sarah Gordon, "Self-Degradation," 816, 825–26, 832; Iversen, 22–25, 113–14; Charlotte Godbe, "A Mormon Lady on the Mormon Leader," *Rev.*, Dec. 15, 1870; The Late Corp. of Church of Jesus Christ of Latter-Day Saints v. United States, 136 U.S. 1 (1890); Murphy v. Ramsey, 114 U.S. 15, 43, 45 (1885); Cott, *Public Vows*, 119.

133 ECS to Elizabeth Smith Miller, June 12, 1871; ECS, "Overland Letters: Salt Lake City," *Rev.*, July 20, 1871; ECS, "Overland Letters: The City of Saints," *Rev.*, July 13, 1871; ECS, "Reminiscences: A Week in Salt Lake City," *Woman's Tribune*, Sept. 13, 1890; ECS, *Eighty Years*, 283–87; Iversen, 25, 40.

134 "City of Saints"; "For Women Only: Mrs. Elizabeth Cady Stanton Discourses on Marriage and Maternity," *SF Chronicle*, July 13, 1871; Iversen, 25.

135 ECS, *Eighty Years*, 283–89; ECS, "Reminiscences: Salt Lake." The case is possibly *Gaines v. New Orleans*, 73 U.S. 642 (1867), denying inheritance rights to the children of a bigamist father in Louisiana, but more likely *Cope v. Cope*, 137 U.S. 682 (1891), directly on point upholding the Edmunds-Tucker Act and its denial of inheritance rights for plural wives and their children. *Cope* had not been decided at the time of Stanton's Salt Lake City trip, but was handed down near the time she published her memoirs.

136 *HWS*, vol. 3, 128; vol. 4, 78, 122, 939–40; Iversen, 28–29; ECS to SBA, Autumn 1879.

137 "City of Saints"; ECS, *Eighty Years*, 283; "Marriage and Divorce," *Chicago Tribune*; Iversen, 25–26.

138 "Overland Letters: Salt Lake City."

139 "City of Saints."

140 *Id.*

141 Iversen, 27.

142 *Id.* at 5, 99–114; Sarah Gordon, "Self-Degradation," 815–19.

143 ECS, "The Central Idea of Woman's Degradation," *Woman's Tribune*, Dec 3, 1884; "City of Saints"; Iversen, 60–61; Cott, *Public Vows*, 120.

144 "City of Saints."

145 ECS, "The Central Idea of Woman's Degradation," *Woman's Tribune*, January 1885; "Marriage and Divorce," *Chicago Tribune.*

146 "Reminiscences: Salt Lake"; ECS, *Eighty Years*, 283–89.

147 "Central Idea."

148 "Reminiscences: Salt Lake."

149 "Kernel."

150 Grossberg, 21–22; Cott, *Public Vows*, 101–3.

151 ECS, "The Need of Liberal Divorce Laws," *No. Amer. Review*, Sept. 1884, 242.

152 Decade Meeting Address, 65–66; "Marriage and Divorce," *Chicago Tribune*; ECS, "Marriage and Divorce," *SF Chronicle*, Aug. 19, 1871.

153 ECS, "Are Homogeneous Laws in All the States Desirable?" *No. Amer. Review* 407, Mar. 1900; ECS, "American Marriage and Divorce," *Humanitarian*, Mar. 1900, 195.

154 Clark, "Bonds," 26.

155 1854 NY Address, 8.

156 Tenth Convention Address, 67; Divorce Bill Address, 6; ECS, "Marriage and Divorce," *Rev.*, Oct. 22, 1868.

157 Tenth Convention, 72; Divorce Bill Address, 10; ECS, "Marriage and Divorce," *Rev.*, Oct. 29, 1868.

158 Clark, "Bonds," 36.

159 Tenth Convention Address, 72.

160 *Id.* at 67; ECS, "Marriage Law," *Omaha Republican*, Mar. 3, 1889; Clark, "Bonds," 37; ECS, "Divorce versus Domestic Warfare," *Arena*, Apr. 1890, 566.

161 ECS, Letter to the Editor, "Mrs. Stanton's Views on Marriage and Divorce," *Nation*, May 26, 1898, 403; ECS, Diary, Jan. 1, 1898, in Stanton and Blatch, vol. 2, 330–31.

162 "Paper on Marriage," 22.

163 "Views."

164 Clark, "Bonds," 35.

165 Tenth Convention Address, 67; Divorce Bill Address; ECS, "Marriage and Divorce," *Rev.*

166 Decade Meeting Address, 64, 67–68; ECS, "Other Things"; Dubler, "Governing," 1909–10.

167 Grossberg, 87.

168 Dubler, "Governing," 1908–12.

169 ECS, "Marriage and Divorce," *Rev.*, Oct. 16, 1870; "Marriage and Divorce," *Chicago Tribune*; "Liberal Divorce Laws," 234.

170 1854 NY Address, 8; Divorce Bill Address, 6; ECS, "Marriage and Divorce," *Rev.*, Oct. 22, 1868.

171 1854 NY Address, 8–9.

172 ECS, "Marriage and Divorce," *Rev.*, Oct. 22, 1868.

173 "Liberal Divorce Laws," 234; ECS, "Good Thoughts in Simple Words," *Pioneer*, July 9, 1870; "Our Girls," *Washington County* (IA) *Press*, Feb. 21, 1880; "Marriage Law"; "Laws for Girls," *Rev.*, June 17, 1869; Decade Meeting Address, 63.

174 "Liberal Divorce Laws."

175 *Id.* at 235.

176 ECS, "About Marrying Too Young," *Rev.*, Oct. 20, 1870; "Good Thoughts."

177 Grossberg, 73–102; Dubler, "Wifely Behavior," 957, 968; *see* Meister v. Moore, 96 U.S. 76 (1877); Fenton v. Reed, 4 Johns 52 (N.Y. Sup. Ct. 1809).

178 Clark, "Bonds," 25–27; Dubler, "Governing," 1908–10; Grossberg, 87–88; Leach, 151.

179 Dubler, "Governing," 1892.

180 "Liberal Divorce Laws," 235.

181 Decade Meeting Address, 68.

182 "Other Things"; Decade Meeting Address, 73.

183 Decade Meeting Address, 73.

184 "Liberal Divorce Laws," 234; "Marriage Law."

185 ECS, "Marriage and Divorce," *Rev.*, Oct. 26, 1870; "Marriage and Divorce," *Chicago Tribune*; Grossberg, 93–94.

186 Maynard v. Hill, 125 U.S. 190, 212–13 (1888).

187 Tenth Convention Address.

188 "Paper on Marriage," 21–22.

189 "Domestic Warfare," 562.

190 "American Marriage," 196.

191 ECS to Lillie Devereux Blake, Jan. 6, 1879; ECS, "Mrs. Stanton to the Women of New York," *Daily Morning Chronicle*, Oct. 18, 1870.

192 "Marriage Law."

193 ECS to Elizabeth Miller, Aug. 11, 1880.

194 "Miss Becker"; "The Man Marriage," *Rev.*

195 Basch, *Eyes of the Law*, 178; Grossberg, 54–55.

196 "Homogeneous"; "American Marriage," 196; Divorce Bill Address, 7: "Marriage and Divorce," *Rev.*, Oct. 22, 1868.

197 ECS, "Bible Marriage," *Rev.*, Apr. 2, 1868.

198 ECS, "Marriage and Divorce," *Rev.*, Oct. 22, 1868; ECS, "A Symposium: Is Marriage a Success?" *Union Signal* (Chicago), May 2, 1889; "Marriage and Divorce," *Janesville Daily Gazette*, Nov. 22, 1870.

199 ECS, "Marriage and Divorce," *SF Chronicle, Aug. 19, 1871.*

200 Harriet Beecher Stowe, "The True Story of Lady Byron's Life," *Atlantic Monthly*, 295, 302, Sept. 1869; Harriet Beecher Stowe, *Lady Byron Vindicated* (Boston: Fields, Osgood, and Co., 1870); T. Austin Graham, "The Slaveries of Sex, Race, and Mind: Harriet Beecher Stowe's *Lady Byron Vindicated*," 41 *New Lit. History* 173 (Winter 2010); White, 151–52.

201 ECS, *Eighty Years*, 88; "Byron Case."

202 Grossberg, 54–56; Decade Meeting Address, 68–70.

203 ECS, "Editorial Correspondence," *Rev.*, Aug. 5, 1869.

204 "Marriage and Divorce," *Chicago Tribune*; Decade Meeting Address, 68–69.

205 Decade Meeting Address, 69; "Editorial Correspondence," Aug. 5, 1869.

206 Mattie H. Brinkerhoff, *Rev.*, Sept. 16, 1869.

207 "The Man Marriage," *Rev.*, Apr. 8, 1869; "Marriages and Mistresses."

208 Decade Meeting Address, 62.

209 "Liberal Divorce Laws," 336; ECS, "Marriage Law"; Fuller, 60.

210 "The Man Marriage," *Rev.*, Apr. 8, 1869.

211 "Infanticide," *Rev.*, Jan. 29, 1868.

212 ECS, "The Man Marriage," *Rev.*, Apr. 8, 1869.

213 Decade Meeting Address, 71.

214 Letter to Seventh National Convention, 88–89.

215 Decade Meeting Address, 77–78.

216 *Id.*; ECS, Speech to a Mass Meeting of Women in New York (ms.), May 17, 1870, *Papers*, vol. 2, 336, 349.

217 "Miss Becker."

218 ECS, Letter to Editor, Matilda Joslyn Gage, *National Citizen and Ballot Box*, June 1878.

219 ECS, "A Story for Wives," *Rev.*, Apr. 6, 1871.

220 "Miss Becker."

221 ECS, "Is Marriage a Success?" *Omaha Republican*, Mar. 24, 1889; "Symposium"; Decade Meeting Address.

222 "Marriage and Divorce," *SF Chronicle*.

223 "Is Marriage a Success?"; "Symposium."

CHAPTER 3. "DIVORCE IS NOT THE FOE OF MARRIAGE"

1 Areen, 30, 61, 67 (citing the first American divorce as Clarke v. Clarke, Ct. Asst., Mass. 1643/44); Blake, 31–32, 38–39, 56, 63, 118–19.

2 Mason, 111; Blake, 134.

3 ECS, Interview on Divorce, *NY Evening Journal*, May 18, 1899.

4 ECS, "Divorce versus Domestic Warfare," *Arena*, Apr. 1890, 566; Interview on Divorce; Clark, "Bonds," 25, 28, 30.

5 Blake, 95.

6 ECS, "The Need of Liberal Divorce Laws," *No. Amer. Review*, Sept. 1884, 243; "Marriage and Divorce," *Chicago Tribune*, Jan. 25, 1871; ECS, "Editorial Correspondence," *Rev.*, Dec. 23, 1869; ECS, "National Law for Divorce," Nov. 15, 1899, unidentified clipping, *Microfilm* 40:227; Interview on Divorce.

7 "Liberal Divorce Laws," 242; "Editorial Correspondence Dec. 23, 1869"; ECS, "Mass Meeting of Women," *World* (NY), May 18, 1870; Grossberg, 85.

8 "Domestic Warfare," 567–68; ECS, "Address at the Decade Meeting on Marriage and Divorce," in Report of Proceedings of the Twentieth Anniversary, Oct. 20, 1870, *Microfilm* 14:1031, 60; ECS, "Progress of the American Woman," 171 *North American Review* 904 (Dec. 1900); "Elizabeth Cady Stanton Says 'No.'" (n.d.), *Microfilm* 45:273.

9 ECS, "Is Marriage a Success?" *Omaha Republican*, Mar. 24, 1889; ECS, "Marriage and Divorce," *Rev.*, Oct. 22, 1868; ECS, "Advice to the Strong-Minded," *Rev.*, May 21, 1868; ECS, "A Short Discussion on the Modern Marriage Problem," *NY American and Journal*, July 13, 1902; Address of Mrs. E. C. Stanton at Tenth National Woman's Rights Convention, May 11, 1860, in *Papers*, vol. 1, 419; Basch, *Divorce*, 69.

10 ECS, *Eighty Years*, 184, 216; ECS, "Reminiscences," *Woman's Tribune*, Mar. 29, 1890.

11 Blake, 64–78; *Papers*, vol. 1, 219.

12 Masson, 163 n. 2, 164.

13 Clark, "Bonds," 28; Pleck, 49, 57; Masson, 63.

14 Declaration of Sentiments, *Report of the Woman's Rights Convention, Held at Seneca Falls, N.Y., July 19th and 20th, 1848*, 8.

15 *Papers*, vol. 1, 163 n. 2.

16 S.F. (ECS), "Divorce," *Lily*, Apr. 1850.

17 *Id.*

18 ECS, *Eighty Years*, 215–16; "Reminiscences"; ECS, "Elizabeth Cady Stanton's Last Plea for Women," *NY American and Journal*, Oct. 29, 1902.

19 ECS, *Eighty Years*, 215–16; ECS, "Temperance—Woman's Rights: An Appeal to the Women of the State of New York," *Carson League*, [July 1, 1852], *Papers*, vol. 1, 201; ECS, "Marriage and Divorce," *Rev.*, Oct. 22, 1868; ECS, "The Unfairness of Laws of Marriage and Divorce," *NY American and Journal*, Aug. 24, 1902.

20 ECS, "Marriage and Divorce," *Rev.*, Oct. 22, 1868; Redelia Bates, "Elizabeth C. Stanton at Home," *Rev.*, Oct. 18, 1870; Interview on Divorce; ECS, *Eighty Years*, 216; "Unfairness of Laws."

21 "Mrs. Stanton's Address, First Annual Meeting of the Woman's State Temperance Society," June 1–2, 1853, *Lily*, June 15, 1853; *HWS*, vol. 1, 496.

22 "Mrs. Stanton's Opening Remarks, Women's Temperance Convention" (Apr. 20–21, 1852), *Lily*, May 1852; Temperance Appeal.

23 *HWS*, vol. 1, 496.

24 Basch, *Divorce*, 58–59.

25 ECS, Letter from Mrs. Stanton to the Women's Temperance Convention, *Lily*, Mar. 1852; ECS, "The Women's Appeal for the Maine Law," *NY Tribune*, Jan. 24, 1853.

26 Letter from Mrs. Stanton to the Women's Temperance Convention at Albany, Jan. 28, 1852.

27 Address of Mrs. Elizabeth Cady Stanton on Woman's Rights, Sept. 1848 (ms.), *Papers*, vol. 1, 94.

28 ECS, "Marriage and Divorce," *Rev.*, Oct. 22, 1868.

29 Temperance Appeal; "Maine Law."

30 Griffith, *In Her Own Right*, 76.

31 "Women's Temperance Convention, Mrs. Stanton's Address," (Apr. 20–21, 1852), *Lily*, May 1852; "Maine Law"; ECS to SBA, Mar. 1, [1852].

32 Temperance Appeal.

33 "Letter from Mrs. Stanton," *Lily*, Mar. 1852; ECS to Gerrit Smith, June 6, 1852.

34 *Papers*, vol. 1, 218 n. 1; Temperance Appeal; "Women's Temperance Meeting," *Rochester Daily American*, Apr. 22, 1852.

35 ECS to SBA, after May 23, 1852.

36 *Papers*, vol. 1, 204 n. 3; "Miss Anthony's Address to the State Temperance Convention," *Lily*, July 1852; Temperance Appeal.

37 SBA Remarks to Women's New York State Temperance Society (Oct. 14, 1852), *Lily*, Nov. 1852.

38 *E.g.,* Woman's State Temperance Convention (Oct. 14, 1852), *Lily*, Nov. 1852 (objections by Mary Vaughan).

39 *Papers*, vol. 1, 219 n. 6.

40 "Maine Law"; SBA to Lucy Stone, Jan. 24, 1853.

41 Temperance Address, June 1–2, 1853, *Lily*.

42 Griffith, *In Her Own Right*, 77; SBA to Lucy Stone, May 1, 1853.

43 ECS to SBA, June 20, 1853.

44 ECS, Address to the Legislature of New-York, Feb. 14, 1854; A Letter from Mrs. Stanton to Gerrit Smith, Dec. 21, 1855; ECS to SBA, July 4, 1858; ECS, "Marriage and Divorce," *Rev.*, Oct. 22, 1868; ECS, "Wife-Beaters," *Boston Investigator*, July 29, 1899.

45 1854 NY Address; SBA, "Hearing before the New York Assembly, Select Committee," *Albany Argus*, Mar. 3, 1854; "Woman's-Rights—Declaration of Claims," *NY Tribune*, Mar. 6, 1854.

46 ECS to Gerrit Smith, June 6, 1852; ECS, "Marriage and Divorce," *NY American and Journal*, Sept. 7, 1902.

47 Clark, "Bonds," 28–29.

48 ECS, *Eighty Years*, 184.

49 "Marriage and Divorce by the Wife of a Presbyterian Minister," *Rev.*, Nov. 19, 1868.

50 Siegel, "'Rule,'" 2128–29.

51 *Id.* at 2162–70. In twenty states, a wife could sue the rum seller who encouraged her husband to drink for damages, if she had previously notified the saloonkeeper not to serve him.

52 *Woman's Journal*, Jan. 28, 1877; "Legal Relief for Assaulted Wives," *Woman's Journal*, Jan. 11, 1879; Pleck, 102–3.

53 Pleck, 108; *Woman's Journal*, June 11, 1881; *Woman's Journal*, July 11, 1885.

54 Pleck, 109, 113, 249. Whipping-post laws were passed in Maryland (1882), Delaware (1901), and Oregon (1905). Stanton's home state of New York considered it in 1895.

55 "Wife-Beaters"; *Woman's Journal*, Apr. 28, 1900. Stanton's remarks followed the ABA's report, Simeon Baldwin, "Whipping and Castration as Punishments for Crime," 8 *Yale Law Journal* 371 (June 1899).

56 *Papers*, vol. 1, 418 n.

57 ECS to SBA, Apr. 24, 1860.

58 Tenth Convention Address.

59 *NY Tribune*, Mar. 1, 5, 6, 12, 17, 19, 24, 28, Apr. 7, 21, 1860; Blake, 82–86, 90–92; Clark, "Bonds," 27.

60 Tenth Convention Address; ECS, "Horace Greeley," *Rev.*, Oct. 29, 1868.

61 Tenth Convention Address.

62 "Marriage and Divorce," *Rev.*, Oct. 29, 1868.

63 Tenth Convention Address, 71–72.

64 *Id.* at 66 (quoting Milton).

65 Hartog, *Man and Wife*, 70–76.

66 Tenth Convention Address, 67; "Horace Greeley."

67 Tenth Convention Address, 70; "Marriage and Divorce," *Rev.*, Oct. 22, 1868; *Papers*, vol. 1, 430 n. 8, 461 n. 4; ECS, "Fashionable Women Shipwreck" Lecture (ms.), [1861], *Microfilm* 10:105.

68 Hartog, *Man and Wife*, 96–97.

69 ECS, "I Have All the Rights I Want" [c. 1859], *Microfilm* 6:501; "A Divorce or a Sewing-Machine," *Rev.*, Sept. 8, 1870.

70 Tenth Convention Address, 70–72; "Marriage and Divorce," *Rev.*, Oct. 22, 1868; "Last Plea."

71 Tenth Convention Address, 73–74; Clark, "Bonds," 41–42.

72 Tenth Convention Address, 84–86.

73 *Papers*, vol. 1, 431, 433–34; *Evening Post*, May 12, 16, 23, 1860; "Marriage and Business," *NY Tribune*, May 14, 30, 1860; *NY Herald*, May 16, 1860; *NY Observer*, May 17, 1860.

74 ECS, "Letter to the Editor: Marriage and Divorce," *NY Tribune*, May 5, 1860.

75 ECS to Wendell Phillips, Aug. 10, 1860; Wendell Phillips to ECS, Aug. 21, 1860; ECS to Wendell Phillips, Feb. 5, 1861; Griffith, *In Her Own Right*, 106 (citing ECS to SBA, [1861]).

76 ECS, "Mrs. Dall's Fraternity Lecture," *Liberator*, Nov. 16, 1860; Clark, "Bonds," 47; DuBois, *Suffrage*, 167–70; Blake, 100.

77 Lucy Stone to SBA, Mar. 22, 1853; SBA to Stone, May 1, 1853; Stone to ECS, Apr. 14, 1853; Stone to ECS, Aug. 14, 1853; Stone to ECS, Mar. 16 [1860]; ECS to SBA, Apr. 24, 1860.

78 "Mrs. Stanton's Address, Anniversary of the NWSA," *Rev.*, May 19, 1870.

79 "A Private Letter," *Rev.*, Nov. 10, 1870.

80 ECS, "Side Issues," *Rev.*, Oct. 6, 1870.

81 *Id.*

82 "Anniversary of NWSA."

83 Blake, 106–7; *Rev.*, July 21, 1870; *Rev.*, Aug. 18, 1870; *Rev.*, July 7, 1870.

84 ECS, "Reminiscences," *Woman's Tribune*, Apr. 5, 1890; ECS, *Eighty Years*, 241–43.

85 "Address of Elizabeth Cady Stanton on the Divorce Bill, before the Judiciary Committee of the New York Senate," Feb. 8, 1861; ECS, "Marriage and Divorce," *New York Daily Tribune*, May 30, 1860; see also ECS, "Marriage and Divorce," *Rev.*, Oct. 29, 1868; ECS, "Reminiscences," *Woman's Tribune*, Mar. 29, 1890 (invited by legislator Lewis Benedict).

86 Divorce Bill Address, 3, 10.

87 *Id.* at 5; ECS, "Editorial Correspondence," *Rev.*, Mar. 17, 1870. Stanton would later incorporate this argument into her "Man Marriage" critique. ECS, "Man Marriage," *Free Parliament, Golden Sun*, Nov. 11, 1871.

88 Tenth Convention Address, 95–97; ECS, "Marriages and Mistresses," *Rev.*, Oct. 15, 1868.

89 "Domestic Warfare," 565.

90 Decade Meeting Address, 67.

91 Divorce Bill Address, 5; "Letter to Editor"; ECS Lecture, "Marriage and Divorce," *Daily Morning Chronicle* (Wash., D.C.), Oct. 18, 1870; "Domestic Warfare," 563.

92 ECS, "Man Marriage," *Golden Sun*; Blake, 49; Friedman, *Private Lives*, 29.

93 Divorce Bill Address; ECS, "Woman's Duty to Vote," *Woman's Tribune*, Dec. 15, 1888; "Domestic Warfare," 563.

94 "Mistresses."

95 Declaration, 8–9.

96 ECS, *Westminster Review* 135 (Jan. 1891); ECS, "Patriotism and Chastity," *Women's Penny Paper*, Dec. 6, 1890.

97 ECS, "Mrs. Elizabeth Cady Stanton's Views of 'The Great Social Earthquake,'" *Chicago Daily Tribune*, Oct. 1, 1874; ECS, "Self-Government" Speech, to NWSA, May 11, 1875, in *Papers*, vol. 3, 178; "The Tilton-Beecher Trial," *NY Tribune*, May 4, 1875; Lutz, 213–31; Fox; White, 205; Korobkin, 1; "Elizabeth Tilton," *NY Times*, Apr. 16, 1878.

98 Victoria Woodhull, *Woodhull & Claflin's Weekly*, Nov. 2, 1872; "What Elizabeth Cady Stanton Says," *Brooklyn Daily Argus*, July 26, 1874; ECS to SBA, July 30, 1874; ECS, *Woodhull & Claflin's Weekly*, Aug. 15, 1874; ECS, *Woodhull & Claflin's Weekly*, Oct. 17, 1874; "Bessie's Testimony," *Rochester Union & Advertiser*, Aug. 24, 1874; "Elizabeth Cady Stanton on Woman," *Newark Sunday Call*, Jan. 2, 1876.

99 "'Great Social Earthquake'"; "A Talk with Mrs. Stanton: Her Opinion Regarding the Great Scandal Trial," *Sun*, July 17, 1875; Blake, 113–15.

100 "Mrs. Stanton to Mr. Hooker," *Rev.*, Feb. 24, 1870.

101 "Marriage and Divorce," *Chicago Tribune*, Jan. 25, 1871.

102 ECS, Speech to a Mass Meeting of Women in New York, May 17, 1870 (ms.), in *Papers*, vol. 2, 336.

103 ECS, "Regarding Divorce," *Omaha Republican*, Feb. 17, 1889.

104 Decade Meeting Address, 65.

105 *Id.* at 65–66, 75; "Short Discussion."

106 "Liberal Divorce Laws," 240; Areen, 41.

107 Tenth Convention Address; "Elizabeth Cady Stanton at Home"; "Marriage and Divorce," *Rev.*, Oct. 29, 1868; "Regarding Divorce;" "Domestic Warfare," 565, 569; "Last Plea."

108 John Milton (1608–1674), *The Doctrine and Discipline of Divorce, Restored to the Good of Both Sexes from the Bondage of Canon Law and Other Mistakes* (1643); John Milton, *The Judgment of Martin Bucer concerning Divorce* (1644); John Milton, *Tetrachordon* (1645); John Milton, *Colasterion* (1645).

109 Blake, 28–29 (citing Milton).

110 Milton, *Divorce*, 130; Areen, 58, 77–78.

111 Tenth Convention Address, 65; ECS, "Marriage and Divorce," *Rev.* 1868; Mass Meeting Speech.

112 Mary Nyquist, "The Genesis of Gendered Subjectivity in the Divorce Tracts and in *Paradise Lost*," in *Re-Membering Milton: Essays on the Texts and Traditions*, Mary Nyquist and Margaret W. Ferguson, eds. (New York: Methuen, 1987).

113 "Domestic Warfare," 569; ECS, "Are Homogeneous Laws in All the States Desirable?" *No. Amer. Review* 409, Mar. 1900.

114 ECS, "Marriage Law," *Omaha Republican*, Mar. 3, 1889; "Domestic Warfare," 564–66; ECS, "The Ideal Marriage of the Future," *NY American and Journal*, Sept. 14, 1902; ECS, Writing about J. William Lloyd's Articles on Divorce (n.d.), *Microfilm* 45:326.

115 "Domestic Warfare," 566; "Mrs. Stanton's Views on Marriage and Divorce," 66 *Nation* 403, May 26, 1898; "Homogeneous," 409; "Ideal Marriage"; ECS, "How Shall We Solve the Divorce Problem?" *NY American and Journal*, Oct. 13, 1902.

116 Cooper, 139, 148; Ganz, 255, 259; A. R. Cazauran, comp., *The Trial of Daniel McFarland for the Shooting of Albert D. Richardson, the Alleged Seducer of His Wife* (New York: W.E. Hilton, 1870).

117 60 U.S. 393 (1857); "Marriage and Divorce," *Chic. Trib.*; ECS, "Woman Suffrage," *NY Times*, May 12, 1870; ECS, "The Disfranchised Sex," *NY World*, May 12, 1870; ECS, Letter to the Editor, *Woodhull & Claflin's Weekly*, Mar. 11, 1871; "Mass Meeting"; [ECS], "The New York Press in Convulsions," *Rev.*, May 26, 1870; "Side Issues."

118 *The Trial*, 226–29; "The M'Farland Divorce: How It Was Obtained in Indiana—the Documents and Evidence Offered in the Case," *NY Times*, Dec. 12, 1869; Ganz, 225–27; Cooper, 5.

119 "The M'Farland Divorce"; *The Trial*, 235–36 (Abby's Affidavit); Ganz, 257; Cooper, 114–21.

120 *The Trial*, 149; Neil R. Feigenson, "Extraterritorial Recognition of Divorce Decrees in the Nineteenth Century," 34 *American Journal of Legal History* 119 (1990).

121 Cooper, 176; Ganz, 278.

122 Cooper, 192–93; Ganz, 259, 286; *The Trial*, 32, 96.

123 Hartog, *Man and Wife*, 221–23; Ganz, 259, 263–64.

124 Hartog, "Unwritten Law," 67, 70–71, 90; Ganz, 266; Cooper, 217; "Lawyer John Graham Dead," *NY Times*, Apr. 10, 1894.

125 "Editorial: The Acquittal of McFarland," *NY Times*, May 11, 1870; *The Richardson-McFarland Tragedy*, 89–90 (Philadelphia: Barclay, 1870); Blake, 103; Cooper, 217–18; Hartog, "Unwritten Law," 88, 93; *The Trial*, 194, 208–09. Following the acquittal, McFarland sued in Indiana to set aside the divorce because of lack of proof of publication, lack of notice to the defendant, and the perjury of witness Lucia Calhoun. 1 *Alb. L. J.* 475–76 (1870). He retained custody of his older son.

126 ECS, "Editorial Corr.," *Rev.*, Dec. 23, 1869.

127 "Woman Suffrage," *NY Times*, May 12, 1870; "Anniversary of NWSA"; ECS, Speech to Suffrage Convention, Founding Meeting of Union Woman's Suffrage Society (ms.), May 10–11, 1870, *Microfilm* 14:723.

128 Basch, *Eyes of the Law*, 69.

129 Catharine E. Beecher to ECS, May 16, 1870.

130 Mass Meeting Speech; "Mass Meeting"; "Bracing the Free Lovers," *Sun*, May 17, 1870; "Mrs. Stanton at Apollo Hall," *Rev.*, May 26, 1870.

131 "The Ladies Attend a Lecture," *Brooklyn Daily Eagle*, May 26, 1870; "Mrs. Stanton at Apollo Hall"; "Bracing the Free Lovers"; "Marriage and Divorce: Mrs. H. B. Stanton on the McFarland Case," *NY Tribune*, May 18, 1870; "'Woman's Right' to Divorce," *NY Times*, May 18, 1870.

132 "On the McFarland Case."

133 "Convulsions."

134 She published it after trial. "Mrs. Richardson's Statement," *NY Tribune*, May 11, 1870, in *The Trial*; Ganz, 255, 279.

135 "Mass Meeting"; ECS, "Reminiscences," *Woman's Tribune*, Apr. 5, 1890; ECS, "Editorial Correspondence," *Rev.*, Dec. 23, 1869; Decade Meeting Address, 70; ECS to Martha Coffin Wright, May 15, 1870.

136 Mass Meeting Speech.

137 "Mass Meeting"; "Disfranchised Sex."

138 "Mrs. Stanton at Apollo Hall."

139 Decade Meeting Address; "Mass Meeting."

140 Haber, 63, 106, 210.

141 See chapter 5.

142 Haber, 134; ECS, "A Few Gentle Taps at Mr. Greeley," *Golden Age*, Sept. 2, 1871.

143 "The Moral of Mrs. Fair's Conviction," *Sun*, Apr. 28, 1871; Haber, 264–65, n. 45.

144 ECS, "Mrs. Stanton on Mrs. Fair," *Golden Age*, Aug. 19,1871; Haber, 136–37; People of the State of California v. Laura D. Fair, 43 Cal. 137 (1872).

145 Haber, 195; Laura Fair, *Wolves in the Fold* (San Francisco: L.D. Fair, 1873), 36–37.

146 Haber, 138; ECS, "Gentle Taps"; ECS, "Woman Suffrage," *Daily Morning Call*, July 13, 1871; ECS, "Laura D. Fair," *SF Chronicle*, July 14, 1871; "Mrs. Stanton on Mrs. Fair"; SBA, Diary, July 13, 1871, *Microfilm* 15:197; "The Acquittal of Mrs. Fair," *NY Times*, Oct. 1, 1872; *Brooklyn Daily Eagle*, Sept. 7, 1871.

147 Lucy Stone to Harriet Robinson, Mar. 4, 1879; Haber, 138.

148 "Elizabeth Cady Stanton at Home."

149 *Id.*; ECS to Isabella Beecher Hooker, May 29, 1870.

150 "Elizabeth Cady Stanton at Home"; ECS to I. B. Hooker.

151 "Marriage and Divorce," *Daily Morning Chronicle*.

152 "Marriage and Divorce," *Chic. Trib.*; ECS, "Marriage and Divorce," *SF Chronicle*, Aug. 19, 1871; Griffith, *In Her Own Right*.

153 Decade Meeting Address, 60–62.

154 *Id.*; "Liberal Divorce Laws," 240; ECS, excerpt, "Marriage and Divorce: Popular Objections Answered" [Feb. 24, 1889], *Microfilm* 27:107; ECS, "A Woman on Divorce," *Omaha Republican*, Feb. 24, 1889.

155 Elizabeth Oakes Smith, "Women's Temperance Meeting," *NY Daily Tribune*, Feb. 4, 1853; "The Marriage Institution," *Lily*, 1855; Blake, 87; Basch, *Eyes of the Law*, 20–27; Decade Meeting Address, 71.

156 "Mrs. Stanton and the Chicago Tribune," *Rev.*, Feb. 9, 1871.

157 Decade Meeting Address, 72.

158 *Id.* at 73; "Liberal Divorce Laws," 241; "National Law"; "Domestic Warfare," 565.

159 Decade Meeting Address, 74–75; "Homogeneous," 409.

160 ECS to SBA, June 27, 1870.

161 ECS to Mrs. Griffing, Dec. 1, 1870; Blake, 104–5.

162 "City Matters: Mrs. Stanton's Lecture," *Milwaukee Sentinel*, Nov. 26, 1870; "Mrs. E. Cady Stanton on Marriage and Divorce, and Other Things," *Wisconsin State Journal*, Nov. 29, 1870; "Mrs. E. Cady Stanton's Lecture," *Madison Daily Democrat*, Nov. 29, 1870; *but see* Eleanor Kirk, "A Word to Abused Wives," *Rev.*, June 18, 1868.

163 "Presbyterian Minister."

164 Lillie Devereux Blake, "The Divorce Question," *Rev.*, July 21, 1870; Blake, 106–7.

165 Clark, "Bonds," 47; Blake, 107; *Woman's Journal*, Oct., 22, 1870; *Woman's Journal*, June 4, 1870.

166 Mary A. Livermore, et al., "Women's Views of Divorce," 150 *No. Amer. Rev.* 111 (1890). Livermore was the president of the AWSA from 1875 to 1878 and an editor for the *Woman's Journal*. Wendy Hamand Venet, *A Strong-Minded Woman: The Life of Mary Livermore* (Amherst: University of Massachusetts Press, 2005).

167 ECS, "Marriage and Divorce," *Rev.*, Oct. 29, 1868; "Mrs. Stanton and the *Chicago Tribune*."

168 ECS, "Marriage and Divorce," *Rev.*, Oct. 29, 1868; "Liberal Divorce Laws," 236; "Domestic Warfare," 566.

169 Blake, 130–31.

170 Theodore D. Woolsey, *Essay on Divorce and Divorce Legislation*, 258–74 (New York: Scribner, 1869); Kay, 2017, 2028–30.

171 ECS, "President Woolsey," *Rev.*, June 10, 1869.

172 ECS, "Editorial Correspondence: Hartford Convention," *Rev.*, Nov. 11, 1869.

173 Blake, 117–29.

174 ECS, "Editorial Correspondence," *Rev.*, Mar. 17, 1870.

175 ECS, "Editorial Correspondence," *Rev.*, Mar. 31, 1870.

176 Friedman, *Private Lives*, 38.

177 *Id.* at 35, 38; Blake, 121, 123, 131.

178 15 *Cong. Rec.* 279 (daily ed. Jan. 8, 1884); Blake, 145. It was only voted on in committee once, in 1892, when the House Judiciary Committee rejected it.

179 Blake, 132–33.

180 Blake, 134; Julia E. Johnsen, ed., *Selected Articles on Marriage and Divorce*, 2 (New York: H.W. Wilson, 1925).

181 Decade Meeting Address, 70; "Marriage and Divorce," *Daily Morning Chronicle*; ECS, "Other Things"; "Liberal Divorce Laws," 234.

182 Which later happened. Williams v. North Carolina, 317 U.S. 287 (1942); Williams v. North Carolina II, 325 U.S. 226 (1945).

183 Interview on Divorce; ECS, "Are Homogeneous Divorce Laws in All the States Desirable?" *Boston Investigator*, Dec. 17, 1898; "Homogeneous," *No. Amer. Rev.*

184 Thomas, "Marriage Amendment," 136; "Domestic Warfare," 560.

185 "Liberal Divorce Laws," 243; ECS, "Degradation of Women—Reply," *Hartford Times*, Apr. 8, 1886; "Marriage Law."

186 "Domestic Warfare," 560; "Solve the Divorce Problem."

187 "Liberal Divorce Laws," 237; "National Law."

188 "Liberal Divorce Laws," 237; *Jelineau, Des.* 45 (S.C. App. 1801); Friedman, "Rights of Passage," 651.

189 ECS to Harriot Stanton Blatch, Sept. 21, 1884.

190 "Domestic Warfare," 560; "Homogeneous," *Boston Inv.*; "Homogeneous," *No. Amer. Rev.*

191 "Domestic Warfare," 561; "Homogeneous," *No. Amer. Rev.*, 408.

192 Thomas, "Federal Marriage Amendment," 146.

193 *E.g.,* ECS, "The Women for Grant," *Connecticut Courant*, Nov. 2, 1872.

194 "Homogeneous," *Boston Inv.*; "Homogeneous," *No. Amer. Rev.*, 407.

195 "Liberal Divorce Laws," 243; "Regarding Divorce"; "Resolutions Presented by Mrs. Stanton," NAWSA 22nd Annual Convention, Feb. 18, 1890, *Microfilm* 28:62; "Is Marriage a Success?"; "National Law"; "Homogeneous," *Boston Inv.*; "Homogeneous," *No. Amer. Rev.*

196 "Liberal Divorce Laws," 243; Livermore, "Women's Views of Divorce," 115.

197 ECS, *Eighty Years*, 218; ECS, "Reminiscences," Mar. 29, 1890.

198 "Solve the Divorce Problem."

199 ECS to William R. Hearst, Oct. 22, 1902.

200 ECS, "An Answer to Bishop Stevens," *NY American and Journal*, Oct. 27, 1902.

201 "Last Plea."

CHAPTER 4. THE "INCIDENTAL RELATION" OF MOTHER

1 "For Women Only: Mrs. Elizabeth Cady Stanton Discourses on Marriage and Maternity," *SF Chronicle*, July 13, 1871.

2 ECS, "The Solitude of Self," to NAWSA Twenty-Fourth Convention, Jan. 18, 1892, in *Woman's Tribune*, Jan. 23, 1892; ECS, Address, Hearing before the House Committee on the Judiciary, Jan. 18, 1892.

3 Clark, "Self-Ownership," 905–9.

4 Hasday, 1469–70; Siegel, "Reasoning," 261, 309.

5 Hasday, 1373, 1472; *e.g.,* Shaw v. Shaw, 17 Conn. 189 (1845); Moores v. Moores, 16 N.J. Eq. 275 (Ch. 1863); Dignan v. Dignan, 40 NYS 320 (Sup. Ct. 1896).

6 1 Matthew Hale, *The History of the Pleas of the Crown* 639 (1736) (Philadelphia: Robert H. Small, 1847 ed.); Hasday, 1396–97.

7 Linda Gordon, *Moral Property*, 55; Linda Gordon, "Voluntary Motherhood," 423.

8 Linda Gordon, *Moral Property*, 55; Linda Gordon, "Why Nineteenth-Century Feminists," 140; Hasday, 1493.

9 Linda Gordon, "Advocates," 27, 28.

10 ECS to SBA, Mar. 1, 1853.

11 Mrs. E. C. Stanton, "Paper on Marriage," *Proceedings of the Yearly Meeting of the Friends of Human Progress* (June 7–9, 1857), 22–23.

12 "Mrs. Stanton to the Women of New York," *Boston Investigator*, Aug. 10, 1870.

13 Linda Gordon, *Moral Property*, 55; Linda Gordon, "Why Nineteeth-Century Feminists," 140; Hasday, 1396–97; *HWS*, vol. 1, 688, 727, May 10–11, 1860 (Antoinette Brown Blackwell).

14 "Marriage" (unpub. ms. c.1856), in Lerner, *Female Experience*, 87–98 (attributing unsigned essay to Sarah Grimké).

15 "Marriage."

16 "Address of Elizabeth Cady Stanton on the Divorce Bill, before the Judiciary Committee of the New York Senate," Feb. 8, 1861, 8; Address of Mrs. E. C. Stanton at Tenth National Woman's Rights Convention, May 11, 1860, in *Papers*, vol. 1, 419.

17 ECS to SBA, July 20, 1857; Hasday, 1401–02.

18 Hasday, 1455.

19 Matilda E. J. Gage, "Is Woman Her Own?" *Rev.*, Apr. 9, 1868; Linda Gordon, *Moral Property*, 67; Siegel, "Reasoning," 305.

20 Thomas Low Nichols and Mary Sargeant Gove Nichols, *Marriage: Its History, Character, and Results* 117 (New York: T.L. Nichols, 1854).

21 Clark, "Self-Ownership," 909; M. S. Gove Nichols to ECS, Aug. 21, 1851; Stanton to Nichols, Aug. 21, 1852; Stanton to Nichols, Aug. 31, 1852.

22 ECS to Gerrit Smith, Dec. 21, 1855; Gerrit Smith to ECS, Dec. 1, 1855; ECS to Gerrit Smith, Jan. 5, 1857; Gerrit Smith to ECS, 1853.

23 ECS to Gerrit Smith, Dec. 21, 1855.

24 Stone to ECS, Oct. 22, 1856.

25 Stone to ECS, Aug. 14, 1853; Stone to SBA, Sept. 11, 1856.

26 Letter from Mrs. Stanton, Nov. 24, 1856, in Proceedings of the Seventh National Woman's Rights Convention, Nov. 25 and 26, 1856, *Microfilm* 8:807.

27 ECS, "What It Means for Women to Own Their Bodies," *Microfilm* 45:301 (n.d.).

28 "The Free Love System: Origin, Progress, and Position of the Anti-Marriage Movement," *NY Times*, Sept. 8, 1855; "A Bad Book Gibbeted," *NY Times*, Aug. 17, 1855; "Free Love: Exposé of the Affairs of the Late 'Unitary Household,'" *NY Times*, Sept. 21, 1860.

29 "Marriage,"

30 Hasday, 1420; Clark, "Self-Ownership," 909.

31 ECS to SBA, July 20, 1857.

32 Clark, "Self-Ownership," 909–11; Griffith, *In Her Own Right*, 42, 68–69.

33 Hasday, 1420.

34 *HWS*, vol. 1, 1842; Hasday, 1422.

35 Matilda Joslyn Gage, "Our Book Tale," *National Citizen Ballot Box*, Jan. 1881, 2.

36 "Marriage."

37 ECS, "Address at the Decade Meeting on Marriage and Divorce," in Report of Proceedings of the Twentieth Anniversary, Oct. 20, 1870, *Microfilm* 14:1031, at 63; ECS, "Woman's Bible: Revised by Woman," *Free Thought Magazine*, Apr. 1895.

38 "What It Means."

39 ECS, "For Women Only: Mrs. Elizabeth Cady Stanton Discourses on Marriage and Maternity," *Daily Iowa State Reg.*, July 29, 1871.

40 *Id.*

41 *Id.*

42 *Id.*

43 Sue Davis, 48–50.

44 ECS, "Marriage and Maternity," *Woodhull and Claflin's Weekly*, Jan. 16, 1875.

45 Gordon, *Moral Property*, 68; Ziegler, "Eugenic," 211.

46 *Id.*

47 *Id.* at 190.

48 Ziegler, "Eugenic," 211.

49 Gordon, *Moral Property*, 68, 84–85, 190; Ziegler, "Eugenic," 244.

50 Hasday, 1440–41.

51 ECS to Gerrit Smith, Dec. 21, 1955.

52 ECS, Letter to the Woman's Rights Convention at Worcester, Oct. 23–24, 1850.

53 Tenth Convention Address.

54 "Mrs. Stanton's Address," *Lily*, May 1852; ECS to SBA, Mar. 1, [1852].

55 Seventh Convention Letter, 89; ECS, "Mrs. Stanton and the Chicago Tribune," *Rev.*, Feb. 9, 1871.

56 ECS, "Divorce versus Domestic Warfare," *Arena*, Apr. 1890, 562, 564.

57 Seventh Convention Letter, 89–90.

58 ECS to SBA, Mar. 1, [1852].

59 "Paper on Marriage," 21–22.

60 "The Woman's Congress," *NY Times*, Oct. 16, 1873; "The Woman's Congress," *NY Tribune*, Oct. 16, 1873; ECS, "The Woman's Congress," *Golden Age* (NY), Oct. 25, 1873.

61 ECS, "The Co-Education of the Sexes," in Papers and Letters Presented at the First Woman's Congress of the Association for the Advancement of Woman, Oct. 17, 1873, *Microfilm* 17:315. "Women's Congress," *NY World*, Oct. 17, 1873.

62 "Women's Congress," *NY World*, Oct. 17, 1873.

63 Mrs. Elizabeth C. Lovering, "Enlightened Motherhood," in Papers of First Woman's Congress, 31, available at Harvard Library; "Women's Congress," *NY World*, Oct. 17, 1873.

64 "Women's Congress," *NY World*, Oct. 17, 1873; "Woman's Congress," *Woodhull & Claflin's Weekly*, Nov. 1, 1873.

65 "Woman's Congress," *NY Tribune*, Oct. 17, 1873; "Woman's Congress," *Woodhull & Claflin*.

66 Diary of Julia Ward Howe, Oct. 16, 1873, Houghton Library, Harvard College Library.

67 "Women's Congress," *NY World*, Oct. 17, 1873; "Woman's Congress," *Woodhull & Claflin*.

68 "Woman's Congress," *Woodhull & Claflin*.

69   "The Woman's Congress," *NY Tribune*, Oct. 17, 1873; "Women's Congress," *NY World*, Oct. 17, 1873; "Woman's Congress," *Woodhull & Claflin's Weekly*, Nov. 1, 1873.

70   "Discourses."

71   Griffith, *In Her Own Right*, 66, 78; Wellman, 219.

72   Caroline Severance to ECS, Oct. 24, 1858; Charles Slack to ECS, Nov. 9, 1858; Caroline Thayer to ECS, Nov. 11, 1858; ECS to Elizabeth Smith Miller, Dec. 1, 1858; Ginzberg, *An American Life*, 94–95; Griffith, *In Her Own Right*, 96–97.

73   Linda Gordon, *Moral Property*, 13, 32; Peter C. Engelman, *A History of the Birth Control Movement in America* 2–10 (Santa Barbara, CA: Praeger, 2011).

74   Gordon, *Moral Property*, 49–51, 111–12; Grossberg, 157–58; Brodie, 204; ECS, Inscription of *The Woman's Bible II* to Foote, *Microfilm* 45:339 (c. 1898); ECS to Edward Bliss Foote [before Feb. 20, 1899].

75   ECS to Martha Wright, June 19, 1871; ECS to Elizabeth Smith Miller, June 12, 1871; Brodie, 131.

76   "For Women Only," *Des Moines Daily Reg.*, July 29, 1871; ECS to Martha Wright, June 19, 1871; ECS, *Eighty Years*, 262.

77   ECS, Extract, in John Cowan, M.D., *The Science of a New Life* 3 (New York: Fowler and Wells, 1870), *Microfilm* 15:883; John Cowan, M.D., *The Science of a New Life* 108–15 (1870); Brodie, 196, 337 n. 48.

78   "Discourses."

79   Griffith, *In Her Own Right*, 65; Banner, 35.

80   Banner, 35; Ginzberg, *An American Life*, 51; Griffith, *In Her Own Right*, 66.

81   Stanton and Blatch, vol. 2, 177.

82   Banner, 35.

83   Stanton and Blatch, vol. 2, 210.

84   Linda Gordon, *Moral Property*, 57; Linda Gordon, "Voluntary Motherhood," 424, 434–35.

85   Linda Gordon, *Moral Property*, 57–59, 66–67; Linda Gordon, "Why Nineteenth-Century Feminists," 145–46.

86   Linda Gordon, *Moral Property*, 57–58; Linda Gordon, "Voluntary Motherhood," 425, 427.

87   Act for the Suppression of Trade in, and Circulation of, Obscene Literature and Articles of Immoral Use, ch. 258, 17 Stat. 598 (1873); Grossberg, 176–77; *see* Marge Piercy, *Sex Wars: A Novel of Gilded Age New York* (New York: William Morrow, 2005) (interweaving fictional stories of Stanton, Woodhull, and Comstock).

88   Grossberg, 155, 170.

89   Banner, 168.

90   Linda Gordon, *Moral Property*, 39–45; Engelman, 8–9.

91   ECS, *Eighty Years*, 369; Lutz, 284; ECS, "Mrs. Annie Besant," *Woman's Tribune*, Dec. 27, 1890.

92   Gage, "Our Book Tale," *National Citizen and Ballot Box*, Nov. 1878.

93   Linda Gordon, "Why Nineteenth-Century Feminists," 147–48; Engelman, xviii, xxi, 23r; People v. Sanger, 222 N.Y. 192 (1918); Maria T. Vullo, "*People v. Sanger* and

the Birth of Family Planning Clinics in America," 9 *Judicial Notice* 43 (Summer 2013); Jean H. Baker, *Margaret Sanger: A Life of Passion* 5 (New York: Hill and Wang, 2011).

94 Mohr, 3–6, 16, 20–47, 94, 200; Siegel, "Reasoning," 220, 285, 297–98.

95 Mohr, 3–6, 16, 20–47, 94, 200; Siegel, "Reasoning," 220, 285, 297–98; Smith-Rosenberg, 217–18; Linda Gordon, *Moral Property*, 25–26; Reagan, 11.

96 Horatio Robinson Storer, *Criminal Abortion: Its Nature, Its Evidence, and Its Law* (Boston: Little, Brown, 1868); Horatio Robinson Storer, *Why Not? A Book for Every Woman* (Boston: Lee and Shephard, 1866).

97 Mohr, 30–39, 157; Siegel, "Reasoning," 282–84, 295–96, 300; Smith-Rosenberg, 125, 230–31; Degler, 232–33, 242.

98 Linda Gordon, *Moral Property*, 1–2; Linda Gordon, "Why Nineteenth-Century Feminists," 146; Smith-Rosenberg, 243.

99 H. S. Pomeroy, *The Ethics of Marriage*, 137–38 (New York: Funk & Wagnalls, 1888); Siegel, "Reasoning," 304, 307–9.

100 Storer, *Why Not?*, 74–76.

101 "The Evil of the Age," *NY Times*, Jan. 12, 1863; "Another Malpractice Case," *NY Times*, Mar. 26, 1867; "The Noble Malpractice Case," *NY Times*, Apr. 1, 1867; "Trunk Mystery," *NY Times*, Aug. 23, 1871; *NY Tribune* in ECS, "Infanticide and Prostitution," *Rev.*, Feb. 5, 1868.

102 Mohr, 51–52, 56–57; Kathleen L. Endres, "'Strictly Confidential': Birth-Control Advertising in a 19th-Century City," *Journalism Quarterly* 748 (1986).

103 1868 N.Y. Sess. Laws § 430; Comstock Act, ch. 258, 17 Stat. 598 (1873); Linda Gordon, *Moral Property*, 32–33; Reagan, 13.

104 N.Y. Rev. Stat., pt. 4, ch. 1, Title. 2, Art. 1, § 9, p. 661, and Title. 6, § 21, p. 694 (1829); 1845 N.Y. Laws, ch. 260, §§ 1–5; 1846 N.Y. Laws ch. 22 § 1, 2; Mohr, 578; Cyril C. Means, Jr., "The Law of New York concerning Abortion and the Status of the Foetus, 1664–1968: A Case of Cessation of Constitutionality," 14 *NY Law Forum* 411, 451 (1968).

105 Mohr, 215.

106 1868 N.Y. Sess. Laws ch. 430, § 1; Mohr, 215–16.

107 1869 N.Y. Laws ch. 631 § 1; 1872 N.Y. Laws ch. 181 §§ 1–4; Mohr, 217–19.

108 Rakow and Kramarae, 7.

109 "Restellism," *Rev.*, Mar. 4, 1869; "Restellism: The Crime of This Age," *Rev.*, May 7, 1868; John, "Shirkers and Workers," *Rev.*, Sept. 3, 1868; "Restellism Rebuked," *Rev.*, Mar. 18, 1869; "Sorosis: Report on Hospitals and Asylums," *Rev.*, Jan. 21, 1869; "Infanticide in Canada," *Rev.*, Feb. 11, 1869; "Thug Doctors," *Rev.*, Mar. 23, 1871.

110 "Letter from Geo. Francis Train," *Rev.*, Oct. 29, 1868; "Terrible Statistics of Crime and Restalism [sic]," *Rev.*, Mar. 4, 1869.

111 Matilda Joslyn Gage, "Is Woman Her Own?" *Rev.*, Apr. 9, 1868; A., "Marriage and Maternity," *Rev.*, July 8, 1869; Mattie Brinkerhoff, "Women and Motherhood," *Rev.*, Sept. 2, 1869; Conspirator, "Child Murder," *Rev.*, Apr. 8, 1868.

112 Hasday, 1437; Mohr, 110–11.

113 Gage, "Own."

114 Response to A., "Restellism," *Rev.*, June 18, 1868.

115 Reagan, 10; Engelman, 17; "Mrs. Lohman's History," *NY Times*, Apr. 2, 1878; People v. Ann Lohman, 2 Barb. 216, 450 (N.Y. Gen. Term 1848), *aff'd*, 1 N.Y. 379 (1848); Clifford Browder, *The Wickedest Woman in New York: Madame Restell, the Abortionist* (Hamden, CT: Archon, 1988).

116 Stacey M. Robertson, *Parker Pillsbury: Radical Abolitionist, Male Feminist* 5–6, 24 (Ithaca, NY: Cornell University Press, 2000); Thomas, "Misappropriating," 58–59.

117 Parker Pillsbury, "The Hester Vaughan Meeting at Cooper Institute," *Rev.*, Dec. 10, 1868; Parker Pillsbury, "Foundling Hospitals Again," *Rev.*, Apr. 30, 1868; Parker Pillsbury, "Foundling Hospitals," *Rev.*, Mar. 26, 1868; Parker Pillsbury, "Quack Medicines," *Rev.*, Mar. 26, 1868; Parker Pillsbury, "Decision Diabolical," *Rev.*, July 29, 1869.

118 Pillsbury, "Quack Medicines"; Parker Pillsbury, "Hester Vaughan Meeting," *NY World*, Dec. 2, 1868.

119 "The Revolution Will Discuss," *Rev.*, Jan. 22, 1868; Mrs. J. B. Jones, MD, Physician, *Rev.*, Nov. 26, 1868; Mrs. Mary Peckenpaugh of St. Louis, *Rev.*, Aug. 6, 1868 (and thirty-three more issues from July 1868–April 1869).

120 Pillsbury, "Foundling Hospitals"; Pillsbury, "Foundling Hospitals Again"; Pillsbury, "The Hester Vaughan Meeting at Cooper Institute"; Pillsbury, "Decision Diabolical"; Pillsbury, "Male Magdalen Asylums," *Rev.*, May 19, 1870.

121 "Infanticide and Prostitution."

122 *Id.*

123 ECS, "Infanticide," *Rev.*, Aug. 6, 1868; ECS, "The Case of Hester Vaughan," *Rev.*, Dec. 10, 1868. Hester's last name was spelled "Vaughn" in most papers, though the *Revolution* spelled it "Vaughan."

124 "Infanticide."

125 *Id.*

126 ECS, "The Working Women's Association," *Rev.*, Nov. 5, 1868; DuBois, *Suffrage*, 126–51; "A Struggle for Life," *NY Times*, Nov. 6, 1868; "Working Women's Association," *Rev.*, Dec. 24, 1868.

127 "Case of Hester Vaughan"; "The Workingwomen of New-York in Behalf of Hester Vaughn, under Sentence of Death in Philadelphia," *NY Times*, Nov. 24, 1868.

128 ECS, "Editorial Correspondence," *Rev.*, Dec. 10, 1868; "Working Women's Association," *Sun*, Dec. 8, 1868.

129 "Editorial Correspondence Dec. 10, 1868."

130 Sarah Gordon, "Infanticide," 55–56; Pillsbury, "Cooper Institute"; "Case of Hester Vaughan"; Eleanor Kirk, "Is Hester Vaughan Guilty?" *Rev.*, Jan. 21, 1869; "Hester Vaughn," *NY Times*, Dec. 2, 1868.

131 "Hester Vaughn"; "Case of Hester Vaughan"; ECS, "Hester Vaughan," *Rev.*, Dec. 10, 1868; "A Western Judge on Hester Vaughan," *Rev.*, Dec. 11, 1868.

132 N.M., "Hester Vaughan and Gen. Cole Again," *Rev.*, Feb. 18, 1869.

133 ECS, Address to the Legislature of New-York, Feb. 14, 1854; ECS, An Appeal to the Women of the State of New York, July 1, 1852; "Hester Vaughn."

134 J.E.B. v. Alabama *ex rel.* T.B., 511 U.S. 127, 132 (1994).

135 *J.E.B.*, 511 U.S. at 133 n. 4; Kerber, *Ladies*, 130; Norton, *Mothers*, 225.

136 1860 NY Address, 7.

137 John H. Colby, *A Practical Treatise upon the Criminal Law and Practice of the State of New York*, 344–45 (Albany, NY: Weare C. Little, 1868).

138 "Case of Hester Vaughan."

139 "Hester Vaughan"; ECS, "The Strong-Minded Women of the Bible," *Rev.*, Feb. 26, 1868.

140 "The Workingwoman's Association," *NY Daily Tribune*, May 28, 1869; Linda Gordon, *Moral Property*, 74–75.

141 Parker Pillsbury, "Hester Vaughan Once More," *Rev.*, Aug. 19, 1869.

CHAPTER 5. RAISING "OUR GIRLS"

1 ECS, "Address at the Decade Meeting on Marriage and Divorce," in Report of Proceedings of Twentieth Anniversary, Oct. 20–21, 1870, *Microfilm* 14:1031; "For Women Only: Mrs. Elizabeth Cady Stanton Discourses on Marriage and Maternity," *SF Chronicle*, July 13, 1871.

2 Clark, "Self-Ownership," 911.

3 ECS, "Miss Becker on the Difference in Sex," *Rev.*, Sept. 24, 1868.

4 ECS, "Woman a Helpmeet," *NY Times*, Feb. 23, 1873.

5 Kerber, *Republic*, 185–220; Norton, *Liberty's*, 298.

6 Kern, 83, 122–23.

7 Julia Crouch, "Babies," *Rev.*, Oct. 29, 1868; ECS, "Bread and Babies," *Rev.*, Nov. 26, 1868.

8 ECS, "The Fountain Rises No Higher Than Its Source," *Commonwealth* (1899).

9 ECS, "Letters to Mothers: Our Babies," *Lily*, Dec. 1851; ECS, "Letters to Mothers: Women, Babies, Mrs. Swisshelm," *Lily*, Apr. 1852; "Bread and Babies"; "Discourses"; ECS, "Something about Babies," in *Buckeye Cookery and Practical Housekeeping*, 2nd ed. (Marysville, OH: Buckeye, 1877); ECS, "Reminiscences: Babies," *Woman's Tribune*, Sept. 7, 1889.

10 Declaration of Sentiments, *Report of the Woman's Rights Convention, Held at Seneca Falls, N.Y., July 19th and 20th, 1848*, 4–5, 9.

11 ECS, "Woman's Rights," *National Reformer*, Sept. 14, 1848; ECS, Address before the U.S. Senate Special Committee on Woman Suffrage (Feb. 8, 1890), *Woman's Tribune*, Feb. 15, 1890.

12 ECS, Address to the New York State Legislature, Mar. 19, 1860, repeated as First Address of Mrs. E. C. Stanton at Tenth National Woman's Rights Convention, May 10, 1860, at 34, in *Microfilm* 9:629.

13 ECS, "Don't Unsex Yourself," *Rev.*, June 24, 1869.

14 ECS, Home Life Lecture (ms. 1878), *Microfilm* 20:449; "Home Life," *Milwaukee Sentinel*, May 21, 1878; "Home News," *Milwaukee Sentinel*, Nov. 8, 1875; *see also* ECS, "The True Republic" Lecture, *Woodhull and Claflin's Weekly*, May 18, 1872.

15 Home Life Lecture; "The Health of American Women: Mrs. Stanton," *No. Amer. Review*, Dec. 1882, 510, 513.

16 Clark, "Self-Ownership," 921–28.

17 Home Life Lecture.

18 "Don't Unsex."

19 Ginzberg, *An American Life*, 76.

20 ECS, *Woman's Bible*, 137–38.

21 ECS, Letter to the Woman's Rights Convention at Worcester, Oct. 23–24, 1850.

22 ECS to Pauline Wright Davis, Dec. 6, 1852.

23 *Id.*; ECS to SBA, June 20, 1853.

24 O'Neill, *Divorce*, 127.

25 "Elizabeth Cady Stanton Says 'No'" [n.d.], *Microfilm* 45:288.

26 ECS, Address, Eleventh National Woman's Rights Convention, May 10, 1866, 13; ECS, "Woman's Duty to Vote," *Woman's Tribune*, Dec. 3, 1888.

27 Special Committee Address.

28 Grossberg, 234–36, 242–43; Mason, xii, 6–7, 13 (1994); William Blackstone, *Commentaries on the Laws of England* (1765) (1979 ed.), 2:452.

29 12 Charles II, c.24 (1660) in Mason, 19.

30 Grossberg, 242–43; Mason, 18.

31 Declaration, 8.

32 Rochester, NY, April 20, 1852.

33 ECS, Address to the Legislature of New-York, Feb. 14, 1854, 14–15.

34 Basch, *Eyes of the Law*, 115.

35 1854 NY Address.

36 *Id.*; Basch, *Eyes of the Law*, 193.

37 Basch, *Eyes of the Law*, 193.

38 1860 NY Address.

39 Laws of NY, Ch. 90 (1860), in Basch, *Eyes of the Law*, 235.

40 People v. Brooks, 35 Barb. 85, 91 (NY 1861); People v. Boice, 39 Barb. 307, 309–10 (NY 1862).

41 Basch, *Eyes of the Law*, 207; HWS, vol. 1, 86–87, 747–78.

42 HWS, vol. 3, 33.

43 HWS, vol. 4, 857.

44 Basch, *Eyes of the Law*, 179–80.

45 "National Woman Suffrage Convention: The Proceedings at Lincoln Hall," *Evening Star*, Jan. 22, 1880; HWS, vol. 3, 152; Mason, 69.

46 HWS, vol. 3, 419.

47 *But see* Kansas Const. art. 15, § 6 (1859) (granting women "equal rights in the possession of their children"); HWS, vol. 4, ch. 24, 458 (noting nine equal custody laws by 1900).

48 Grossberg, 246; Mason, 57; *Brooks*, 35 Barb. at 90.

49 Grossberg, 247.

50 *Rex v. Delaval*, 3 Burr. 1434 (K.B. 1763); Grossberg, 236–37.

51 Ahrenfelt v. Ahrenfelt, Hoff. Ch. 4976, 6 N.Y. Ch. Ann. 1221 (1840).

52 Grossberg, 236–37; Mason, xiii.

53 Grossberg, 234–38.

54 J.N.H., "A Court Scene," *Rev.*, Feb. 24, 1870 (reporting on *In re Euene A. Dreselski*).

55 *HWS*, vol. 1, 229 n. 48; Dorothy E. Zaborszky, "Domestic Anarchy and the Destruction of the Family: Caroline Norton and the Custody of Infants Act," 7 *Int'l J. Women's Studies* 397 (1989).

56 Grossberg, 209.

57 *Id.* at 241.

58 *Id.* at 249–50; Mason, xii; ECS, "Mrs. Annie Besant," *Woman's Tribune*, Dec. 27, 1890.

59 ECS, "Divorce versus Domestic Warfare," *Arena*, Apr. 1890, 567.

60 Grossberg, 248–49, 300–301; "Mrs. Stanton to the Mothers' Congress," *Woman's Journal*, May 26, 1900.

61 ECS, "Our Young Girls," *Rev.*, Jan. 29, 1868.

62 "Begin at the Beginning: Elizabeth Cady Stanton's Advice to Moral Reformers," *Omaha Bee* (NE), Apr. 7, 1889; Hogan and Hogan, 415; Strange, "Dress Reform," 1.

63 ECS, "Our Young Girls," *Rev.*, Jan. 29, 1868; "Our Girls" Speech [1872–80] (ms.) in *Papers*, vol. 3, 484; "The Health of American Women," 510.

64 Letter from Mrs. Elizabeth Cady Stanton, Proceedings of the Woman's Rights Convention Held at Akron, Ohio, May 28 and 29, 1851, *Microfilm 7:79*; ECS, "Our Young Girls: An Essay Read before the Seneca Falls Conversational," in *Lily*, Mar. 1, 1853.

65 "Our Young Girls," *Rev.*, Jan. 29, 1868; ECS, "Our Young Girls," *Rev.*, June 25, 1868; "Our Young Girls Lecture," *Dubuque Daily Times*, Dec. 4, 1869; "Our Young Girls," *Daily Missouri Republican*, Dec. 29, 1869; ECS, "Our Girls" Speech; "The Lectures of Mrs. Elizabeth Cady Stanton," *Grand Rapids Democrat*, Jan. 11, 1870; ECS, "The Girls of the Period," *NY Times*, Oct. 25, 1873; ECS, "The Girls," *Milwaukee Sentinel*, Apr. 18, 1877; "Our Girls," *Indianapolis Sentinel*, Jan. 19, 1879; "The Lectures," *Greenfield Transcript*, Jan. 24, 1880; "Sister Stanton," *Washington County Press*, Feb. 25, 1880; "The Health of American Women," 510.

66 Our Girls ms.; "The Girls"; "Sister Stanton"; "The Lectures."

67 Strange, "Dress Reform," 2, 7; Hogan, 419–20.

68 Address of Mrs. Elizabeth Cady Stanton on Woman's Rights, Sept. 1848 (ms.), *Papers*, vol. 1.

69 "The Girls"; ECS, "The Question of Marriage," *Omaha Republican*, Mar. 31, 1889.

70 Our Girls ms.; Akron Letter.

71 "The Lectures."

72 Akron Letter; "The Health of American Women," 511; "The Girls"; "Sister Stanton."

73 "The Health of American Women," 512.

74 ECS, "The Era of the Bicycle," *American Wheelman*, Aug. 1895; ECS, "Shall Women Ride the Bicycle?" *American Wheelman* [May 1896]; ECS, "Shall Women Ride the Bicycle?" *SF Examiner*, Sept. 16, 1896; Lisa S. Strange and Robert S. Brown, "The Bicycle, Women's Rights, and Elizabeth Cady Stanton," 31 *Women's Studies* 609, 613–14, 622 (2002).

75 Griffith, *In Her Own Right*, 69; ECS to Elizabeth Smith Miller, Sept. 11, 1862.

76 "Our Young Girls," *Dubuque*; "Our Young Girls," *Missouri*.

77 "The Health of American Women," 511.

78 Mary F. Eastman, *The Biography of Dio Lewis* (New York: Fowler and Wells, 1891).

79 Address of ECS, in Proceedings of the First Anniversary of the AERA, May 9, 1867.

80 Dio Lewis, *Our Girls* (New York: Harper and Brothers, 1871).

81 "The Lectures."

82 "Our Young Girls," *Rev.*; "Sister Stanton"; "The Lectures."

83 "Girls of the Period"; "The Girls"; "The Lectures"; "Our Young Girls," *Dubuque*; Strange, "Dress Reform," 3, 11.

84 ECS, "Bloomerism in the Mills," *Lily*, July 1851; ECS, "Our Costume," *Lily*, July 1851.

85 "Female Attire," *Lily*, Feb. 1851; "Female Attire," *Lily*, Mar. 1851.

86 Strange, "Dress Reform," 2.

87 "Our Costume"; ECS, *Eighty Years*, 201; Gerrit Smith to ECS, Dec. 1, 1855; Gerrit Smith to ECS, Dec. 19, 1855.

88 A Letter from Mrs. Stanton to Gerrit Smith, Dec. 21, 1855.

89 Strange, "Dress Reform," 9.

90 ECS, "Our Young Girls," *Rev.*, June 25, 1868; Our Girls ms.

91 "Our Young Girls," June; Our Girls ms.

92 Our Girls ms.; "Our Young Girls," *Dubuque*; "The Lectures"; "Our Young Girls," *Missouri*.

93 Our Girls ms.; "Our Young Girls," *Rev.*, Jan. 29, 1868.

94 "Our Young Girls," Jan. 1868; Akron Letter.

95 "Mrs. Elizabeth Cady Stanton," *Dubuque Daily Herald* (IA), Dec. 4, 1869.

96 ECS, "Our Boys" [1875] (ms.), *Microfilm* 45:75.

97 Hogan and Hogan, 415–17; *Geneva Gazette*, Dec. 14, 1877.

98 ECS, "The Boys of Our Village," *Lily*, Sept. 1851.

99 ECS to SBA, Jan. 20, 1854.

100 *Id.*; ECS, *Eighty Years*, 163; to Elizabeth Smith Miller, Sept. 11, 1862.

101 Griffith, *In Her Own Right*, 173; Margaret Stanton Lawrence, "As a Mother," *New Era*, Oct. 1, 1885, in *Woman's Tribune*, July 25, 1891.

102 ECS, "Our Boys on Sunday," 1 *Forum* 191, Apr. 1886; ECS to Margaret Stanton, Nov. 26, 1877; Hogan and Hogan, 415–16, 425.

103 ECS, Home Life Lecture (ms. 1878), *Microfilm* 20:449.

104 "Our Boys" ms.; "Our Boys: Lecture by Mrs. Elizabeth Cady Stanton," *Chicago Daily Tribune*, Feb. 15, 1875; ECS, "The Rights of Children," *Milwaukee Sentinel*, Mar. 4, 1878; *Geneva Gazette*, Dec. 14, 1877; Hogan, 415–16, 420–21, 431.

105 "The Girls."

106 ECS to Margaret Stanton, Dec. 1, 1872.

107 ECS, "How to Make Woman Independent," *Una*, Sept. 1855; First Anniversary AERA Address, 12; "The Disability of Sex and Marriage," *Rev.*, Mar. 3, 1870; ECS, "A Short Discussion on the Modern Marriage Problem," *NY American and Journal*, July 13, 1902.

108 "Make Woman Independent"; Eleventh Convention Address, 7; First Anniversary AERA Address, 11.

109 "Women's Temperance Convention, Mrs. Stanton's Address" (Apr. 20–21, 1852), *Lily*, May 1852; "The Lectures."

110 Cott, *Bonds*, 101–3.

111 ECS, "Home Life a Century Ago," *Press*, Dec. 8, 1901.

112 "Century Ago."

113 Kern, 84.

114 ECS, *Eighty Years*, 35; Griffith, *In Her Own Right*, 17.

115 ECS, "The Co-education of the Sexes," Papers and Letter Presented at the First Woman's Congress of the Association for the Advancement of Woman, Oct. 17, 1873; Kathi L. Kern, "Gray Matters: Brains, Identities, and Natural Rights," in *The Social and Political Body* 103–6, Theodore Schatzki and Wolfgang Natter eds. (New York: Guilford Press, 1996).

116 "Co-education."

117 "The Health of American Women," 513; First Anniversary AERA Address, 11, 13.

118 "Our Young Girls," *Missouri*.

119 ECS, Address, Eleventh National Woman's Rights Convention, May 10, 1866; ECS to Second Convention at Worcester, in *Liberator*, Nov. 7, 1851.

120 Kay, 2033; Cott, *Bonds*, 35, 48–49.

121 Cott, *Bonds*, 35, 46, 48–49.

122 ECS, "Advice to the Strong-Minded," *Rev.*, May 21, 1868; "Our Young Girls," June.

123 Worcester Letter, *Liberator*.

124 Eleventh Convention Address.

125 *Id.*

126 ECS, "The Degradation of Woman," *Rev.*, Jan. 15, 1868.

127 *Id.*

128 "Woman's Rights Convention," *North Star*, Aug. 11, 1848.

129 "Sister Stanton."

130 Thirty-First Convention, Feb. 10, 1900, *Woman's Tribune*, Mar. 10, 1900.

131 "Sister Stanton."

132 Cott, *Bonds*, 20.

133 "Home Life" Lecture

134 Temperance Address, 1852; Worcester Letter.

135 "The Girls."

136 "The Health of American Women," 513.

137 Our Girls ms.

138 "Co-education"; Griffith, *In Her Own Right*, 175; Blatch, 36.

139 "The Girls"; "Our Young Girls," *Dubuque*; Our Girls ms.

140 ECS, "The Strong-Minded Women of the Bible," *Rev.*, Feb. 26, 1868.

141 ECS, "The Solitude of Self," to NAWSA Twenty-Fourth Convention, Jan. 18, 1892, in *Woman's Tribune*, Jan. 23, 1892; ECS, Address, Hearing before the House Committee on the Judiciary, Jan. 18, 1892; ECS, "The Solitude of Self," *Boston Investigator*, Jan. 12, 1901.

142 Clark, "Religion," 51.

143 "Our Young Girls: An Essay Read before the Seneca Falls Conversational"; Temperance Address, 1852.

144 Our Girls ms.; ECS, "The Parable of the Ten Virgins," *Ballot Box*, Dec. 1877.

145 "Solitude of Self."

146 Worcester Letter.

147 *Id.*

148 *Id.*

149 "Strong-Minded Women."

150 ECS, "Why We Need Women as Physicians," *Phosphorus Phrenological Journal* 347 (May 1871).

151 Our Girls ms.

152 "Make Woman Independent."

153 83 U.S. 130 (1872).

154 *Id.*

155 ECS, "The Subjection of Woman" Speech, [1873], in *Papers*, vol. 2, 621, 625.

156 *HWS*, vol. 2, 644, 656, 673.

157 Karen Berger Morello, *The Invisible Bar: The Woman Lawyer in America, 1638 to the Present* 37–38 (New York: Random House, 1986) (Iowa, Missouri, Michigan, Maine, Utah, and D.C.).

158 In re Goodell, 39 Wisc. 232 (1875); In re Lockwood, 9 Ct. Cl. 346; Supreme Court of the United States, *Minutes*, Nov. 6, 1876; Letter from Mrs. Stanton, *Ballot Box*, Feb. 1877; Ex Parte Lockwood, 154 U.S. 116 (1894); *HWS*, vol. 3, 107.

159 ECS, "Introduction," *Woman's Bible*, Pt. I, 7.

160 ECS, "The Chief Obstacle in the Way of Woman's Suffrage," *Woman's Tribune*, Oct. 27, 1888; ECS, "The Duty of the Church to Woman at This Hour," *Free Thought* 189, 191 (Apr. 1902); Kern, 98–99.

161 Strange, "*Woman's Bible*," 19; Hersch, 6, 23; Sarah Grimké, *Letters on the Equality of the Sexes, and the Condition of Woman* (Boston: Isaac Knapp, 1838), 40; Lucretia Coffin Mott, "Discourse on Woman" (1849) in Campbell, 75.

162 Maureen Fitzgerald, "The Religious Is Personal Is Political: Foreword to the 1993 Edition of *The Woman's Bible*," *Woman's Bible* xi–xii (1993 ed.); "Sister Stanton."

163 *Woman's Bible*, Pt. I, 61; Kern, 12.

164 ECS, "The Degraded Status of Woman in the Bible," 14 *Free Thought Magazine* 539 (Sept. 1896).

165 "Helpmeet"; "Subjection" Speech; "Sister Stanton"; Strange, "*Woman's Bible*," 20.

166 Strange, "*Woman's Bible*," 15.

167 Hamlin, 25.

168 "Ten Virgins"; ECS, "The Origin of Woman," *Rev.*, Apr. 30, 1868; ECS, *Woman's Bible*, 7, 24.

169 Genesis 1:37–38.

170 *Papers*, vol. 4, 278, later published as ECS, "Woman's Position in the Christian Church," *Boston Investigator*, May 18, 1901.

171 "Subjection" Speech; "Sister Stanton"; "Degraded Status"; ECS, "Man and Woman Made Equal," *Sun*, May/June 32, 837.

172 Kern, 59–62; ECS, "Has Christianity Benefited Woman?" *No. Amer. Rev.* 389, 395 (May 1885); ECS, Speech, Fourteenth Annual Meeting, Free Religious Association, *Index*, June 23, 1881.

173 "Woman's Position"; "Helpmeet"; "Man and Woman Made Equal"; Kern, 54–55.

174 "An Old Story: Letter from Mrs. Stanton," *Woman's Journal*, Apr. 5, 1873.

175 "Our Young Girls," *Rev.*, Jan. 29, 1868; "Old Story."

176 "Subjection" Speech; "The Health of American Women."

177 "Old Story."

178 "Helpmeet."

179 ECS, "Mass Meeting Protest, McFarland Trial," *World*, May 17, 1870.

180 Decade Meeting Address; "Discourses."

181 Kern, 53; ECS to SBA, Aug., 1883; *HWS*, vol. 3, 928; "Woman's Position."

182 "Christianity Benefited"; ECS, "Degradation of Women: Reply," *Hartford Times*, Apr. 8, 1886; Kern, 53.

183 Kern, 53, 96; ECS to SBA, Aug. 31, 1883; ECS, *Eighty Years*, 356; ECS, "Church Action," *National Citizen Ballot Box*, Mar. 1881; "Christianity Benefited"; ECS, "The Christian Church and Woman I," *Index*, Oct. 30, 1884; ECS, "The Christian Church and Woman," *Free Thought*, Nov. 1896; ECS, "Bible and Church Degrade Woman," *Microfilm:* 39:651; "Degradation: Reply."

184 "NY Woman's Temperance Meeting, June 1, 1853," *Lily*, June 15, 1853; Letter from Mrs. Elizabeth C. Stanton to the Woman's Rights Convention Held at Syracuse, Sept. 6, 1852.

185 ECS, *Eighty Years*, 382; "Church Action"; "Woman's Position"; Kern, 97.

186 "Woman's Position"; ECS, "The Christian Church and Woman, III," *Index*, Dec. 4, 1884.

187 "Christianity Benefited"; "Woman's Position.".

188 ECS, "A Woman's Thoughts about Women," *Golden Age*, Feb. 7, 1874.

189 "Woman's Position"; "Benefited."

190 Fitzgerald, xxi–xxii.

191 ECS, "Woman Suffrage and the Church," *Index*, Mar. 25, 1886; ECS, "The Duty of the Church to Woman at This Hour," *Boston Investigator*, May 4, 1901; ECS, "The Duty of the Church to Woman at this Hour," *Free Thought* 189 (Apr. 1902).

192 ECS, "The Matriarchate, or Mother-Age," National Council of Women, Feb. 22–25, 1891, at 218, 227, *Microfilm* 28:1009; "Her Political Status," *Evening Star*, Feb. 25, 1891; "The Matriarchate Mother-Age," *Woman's Tribune*, Feb. 28, 1891; "The Matriarchate or Mother-Age," *National Bulletin*, Feb. 1892; ECS, "Wyoming," *Woman's Tribune*, July 5, 1890; ECS, "Wyoming Admitted as a State into Union," 134 *Westminster Review* 280 (Sept. 1890); ECS, "The Antagonism of Sex," *National Bulletin*, June 1893; "Mrs. Stanton on Our Foremothers," *Woman's Journal*, Dec. 29, 1894; ECS and SBA, "Women's Rights," in *Johnson's Universal Cyclopedia* vol. 8. Charles Kendall Adams, ed. (New York: A.J. Johnson, 1895).

193 Johann Jakob Bachofen, *Mother Right: A Study of the Religious and Juridical Nature of Gynecocracy in the Ancient World* (1861) (Princeton, N.J.: Princeton University Press, 1967); Friedrich Engels, *Origin of the Family, Private Property, and the State* (1884) (New York: International Publishers, 1972).

194 ECS, "Karl Pearson on the Matriarchate," *Women's Penny Paper*, Nov. 8, 1890; "Matriarchate," National Council of Women; "Antagonism of Sex," *National Bulletin*; ECS, "Then Woman Said: 'I Will,'" *NY Tribune*, Dec. 23, 1894; ECS, "Moral Power, or Brute Force?" *Boston Investigator*, Feb. 25, 1899; ECS, "The Antagonism of Sex," *Boston Investigator*, Mar. 16, 1901; ECS, *Woman's Bible*, 25; Cynthia Eller, *Gentlemen and Amazons: The Myth of Prehistory, 1861–1900*, 6–7 (Berkeley: University of California Press, 2011); Cynthia Eller, *The Myth of Matriarchal Prehistory* 3–15 (Boston: Beacon, 2000).

195 ECS to Clara Colby, Feb. 21, 1891; ECS, "Reminiscences," *Woman's Tribune*, Mar. 19, 1892.

196 Fitzgerald, xxi; Kern, 67; *HWS*, vol. 1, 753; Matilda Joslyn Gage, "The Matriarchate," *Open Court* 1480–81, Jan. 5, 1889. Gage's son-in-law, Frank Baum, actualized Gage's theory of matriarchal power in his "Wizard of Oz" book series.

197 "Matriarchate," National Council of Women, 227; "Antagonism," *National Bulletin*; ECS, *Woman's Bible*, 25; Eller, *Amazons*, 123, 130–32.

198 Gloria Steinem, "Wonder Woman," in Eller, *Myth*, 1–2; Merlin Stone, *When God Was a Woman* (New York: Dial, 1976); Riane Eisler, *The Chalice and the Blade* (Cambridge, MA: Harper and Row, 1987).

199 Fitzgerald, viii; Kern, 45.

200 Lutz, 292.

201 ECS, "Address at the Metropolitan Opera House on Her Eightieth Birthday," Nov. 12, 1895, *Microfilm* 34:479; Strange, "*Woman's Bible*," 15–16.

202 ECS, "The Central Idea of Woman's Degradation," *Woman's Tribune*, Dec 3, 1884.

203 "Degraded Status."

204 "Helpmeet"; "Sister Stanton"; "Central Idea"; ECS to Mr. E. H. Slagle, Dec. 10, 1885; ECS, "The Woman's Bible," *Woman's Tribune*, Oct. 1886.

205 "Woman's Position."

206 ECS, "The Woman's Bible," *Index*, Oct. 21, 1886; "Introduction: *Woman's Bible*," 10–11; Fitzgerald, xxiii.

207 Kern, 51, 71, 78.

208 ECS, *Woman's Bible*, Pt. I, 149–51; Emily Sampson, *With Her Own Eyes: The Story of Julia Smith, Her Life, and Her Bible* 133–34 (Knoxville: University of Tennessee Press, 2006).

209 "Bible," *Index*, Oct. 1886; ECS, "Reminiscences: The Woman's Bible," *Woman's Tribune*, Sept. 5, 1891; Fitzgerald, xxvi; Strange, "*Woman's Bible*," 25–26; Kern, 137–38.

210 Strange, "*Woman's Bible*," 28.

211 *Id.*; Kern, 173.

212 Kern, 3.

213 *Id.* at 121.

214 ECS, *Eighty Years*, 392; ECS to SBA, 1896; Kern, 99.

215 ECS, *Woman's Bible*, vol. 2, 215; Strange, "*Woman's Bible*," 28–29: Kern, 181–90.

216 Kern, 1.

217 *Id.* at 198; Stanton and Blatch.

218 ECS, *Woman's Bible*, Pt. 1, 467.

219 Griffith, *In Her Own Right*, 212; Kern, 171.

220 Strange, "*Woman's Bible*," 17.

221 *Id.* at 31–32; Fitzgerald, xxvii; Kern, 8; see Mary D. Pellauer, *Toward a Tradition of Feminist Theology: The Religious Social Thought of Elizabeth Cady Stanton, Susan B. Anthony, and Anna Howard Shaw* (Brooklyn, NY: Carlson, 1991).

222 Fitzgerald, vii; Angela L. Padilla and Jennifer J. Winrich, "Christianity, Feminism, and the Law," 1 *Columbia J. Gender and Law* 67 (1991).

CONCLUSION

1 Grossman and Friedman, 14, 164–66, 172, 178; Kay, 2033, 2035, 2041, 2050.

2 Grossman and Friedman, 80; D. Kelly Weisberg and Susan Frelich Appleton, *Modern Family Law* 213–15 (New York: Kluwer, 5th ed. 2013); Grossberg, 34–61; Dubler, "Wifely Behavior," 964, 994, 1001–03.

3 Grossman and Friedman, 196–97; *Modern Family Law*, 557–58.

4 *Modern Family Law*, 194–95; U.S. Decennial Census (1890–2000); U.S. Census Bureau 2009–2013 American Community Survey 5 Year Estimates; Vivian E. Hamilton, "The Age of Marital Capacity: Reconsidering Civil Recognition of Adolescent Marriage," 92 *Boston University Law Review* 1817, 1843–50 (2012); June Carbone, "Age Matters: Class, Family Formation, and Inequality," 48 *Santa Clara Law Review* 901 (2008); Jonathan Todres, "Maturity," 48 *Houston Law Review* 1107 (2012).

5 Suzanne A. Kim, "Marital Naming/Naming Marriage: Language and Status in Family Law," 85 *Indiana L.J.* 893 (2010); Omi, "The Problem That Has No Name," 4 *Cardozo Women's L.J.* 321 (1998); *but see* Forbush v. Wallace, 405 U.S. 970 (1972).

6 *Modern Family Law*, 674–91, 703–6; Watts v. Watts, 350 N.Y.S.2d 285 (Fam. Ct. 1973); King v. Vancil, 341 N.E.2d 65 (Ill. 1975); Fineman, *Illusion*, 82–186; Elizabeth S. Scott and Robert E. Emery, "Gender Politics and Child Custody: The Puzzling Persistence of the Best Interest Standard," 77 *Law and Contemporary Problems* 69 (2014).

7 Grossman and Friedman, 15, 187; *Modern Family Law*, 499; Scott Keyes, "Conservatives Aren't Just Fighting Same-Sex Marriage: They're Also Trying to Stop Divorce," *Washington Post*, Apr. 11, 2014; Amanda Marcotte, "Republicans Are Quietly Trying to Kill No-Fault Divorce," *Slate*, April 14, 2014.

8 Herbert Jacob, *Silent Revolution: The Transformation of Divorce Law in the United States*, 168–70 (Chicago: University of Chicago Press, 1988); Williams v. North Carolina, 317 U.S. 287 (1942); Williams v. North Carolina, 325 U.S. 226 (1945); Sherrer v. Sherrer, 334 U.S. 343 (1948); Estin v. Estin, 334 U.S. 541 (1948).

9 208 U.S. 412 (1908); Tracey Jean Boisseau and Tracy A. Thomas, "After Suffrage Comes Equality? ERA as the Nineteenth Amendment's Next Logical Step," in *100 Years of the Nineteenth Amendment: An Appraisal of Women's Political Activism*, Lee Ann Banaszak and Holly J. McCammon, eds. (New York: Oxford University Press, forthcoming); Nancy Woloch, *A Class by Herself: Protective Laws for Women Workers, 1890s–1990s* (Princeton, NJ: Princeton University Press, 2015).

10 Thomas and Boisseau, *FLH*, 10–12; Kay, 2048–49.

11 Gloria Steinem, "An Introductory Statement," in Caroline Bird, *What Women Want: From the Official Report to the President, the Congress, and the People of the United States* 10, 13–14 (New York: Simon and Schuster, 1979); Bird, 55.

12 Ziegler, "Incomplete," 261; "Homemakers," in Bird, 129

13 Cynthia Eller, *The Myth of Matriarchal Prehistory* 1–3 (Boston: Beacon, 2000).

14 Letter from Mrs. Elizabeth C. Stanton to the Woman's Rights Convention Held at Syracuse, Sept. 6, 1852.

15 Frances E. Willard and Mary A. Livermore, eds., "Mrs. Ada Miser Kepley," *A Woman of the Century*, 434 (1893); "Phoebe Couzins Dies at 72," *NY Times*, Dec. 7, 1913; Drachman, 157.

16 ABA Commission on Women, *A Current Glance at Women in the Law*, www.americanbar.org (July 2014); NAWL, *Eighth Annual National Survey on Retention and Promotion of Women in Law Firms*, www.nawl.org (Feb. 2014); Center for Women in Government and Civil Society, SUNY, *Women in Federal and State-Level Judgeships*, www.albany.edu (Summer 2012); Rutgers, "Current Numbers of Women Officeholders," Center for American Women and Politics, www.cawp.rutgers.edu.

17 JEB v. Alabama, 511 U.S. 127, 132 (1994); Taylor v. Louisiana, 419 U.S. 522, 537 (1975); Hoyt v. Florida, 368 U.S. 57, 62 (1961); Fay v. New York, 332 U.S. 261, 289 (1947); Ballard v. United States, 329 U.S. 187, 193–34 (1946); Grossman, "Jury," 1115, 1134–35.

18 Joan Williams, "Jumpstarting," 1267, 1267; Neil S. Siegel and Reva B. Siegel, "Struck by Stereotype: Ruth Bader Ginsburg on Pregnancy Discrimination as Sex Discrimination," 59 *Duke Law Journal* 771 (2010); Neil S. Siegel, "'Equal Citizenship Stature': Justice Ginsburg's Constitutional Vision," 43 *New England Law Review* 799 (2010); Nina Totenburg, Lecture, "*Reed v. Reed* at 40: Equal Protection and Women's Rights," 20 *American U.J. Gender Social Policy and Law* 315 (2012).

19 Reed v. Reed. 404 U.S. 71 (1971); Frontiero v. Richardson, 411 U.S. 677 (1973); United States v. Virginia, 518 U.S. 515 (1996).

20 Thomas, "Struggle," 165.

21 Catharine A. MacKinnon, *Sexual Harassment of Working Women: A Case of Sex Discrimination* (New Haven, CT: Yale University Press, 1979); Carrie Baker, *The Women's Movement against Sexual Harassment* 20–26 (New York: Cambridge University Press, 2007).

22 Linda Greenhouse and Reva B. Siegel, *Before Roe v. Wade: Voices That Shaped the Abortion Debate before the Supreme Court's Ruling*, 24 (New York: Kaplan, 2010); Model Penal Code Sec. 207.11 (Tent. Draft No. 9, 1959).

23 Betty Friedan, "Abortion: A Woman's Civil Right," *Before Roe v. Wade*, 38–40.

24 Grossberg, 192.

25 381 U.S. 479 (1965); 405 U.S. 438 (1972); Cathering G. Roraback, "*Griswold v. Connecticut*: A Brief Case History," 16 *Ohio Northern University Law Review* 395 (1989).

26 410 U.S. 113 (1973).

27 City of Akron v. Akron Center for Reproductive Health, Inc., 462 U.S. 416 (1983); Planned Parenthood of Southeastern Pennsylvania v. Casey, 505 U.S. 833, 876 (1992); Gonzales v. Carhart, 550 U.S. 124, 185 (2007); Thomas, "Regulating Abortion," 47, 51.

28 *E.g.,* Mike Pence (R-Ind.), 32 *Congressional Record*, H9802 (daily ed. Oct. 21, 2003).

29 Mary Krane Derr et al., eds., *ProLife Feminism: Yesterday and Today* (Kansas City: Feminism and Nonviolence Studies Assoc., 2nd ed., 2005), 219–27; Linda C. McClain, "Equality, Oppression, and Abortion: Women Who Oppose Abortion Rights in the Name of Feminism," *Feminist Nightmares: Women at Odds; Feminism and the Problem of Sisterhood*, Susan Ostrov Weisser and Jennifer Fleischner eds. (New York: NYU Press, 1994), 159, 165; Lynette Clemetson and Robin Toner, "Antiabortion Advocacy of Wife of Court Nominee Draws Interest," *NY Times*, July 23, 2005; Marisa McQuilken, "Not Your Mom's Feminists," *Legal Times*, June 19, 2006.

30 *ProLife Feminism*; Serrin M. Foster, "The Feminist Case against Abortion," *American Feminist* (FFL), reprinted in *Great Speeches in History: Women's Rights*, Jennifer A. Hurley ed. (Farmington Hills, MI: Cengage Gale, 2001), 19.

31 Thomas, "Misappropriating," 4; Foster, "Feminist Case"; Suzanne Schnittman, "Elizabeth Cady Stanton: Feminist, Wife, and Mother of Seven," *American Feminist*, Fall 2003–Winter 2004, 24, www.feministsforlife.org; Serrin M. Foster, "Why Is This Bill Named after Elizabeth Cady Stanton?" www.feministsforlife.org.

32 Brief for Feminists for Life in: Bray v. Alexandria Women's Health Clinic, 506 U.S. 263 (1993); *Casey*, 505 U.S. 833 (1992); Webster v. Reproductive Health Services, 492 U.S. 490 (1989); *City of Akron*, 462 U.S. 416 (1983).

33 Foster, "Feminist Case."

34 Thomas, "Misappropriating," 3; *ProLifeFeminism*, 17; Feminists for Life Website, www.feministsforlife.org (last visited Aug. 12, 2015).

35 Thomas, "Misappropriating," 15; Ann Gordon and Lynn Sherr, "Sarah Palin Is No Susan B. Anthony," On Faith, *Washington Post,* www.washingtonpost.com, May 21, 2010; Stacy Schiff, "Desperately Seeking Susan," Op-Ed, *NY Times,* Oct. 13, 2006; Christine Stansell, "Meet the Anti-Abortion Group Pushing Presidential Politics to the Extreme Right," *New Republic,* July 11, 2011; Cat Clark, "The Truth about Susan B. Anthony: Did One of America's First Feminists Oppose Abortion?" *American Feminist* 1 (2007).

36 ECS, "Infanticide and Prostitution," *Rev.,* Feb. 5, 1868; "Infanticide," *Rev.,* Jan. 29, 1868; "Child Murder," *Rev.,* Mar. 12, 1868; *ProLife Feminism,* 48–51; Thomas, "Misappropriating," 57–64.

37 Parker Pillsbury, "Quack Medicines," *Rev.,* Mar. 26, 1868; Griffith, *In Her Own Right,* 133; Letter from Mrs. Stanton, Nov. 24, 1856, in Proceedings of the Seventh National Woman's Rights Convention, Nov. 25 and 26, 1856, 89, *Microfilm* 8:807.

38 "Infanticide and Prostitution."

39 "Infanticide and Prostitution."

40 Seventh Convention, 89.

41 "Restellism: The Crime of This Age, *Rev.,* May 7, 1868; "Women as Jurors," *Rev.,* Dec. 1868; *NY World,* Dec. 2, 1868, at 1; "Hester Vaughn," *NY Times,* Dec. 2, 1868.

42 Thomas, "Misappropriating," 36–37; FFL website, www.feministsforlife.org, citing "Letter to Julia Ward Howe, October 16, 1873, recorded in Howe's diary at Harvard University Library"; Cat Clark, "Did Elizabeth Cady Stanton Say That?" (2011), at www.feministforlife.org; Suzanne Schnittman, "Elizabeth Cady Stanton Honored by FFL of Western New York," *American Feminist,* Spring 1996.

43 Diary of Julia Ward Howe, Oct. 16, 1873, Houghton Library, Harvard College Library; "The Woman's Congress," *NY Times,* Oct. 16, 1873; "The Woman's Congress," *NY Tribune,* Oct. 16, 1873; "Woman's Congress," *Woodhull and Claflin's Weekly,* Nov. 1, 1873.

44 S. 1966, 109th Cong. (2005); H.R. 4265, 109th Cong. (2005); Serrin M. Foster, Op-Ed., "Pregnant Student Services Act," *Washington Times,* Nov. 20, 2005; Foster, "Named After."

45 Patient Protection and Affordable Care Act, Pub. L. No. 111–148, §§ 10211–10214, 124 Stat. 119 (2010); Thomas, "Misappropriating," 16–18.

46 Patrick D. Healy, "Clinton Seeking Shared Ground over Abortions," *NY Times,* Jan. 25, 2005; William Saletan, "Safe, Legal, and Never: Hillary Clinton's Anti-Abortion Strategy," *Slate,* Jan. 26, 2005; "Hillary in the Middle on Values Issues," *Washington Times,* Jan. 26, 2005; Peter Baker and Susan Saulny, "At Notre Dame, Obama Calls for Civil Tone in Abortion Debate," *NY Times,* May 17, 2009.

47 Thomas, "Misappropriating," 66–68.

48 D'Vera Cohn, et al., "Barely Half of US Adults Are Married: A Record Low," Pew Research Center, Dec. 14, 2011; U.S. Census Bureau, Number, Timing, and Duration of Marriages and Divorces: 2009 (May 2011); U.S. Census Bureau, Marital

Events of Americans: American Community Survey Reports (Aug. 2011). All sources available online.

49 Brady E. Hamilton et al., "Births: Preliminary Data for 2013," National Vital Statistics Reports, May 29, 2014, 1, 4 (40.6 percent in 2013), available online; Clare Huntington, "Postmarital Family Law: A Legal Structure for Nonmarital Families," 67 *Stanford Law Review* 167 (2015); Isabel V. Sawhill, *Generation Unbound: Drifting into Sex and Parenthood without Marriage* (Washington, D.C.: Brookings Institute Press, 2014).

50 Census Bureau, Marital Events; Betsey Stevenson and Justin Wolfers, "Trends in Marital Stability," *Research Handbook on the Economics of Family Law*, Lloyd R. Cohen and Joshua D. Wright eds. (Northhamptom, MA: Elgar, 2011), 96.

51 Maanvi Singh, "Young Women and Men Seek More Equal Roles at Work and Home," NPR Blog, Jan. 23, 2015, http://www.npr.org; Claire Camp Dush, "The Origins of Gender Inequalities in Dual-Earner, College Educated Couples," Council on Contemporary Families, May 7, 2015, https://contemporaryfamilies.org; Arlie Hochschild and Anne Machung, *The Second Shift* (New York: Viking, 1989).

52 Betsey Stevenson and Justin Wolfers, "Marriage and Divorce: Changes and Their Driving Forces," 21 *Journal of Economic Perspectives* 27 (Spring 2007).

53 June Carbone and Naomi Cahn, *Marriage Markets: How Inequality Is Remaking the American Family* 15 (Oxford: Oxford University Press, 2014); June Carbone and Naomi Cahn, *Red Families v. Blue Families: Legal Polarization and the Creation of Culture* (Oxford: Oxford University Press, 2010); Kay Hymowitz et al., "Knot Yet: The Benefits and Costs of Delayed Marriage in America," National Marriage Project at the University of Virginia, 2013, http://twentysomethingmarriage.org/.

54 Joan Williams, *Unbending Gender: Why Family and Work Conflict and What to Do about It* 2 (New York: Oxford University Press, 2000).

55 Fineman, *Autonomy*.

56 Joan C. Williams and Nancy Segal, "Beyond the Maternal Wall: Relief for Family Caregivers Who Are Discriminated Against on the Job," 26 *Harv. Women's L.J.* 77, 115 (2003).

57 Grossman and Friedman, 218.

58 Wayne Grudem, *Countering the Claims of Evangelical Feminism: Biblical Responses to the Key Questions* (Colorado Springs, CO: Multnomah, 2006).

59 Deborah A. Widiss, "Changing the Marriage Equation," 89 *Washington University Law Review* 721, 721–22 (2012).

60 Stephanie Coontz, "Why Gender Equality Stalled," *NY Times*, Feb. 17, 2013.

61 Kara Jesella, "Mom's Mad: And She's Organized," *NY Times*, Feb. 22, 2007.

62 Susan J. Douglas and Meredith W. Michaels, *The Mommy Myth: The Idealization of Motherhood and How It Has Undermined All Women* (New York: Free Press, 2004); Ann Crittenden, *The Price of Motherhood: Why the Most Important Job in the World Is Still the Least Valued* (New York: Holt, 2000).

63 Naomi Wolf, *The Beauty Myth* (New York: Morrow, 1991).

64 Sarah Palin, *America by Heart: Reflections on Family, Faith, and Flag* 171 (New York: Harper, 2010).

65 Coontz, "Stalled."

66 Cary L. Franklin, "Inventing the 'Traditional Concept' of Sex Discrimination, 125 *Harvard Law Review* 1307, 1318 n. 36 (2012).

67 Baker, *Sexual Harassment*, 115–31.

68 Deborah L. Brake, *Getting in the Game: Title IX and the Women's Sports Revolution* (New York: NYU Press, 2010).

69 Jesella, "Mom's Mad."

70 Williams and Segal, "Maternal Wall," 80.

71 Claudia Wallis, "The Case for Staying Home," *Time*, Mar. 22, 2004, 50; Bernie D. Jones, ed., *Women Who Opt Out: The Debate over Working Mothers and Work-Family Balance* (New York: NYU Press, 2012).

72 *E.g.,* Young v. United Parcel Service, Inc., 138 S.Ct. 1338 (2015); Ames v. Nationwide Mutual Insurance Co. (S.D. Iowa 2012), *aff'd* 747 F.3d. 509 (8th Cir. 2014), *reh'g*, 760 F.3d 763, *cert. denied*, 135 S.Ct. 947 (2015).

73 42 U.S.C. § 2000e(k) (1978); General Electric Co. v. Gilbert, 429 U.S. 125 (1976); Geduldig v. Aiello, 417 U.S. 484 (1974).

74 29 U.S. Code § 2612.

75 Jesella, "Mom's Mad."

76 Joan Williams, "'It's Snowing down South': How to Help Mothers and Avoid Recycling the Sameness/Difference Debate," 102 *Columbia Law Review* 812, 826, 828 (2002).

77 *Id.*; Harris v. Quinn, 134 S.Ct. 2618 (2014).

78 Coontz, "Stalled."

79 Jeff Landers, "What Divorcing Women Need to Know about Divorce 'Reform,'" *Forbes*, May 17, 2013, http://www.forbes.com; Stacie Sherman and Terrence Dopp, "Christie Signs Bill to Eliminate Alimony Sooner in New Jersey," *Bloomberg Business News*, Sept. 11, 2014; Jess Bidgood, "Alimony in Massachusetts Gets Overhaul, with Limits," *NY Times*, Sept. 26, 2011.

80 American Law Institute, *Principles of the Law of Family Dissolution* §§ 5.04, 5.05 (2002); Ira Mark Ellman, "The Theory of Alimony," 77 *California Law Review* 1, 42–43, 50–51 (1989).

81 Cynthia Lee Starnes, *The Marriage Buyout: The Troubled Trajectory of U.S. Alimony Law* (New York: NYU Press, 2014); Jane Rutherford, "Duty in Divorce: Shared Income as a Path to Equality," 58 *Fordham Law Review* 539, 564–74 (1990); Joan Williams, "Is Coverture Dead? Beyond a New Legal Theory of Alimony," 82 *Georgetown Law Journal* 2227 (1994).

82 Deborah Rhode and Martha Minow, "Reforming the Questions: Questioning the Reforms: Feminist Perspectives on Divorce Reform," *Divorce Reform at the Crossroads*, Herma Hill Kay and Stephen S. Sugarman eds. (New Haven, CT: Yale University Press, 1990), 192.

83 ECS Diary, Feb. 25, 1892, in Stanton and Blatch, vol. 2, 282–83.

SELECTED BIBLIOGRAPHY

STANTON PAPERS

The Elizabeth Cady Stanton–Susan B. Anthony Reader: Correspondence, Writings, Speeches, rev. ed. Ellen Carol DuBois, ed. Boston: Northeastern University Press, 1992.

The Papers of Elizabeth Cady Stanton and Susan B. Anthony, Microfilm Collection, reels 1–45. Ann D. Gordon, ed. New Brunswick, NJ: Rutgers University Press, 1991. Referred to in the Notes as *Microfilm*.

The Selected Papers of Elizabeth Cady Stanton and Susan B. Anthony, vols. 1–6. Ann D. Gordon, ed. New Brunswick, NJ: Rutgers University Press, 1998–2012. Referred to in the Notes as *Papers*.

Stanton, Elizabeth Cady. *Eighty Years and More: Reminiscences, 1815–1897*, 1898. New York: Humanity Books, 2002.

———. *The Woman's Bible*, 1895. Boston: Northeastern University Press, 1993.

Stanton, Elizabeth Cady, Susan B. Anthony, and Matilda Joslyn Gage, eds. *History of Woman Suffrage*, vols. 1–3. Rochester, NY: Charles Mann, 1881–1922. Referred to in the Notes as *HWS*.

Stanton, Elizabeth Cady, Susan B. Anthony, and Parker Pillsbury, eds. *The Revolution*, 1868–1870, in *Microfilm*, vols. 1–3. Referred to in the Notes as *Rev*.

Stanton, Theodore, and Harriot Stanton Blatch, eds. *Elizabeth Cady Stanton as Revealed in Her Letters, Diary, and Reminiscences,* vols. 1–2. New York: Harper and Brothers, 1922.

SECONDARY SOURCES

Areen, Judith. "Uncovering the Reformation Roots of American Marriage and Divorce Law." 26 *Yale J. Law and Feminism* 29 (2014).

Banner, Lois W. *Elizabeth Cady Stanton: A Radical for Woman's Rights*. Boston: Little, Brown, 1980.

Basch, Norma. *Framing American Divorce: From the Revolutionary Generation to the Victorians*. Berkeley: University of California Press, 1999.

———. *In the Eyes of the Law: Women, Marriage, and Property in Nineteenth-Century New York*. Ithaca, NY: Cornell University Press, 1982.

Blake, Nelson Manfred. *The Road to Reno: A History of Divorce in the United States*. New York: Macmillan, 1962.

Blatch, Harriot Stanton, and Alma Lutz. *Challenging Years: The Memoirs of Harriot Stanton Blatch*. New York: Putnam's, 1940.

Brodie, Janet Farrell. *Contraception and Abortion in Nineteenth-Century America*. Ithaca, NY: Cornell University Press, 1994.

Campbell, Karlyn Kohrs. *Man Cannot Speak for Her*. Vol. 1, *A Critical Study of Early Feminist Rhetoric*. Westport, CT: Greenwood, 1989.

Chamallas, Martha. *Introduction to Feminist Legal Theory*, 2d ed. New York: Aspen, 2003.

Chused, Richard H. "Married Women's Property Law: 1800–1850." 71 *Georgetown L.J.* 1359 (1983).

Clark, Elizabeth B. "Matrimonial Bonds: Slavery and Divorce in Nineteenth-Century America." 8 *Law and History Review* 25 (1990).

———. "Religion, Rights, and Difference in the Early Woman's Rights Movement." 3 *Wisconsin Women's L.J.* 29 (1987).

———. "Self-Ownership and the Political Theory of Elizabeth Cady Stanton," 21 *Connecticut Law Review* 905 (1988).

Cole, Phyllis. "Stanton, Fuller, and the Grammar of Romanticism," 73 *New England Quarterly* 553 (2000).

Cooper, George. *Lost Love: A True Story of Passion, Murder, and Justice in Old New York*. Delanco, NJ: Notable Trials Library, 1994.

Cott, Nancy F. *The Bonds of Womanhood: "Woman's Sphere" in New England, 1780–1835*. New Haven, CT: Yale University Press, 1977.

———. "Comment on Karen Offen's 'Defining Feminism: A Comparative Historical Approach.'" 15 *Signs* 205 (1989).

———. *The Grounding of Modern Feminism*. New Haven, CT: Yale University Press, 1987.

———. *Public Vows: A History of Marriage and the Nation*. Cambridge, MA: Harvard University Press, 2000.

Davis, Angela Y. *Women, Race, and Class*. New York: Vintage, 1981.

Davis, Sue. *The Political Thought of Elizabeth Cady Stanton: Women's Rights and the American Political Tradition*. New York: NYU Press, 2010.

Degler, Carl N. *At Odds: Women and the Family in America from the Revolution to the Present*. New York: Oxford University Press, 1980.

Dowd, Nancy E., and Michelle Jacobs, eds. *Feminist Legal Theory: An Anti-Essentialist Reader*. New York: NYU Press, 2003.

Drachman, Virginia G. *Sisters in Law: Women Lawyers in Modern American History*. Cambridge, MA: Harvard University Press, 1998.

Dubler, Ariela R. "Governing through Contract: Common Law Marriage in the Nineteenth Century." 107 *Yale L.J.* 1885 (1998).

———. "In the Shadow of Marriage: Single Women and the Legal Construction of the Family and the State." 112 *Yale L.J.* 1642 (2003).

———. "Wifely Behavior: A Legal History of Acting Married." 100 *Columbia Law Review* 957 (2000).

DuBois, Ellen Carol. "Feminism and Free Love." H-Net Women, 2001. www.h-net.org.

———. *Feminism and Suffrage: The Emergence of an Independent Women's Movement in America, 1848–1869.* New York: NYU Press, 1978.

———. *Harriot Stanton Blatch and the Winning of Woman Suffrage.* New Haven, CT: Yale University Press, 1997.

———. "On Labor and Free Love: Two Unpublished Speeches of Elizabeth Cady Stanton." 1 *Signs* 257 (1975).

DuBois, Ellen Carol, and Richard Candida Smith, eds. *Elizabeth Cady Stanton: Feminist as Thinker: A Reader in Documents and Essays.* New York: NYU Press, 2007.

Fineman, Martha Albertson. *The Autonomy Myth: A Theory of Dependency.* New York: NYU Press, 2004.

———. "Beyond Identities: The Limits of an Antidiscrimination Approach to Equality." 92 *Boston University Law Review* 1713 (2012).

———. "Feminism, Masculinities, and Multiple Identities." 13 *Nevada Law Review* 619 (2013).

———. *The Illusion of Equality: The Rhetoric and Reality of Divorce Reform.* Chicago: University of Chicago Press, 1991.

———. "Implementing Equality: Ideology, Contradiction, and Social Change: A Study of Rhetoric and Results in the Regulation of the Consequences of Divorce." 1983 *Wisconsin Law Review* 789, 801.

Fineman, Martha Albertson, and Isabel Karpin, eds. *Mothers in Law: Feminist Theory and the Legal Regulation of Motherhood.* New York: Columbia University Press, 1995.

Fox, Richard Wightman. *Trials of Intimacy: Love and Loss in the Beecher-Tilton Scandal.* Chicago: University of Chicago Press, 1999.

Friedman, Lawrence M. *Law in America: A Short History.* New York: Random House, 2002.

———. *Private Lives: Families, Individuals, and the Law.* Cambridge, MA: Harvard University Press, 2004.

———. "Rights of Passage: Divorce Law in Historical Perspective." 63 *Oregon Law Review* 649 (1984).

Fuller, Margaret. *Woman in the Nineteenth Century.* New York: Greeley and McElrath, 1845.

Ganz, Melissa J. "Wicked Women and Veiled Ladies: Gendered Narratives of the McFarland-Richardson Tragedy." 9 *Yale J. Law and Feminism* 255 (1997).

Ginzberg, Lori D. *Elizabeth Cady Stanton: An American Life.* New York: Hill and Wang, 2009.

———. *Untidy Origins: A Story of Woman's Rights in Antebellum New York.* Chapel Hill: University of North Carolina Press, 2005.

Gordon, Ann D. "Stanton and the Right to Vote: On Account of Race or Sex," in *Feminist as Thinker*, 111. 2007.

Gordon, Linda. *The Moral Property of Women: A History of Birth Control Politics in America.* Urbana: University of Illinois Press, 2007.

———. "Nineteenth-Century Women's-Rights Advocates on Abortion." 36 *Seattle Law Review SUpra* 27 (2013).

———. "Voluntary Motherhood: The Beginnings of Feminist Birth Control Ideas in the United States." Rima D. Apple and Janet Golden, eds. *Mothers and Motherhood: Readings in American History.* Columbus: Ohio State University Press, 1997.

———. "Why Nineteenth-Century Feminists Did Not Support 'Birth Control' and Twentieth-Century Feminists Do: Feminism, Reproduction, and the Family." Barrie Thorne with Marilyn Yalom, eds. *Rethinking the Family: Some Feminist Questions.* Boston: Northeastern University Press, 1992. 140–54.

Gordon, Sarah Barringer. "Law and Everyday Death: Infanticide and the Backlash against Woman's Rights after the Civil War." Austin Sarat, Lawrence Douglas, and Martha Merrill Umphrey, eds. *Lives in the Law.* Ann Arbor: University of Michigan Press, 2002.

———. "'The Liberty of Self-Degradation': Polygamy, Woman Suffrage, and Consent in Nineteenth-Century America," 83 *J. American History* 815 (1996).

———. *The Mormon Question: Polygamy and Constitutional Conflict in Nineteenth-Century America.* Chapel Hill: University of North Carolina Press, 2002.

Gornick, Vivian. *The Solitude of Self: Thinking about Elizabeth Cady Stanton.* New York: Farrar, Straus and Giroux, 2005.

Griffith, Elisabeth. "Elizabeth Cady Stanton on Marriage and Divorce: Feminist Theory and Domestic Experience." Mary Kelley, ed. *Woman's Being, Woman's Place: Female Identity and Vocation in American History.* Boston: G.K. Hall, 1979.

———. *In Her Own Right: The Life of Elizabeth Cady Stanton.* New York: Oxford University Press, 1984.

Grossberg, Michael. *Governing the Hearth: Law and the Family in Nineteenth-Century America.* Chapel Hill: University of North Carolina Press, 1985.

Grossman, Joanna L. "Women's Jury Service: Right of Citizenship or Privilege of Difference?" 46 *Stanford Law Review* 1115 (1994).

Grossman, Joanna L., and Lawrence M. Friedman. *Inside the Castle: Law and the Family in Twentieth-Century America.* Princeton, NJ: Princeton University Press, 2011.

Haber, Carole. *The Trials of Laura Fair: Sex, Murder, and Insanity in the Victorian West.* Chapel Hill: University of North Carolina Press, 2013.

Hamlin, Kimberly A. *From Eve to Evolution: Darwin, Science, and Women's Rights in Gilded Age America.* Chicago: University of Chicago Press, 2014.

Harris, Angela P. "Race and Essentialism in Feminist Legal Theory." 42 *Stanford Law Review* 581 (1990).

Hartog, Hendrik. "Lawyering, Husbands' Rights, and 'the Unwritten Law' in Nineteenth-Century America." 84 *J. American History* 67 (June 1997).

———. *Man and Wife in America: A History.* Cambridge, MA: Harvard University Press, 2000.

Hasday, Jill Elaine. "Contest and Consent: A Legal History of Marital Rape." 88 *California Law Review* 1373 (2000).

Hersch, Blanche Glassman. *The Slavery of Sex: Feminist-Abolitionists in America*. Chicago: University of Illinois Press, 1978.

Hogan, Lisa S., and J. Michael Hogan. "Feminine Virtue and Practical Wisdom: Elizabeth Cady Stanton's 'Our Boys.'" 6 *Rhetoric & Public Affairs* 415 (2003).

Holton, Sandra Stanley. "'To Educate Women into Rebellion': Elizabeth Cady Stanton and the Creation of a Transatlantic Network of Radical Suffragists." 99 *American Historical Review* 1112 (October 1994).

Isenberg, Nancy. *Sex and Citizenship in Antebellum America*. Chapel Hill: University of North Carolina Press, 1998.

Iversen, Joan Smyth. *The Antipolygamy Controversy in U.S. Women's Movements, 1880–1925: A Debate on the American Home*. London: Routledge, 1997.

Jones, Carolyn C. "Dollars and Selves: Women's Tax Criticism and Resistance in the 1870s." 1994 *University of Illinois Law Review* 265.

Kay, Herma Hill. "From *The Second Sex* to the Joint Venture: An Overview of Women's Rights and Family Law in the United States during the Twentieth Century." 88 *California Law Review* 2017 (2000).

Kerber, Linda K. *No Constitutional Right to Be Ladies: Women and the Obligations of Citizenship*. New York: Hill and Wang, 1998.

———. *Women of the Republic: Intellect and Ideology in Revolutionary America*. Chapel Hill: University of North Carolina Press, 1980.

Kern, Kathi. *Mrs. Stanton's Bible*. Ithaca, NY: Cornell University Press, 2001.

Korobkin, Laura Hanft. "The Maintenance of Mutual Confidence: Sentimental Strategies at the Adultery Trial of Henry Ward Beecher." 7 *Yale J. Law and Humanities* 1 (1995).

Kraditor, Aileen. *The Ideas of the Woman Suffrage Movement: 1890–1920*. New York: Columbia University Press, 1965.

Leach, William. *True Love and Perfect Union: The Feminist Reform of Sex and Society*. New York: Basic Books, 1980.

Lerner, Gerda. *The Female Experience: An American Documentary*. Indianapolis: Bobbs-Merrill, 1977.

———. *The Grimké Sisters from South Carolina: Pioneers for Women's Rights and Abolition*. Chapel Hill: University of North Carolina Press, 2004.

Lind, JoEllen. "Symbols, Leaders, Practitioners: The First Women Professionals." 28 *Valparaiso Univ. Law Review* 1327, 1338 (1994).

Lutz, Alma. *Created Equal: A Biography of Elizabeth Cady Stanton, 1815–1902*. New York: Octagon Books, 1940.

Marshall, Megan. *Margaret Fuller: A New American Life*. New York: Houghton Mifflin Harcourt, 2013.

Mason, Mary Ann. *From Father's Property to Children's Rights: The History of Child Custody in the United States*. New York: Columbia University Press, 1994.

Masson, Erin M. "The Woman's Christian Temperance Union, 1874–1898: Combatting Domestic Violence." 3 *William and Mary J. Women and Law* 163 (1997).

McClain, Linda C., and Joanna L. Grossman, eds. *Gender Equality: Dimensions of Women's Equal Citizenship*. New York: Oxford University Press, 2009.

McMillen, Sally G. *Seneca Falls and the Origins of the Women's Rights Movement*. New York: Oxford University Press, 2008.

Mill, John Stuart. *The Subjection of Women*. London: Longmans, Green, Reader, and Dyer, 1869.

Miller, Diane Helen, "From One Voice a Chorus: Elizabeth Cady Stanton's 1860 Address to the New York State Legislature." 22 *Women's Studies Communications* 152 (1999).

Minow, Martha. "Rights of One's Own: *In Her Own Right; The Life of Elizabeth Cady Stanton*." 98 *Harvard Law Review* 1084 (1985).

Mitchell, Michele. "'Lower Orders,' Racial Hierarchies, and Rights Rhetoric: Evolutionary Echoes in Elizabeth Cady Stanton's Thought during the Late 1860s." *Feminist as Thinker*, 128. 2007.

Mohr, James C. *Abortion in America: The Origins and Evolution of National Policy*. New York: Oxford University Press, 1978.

Newman, Louise Michele. *White Women's Rights: The Racial Origins of Feminism in the United States*. New York: Oxford University Press, 1999.

Norton, Mary Beth. *Founding Mothers and Fathers: Gendered Power and the Forming of American Society*. New York: Knopf, 1996.

———. *Liberty's Daughters: The Revolutionary Experience of American Women, 1750–1800*. Ithaca, NY: Cornell University Press, 1996.

Offen, Karen. "Defining Feminism: A Comparative Historical Approach." 14 *Signs* 119 (1988).

O'Neill, William L. *Divorce in the Progressive Era*. New Haven, CT: Yale University Press, 1967.

———. *Feminism in America: A History*. New Brunswick, NJ: Transaction, 1989.

Passet, Joanne E. *Sex Radicals and the Quest for Women's Equality*. Urbana: University of Illinois Press, 2003.

Pleck, Elizabeth. *Domestic Tyranny: The Making of American Social Policy against Family Violence from Colonial Times to the Present*. Chicago: University of Illinois Press, 2004.

Rabkin, Peggy A. "The Origins of Law Reform: The Social Significance of the Nineteenth-Century Codification Movement and Its Contribution to the Passage of the Early Married Women's Property Acts." 24 *Buffalo Law Review* 683 (1975).

Rakow, Lana F., and Cheris Kramarae, eds. *The Revolution in Words: Righting Women, 1868–1871*. London: Routledge, 1990.

Reagan, Leslie. *When Abortion Was a Crime: Women, Medicine, and Law in the United States, 1867–1973*. Berkeley: University of California Press, 1998.

Reid, Charles J., Jr. "The Journey to Seneca Falls: Mary Wollstonecraft, Elizabeth Cady Stanton, and the Legal Emancipation of Women." 10 *Univ. St. Thomas L.J.* 1123 (2013).

Rice, Arthur. "Henry B. Stanton as a Political Abolitionist." Ph.D diss., Columbia University, 1968.

Salmon, Marylynn. *Women and the Law of Property in Early America.* Chapel Hill: University of North Carolina Press, 1986.

Siegel, Reva B. "Home as Work: The First Woman's Rights Claims concerning Wives' Household Labor, 1850–1880." 103 *Yale L.J.* 1073 (1994).

———. "The Modernization of Marital Status Law: Adjudicating Wives' Rights to Earnings, 1860–1930." 82 *Georgetown L.J.* 2127 (1994).

———. "Reasoning from the Body: An Historical Perspective on Abortion Regulation and Questions of Equal Protection." 44 *Stanford Law Review* 261 (1992).

———. "'The Rule of Love': Wife Beating as Prerogative and Policy." 105 *Yale L.J.* 2117 (1996).

———. "She the People: The Nineteenth Amendment, Sex Equality, Federalism, and the Family." 115 *Harvard Law Review* 945 (2002).

Smith-Rosenberg, Carroll. *Disorderly Conduct: Visions of Gender in Victorian America.* New York: Oxford University Press, 1986.

Solomon, Martha. "Autobiographies as Rhetorical Narratives: Elizabeth Cady Stanton and Anna Howard Shaw as 'New Women,'" 42 *Communications Studies* 354 (1991).

Stansell, Christine. *The Feminist Promise, 1792 to the Present.* New York: Modern Library, 2010.

———. "Missed Connections: Abolitionist Feminism in the Nineteenth Century." *Feminist as Thinker* 32 (2007).

Stanton, Henry B. *Random Recollections.* New York: Harper and Brothers, 1883.

Strange, Lisa S. "Dress Reform and the Feminine Ideal: Elizabeth Cady Stanton and the 'Coming Girl.'" 68 *Southern Communication J.* 1 (2002).

———. "Elizabeth Cady Stanton's *Woman's Bible* and the Roots of Feminist Theology." 17 *Gender Issues* 15 (1999).

———. "Pragmatism and Radicalism in Elizabeth Cady Stanton's Feminist Advocacy: A Rhetorical Biography." Ph.D. diss., Indiana University, 1998.

Tetrault, Lisa. *The Myth of Seneca Falls: Memory and the Women's Suffrage Movement, 1848–1898.* Chapel Hill: University of North Carolina Press, 2014.

Thomas, Tracy A. "Back to the Future of Regulating Abortion in the First Term." 29 *Wisconsin J. Law, Gender, and Society* 47 (2014).

———. "Elizabeth Cady Stanton and the Notion of a Legal Class of Gender." *Feminist Legal History: Essays on Women and Law.* New York: NYU Press, 2011.

———. "Elizabeth Cady Stanton on the Federal Marriage Amendment: A Letter to the President." 22 *Constitutional Commentary* 137 (2005).

———. "Misappropriating Women's History in the Law and Politics of Abortion." 36 *Seattle University Law Review* 1 (2012).

———. "Sex versus Race, Again." Johnnetta Betsch Cole and Beverly Guy-Sheftall, eds. *Who Should Be First? Feminists Speak Out on the 2008 Presidential Campaign.* Albany: SUNY Press, 2010.

———. "The Struggle for Gender Equality in the Northern District of Ohio." Paul Finkelman and Roberta Sue Alexander, eds. *Justice and Legal Change on the Shores of Lake Erie: A History of the Northern District of Ohio.* Athens: Ohio University Press, 2012.

Thomas, Tracy, and Tracey Jean Boisseau, eds. *Feminist Legal History: Essays on Women and Law.* New York: NYU Press, 2011.

———. "Law, History, and Feminism." *Feminist Legal History* 3 (2011).

Venet, Wendy Hamand. *Neither Ballots nor Bullets: Women Abolitionists and the Civil War.* Charlottesville: University of Virginia Press, 1991.

Waggenspack, Beth M. *The Search for Self-Sovereignty: The Oratory of Elizabeth Cady Stanton.* Westport, CT: Greenwood Press, 1989.

Warbasse, Elizabeth Bowles. *The Changing Legal Rights of Married Women, 1800–1861.* New York: Garland, 1987.

Ward, Geoffrey C., and Ken Burns. *Not for Ourselves Alone: The Story of Elizabeth Cady Stanton and Susan B. Anthony.* New York: Knopf, 1999.

Wayne, Tiffany K. *Woman Thinking: Feminism and Transcendentalism in Nineteenth-Century America.* New York: Lexington Books, 2005.

Wellman, Judith. *The Road to Seneca Falls: Elizabeth Cady Stanton and the First Woman's Rights Convention.* Chicago: University of Illinois Press, 2004.

Welter, Barbara. "The Cult of True Womanhood, 1820–1860." 18 *American Quarterly* 151 (1966).

White, Barbara A. *The Beecher Sisters.* New Haven, CT: Yale University Press, 2003.

Williams, Joan C. "Jumpstarting the Stalled Gender Revolution: Justice Ginsburg and Reconstructive Feminism." 63 *Hastings L.J.* 1267 (2012).

Williams, Wendy. "The Equality Crisis: Some Reflections on Culture, Courts, and Feminism." 7 *Women's Rights Law Reporter* 175 (1982).

Winkler, Adam. "A Revolution Too Soon: Woman Suffragists and the 'Living Constitution.'" 76 *NYU Law Review* 1456 (2001).

Yalom, Marilyn. *A History of the Wife.* New York: HarperCollins, 2001.

Ziegler, Mary. "Eugenic Feminism: Mental Hygiene, the Women's Movement, and the Campaign for Eugenic Legal Reform, 1900–1935." 31 *Harvard J. Law and Gender* 211 (2008).

———. "An Incomplete Revolution: Feminists and the Legacy of Marital-Property Reform," 19 *Michigan J. Gender and Law* 259, 260 (2013).

INDEX

abolition, 5–6, 8, 10, 77, 113; male leaders, 124. *See also* Garrison, William Lloyd; Phillips, Wendell

abortion, 159, 174, 176–81, 211, 235; advertisements, 179–80, 235; Anthony on, 233–34; history, 176–78; misappropriation of Stanton on, 232–35; modern developments, 231–33; New York law, 178–81; Pillsbury on, 235; in *Revolution*, 277n109, 277n111; Stanton on, 159, 167, 173, 180–81, 235. *See also* Feminists for Life

adultery, 127–28

alimony, 126–27, 240

Amazons, 210

American Anti-Slavery Society, 8, 10

American Civil Liberties Union Women's Rights Project, 230

American Equal Rights Association, 11, 13, 15

American Law Institute (ALI), 231

American Medical Association (AMA), 177

American Woman Suffrage Association (AWSA), 13, 96, 123–24, 138. See also *Woman's Journal*

amphiarchate, 222. *See also* matriarchate

Andrews, Stephen Pearl, 119

Angelou, Maya, 229

Anthony, Susan B., 96, 165, 182, 209; Birthplace Museum, 234; coin, 225; on divorce, 115–16, 122; friendship with Stanton, 8–10, 16; on marital property petitioning, 48, 57–58; on temperance, 113, 115–16; on suffrage, 224–25; voting, 69. *See also* abortion: Anthony on

apartment living, 190

apprentice, 57, 191–92, 194; in law, 4, 41–42, 250n124

Auclert, Hubertine, 19, 248n61

babies, 168, 187–88

Bachofen, Johann Jakob, 221

Barry, Francis, 93

Baum, Frank, 286n196

Bayard, Edward, 4

beauty myth, 202, 238

Beecher, Henry Ward, 129–30

Beecher-Tilton trial, 129–30

Besant, Annie, 175

Bible: feminist interpretation, 223; women in, 220, 224

biblical critique, 1, 216–20, 223; of church institution, 220–22; creation and Eve, 21, 217–18; gender duality of God, 217–18; of marriage sacrament, 98; maternal curse, 218; Trinity, 217–18. *See also* Free Thought; *The Woman's Bible*

bicycling, 200

Bingham, John, 70–71

birth control, 171–75, 177, 231; Stanton's views, 173

Bishop, Joel, 250n124

Blackstone, William, 31, 71, 191, 214

Blackwell, Antoinette Brown, 83; divorce debate, 121–22; on marital property, 54

Blackwell, Henry, 13, 83

ABOUT THE AUTHOR

Tracy A. Thomas is a professor of law at the University of Akron, where she holds the Seiberling Chair of Constitutional Law and directs the Center for Constitutional Law. She is editor of the Gender and the Law Prof Blog and coeditor of *Feminist Legal History*.